Black Women in the Academy

Black Women in the Academy
Promises and Perils

Edited by Lois Benjamin

University Press of Florida

Gainesville Tallahassee Tampa Boca Raton

Pensacola Orlando Miami Jacksonville

02 01 00 99 98 97   6 5 4 3 2 1

Library of Congress Cataloging-in-Publication Data

Black women in the academy: promises and perils / edited by Lois Benjamin.
  p. cm.
Includes index.
ISBN 0-8130-1500-6 (alk. paper)
1. Afro-American women college teachers. 2. Afro-American women college administrators. 3. Discrimination in higher education—United States. 4. Sex discrimination in higher education—United States. I. Benjamin, Lois, 1944- .
LB2332.3.B53 1997
378.1'2'082—dc21 96-47388

The following chapters have been edited since their original publication and are reprinted herein by permission of the copyright holders:
Chapter 1, "A Troubled Peace: Black Women in the Halls of the White Academy" by Nellie Y. McKay, was originally published in *Bucknell Review* 36, no. 2 (1992): 21–37.
Chapter 2, "Black Women in Academe: Issues and Strategies" by Yolanda T. Moses, was originally published by the Project on the Status and Education of Women, Association of American Colleges, Washington, D.C., 1989.
Chapter 9, "Tranforming the Academy: A Black Feminist Perspective" by Beverly Guy-Sheftall, was originally published in *Changing Classroom Practices: Resources for Literary and Cultural Studies*, edited by David B. Downing (Urbana, Ill.: National Council of Teachers of English, 1994).

The University Press of Florida is the scholarly publishing agency for the State University System of Florida, comprised of Florida A & M University, Florida Atlantic University, Florida International University, Florida State University, University of Central Florida, University of Florida, University of North Florida, University of South Florida, and University of West Florida.

University Press of Florida
15 Northwest 15th Street
Gainesville, FL 32611

This work is dedicated to Frances Howard Hawkins,

who labored in the academic vineyard for over thirty-two years.

Contents

Preface

In this edited volume, black women administrators and faculty, exploring the thematic issues of identity, power, and change, examine the impact of racism and sexism in higher education. From a holistic framework, these academicians utilize multiple approaches — conceptual, empirical, and experiential — to understand and document racism and sexism, while weaving stories of windows of opportunity and the woes and wounds of the warriors who make their sojourn inside the sacred grove. While critiquing the ways of thinking and knowing of the Eurocentric patriarchal paradigm, these new voices offer insights into black women's communal values and their more spiritual and intuitive ways of viewing the world. Black women's ontological and epistemological assumptions should balance the present-day academy's emphasis on individualism and its reductionistic Western scientific thinking.

Too often, black women's voices have been absent from the literature, particularly in women's studies, black studies, ethnic studies, and multicultural studies. This work should help fill that knowledge void of the intersection of race, gender, class, and ethnicity in the aforementioned areas and in the transdisciplines of anthropology, history, political science, philosophy, psychology, and sociology as well as the general audience.

I am enormously indebted to the contributors who took time from their busy schedules to help fill this knowledge gap. In meeting their deadlines for this work, they juggled competing demands of time, family, and career. For some contributors, it gave them a chance to reflect on their ambiguous status in the academy.

Words cannot express my indebtedness to Frances Howard Hawkins, retired university administrator, for her immeasurable contribution to this project. She played a major role as cheerleader, boosting my spirits throughout this project. She had much faith in the value of such a volume in adding new knowledge to the academy and in contributing to future black women academics. It was at her urging that I undertook this project. In addition to Frances's emotional and moral support, she went beyond the call of duty, providing superb editorial, typing, and other technical assistance. Without her commitment and dedication, this project would have been difficult to complete in a timely manner. Thank you, Frances.

Deep appreciation is also expressed to Richelle Payne for her editorial assistance.

Finally, I wish to thank members of my family for their support: my parents; my brothers, Joseph and Andrew Benjamin; my sisters, Thelma P. Melton and Carolyn Beal; and especially my sister and brother-in-law, Bernice and Walter Fortson, who have always been supportive and have believed in me.

Introduction

Lois Benjamin

The need for this volume was underscored by the historic convergence of two thousand black women academics on the campus of the Massachusetts Institute of Technology in January 1994 for the conference entitled "Black Women in the Academy: Defending Our Name, 1894–1994," convened by historians Robin Kilson and Evelynn Hammonds. This "event of the century," as it was designated in the *Chronicle of Higher Education* by Nellie Y. McKay, professor of American and Afro-American history at the University of Wisconsin, became the venue for exchange about the promises and perils of the academic marketplace. Women from historically black and white, public and private, large and small institutions attended.

In this volume, African American women administrators and faculty address the issues of identity, power, and change. The holistic approach is reflective of the contributors' conceptual, empirical, and stream-of-consciousness and experiential pieces that weave a completed fabric of promises and perils inside the academy. They come from predominantly black and white institutions, public and private, research and teaching, coeducational and women's colleges, and from diverse disciplines, regions, and age strata. This work should make their voyage in the academy closer to a mosaic celebration and liberation. It should also prepare future black women academicians for the rough spots along the road, ease the journey of those presently climbing the hill, and allow those who have traversed over the hill to stop, look back, and tell the stories of the stony road we've trod.

The volume consists of seven parts, each addressing the core issues of identity, power, and change:

Part 1, "Black Women in the Academy: An Overview," explores the general academic climate and racial and sexual stereotyping.

Part 2, "Alternative Paradigms for Black Women in the Academy: Epistemological and Ontological Issues," focuses on the racist and sexist assumptions underlying concepts, theoretical frameworks, methodologies, organizational structures, and organizing assumptions in the academy and examines alternative paradigms for deconstructing and balancing Western ways of thinking and knowing.

Part 3, "Black Women Faculty: Issues in Teaching and Research," analyzes the important theoretical and methodological assumptions about pedagogy, curricula, and research orientation from a multidisciplinary perspective of black women in education, humanities, natural sciences, and the social sciences.

Part 4, "Black Women Administrators in the Academy," examines the status of black women in higher education administration and the specific barriers they face in overcoming racial and sexual prejudice.

Part 5, "The Social Dynamics of Academic Life," focuses on issues of recruitment and retention, tenure and promotion, gender and sexual harassment, mentors and support systems, and collegiality among faculty.

Part 6, "Black Women in Diverse Academic Settings," looks at the interplay of racism and sexism in predominantly white institutions and the issues of sexism in predominantly black institutions both public and private, research and teaching, and women's colleges.

Part 7, "The Future of Black Women in the Academy," concludes with an experiential case history by Darlene Clark Hine, John A. Hannah Professor, Michigan State University, which illustrates how the richness and depth of black women's perspectives and experiences can add to the academy. Additional issues treated in this section are problems and prospects for the future.

Marginalized, misnamed, maligned, and made invisible in the academy, African American women, the "Queens of Multiple Juxtapositions,"[1] as Beverly M. John denotes, attended the landmark MIT conference in order to challenge the Kings of the Eurocentric patriarchal hill for denied space and to level off the playing field. This space and playing field exclude black women's values, voices, and visions while embracing the Western patriarchal perspective. Such a worldview values competition, individualism, and control over nature — the physical environment as well as social relationships. Objectivity is *the* way of knowing. Underlying this epistemology are two tenets — the belief in the separation of the observers from the observed and the belief in the separation of mind, spirit, and matter. This angle of vision for knowing and understanding the world has blind spots because it excludes, devalues, or ignores black women as well as other men and women of color. This Eurocentric and androcentric perspective perpetuates a hierarchy: unearned privileges, based on white skin and maleness, accrue to those within the presumed normative experience.

Unlike people in the Eurocentric male matrix, many black women on the academic hill view the world from a more inclusive Afrocentric and matricentric angle, although their perspective is filtered through a labyrinth of oppression of race, gender, and class. Underlying this worldview and tradition is a holistic approach to knowing and understanding the world. In this approach, the individual and community, as well as all living elements, are linked in the cosmos. Thus such values as cooperation, collectivity, harmony, and interdependence with the environment are important. Subjectivity is *a* way of knowing. Emotions, intuition, and spirituality are therefore not detached from human affairs. As black women's ontological and epistemological ways of understanding, thinking, feeling, and behaving become added threads in the academy's fabric, mountains of multiple realities, values, visions, and voices will transform the oppressive Eurocentric patriarchy's molehill and lift the myopic veil that distorts social vision.

Too often, impaired social vision distorts reality and dulls the senses. "When the senses are dulled to racial [gender and class] oppression[s], one looks, but does not see; one tastes, but does not savor; one touches, but does not feel; hears, but does not understand."[2] Witness this reaction of Alice Walker, Pulitzer Prize novelist and author of *The Color Purple*, who was named a California "state treasure" for literature and was awarded a statuette—"a foot-tall sculpture of a woman's torso, without arms, legs, or head." *Warrior Marks*, one of her most recent works, is a film and companion book about female mutilation. As quoted in the *San Francisco Chronicle*, Walker said, "Imagine my horror when, after years of thinking about the mutilation of women, I was presented with a decapitated, armless, legless woman, on which my name hung from a chain." A spokesman for the artist who created the statuette called it "fine art that will increase in value." Responding, Walker stated that "though these mutilated figures are prized by the museum and considered art by some, the message they deliver is domination, violence, and destruction."[3]

The academy is another medium for this message to black women. Here race and sex are used as justification for domination, violence, and destruction. The much-maligned, mutilated, and misnamed images—mammy, matriarch, Jezebel, and welfare queen[4]—contribute to our marginal status in the academy. This Eurocentric and androcentric way of devaluing, denigrating, and distorting others' reality is also physically, psychologically, and socially costly to oppressors and oppressed. While we focus primarily on its price for the oppressed victims, such perverted reality creates a spiritual vacuity and presents an existential crisis of alienation and inauthenticity of selves and institutions. Like the disavowal of the impact of oppression on the oppressor, the survivability, strengths, and resiliency of the oppressed are also understated.

Within the oppressive enclave of the Eurocentric academy, the black woman, along with the black man, can fulfill the historic role of freedom fighter. In our increasingly mosaic global village, we can learn much from the strength and resistance of such figures as Fannie Lou Hamer, Ida B. Wells, Martin Luther King, Jr., Winnie Mandela, and Nelson Mandela. As the voice of black South Africa's women and children, an anchor for the freedom movement, and the keeper of Nelson Mandela's name for twenty-seven years, Winnie Mandela played a central role in black South Africa's liberation struggles, which contributed to Nelson Mandela's rise to the presidency of South Africa. (Survivors like Winnie Mandela are not immune to personal weaknesses. She apologized for her role in the murder of a young South African man.) Completing the thirty-one-year journey from prisoner to politician, Nelson Mandela, the newly elected president of South Africa, lit the freedom flames for all South Africans in his inaugural address, heard by a billion of the world's population. "We have triumphed in the effort to implant hope in the breasts of millions of our people," he said. "We enter into a covenant that we shall build the society in which all South Africans, both black and white, will be able to walk tall, without any fear in their hearts, assured of their inalienable right to human dignity—a rainbow nation at peace with itself and the world. . . . Never, never, and never again shall it be that this beautiful land will again experience the oppression of one by another and suffer the indignity of being the skunk of the world. The sun shall never set on so glorious a human achievement."

Can "so glorious a human achievement"—a multiracial, multiethnic, gendered montage of equal peoples—be translated into an authentic reality in the academy? Who can and will lead the way? Will the "Queens of Multiple Juxtapositions?" Balancing between two value systems—Afrocentrism and Eurocentrism—and experiencing the double jeopardy and double bind give black women a double angle of vision to equip them as a liberating force for race, gender, and class struggles. We must, therefore, understand their contribution to the academy and their role as liberator in that light. Unlike Sisyphus, we must "never, never, and never again" condemn ourselves to the fate of the Western patriarch's gods, to ceaselessly rolling oppressive boulders to the top of the hill only to have the stones roll back.

As liberators, we must be the beacon that leads the way out of inauthenticity and social blindness to authenticity and illumination and away from dualism toward holism, from competition toward cooperation, and from individualism toward community. Such an epochal shift would synchronize the union of opposites, which would require a transformation of the present-day academy and its unauthentic claims that it pursues knowledge and truth, free inquiry, value objectivity, meritocracy and excellence, fairness, and reason.

If the academy, the official knowledge architect, is to remain viable in the twenty-first century, it must draw from diverse blueprints. But in the closing decade of the twentieth century, white males are still those official knowledge builders. They comprise 39.2 percent of the United States population but account for 70 percent of tenured college faculty.[5] In the total full-time tenure-track faculty, white males make up 71.4 percent. White women comprise 19.4 percent; African American men, 2.1 percent; African American women, 1.4 percent; and other people of color, 5.7 percent. White males also make up 61 percent of the full-time faculty, both tenured and nontenured; white females, 26.5 percent; African American men, 2.4 percent; and African American women, 2.1 percent.[6] But is this unequal makeup of higher education based solely on excellence or merit? Should excellence also include other knowledge producers—those who are socially and politically defined as qualified producers of ways of knowing—or canons of the academy? Does meritocracy mean unearned advantage and conferred dominance because of white male skin privilege?[7]

This country is witnessing a demographic shift in the population of people of color. The census estimates that by the year 2000, 30 percent of the population will be people of color; by the year 2150, 45 percent will be. The majority of workers entering the job market by the year 2000 will be men and women of color and white women. But how will this demographic shift be reflected in university faculty and student populations?

Such demographic trends also affect higher education. Students who are ethnically and racially diverse by class and gender will have distinctly different styles of thinking, learning, communicating, decision making, and different ways of knowing. Will there be an adequate supply of faculty and administrators to meet higher educational needs and demands?

African American women bring to the academy a rich matricentric tradition of inclusiveness around issues of education and empowerment. In her position paper, sociologist Elizabeth P. Morgan reminds us that black women are well-suited as facilitators for the future academy:[8]

Many African American women were given some preparation for careers in academic institutions by the parenting to which they were subjected in their families and in their communities. . . . Among the social obligations extended to kin and non-kin after slavery were "considering free schooling for the poor neighbor's widow's children."[9] Continuing to the present, education is the traditional opportunity through which black families find their place in life.

In my own research in 1974, parents' responses in interviews suggested that their primary concern in parenting was to help their children develop in a supportive environment and achieve the ability to make choices from as broad a range of alternatives as possible. According to recent scholarship, parents' belief in the importance of education continues. One of the strategies operative in the expression of commitment to education was the creation of institutions of higher learning by blacks and for blacks since slavery.

In the tradition of black colleges, everyone was included in the process of education. Perhaps the most basic education for children is in the observation of the roles of individuals and family. . . . Billingsley has noted the strong egalitarian relationship among black married couples.[10] The female children had early models to promote self-confidence, as well as examples of doing whatever is necessary to promote family or other organizational stability.

Black women's long traditional role as educators—as agency, administrator, teacher—in empowering themselves and others offers a liberating compass for navigating through the "isms" in higher education. In critiquing the Eurocentric patriarchy, its pedagogies, paradigms, methods, and canons, we can balance the conceptual foundations of the Western scientific mind, which postulates that knowledge can be derived through procedures that are free of race, gender, ethnicity, class, age, or other such contexts. The holistic perspective recognizes that scientific knowledge and truth are products of human interpretative structures and are therefore relative to the observer, theoretical dogmas, physical and social context, cultural beliefs, and prevailing paradigms, which are self-validating. Richard Tarnas has observed that "the Paradigm acts as a lens through which every observation is filtered, and is maintained as an authoritative bulwark by common convention. Through teacher and texts, scientific pedagogy sustains the inherited paradigm and ratifies its credibility."[11]

Western scientific conceptual systems are, in essence, antithetical, mechanistic, and reductionistic. Linda Jane Myers noted that "an antithetical system that separates spirit and matter, assumes no natural order, seeks to control nature, and operates as if experiences were an accumulation of discrete events, would be seen as yielding false knowledge to the holist."[12] Knowledge and truth are therefore discovered in the intersection among diverse knowledge systems and differentially empowered groups. Hence antithetical and reductionistic scientific thinking is inadequate, concludes Cindy Cowden, a U.S. natural scientist, "to understand organisms, whether they are spiders, starfish, or women; . . . we can only understand organisms by seeing with a loving eye."[13]

In a transformed academy, "a loving eye" improves our angle of vision. In the global village, our physical and social survivability depends also on the eye of equality, justice, and peace, which is strengthened through diversity. Thus it is the responsibility of the academy to acknowledge pieces of this mosaic diversity and prepare for the twenty-first century. We must move beyond a Mayflower education and aspire to a more global celebration.

Notes

1. See chapter 4.

2. Lois Benjamin, *The Black Elite: Facing the Color Line in the Twilight of the Twentieth Century* (Chicago: Nelson-Hall, 1991), 251–52.

3. These quotes from the *San Francisco Chronicle* appeared in the *Daily Press* (Newport News, Va.), April 18, 1994, A2.

4. Sue K. Jewell, *From Mammy to Miss America and Beyond: Cultural Images and the Shaping of U.S. Social Policy* (New York: Routledge, 1993).

5. David Gates, "White Male Paranoia," *Newsweek*, March 29, 1993.

6. Deborah J. Carter and Reginald Wilson, "Special Focus: Racial and Ethnic Trends in Academic Employment," *Minorities in Higher Education*, Tenth Annual Status Report (Washington, D.C.: American Council on Education, 1992), tables 19–20. See also Alexander W. Astin, William S. Korn, and Eric L. Dey, *The American College Teacher: National Norms for the 1989–90 HERI Faculty Survey* (Los Angeles: Regents of the University of California, Higher Education Research Institute, 1991); Hugh R. Fordyce, *1993 Statistical Report* (New York: United Negro College Fund, 1993). Statistical data in parts 1 through 6 are based on these reports.

7. Peggy McIntosh, "White Privilege and Male Privilege," in *Race, Class and Gender*, edited by Margaret L. Andersen and Patricia Hill Collins (Belmont, Calif.: Wadsworth Press, 1992), 78.

8. Elizabeth P. Morgan, unpublished position paper, February 1994.

9. Herbert G. Gutman, *The Black Family in Slavery and Freedom, 1750–1925* (New York: Vintage, 1977), 229.

10. Andrew Billingsley, *Climbing Jacob's Ladder: The Enduring Legacy of African American Families* (New York: Simon and Schuster, 1992).

11. Richard Tarnas, *The Passion of the Western Mind* (New York: Ballantine, 1991), 360–61.

12. Linda James Myers, "Expanding the Psychology of Knowledge Optimally: The Importance of World View Revisited," in *Black Psychology*, edited by Reginald L. Jones (Berkeley: Cobb and Henry, 1991), 23.

13. Shulamit Reinharz, *Feminist Methods in Social Research* (New York: Oxford University Press, 1992), 3.

Part One
Black Women in the Academy
An Overview

During the past thirty years, a demographic and cultural shift has occurred in higher education. Black women, black men, other men and women of color, and white women have entered the teaching force in greater numbers than ever before. Although the number of black women in the academy has increased, however, we still remain largely invisible. According to the American Council on Education, we constituted only 2.1 percent of full-time faculty and 2.4 percent of part-time faculty in 1989, compared to 2.0 percent and 2.3 percent, respectively, in 1979. In 1989 only 0.7 percent of black women working in higher education were full professors; 1.6 percent associate professors; 2.7 percent assistant professors; 3.3 percent instructors, lecturers, and other faculty; and 4.2 percent administrators. Black women administrators and faculty are largely concentrated in predominantly black institutions. Whether in black or white institutions, we face barriers of racial and sexual discrimination. While black women in historically black colleges and universities (HBCUs) encounter sexual discrimination, we battle both sexual and racial obstacles in white academic milieus.

Nellie Y. McKay's "A Troubled Peace: Black Women in the Halls of the White Academy" gives experiential credence to the "promises and perils" of black women in the academy. Among the first cohort of black women scholars who entered white academia in the late 1960s and early 1970s, she writes about two decades of gender and racial "difficulties and discomforts" as well as triumphs, of being isolated and marginalized, and of competing for contested space in the Eurocentric patriarchal academy.

Yolanda T. Moses's "Black Women in Academe: Issues and Strategies" gives the reader a detailed empirical and experiential portrayal of the status of black women in both predominantly black and predominantly white institutions. She discusses how race and gender stereotypes intertwine to create double barriers. Moses explores such issues as professional climate, affirmative action, tokenism, mentoring and support systems, sexuality and sexual harassment, balancing competing obligations, collegiality, research, teaching and tenure, recruitment, and retention.

Chapter 1

A Troubled Peace

Black Women in the Halls of the White Academy

Nellie Y. McKay

In the early 1980s, I read a short paper at an MLA convention entitled "Black Woman Professor—White University," which addressed some of the difficulties and discomforts I felt other black women and I were experiencing at that time in our new roles as college and university professors in predominantly white institutions of higher education. The conclusion to that essay reads, "To be a black woman professor in a white university is difficult and challenging, but it is exciting and rewarding, and black women professors like it here. We aim to stay!" At the time, I did not ask, At what price?

Although I spoke largely out of my own experiences, I was part of a generation of black women with shared academic experiences. Most of us had gone to white graduate schools between the late 1960s and early 1970s and were the first, as a group (by race and sex), to find employment in predominantly white colleges and universities. And it was clear, as the premise of my text indicated, that as a rule, black women did not feel welcome or appreciated in their new positions, but having broken the barriers of this stronghold of sex prejudice, they planned no retreat from gains hard won.

The exception to this individual racial isolation in the workplace of white academia occurred when a black faculty member was part of a black studies program, the cause that brought the largest number of black faculty into a new space for them. Then the danger was group isolation, for chances were that all black faculty in his/her institution were located in black studies, as though black scholars had not received the same training as their white peers in history and literature and sociology. But this did not matter. In breaking down the barriers that had relegated even such figures as W. E. B. DuBois, Alain Locke, and other great black lights of an earlier era to the historically black colleges, these scholars made a crucial discovery. They learned firsthand that the gains of the civil rights movement did not constitute a reform of racial attitudes toward black people. Few white institutions were interested in them other than for the calm they could bring to troubled campuses by way of black studies classes to satisfy the demands of obstreperous black undergraduates. Only a small number held appointments in black studies *and* their disciplinary departments, and an even smaller number were hired solely in their disciplines.

Nevertheless, this segregation had advantages for the new field's development other than bringing black scholars from different disciplines together in intense situations. Among these advantages were that faculty could concentrate on learning for themselves what had been left out of their graduate education, and they could focus exclusively on the needs of a new interdisciplinary curriculum. This was helpful. It eliminated the possibilities of split loyalties to other departments and lessened racial confrontations within departmental work space. Black scholars who especially favored this isolation defended its merits by denouncing racism within the discipline departments.

In spite of these benefits, some black studies scholars were ambivalent about their positions outside of their home disciplines. They questioned the effects of the separation on the new field for the long term, on their personal intellectual growth, and on cross-racial relations with other faculty with whom they shared interests. Those in this situation would have preferred the dual-appointment model, like that of Yale and a few other institutions, which followed the patterns of African studies and American studies. All, however, agreed strongly, and correctly, that having been excluded from the academic curriculum until then, black studies absolutely required its own space to develop its own academic and political agendas and to carry out the intensive re-education that students and faculty needed in order to recuperate the intellectual dimensions of the black experience. Regardless of where black faculty were positioned within the structures of their institutions in their relationships to dominant traditional educational programs, these teachers rejected ideas of token status in the academy and its oppositional alienation from the center of the authority of the black intellectual tradition.

Personally, I endorsed a separate interdisciplinary space for black studies but favored a structure that insured black intellectual interaction with the community at large. A segregated black studies would operate only within the boundaries of its own marginality and increase the difficulties of making significant educational and political changes with the systems of power in the academy. Such changes would come only through the engagement between those located at the boundaries of the exclusive accepted knowledge we opposed and those at its center.[1] I understood black studies and my place in the white academy as a complex interweaving of political and educational issues. Like many of my colleagues, I was caught up in the fervor of reform. I wanted black studies to grow and develop into a force on college and university campuses across the country, but I was also concerned that our scholarship and teaching permeate the disciplines in the arts and sciences curriculum and thus completely transform them. The ideal goal was to reform conventional American education from outside and inside. Options on strategies to this end differ as widely today as they did then, but in the late 1960s and 1970s, for many black scholars, there was no choice. Black studies programs were the only spaces available to them in white colleges and universities.

Nor, in the academic ghetto of black studies, did the militant political rhetoric that so dramatically challenged racism build bridges between the new field and its discipline departments. Furthermore, in response to the unsettling presence of the revolutionary-minded inhabitants of this ghetto, white faculty threatened by curricular changes and the loss of the hegemony of Eurocentric-based knowledge defended the sovereignty of Western tradition on the basis that black studies was unsound academically and its fledgling faculty intellectually inferior to the rest of their campus colleagues. Obviously, this racist defense of the status quo increased hostilities between the opposing sides. Only many years later, with the emergence of more politically moderate black scholars as spokespeople for the field, with records of "acceptable" scholarship behind them, did large numbers of white faculty begin to acknowledge the merits of black studies. The Norton Anthology of Afro-American Literature,[2] the white literary establishment's final endorsement of this field, was one of the single most significant events in the history of black studies.

Historically, education is familiar ground for black women since it was always one of the few respectable professions open to the group. In the nineteenth century, middle-class black women were schoolteachers among free blacks before and after emancipation, and few obtained positions higher than employment in black elementary and secondary schools. Still today, black women in education and all black people point with pride to a long list of distinguished black women educators from earlier times: Fanny Coppin, Lucy Moten, Frances Watkins Harper, Margaret Washington, Mary Church Terrell, and Anna Julia Cooper, to name some of the best-known. Without the efforts of these women between the 1850s and the early part of this century, their race would never have produced the women and men who held high the torch of freedom and literacy for black people from the mid-nineteenth century through the 1950s and beyond. For although on all levels, until our time, racism remanded black women and men to historically black schools, and black male sexism consigned the handful of black women in the historically black colleges to activities associated with the female arts—teaching home economics, for instance, or performing specific duties closely linked to the interests of women students—these women provided the shoulders on which today's black women educators stand. They are our most revered role models.

In 1983 I was a professor, five years into my first job after graduate school and desperately struggling to qualify for tenure, the hardest test that a faculty member ever faces in pursuit of an academic career. No one told me then that for all of its difficulties, achieving tenure was only the end of one struggle that would lead to another, and another, and another, each increasingly less defined or concrete. No one could have explained what it really meant to be a black woman professor in a white college or university for the long haul. The following incident illustrates this point.

In my office, I was engaged in conversation with a black woman colleague in the Afro-American Studies Department. She was standing just inside my door. A white male professor from another department stopped at the door and, without apology, pushed his way past my colleague. Before either she or I realized what had happened, he preempted her presence in our space to make a request of me. I had scarcely grasped the politics of the situation before it was over—he was gone and my female colleague had retreated to her office across the hall. It was another everyday incident, in our days of such incidents, when white colleagues, without even trying, asserted the privilege of whiteness, especially male whiteness, over those they perceived to be unequal to themselves by the authority of race and/or sex.

Unfortunately, white male professors and administrators are not the only group that offend black women by their racist verbal expressions. White women faculty are equally guilty. The black woman is often told by the white woman that she would be happier if she "returned" to a historically black college (in most cases, she had not come from one). This advice is further emphasized when the white woman notes that the black woman's contact with the white academy—her education in a white college or university and her subsequent employment by another such institution—gives her added prestige in the historically black college. I received this advice shortly after I was tenured. My Ivy League graduate training, my colleague told me, would make me a "queen" at a historically black college.

Such anecdotes are not isolated or unusual events. They occur daily in many variations in the lives of black women professors.

The second incident noted is perhaps the most difficult to cope with because the suggestion is usually made by a white woman whom one knows and likes reasonably well and with whom one must also make alliances in the struggle against sexism in the academy. Consider that a senior black faculty member in my university recently asked me why she always feels "at home" when she visits historically black colleges as opposed to how she feels in our university, which, technically, is "home" for us. She followed that inquiry with another question: Why do we remain in the predominantly white university, where many abuses constantly beset our sensitiveness?

To the first part of her query, I replied that in the white academy, our location is always contested space even though it is as rightfully our space as that of others in the academy. When we visit historically black colleges, the space is uncontested. In one, our occupancy is conditional; in the other, it is unconditional. In one, there is everything to prove over and over again; in the other, we have nothing to prove. In black-dominated space, we are who we are. In that context, we can understand, but never accept, the impulse of the white suggestion that we "return" to the historically black colleges.

To my colleague's second question, I suggested that we choose to remain in these contested spaces because as black women (and men) we know that we have a right to occupy them and will not be driven out by those who would gladly see us go. We have not rejected the historically black colleges, and our anger boils when white people imply that they are inferior. But this knowledge does not make life easier on the white campus, and black women must always weigh the cost of their choices against the balance of energy, will, and the determination to survive with human dignity. Each woman must learn to identify her own limits.

For me, even after living this reality for many years and coming to understand much more than I did a decade ago of what it means to be who I am in the place that I am in, I find it impossible to conceive of myself in the state of complete "otherness," implied in the anecdotes above, that I represent in the world of whiteness. For what those in my racial and sexual group know but sometimes fail to remember is that the academy is a microcosm of the larger society in which we live and that America and all Western society remain provinces in which white men, and some white women, of a particular class and with particular dominant ideologies determine the nature of all of our existences. Thus, even without deliberate intentions to enforce dominance over others, the relations between whites and the "other" in white institutions of higher education develop and emerge out of a dynamic that reifies racist and sexist paradigms of power and powerlessness. How then has it been for black women in these last years of the twentieth century to live, work, and sometimes even claim success in the predominantly white academy?

I see our present in the context of more than two decades of my own constant struggle to minimize loss of personal dignity and find as much fulfillment as possible in my life in the work I have chosen to do. Today I, and many of the black women in the group I spoke of and for in the early 1980s, have scaled several resisting walls, and we have lasting scars to prove our efforts. Racism, sexism, and classism are unrelenting adversaries. No skirmish is minor. Each is a major confrontation with powerful forces of tradition, and there is always a price to pay for having been there. Nevertheless, in spite of or because of our bruises, we are on the other side from where we were a decade ago, and on that side, our white colleagues were forced, even if sometimes only perfunctorily, to acknowledge us as colleagues. For a short time, many of us, reaching this other side, experienced a strange sense of dislocation when, following our positive tenure reviews, we surmised that the "we" and "they" division in which we were positioned in our first years in the academy had disappeared. By virtue of our new standing, some of us thought (and such thoughts were very unsettling) we had become a part of "them," that having fulfilled the requirements of the game as they defined it, we now shared their legitimacy. Our discomfiture, however, was hardly warranted. We soon realized that although our status vis-à-vis such things as job security had altered appreciably, we were still excluded from the centers of power vested in the premises of white maleness.

The years have taught us that "we" are neither "them" nor who we were—that is, completely vulnerable in some areas of our lives. Blackness and femaleness insure that we can *never* be them, and we cannot, nor would we if we could, return to our early struggles. Experience tells us we occupy our own space: sometimes on the margins of all that goes on around us, oftentimes in the buffer zone between "them" and those who have taken our former places on the lines of anxiety and uncertainty. But we are always on a battleground trying to determine the nature of the fray and deciding how best to spend our valuable, but decidedly depletable, physical energies and psychological resources. Today, for the women who have followed us, we hope that we hold the door to professional success slightly more ajar than it had been for us. We hope that instead of reinventing the wheel, black women professors now entering the white academy strengthen the positions we set in place.

Yet for all of these hopes, I am not as optimistic about material changes in our situation as I was a decade ago. The quality of this peace disturbs me. True, over the last decade and a half, such things as open racial hostilities toward black and other minority group faculty have decreased considerably among faculties of mixed racial groups. Not even the most rabid bigot wants to be branded a racist. But many of those early hostilities have not dissolved; they have only become more subtle and dangerous. It is infinitely more sophisticated to attack affirmative action and like initiatives from behind the banner of "'quality' without quotas" than to make frontal attacks on minority groups. The result is a continuing disease among black and other minority group faculty within the halls of the white academy.

Earlier I was confident that we could collectively find a solution to some of the problems of race, class, and sex in the academy; today I am doubtful that we will ever achieve that goal. This reevaluation of the state of black women in the white university admits to grave disappointments, unfulfilled dreams, and deep frustrations on the part of most of the women I know. Change will not come until those responsible for the current conditions decide to end the impact that racism, classism, and sexism among white faculty and administrators have on the lives of others. My pessimism springs from feeling that nothing we have seen over the last twenty-five years indicates such action. While individual white faculty and administrators have made valiant efforts toward change, nevertheless, domination, empowerment, legitimacy, and authority remain in the places they have always been. Minorities and, to a large extent, white women are excluded from these places. After almost two decades of service in white colleges and universities, by dint of race, class, and sex, at best, black women and minority group others now experience themselves in the peculiar situation of outsiders within the white academy.

Some people will find it difficult to understand this distress among black women faculty and others. When we stand in certain places, like the major white research universities in the country, and survey faculty opportunities in higher education today, no one can deny that some earlier conditions of the work lives of black women educators have changed for the better. A more critical appraisal, however, reveals the disquieting statistics that even now only a small number of the professorate in the country are black women, and the overwhelming majority of these are still employed in historically black colleges, not always by their choice. Researchers generally estimate that black women compose less than one percent of the faculty in all colleges and universities, and half of that number are still in historically black colleges. For those who wish to enter white institutions, deep-seated social prejudices against blacks and women still work more effectively against black women. These women have an even harder time than black men or white women in gaining access to highly competitive graduate schools and in finding employment in institutions with resources to nurture research careers. In addition, those who are able to enter such colleges and universities on the junior level have a more difficult time achieving tenure because, until they become well known, their work is usually undervalued. The majority of black women in the academy are part of the negative statistics.

Why then does the world of blacks in higher education look more promising at a first glance from some perspectives? The answer lies in the view one gets from a position that easily blinks out the grim reality of most black experiences. From a more privileged place, one sees that a number of black women and men have risen above the difficulties I have described. These scholars, with a few exceptions, were fortunate enough to have gained admission to and to have succeeded in highly competitive and/or prestigious East and West Coast graduate programs in the 1970s and early 1980s. Now they hold appointments, even chair professorships, in institutions that are recognized as the most desirable in the profession. Everyone has heard that in this time, for all the ubiquitous problems of racial and sexual prejudices in university hiring, every major and hundreds of minor white institutions of higher education in the country are in competition for today's small pool of successful black scholars (especially women), and some are investing generously in some of those whom they identify as the most promising younger black scholars through postdoctoral fellowships, research funds, reduced teaching loads, generous leave policies, and so on.

What appears to be an unprecedented "buyer's market" for black women and men scholars, however, is anything but the true state of affairs for the majority of the group seeking academic careers outside of the historically black colleges. These well-publicized gestures toward a highly visible small group of brilliant, ambitious, achieving scholars now in well-placed positions in a few institutions signal no major changes in the general status of black women or men in higher education. Most white college and university administrators and faculty, including those who claim a willingness to hire black scholars if only they could find "qualified" ones or could afford one of the "stars," do not know and cannot comprehend that if such a thing as color/class/race/sex-blind hiring existed, those now excluded would bring tremendous enhancement. Instead, they still consider the possible employment of those from these groups as an affirmative-action duty or, worse, as evidence of their liberal attitudes in educational matters. Never do they see the potential richness of experience in diversity and openness.

Recent controversies over the values of multicultural education have more clearly defined the dragon that lurks at the heart of the problem, which has kept large numbers of people of color out of faculty positions in the majority of white colleges and universities in America and continues to treat those within as second-class citizens. When the barricades in the struggle for black studies in these institutions came down in the 1960s and early 1970s in response to pressure brought to bear as a result of the black revolution of that era, a new area of study entered the academy. And while black studies units have had a history of academic and political successes and failures in the white academy, the field opened up the way for a generation of young black scholars to enter these institutions. Those who have succeeded defined and developed careers that would have been almost impossible for them otherwise. Other fields— women's studies, Chicano studies, Native American studies—as well as a host of white ethnic studies programs have benefited from the battles fought by black studies in the late 1960s and early 1970s.

Although no active coalition exists between these "studies" groups except as "ethnic studies" on a few campuses, together they present a force reminiscent of but collectively more potentially threatening than black studies alone was in the 1960s. In many quarters, the response from those who still promote higher education predicated on the "Great Books" theory of the primacy of Western civilization is an elevation of the tactics of the earlier time. The controversies over the value of a diversified curriculum, now being waged on many campuses and in some popular as well as scholarly journals and magazines, initiated under the auspices of such groups as the National Association of Scholars, are struggles to maintain and privilege Euro-American concepts of knowledge as the only "Truth." They indicate how deeply embedded are the roots of racial, class, and sex prejudices in the centers of white academic power. While sometimes less dramatically experienced, black women endured these pressures for more than two decades.

Even in those institutions in which they are treated well, black women professors in white colleges and universities are always aware that their presence represents a disruptive incursion into spaces never intended for them. Whatever their ranks, some students, faculty, and administrators are always poised to undermine their professional authority. The vicious, obscene attack on a black woman historian at Princeton University by a group of students in the fall of 1990 bears out this point. Under the banner of the secret (for fear of reprisals) "National Association for the Advancement of White People, Princeton Chapter," and claiming the authority of the "Shockley Report,"[3] the group distributed flyers, including one in the professor's mailbox, in which Martin Luther King Jr., Winnie Mandela, the professor in question, and affirmative action were called filthy names, and the female professor was singled out as an intellectual incompetent. While this was clearly a racist attack, on other campuses black women professors (and white women, too) have also been sexually harassed by white and black men seeking to intimidate them. Often women are uncertain of how to respond to such racist and sexual outrages—this other kind of rape. Unfortunately, too many women, as in cases of physical rape, remain silent, internalizing their victimization. Women must learn to scream loudly, and other colleagues and college/university administrators must be actively involved in the processes that counter such harassment tactics. Even when a few black women appear to be accepted and rewarded on their merit through prizes and awards, praise for good scholarship, and/or appointments to important positions and committees, for instance, incidents surrounding them indicate tolerance rather than full recognition of them as equals. Perhaps the low number of available black faculty for positions in white colleges and universities is the clearest indication of the level of threat the presence of black women and black men presents to higher education outside of the historically black colleges.

The small number of black women and men on white college and university faculties is appalling. None of these institutions, to my knowledge, has an aggregate black faculty that is a respectable proportion of its overall faculty population. Even in institutions conscious of the politics of the situation, dozens of departments remain all-white enclaves; and some white colleges and universities still have few black faculty not associated with black studies. In the new "hot" market for star black women and men faculty, department heads and university and college administrators blame the small pool of available candidates for the odiousness, at times, of the competition for these faculty; sometimes they also use the numbers as an excuse for the absence of blacks on their faculties. Few, if any, seem to realize they are consciously and/or unconsciously complicitous in maintaining the size of that pool. Nor do they acknowledge the devastating implications of their inertia in attacking the problem at its roots—not at Ph.D. commencements, but at the junior high school level. How otherwise do we account for the state of black graduate affairs such as exists in the English department of my own university? Each fall I receive dozens of telephone calls and letters from colleagues across the country requesting that I recommend to my newly or nearly graduated black English department Ph.D. students faculty positions in the schools of the callers and writers (usually to teach courses in black literature as part of their workload). Had I twenty-five such students in any year, I could guarantee each one a job in the college or university of her/his choice. Yet in my thirteen years here, the department has had a total of two such graduates from its program, separated in time by approximately nine years. My university is no worse than any other comparable Ph.D.-granting institution with which I am familiar.

Why this absence of black graduate students from English departments when there is such a demanding market for them? Is there a connection between the desperate competition of discipline departments in white universities and colleges for the few available black faculty and the absence of candidates to fill those positions? In comparison to the numbers of black graduates in engineering, law, and business during the period of my Wisconsin tenure, after more than twenty-five years of black studies in the academy, I have no doubt that white colleges and universities have a vested interest in maintaining the minuscule size of the number of black Ph.D.s in arts and sciences. Nor do I deny that engineering, law, and business have been more attractive to black undergraduates for several years. But I am also aware that many potential black graduate students have been turned away from pursuing Ph.D.s in my discipline by admissions policies that fail to keep up with the currents of the times and thus, ultimately, perpetuate the racist problems of the past.

Black women everywhere suffer race, sex, and class discrimination because they are black and women, and the halls of the academy provide no safe sanctuary. In white universities and colleges, these women experience the workplace as one of society's exclusive clubs to which, even though they have as much right as everyone else to be there, they will never gain full membership—at least, not in the lifetime of this generation of scholars. Given the record of the past, their numbers will always be small; they will be mere tokens in most institutions. The black women I know complain constantly of overwork: more is expected of them than of others by students, other faculty, administrators, and the professional organizations to which they belong. And that work is infinitely varied, including the expectation that they will assume responsibility for working out the problems that black and Third World students encounter in the academy. Students (even white ones) in need of counseling on academic issues as well as psychological ones continually appear on the doorstep of the black mother, the great bosom of the world. The black women feel sure, too (or is this paranoia?), that their performances are more carefully scrutinized than those of some others.

In addition to work expectations, black women faculty often find themselves bearing the brunt of jokes and other overt ethnic and gender insensitivities of their colleagues, which does little to enhance their comfort levels among their peers. The energy they spend on extra work that serves the needs of their institutions and the psychological toll of coping with the racism and sexism of colleagues are barriers to growth and success in the profession of their choice. These problems have a direct relationship to the difficulty many of the women face in completing sufficient research for tenure.

But if the obstacles they face in the white academy are daunting, black women have not been impotent. Looking back over the years since the first group of black women entered this arena, it is possible to see that their presence, like that of all minorities in the same space, has changed the face of American education and revised the premises of previously accepted knowledge to include materials long excluded from such considerations. In their interactions with students and faculty, they have also made major positive impact on many lives. They know that, despite the cost, these years have not been wasted ones.

Still, underlying any possible successes, a troubled peace exists between black women and the various constituencies of the white academy they serve. This state is neither energizing nor creative, for it reflects the wastefulness of marginalized work and devalued selfhood—commodities our world can ill afford to spend this way. White educators must assume leadership and responsibility to deal effectively with the debilitating forces of race, class, and sex that have brought us to this pass. Only then will the troubled peace black women now experience inside these halls dissipate. At that time, to take liberties with the words of the great black woman educator Anna Julia Cooper, the whole race of those with rights to be there, with privilege to none, will enter a new space of equality with them and share in opportunities to do the long-neglected work without which the survival of our world will always be in doubt.[4]

Notes

1. Helene Moglen, "Power and Empowerment," in *Women in Academe*, edited by Resa L. Dudovitz (Oxford: Pergamon, 1984), 132.

2. Henry Louis Gates, ed., *Norton Anthology of Afro-American Literature* (New York: Norton, 1990).

3. William Shockley, winner of a Nobel Prize in physics, argued that people of African origin are lower on the evolutionary scale. Expression of his views was confined to speeches before lay audiences.

4. Anna Julia Cooper, *A Voice from the South by a Black Woman of the South* (New York: Oxford University Press, 1988), 31.

Chapter 2

Black Women in Academe
Issues and Strategies

Yolanda T. Moses

This chapter explores the climate for black women faculty members and administrators in both predominantly white colleges and universities and historically black ones. It focuses on the subtle and not so subtle ways that race and gender stereotypes can combine to create double obstacles for black women. While the chapter does not specifically mention black women students and staff members (that is, secretaries, clerical workers, custodians, and others), several of the problems discussed and issues raised for black women faculty members and administrators pertain also to black students and staff members. These problems include stereotyping, disrespect, isolation, and lack of support networks.

Black women have been participants in higher education for more than a century, but they are almost totally absent from the research literature; rarely is the impact of racism and sexism on black women in academe examined.[1] This chapter will provide such an examination. In addition, it will serve to help institutions be more supportive and aware of the needs of black women faculty members and administrators.[2]

Many misconceptions surround the status of black women on campus, in large part because there is very little research specifically concerning black women in academe, how they are faring, and what issues are of concern to them.[3] Research on minorities and women often ignores the unique position and experiences of black women. The result is that black women are virtually invisible.

In order to create a more hospitable climate for black women on the campuses of this country, we must know about their needs and concerns. Most research conducted on racial/ethnic minority issues continues to treat minority groups as sexually monolithic; it assumes that what is true for minority men is also true for minority women. For example, a review of four national reports on higher education shows that in only one of the reports, *The New Agenda of Women for Higher Education*, were the issues of race and gender integrated throughout.[4]

Professional Climate Issues

Black women faculty members and administrators face numerous barriers to their growth and success in academe. Issues such as support, retention, research, teaching, and tenure are affected by the climate for black women at both predominantly white institutions and historically black ones. Equally, the leadership, advocacy, and career satisfaction black women administrators strive for are affected in subtle ways by a sometimes chilly and unwelcoming environment. To effectively recruit and retain more black women faculty members and administrators, colleges and universities need to understand these barriers and institute policies and programs to overcome them.[5]

Between 1977 and 1986, the number of blacks earning doctorates declined by 27 percent. Experts foresee severe shortages of minority faculty members for years to come. There has been a shift in the male-female proportions of the black doctorate pool. After a slump in 1977, black women substantially increased their share of doctoral degrees.[6] In 1986 they received almost 61 percent of all doctorates awarded to black candidates, compared to 39 percent in 1977.[7] Black women who attain doctorates tend to be older than the average student and take longer to get their degrees; they tend to be married and to have parents with limited educational attainment; and they are most likely to earn their doctorates in education, the social sciences, and the professions.

More than 70 percent of all blacks with doctorates are employed in academe. Blacks in general have the lowest faculty progression, retention, and tenure rates in academe, with black women most concentrated in the lower academic ranks. Black women faculty members are also concentrated in two- and four-year colleges and universities (including historically black schools) rather than in research universities.[8] Black women constituted 1.9 percent of full-time faculty in higher education in 1985; they made up 0.6 percent of full professors, 1.4 percent of associate professors, 2.7 percent of assistant professors, and 3 percent of instructors, lecturers, and others.[9]

Although black women have had a rich tradition of leadership in higher education of blacks in the United States, their current status as administrators is not impressive.[10] In 1985 only 3.4 percent of administrators in higher education were black women; white women constituted 30.4 percent.[11] The majority of black women administrators are employed on black campuses and are generally concentrated at the lower administrative levels (below dean). They are concentrated in student affairs and specialized positions such as affirmative action officer and assistant to the president.[12] Like black female faculty members, black female administrators tend to be older than white female administrators; most are married; and they are concentrated in two-year rather than four-year institutions.[13] Twenty-two colleges and universities in the United States are headed by black women.[14] Black women administrators generally earn 15 percent less than their male counterparts.[15]

Affirmative Action Dilemma

The values of the university administration and those of the faculty and staff are often in conflict over affirmative action issues; black women get caught in the middle. For example, James E. Blackwell and William Moore Jr. note that the attitudes of faculty members on affirmative action are highly complex and lack uniformity.[16] Blackwell states, "People are motivated by economic self-interest; hence their responses to programs like affirmative action will be dictated in large part by perceptions, real or imagined, of the threats to their own sense of economic entitlements imposed by the implementation of such programs." Verbal support for affirmative action does not necessarily transform itself into support of a program or of new minority employees once they are hired. Some faculty members may believe that black women are hired only because of affirmative action, not because of their qualifications. Black women may be stereotyped, resented, or even treated with disrespect because they are perceived as less qualified. Responses from a questionnaire sent out by the Project on the Status and Education of Women (PSEW) bear this out. A faculty respondent notes, "My appointment was seen as an affirmative action hire. People did not expect me to be successful. But I was. Some were actually rude enough to tell me so—thinking it was a compliment."

Double Discrimination: Racism and Sexism

Black women, including faculty and administrators on historically black campuses, experience and must deal with not only the effects of racism but also those of sexism. Racism and sexism may be so fused in a given situation that it is difficult to tell which is which. As one faculty member says, "It is difficult for me, as a black woman, to have the issue of sexism treated as a legitimate topic by my colleagues. While they understand the interconnections of racism and sexism at an intellectual level, at the operational level they tend to ignore it, or dismiss it, as not pertaining to themselves."

Black women may also be ignored, isolated, or passed over for promotion in favor of less qualified people. For example, one respondent reports, "I have been upset by the racist and sexist treatment that I have received from both white men and white women unable to deal with a black woman in a position of authority. Frequently they would attempt to go over my head or around me to keep from dealing with me."

The "Token" Syndrome

In higher education administration, as in society, the numerically dominant group controls the academy and its culture. The small number of people from other ethnic or racial groups are often seen by the dominant group to be "tokens and are, thus, treated as representatives of their group or as symbols rather than individuals."[17] Black women faculty members and administrators often find themselves in the position of being tokens. Because there are so few of them, there is a tendency for the majority to see these women as spokespersons for all blacks rather than as individuals with other qualifications. Black women are often asked to sit on committees as experts on blacks, and they are asked to solve problems or handle situations having to do with racial difficulties that should be dealt with by others. There is often no reward for this extra work; in fact, black women may be at a disadvantage when they are eligible for promotion or tenure because so much of their time has been taken up with administrative assignments. A respondent to the PSEW questionnaire offers this example: "When I first arrived at the university (my first professional appointment), I enjoyed the attention I received. After a short while, however, I realized that the responsibility associated with being the only black female in my college, and only one of a handful in the university, was overwhelming. I have suffered several instances of burnout and exhaustion. As a consequence, I have learned to maintain a less visible profile as a coping and survival strategy."

Mentoring and Support Systems

One of the consistent themes in this report is that women in higher education are often viewed as "others" or "outsiders." As a result, they are rarely included in university networks. They are less likely to be familiarized with the practical aspects of their jobs or receive support for their efforts. Joyce Bennett Justus, Sandra Freitag, and L. Leann Parker talk about the lack of mentors and sponsorship as a major stumbling block to the attainment of a successful academic career for women.[18]

Mentoring is especially useful early in the development of a career, with senior faculty members mentoring their junior colleagues. Sponsorship is typically more useful in the later stages of a career—for example, when a junior administrator wants to move up and needs a well-established senior person to promote her accomplishments, both on and off the campus. White males have been the usual beneficiaries of this kind of support. Many women and minority members have pointed out that the lack of collegiality in their departments or offices isolates them from professional networks, research grants, and publishers. To move up the academic ladder, one depends heavily on the support of departmental colleagues. Without this sponsorship, many women and members of minority groups need to develop alternative avenues of support, such as finding mentors in other departments or at other institutions.[19] One faculty respondent to the PSEW questionnaire comments, "I have had to create a strong and well-integrated network across the nation, which means I am far from isolated, but I'm in a university where I [do not feel comfortable asking] the person next to me to go to lunch." Another says, "I have gotten a great deal of support from black female staff members. Although there has been some tension, my overall involvement with black female students (both graduate and undergraduate) has been positive. These women have provided—though to a limited extent—the kind of support and encouragement system missing from my interactions with the faculty in my department."

Black female administrators face similar situations. A respondent to the PSEW questionnaire notes, "In my position, I have been able to hire some dynamic black women in professional positions. I have also taken the responsibility for offering to act as mentor to them. I know how lonely it was for me starting out in administration several years ago."

Historically Black Colleges

Despite some real progress, black women faculty members and administrators in historically black colleges often face gender inequities.[20] From the early establishment of black colleges, more than a century ago, the actions of women faculty members and administrators have been a focal point of campus life.[21] Ruth N. Swann and Elaine P. Witty, in their 1980 study of black women on historically black campuses, noted that these women are "both competent and secure in dealing with men as equals, because they have been working seriously for so long."[22] Swann and Witty found that women on these campuses constituted 32 percent of full professors, 30 percent of associate professors, 39 percent of assistant professors, and 79 percent of instructors.

Studies of black women in black institutions indicate that there are fewer women in top administrative positions. Lea E. Williams, in her study of chief academic officers (CAOs) of private and public black colleges and universities, found that chief academic offices were generally held by middle-aged black males; on the average, women CAOs were slightly older and had worked in their current institutions longer than men; at public universities, female CAOs earned less than males; and at private institutions, female CAOs earned more than males. None of the female CAOs surveyed aspired to the office of president, and none of them was likely to be chosen as chief executive officer in the president's absence; the opposite was true for males.[23] Finally, while men and women CAOs at black colleges have similar career paths to the top academic offices, female CAOs take longer to achieve these positions and, once there, have different salaries and administrative responsibilities than their male counterparts. Williams suggests that black schools need to examine these inequities by looking at their policies concerning recognition and promotion as well as by examining attitudes that impede women's career progress. More research needs to be done on the quality of the campus environment and career satisfaction for both black women faculty and staff.[24]

Women's Worth in a Man's World

It is generally accepted in our culture that men can be powerful, assertive, ambitious, and achieving. Many people, however, are uncomfortable when black women exhibit these traits. In view of the devalued status that black women have in our society, their presence in positions of authority on campus is a problem for some people. For example, a faculty member talks about a white male student who came up to her after the first day of class and said, "I was ready to check out of this class when I saw you walk in as the teacher. But I sat through your class and you really know your stuff; I am going to keep the class."

Gender—especially in academic settings—influences perception and evaluation of behavior and achievement.[25] A woman's work is often not given the same credit as a man's; her accomplishments may be ignored or, conversely, scrutinized very carefully, or she may be perceived as "moving too fast." Respondents to PSEW's questionnaire illustrate these points. A black female president at a predominantly white institution said, "I was given a 'review' by the powerful local conservative newspaper. It was a true witch-hunt, but they did not find anything. By the way, the paper has not done a similar review of the president [a white male] of the other regional university." According to another, "Management behavior that is tolerated from black men is not tolerated from black women. Strong black female managers are not looked upon favorably. Black women who supervise other black women come under particular scrutiny. This also holds true in comparison to white women."

Sexuality and Sexual Harassment

Some people relate to women in terms of their sexuality rather than as professionals. For black women, as for white women, this can lead to incidents of sexual harassment—"unwelcome sexual advances, requests for sexual favors, and other verbal or physical conduct of a sexual nature."[26] Some men have difficulty distinguishing between friendship and sexuality and may misread demonstrations of the former as sexual overtures. Some men have difficulty seeing women in anything but a sexual role and may abuse their power as faculty members or administrators. Although it is not clear how many women faculty members and administrators experience sexual harassment, a study at Harvard University found that 32 percent of the tenured faculty women there had experienced it, and 49 percent of the untenured female faculty had been sexually harassed.[27]

Because of a perceived lack of status and power, minority women in general—and black women in particular—are especially likely to be treated in a superficial manner or viewed in terms of their sexuality by both white and minority men. This can result in sexual harassment, social distancing, and a lack of collegiality.[28] The only praise some black women receive may be for their attractiveness—not their achievement. The respondents to PSEW's questionnaire offer some examples. One woman reports, "One of my white colleagues used to tell me how nice I looked all the time. Maybe it was his way of paying me a compliment. But it made me feel as though he did not care about my contributions to the department." Another says, "The most frustrating experience is working with black males who refuse to see the chauvinism and subtle harassment in their interaction with black women. Because these men are black, this experience is even more upsetting." And a third notes, "The senior vice president and provost commented positively on my dress on several occasions, and there had been a brief discussion about where I shopped. Later, when I requested funds from him to go to an international conference to present a paper, his response to my request was, 'If you didn't buy so many clothes, you would have money to travel.' Although I was given the money to make the trip, the comment was certainly out of order."

Balancing Competing Obligations

Another obstacle for both black women faculty members and administrators is the tug-of-war they experience in trying to balance professional with family and community responsibilities.[29] Black women have a long tradition of managing family, work, and community responsibilities; however, like white women, they do it at a cost. Black women tend to engage in more teaching, counseling of students, and committee work than do white males and females. As a result, they may do less research and write fewer publications than their white male or female counterparts. This presents dilemmas for faculty members and administrators who want to pursue an academic career, as they clearly express in responses to the PSEW questionnaire. One explains:

> To have civic consciousness and involvement, to have a family, to teach with social responsibility and vision, to pursue socially pertinent research and writing, to actively render service to one's profession—to do all of these things would be to be a whole, multifaceted, well-rounded person. However, in light of the imbalances in academia (for example, the focus on publications at the expense of teaching integrity), to do all of the above is to risk chronic burnout and frustration. I am still learning how to reach a comfortable balance. But if I do, it will be because of my own drive and convictions rather than because of any support from the university.

A second says, "Black women scholar/teachers who are also mothers and wives have a very difficult time. The standards, demands, and pressures of academic work reflect 'Yuppie' value orientations, and they are androcentric to boot! To remain competitive in the Ph.D. academic market . . . often translates into sacrificing family, personal life, and so on for career development (particularly with the 'publish or perish' syndrome of research universities)." By another respondent's account, "There are subtle discrimination and disadvantages that affect black women during childbearing years. Beyond the problems related to race, I find that being a mother of small children puts me at a professional disadvantage because the standards and expectations [of the academy] do not reflect or respect the realities of a parent/professional. Maternity benefits and leaves need to be adjusted for faculty who cannot afford to be penalized (momentarily or in terms of promotions) for having a baby."

One solution to this problem of balance may be heightened institutional recognition of the value of extra work in the academic community. A publication by Joyce Bennett Justus and others calls for redefining traditional notions of productivity so that teaching, counseling, community work, and advising are weighed more heavily in the promotion and tenure processes.[30]

Collegiality Among Faculty

One of the best sources of support that faculty members can get is the respect and validation of their peers. Collegiality fosters a sense of community as well as an atmosphere of creativity in which people can share ideas, collaborate, and generally benefit from working together. For many black women, especially those on predominantly white campuses, this essential ingredient is missing from their professional experience. Because of stereotypes based on racist and sexist attitudes, black women's contributions to their departments are not always recognized or valued. Black women respondents to the PSEW questionnaire talk about the ways in which they have been excluded from the academy. One describes her situation thus: "Beyond the collegiality expressed by a few faculty members, I am invisible except for the important role that I play as a documentary, legitimizing category for affirmative action purposes. Faculty whose specialties are similar to my own (outside my department) rarely seek me out for exchanges or for participation in symposia and other such things. I work pretty much in isolation, dependent upon extra-university cross-fertilization and moral support." Another reports, "When I came to the university in 1984, I was generally amazed at the callous, arrogant, and disrespectful way that white staff spoke to me. I assumed they had no 'home training' in manners or were just not used to addressing black women in a professional manner. Now I understand that they pick up their cues from their administrative superiors."

Some black women at both historically black and predominantly white schools report feelings of neglect, ostracism, and isolation. A professor in a predominantly male department at a public, coeducational, historically black college says, "I have been in this department for a long time, and it is very male-oriented. They do most of the committee work and write most of the joint proposals. Usually the women, including myself, are not invited to participate. Also, all other opportunities are usually awarded by the department chairman or the dean to men in the department. I have turned to 'hard' teaching and writing and research on my own. Having these outlets has enabled me to get along with the men and keeps them from being threatened."

Research, Teaching, and Tenure

Black women tend not to be included in collaborative research projects with their peers; they lack sponsorship and therefore have less access to sources for research.[31] Jackie Mitchell also talks about the problem of having research trivialized and devalued if it focuses on black issues or issues of a social, activist nature.[32] She further notes that a successful academic career is "the product of not only the intelligence and ability to do outstanding scholarship, but also of ambition, dedication, hard work, circumstances that foster an orientation toward scholarship, and acceptance into a small fraternity of scholars." Black

women have a difficult time winning that acceptance, especially in predominantly white colleges and universities. Some examples from respondents to the
PSEW questionnaire include the following: "There is still the tendency either
to criticize my research efforts or believe that ethnic professional associations,
conferences, and workshops are not as worthy as predominantly nonethnic ones."
"I have gotten a lot of criticism about the fact that I am doing research [on
social issues that affect black women in a cross-cultural context] that is not
rigorous or relevant to the thrust of the department." "I have survived because I
do two sets of research: one on black women's issues and one that is main-
streamed within my profession. It is the only way I will have legitimacy when
tenure time comes."

Typically, minority men and all women spend a higher proportion of their
time teaching and advising rather than engaging in original research. This has
happened in part because they are clustered in two- and four-year colleges rather
than in research institutions.[33] Many women who responded to the PSEW questionnaire stated that teaching was one of the most rewarding experiences of
their professional careers. Here is one example: "My consistently positive experiences have been my relationships with students. This university has a primarily working-class student body, and I identify with those students. I also work
in several programs that allow me to interact with the relatively small minority
population."

Some faculty members expressed conflict in their teaching experiences: "On
several occasions, I have had black students become upset when they expected
special treatment from me in class—and they did not get it. I told them I would
work with them one-on-one but that there would be no special favors." "I find
that students (mostly white) seem to resist the intellectual and pedagogical authority of a black female professor."

James E. Blackwell and others discuss the reasons for the low numbers of
blacks (men and women) who receive tenure and the time it takes them to
receive it compared to the time it takes for white males, white females, and
other ethnic/racial groups.[34] Black women also face distinct disadvantages as
"outsiders" who want to join the club. Responses from the PSEW question-
naires show that, like black males, other people of color, and white women,
these black women have a hard time getting tenure. One relates: "When I first
came up for tenure, my effort was met with opposition on many fronts. I clearly
got the sense that I was stepping out of my 'place,' or the place that others had
assigned to me in their minds. This was very upsetting. I don't think that I have
unduly high expectations for collegial relationships, but I do want to be given

the rewards I've earned. I guess this was an opportunity to mourn the fact that my professional relationship with my colleagues is limited because people cannot cope with who I am." Another says, "Service contributions are not weighed heavily in merit and promotion decisions at my university since it is regarded as a research institution. As a consequence, the multiple roles that black female professors like myself are forced to maintain and the university/ethnic/gender service obligations that we are required to fulfill erode sacred research time."

Retention

The recruitment and retention of black women faculty members is critical not only to the careers of the women themselves but to the successful recruitment and retention of black women students. Some university administrators have stepped up efforts to recruit, hire, and grant tenure to black female faculty members in greater numbers. Until top administrators are more effective in insuring job satisfaction and an environment free from hostility, arrogance, and devaluation of diversity, however, black women may choose not to enter academia or to remain there. There is already some indication that, as a group, blacks are beginning to avoid careers in academia.[35] By offering more money and better working conditions, business and private industry may be claiming the best and brightest black students.

Despite a demonstrably chilly climate on many campuses, many black women enjoy their jobs in academia. Respondents to the PSEW questionnaire, for example, find many aspects of their experiences quite positive: "A new department chair has asked me to put some of my thinking into practice. This way, I can work to help the institution be more sensitive to the needs of women and people of color." "Once accepted . . . I have been treated fairly well by other faculty and administrators (for example, I have gotten release time privileges and I have gotten respect for my ideas)." "Usually the dean of the college will give me money to travel to conferences or to put on a conference here. Also, the vice president for academic affairs (a woman) financially supports my projects. The affirmative action officer and faculty union representative also are helpful."

Other black female faculty members recognize the existence of racism but feel that the good aspects of their position outweigh the bad: "Yes, I am staying here. I have a great job and good colleagues. I do what I want for the most part. I also have some racist, vicious colleagues, but the good outweighs the bad most of the time." "I plan to stay here because this is a major city where I can live comfortably as a black female professional. I have a good teaching situation, good colleagues in my field, and an opportunity to work with a center with a national reputation. I think I recognize that racism and sexism are everywhere; thus I have no illusion of seeking a place where they do not exist."

Leadership and Advocacy: Critical Skills

The ability to lead is perhaps the primary quality of an administrator. In her review of the literature on black women administrators, Patricia A. Harvard lists three major barriers to women in seeking and maintaining administrative positions: (1) sex role stereotypes, (2) organizational barriers, and (3) internalization of traditional female behaviors.[36]

Harvard found that successful administrators had obtained their doctorates and described them as committed, independent, dominant, active, adventurous, sensitive, secure, and self-confident.[37] Other researchers point out other important components of successful leadership such as self-confidence, technical and interpersonal skills, awareness of organizational attitudes, and conformity to the culture; having mentors both inside and outside the university is also important.

Having achieved their goals, many black women administrators in positions of leadership find that, while they may have the title and the responsibility, they often do not have the authority or the backing they need to make decisions or implement their ideas. They may be undercut by colleagues as well as superiors. When asked about their reception as leaders, the administrators in our survey talked about the problems of nonrecognition of their power and authority: "I feel that I am unwittingly used to validate personal and institutional racism. It took me a while to discover that I was being 'set up' to fail. In meetings that I am not chairing, my remarks are sometimes treated as trivial and unworthy of discussion. There have also been times people have gone behind my back when I was away from campus and attempted to change the direction of projects for which I was responsible." "My [opportunity for] leadership is lessened because I am frequently not included in activities (for example, meetings and conferences where I have direct responsibility). I often receive information secondhand." "I have been upset when I have not been consulted about major decisions that affect my area of responsibility, or when decisions are made that will reflect back on me."

Do women and minorities move into leadership positions and maintain the status quo, or do they advocate change? Black women, as mentioned earlier in this chapter, have a long history of educational advocacy and activism. Responses to PSEW's questionnaire regarding the most positive aspects of their jobs show their active involvement in their students' lives and an optimism about the potential for change. An associate vice president for student affairs talks about a larger goal: "In addition to my regular work, I enjoy working with students. I enjoy introducing them to the black perspective and to the women's perspective. Seeing females (especially minority ones) grow and develop in all areas of their lives is such a reward for me."

Many of the women who responded to the PSEW questionnaire are very comfortable talking about their plans for change. They see their positions in higher education administration as one of the major ways to effect change in their students' lives and ultimately in society.

Conclusion

The issues and examples in this chapter demonstrate clearly that black women faculty members and administrators do not perceive themselves and their concerns as integrated into the missions, goals, and social structures of college campuses. The job of integration is not one that black women can or should tackle alone; it will take the hard work of many members of the academic community. It must be done if we are to encourage black women students in this country to pursue higher education and professional careers as faculty members or administrators in academia.

Notes

1. For an overview of research on faculty, see James E. Blackwell, "Faculty Issues Affecting Minorities in Education," in *From Access to Achievement: Strategies for Urban Institutions: Proceedings from a National Invitational Conference*, edited by Richard C. Richardson Jr. and Alfredo G. de Los Santos Jr. (Washington, D.C.: National Center for Postsecondary Governance and Finance, 1988), 165–98; Joyce Bennett Justus, Sandra Freitag, and L. Leann Parker, *The University of California in the Twenty-First Century: Successful Approaches to Faculty Diversity* (Berkeley: University of California Press, 1987); McLean Tobin, *The Black Female Ph.D.: Education and Career Development* (St. Louis: Washington University Press of America, 1981); William H. Trent et al., "Making It to the Top: Women and Minority Faculty in the Academic Labor Market," *American Behavioral Scientist* 27 (January–February 1984), 301–24; and William Moore Jr. and Lionel Wagstaff, "The Black Woman in Higher Education," in their *Black Educators in White Colleges* (San Francisco: Jossey-Bass, 1974).

For an overview of research on black women administrators, see Ruth N. Swann and Elaine P. Witty, "Black Women Administrators at Traditionally Black Colleges and Universities: Attitudes, Perceptions, and Potentials," *Western Journal of Black Studies* 4 (Winter 1980): 261–70; Constance M. Carroll, "Three's a Crowd: The Dilemma of Black Women in Higher Education," in *All the Women Are White, All the Men Are Black, But Some of Us Are Brave: Black Women's Studies*, edited by Gloria Hull, Patricia Bell-Scott, and Barbara Smith (New York: Feminist Press, 1982), 115–21; Myrtle Hall Mosley, "Black Women Administrators in Higher Education: An Endangered Species," *Journal of Black Studies* 10

(March 1980): 295–310; and Lea E. Williams, "Chief Academic Officers at Black Colleges and Universities: A Comparison by Gender," *Journal of Negro Education* 55 (Fall 1986): 443–52.

2. This chapter draws from extensive files and previous reports of the Project on the Status and Education of Women (PSEW) as well as informal interviews PSEW conducted with black women and anecdotal material it collected through an informal questionnaire on black women faculty members and administrators around the country. The eleven-item, open-ended questionnaire was sent out to approximately eighty black women students, faculty members, and administrators in spring 1988. The sample included women from public, private, historically black, and predominantly white colleges and universities across the country. There was a 50 percent response rate to the survey.

3. Deborah Carter, Carol Pearson, and Donna Shavlik, "Double Jeopardy: Women of Color in Higher Education," *Educational Record* 68–69 (Fall 1987–Winter 1988): 99–100.

4. *The New Agenda of Women for Higher Education* (Washington, D.C.: American Council on Education, 1987); *Minorities on Campus: A Handbook for Enhancing Diversity* (Washington, D.C.: American Council on Education, 1989); *One Third of a Nation: A Report on the Commission on Minority Participation in Education and American Life* (Washington, D.C.: ACE Education Commission of the States, 1987); *From Access to Achievement: Strategies for Urban Institutions* (Washington, D.C.: National Center for Postsecondary Governance and Finance, 1988).

5. See Bernice Sandler, *The Campus Climate Revisited: Chilly for Faculty, Administrators, and Graduate Students* (Washington, D.C.: Association of American Colleges/Project on the Status and Education of Women, 1986).

6. Shirley Vining Brown, *Increasing Minority Faculty: An Elusive Goal* (Princeton: Educational Testing Service, 1988), 6.

7. *Summary Report 1986 Doctorate Recipients from U.S. Universities* (Washington, D.C.: National Research Council, 1986).

8. Ibid., 25.

9. "EEO-6 Higher Education Staff Information Surveys, 1985, U.S. Equal Employment Opportunity Commission," in *Minorities in Higher Education, Seventh Annual Status Report 1988* (Washington, D.C.: American Council on Education), 33–34.

10. Patricia Bell-Scott, "Schoolin' 'Respectable' Ladies of Color," *Journal of the National Association of Women Deans, Administrators, and Counselors* 43 (Winter 1980): 1.

11. "EEO-6 Higher Education," 36.

12. Adrian Tinsley, Cynthia Secor, and Sheila Kaplan, eds., *Women in Higher Education Administration* (San Francisco: Jossey-Bass, 1984), 7.

13. Patricia Harvard, "Successful Behaviors of Black Administrators in Higher Education: Implications for Leadership," paper presented at the meeting of the American Educational Research Association, San Francisco, April 1986.

14. "Growth Slows in Number of Women Heading Colleges," *Higher Education and National Affairs* 37 (March 14, 1988): 1–5.

15. Harvard, "Successful Behaviors," 7.

16. William Moore Jr., "Black Faculty in White Colleges: A Dream Deferred," *Educational Record* 68–69 (Fall 1987–Winter 1988): 117; and James E. Blackwell, "Issues Affect-

ing Minorities in Higher Education," paper presented at the conference "From Access to Achievement: Strategies for Urban Institutions," Los Angeles, November 15–17, 1987, 20.

17. Harvard, "Successful Behaviors," 8.

18. Justus, Freitag, and Parker, *University of California*, 23.

19. Ibid. See also Margaret Wilkerson, "Lifting as We Climb: Networks for Minority Women," in *Women in Higher Education Administration*, 59–66.

20. See Bell-Scott, "Schoolin'," 22–28; Moore and Wagstaff, *Black Educators*; and Mosley, "Black Women Administrators," 295–310. See also Williams, "Chief Academic Officers."

21. Bell-Scott, "Schoolin'," 27.

22. Swann and Witty, "Black Women Administrators," 262.

23. Williams, "Chief Academic Officers," 451.

24. Jacqueline Fleming, *Blacks in College: A Comparative Study of Students' Success in Black and White Institutions* (San Francisco: Jossey-Bass, 1984); and Walter Allen, *Gender and Race Differences in Black Student Academic Performance, Racial Attitudes and College Satisfaction* (Atlanta: Southern Education Foundation, 1986).

25. Sandler, *Campus Climate Revisited*, 6.

26. Ibid., 9.

27. Ibid., 10.

28. Ibid., 13.

29. Justus, Freitag, and Parker, *University of California*, 25.

30. Ibid., 27.

31. Justus, Freitag, and Parker, *California*, 23; see also Brown, *Increasing Minority Faculty*, 25.

32. Jackie Mitchell, "Visible, Vulnerable, and Viable: Emerging Perspectives of Minority Professors," in *Teaching Minority Students*, edited by James H. Cones III, John F. Noonan, and Denise John (San Francisco: Jossey-Bass, 1983), 17–28

33. Ibid.

34. Blackwell, "Issues Affecting Minorities in Higher Education," 23; and Brown, *Increasing Minority Faculty*, 25.

35. Brown, *Increasing Minority Faculty*, 25.

36. Harvard, *Successful Behaviors*, 46.

37. Ibid., 15.

Part Two

Alternative Paradigms for Black Women in the Academy

Epistemological and Ontological Issues

As more black women have entered the academy, we have begun to challenge the Eurocentric and androcentric ways of thinking and knowing. Specifically, the knowledge about black women and other men and women of color has been largely generated by white supremacy and male superiority. In the United States, as the American Council on Education noted, whites comprised 88.5 percent of the full-time faculty in higher education in 1989, of which 62 percent were males. Since we black women have been excluded, until recently, from the academy as definers, producers, and dispensers of knowledge about our realities, the Anglo-male orientation, which distorts our realities and images, is reflected in curricula, scholarly journals and textbooks, pedagogies, concepts and paradigms, organizational structures, and organizing assumptions.

Black women have historically resisted, individually and collectively, these imposed definitions and images of our racial and sexual being. Bell Hooks notes in *Talking Back: Thinking Feminist, Thinking Black* that "oppressed people resist by identifying themselves as subjects, by defining their reality, shaping their new identity, naming their history, telling their story." In this section, Shelby F. Lewis's "Africana Feminism: An Alternative Paradigm for Women in the Academy" continues that redefinition of ourselves and our realities. She argues that the racist, classist patriarchy is the underlying foundation of a global hegemonic paradigm, which operates in the academy, as well as other arenas, to protect elite white male privilege. In the academy, white males control the production and dissemination of information. On the question of gender, Lewis writes that white women "own the realm of theory," which excludes other voices. She proposes that black women academicians begin deconstructing the Eurocentric classist, racist patriarchy. She maintains we can start by embracing an Afrocentric perspective and "naming ourselves African American." This redefinition, according to Lewis, reinforces the African linkage, a necessary paradigm to shape a global liberation struggle against racism, sexism, and classism.

While Lewis posits an alternative paradigm for black women in the academy, Beverly M. John's "The African American Female Ontology: Implications for Academe" addresses the origin and importance of an African American female ontology, born of the multiple juxtapositions of culture, gender, and race, in the survival of the academy, the United States, and the global community. John calls for an inclusion of this way of viewing the world in creating a more humane academy and world community.

Chapter 3

Africana Feminism

An Alternative Paradigm for Black Women in the Academy

Shelby F. Lewis

In the foreword to the 1983 book *Feminist Theories*, Dale Spender notes that
central issues in theories for liberation are who controls the channels of communication and who decides what we know.[1] She suggests that males own the
realm of theory and that society legitimates male-oriented theories because males
control information, are able to put forward their own version of facts, and can
suppress alternative versions.

While this analysis of male hegemony is insightful, Spender has neglected
to acknowledge African American women's knowledge and theories. This form
of marginalization highlights the critical reality that on questions of gender,
white women own the realm of theory. White male hegemony in the larger
society is replaced by white female hegemony in the feminist arena.[2] Though
alternative versions of gender-related facts are not always suppressed, a hostile
climate is created for other female voices, leading a number of scholars to assert that white female hegemony is a central issue in Western feminist theories
of liberation.[3]

In the academy, including the black academy, where white versions of facts
are disseminated in the literature used for research and in that assigned to students, seemingly the areas of control collectively enjoyed by white males and
white females contribute to racial dominance. How racial hegemony was attained and how it is maintained are questions that should be addressed. It is
also important to address the need for black women to deconstruct and overcome the basic assumptions underlying white hegemony.

This chapter addresses the question of hegemony in the academy and explores the premise that racist/capitalist patriarchy forms the pillars of a global
paradigm of oppression. This paradigm operates in the academy to support and
protect the interests and concerns of rich white males, except on questions of

gender, where white females constitute the dominant class. Three major issues are examined: (1) the hegemonic paradigm that structures a hierarchy of inequity in the academy; (2) the historical development of white female hegemony on questions of gender; and (3) ways that black women can break out of this paradigm and create an alternative, emancipatory model.

The Hegemonic Paradigm

When the *Handbook for Achieving Sex Equity Through Education* was published in 1985,[4] it devoted a sixty-nine-page section entitled "Sex Equity Strategies for Specific Populations" to the question of minority, handicapped, and other nonmainstream women. I was asked to do the chapter "Achieving Sex Equity for Minority Women," which I elected to do because I felt that alternative voices and perspectives were needed in the volume. So, through collaborating with Native American, Hispanic, Asian, and African American women from various disciplines and backgrounds, I completed a chapter that made a number of interesting points about the role of educational systems in societies. The major premise of the chapter is reflected in the following abstract:

> Educational systems reflect the values and practices of the larger society. If the larger society is sexist, racist, and based on economic, cultural, and historical inequities, it is unrealistic to expect educational systems to be devoid of these inequities. Educational systems, after all, are the formal, institutionalized, systematized vehicles through which the larger society socializes youth to the values held by the dominant or ruling group. . . . defining the very narrow dimension of the formal educational system as the arena within which a struggle for equity is concentrated raises strategic as well as theoretical questions. . . . alternative theoretical constructs must be developed for measuring, evaluating, and linking the causes, relationships, and consequences of inequity in the various dimensions of society.[5]

The basic assumption of this analysis is that black females in the academy are imprisoned in a dysfunctional paradigm because they are paralyzed by its logic, structures, and biased knowledge base. Just as the formidable illusions around the Wizard of Oz were powerful enough to control and channel minds, the academy, as a consequence of such illusion, is viewed through a glass darkly. The smoke and mirrors that make the system work day in and day out are not easily perceived because only the hegemonic versions of reality are reflected in the mirrors.

The instrumental values that shape the mirrored images are race, class, and gender.[6] Although rich white male images shine brightest, rich white female images also shine, as do other sanctioned images of the model. But the images of impoverished black females do not shine because the mirrors are grounded to deflect their contributions.

What role does the academy play in creating and sustaining the global hegemonic paradigm? A contaminated knowledge base is the fuel for the establishment of hegemony in the academy. Data in the knowledge base are generated, analyzed, vetted, stored, and valued on the basis of the needs and goals of racist/capitalist patriarchy. Because of the purpose and role of the contaminated academic knowledge base, one understands that the academy is not a place where truth reigns supreme. The data are not required to be objective, complete, or accurate; what is required is the exoneration of the history, aspirations, views, contributions, and interests of the hegemonic class and the diminution of the accomplishments of marginalized groups, even if this means total distortion of history and complete fabrication of material reality. An example is the falsification of the relative differences in the sizes of the continents so that Africa would not take its prominent place on the map of the world. The curriculum, pedagogy, research methodologies, organizational structures, and organizing assumptions of American education are also integral to sustaining the hegemonic paradigm. The illusion of objectivity, including biased standards for measuring qualifications for entry and upward mobility, very nearly insulates the academy from the critical thinking necessary to expose the contrived reality. This process is most noticeable when the standard biases of traditional disciplines are stringently applied to nontraditional, primarily interdisciplinary approaches to the generation and dissemination of knowledge. The assessment and ratings for the work and publications of those who represent nontraditional disciplines, such as black studies and women's studies, are generally low;[7] this is because scholars in the academy are programmed to denigrate alternative versions of facts and because the new disciplines have not yet been adequately programmed to reflect the preferred images of the hegemonic paradigm.

Scholars who attempt to raise basic questions and set norms may be excluded from significant research projects and funding; their methodologies, analyses, and findings may be carefully critiqued and denounced, and their academic qualifications may be questioned. When subtle attacks under the guise of "academic standards" and "legitimacy" are ineffective, character assassination may take place, and livelihoods may be threatened. For example, through media attacks, political action, and academic pressure, Dr. Leonard Jeffries, former chair of black studies at City College of New York, was victimized and made an example to all who would question the established versions of historical fact.

Understanding the reason for the "established standards" enables suppressed groups in the academy to reject academic imperialism and to frame discourse that unveils the smoke and mirrors and undermines the basis of global racist hegemony in the academy.

White Female Hegemony in the Academy

Two common feminist themes are oppression, or denial of power, and struggle, or quest for power. These themes have always been present in American liberation struggles. Native American women, Hispanic women, both free and enslaved African women, both indentured and free European women, and contemporary women of all shapes and sizes continuously focus on powerlessness and empowerment. It is part of a primordial cry for liberation.

Because of the racial dichotomy in American history, there are two Americas and two American feminisms, one revolutionary and the other reformist, one focusing primarily on gender and one linking all forms of oppression, one exclusive and the other inclusive.

This bifurcation is very real in the academy. White American feminist history has been, for the most part, reformist, and white feminists have been able to use mainstream channels of communication to disseminate and legitimize their versions of facts and establish dominance over the realm of theory and questions of gender in the academy because of their relations, and sometimes solidarity, with white male power holders in the state and in the academy.

Mainstream feminism roughly parallels the mainstream women's movement, which can be divided into two waves. The first wave has its roots in the abolitionist movement of the nineteenth century, and the second wave is rooted in the civil rights movement of the twentieth century. The first wave split into two groups in the 1860s. One group sought to combine the demand for black suffrage with women's suffrage by advocating universal adult suffrage.[8] This group saw a strong and direct relationship between black struggle and gender struggle.

The second group was made up of a strong contingent of white women who opposed the ratification of the Fourteenth and Fifteenth Amendments in the name of women's rights. This group felt betrayed by what it saw as congressional efforts to prioritize the needs of black men over those of white women.[9] It is this branch of the women's movement that provides the defining tenets of mainstream American feminism in the absence of an overarching framework for revolutionary change and within the context of racial discord.

Analyses of this aspect of mainstream feminism have been fragmented, tentative, and generally uncritical primarily because of the location of white women in the hegemonic paradigm. They are essentially locked in a family struggle against their fathers, husbands, brothers, and friends; rather than undermining the power of the white family, they have sought a redistribution of that familial power.

Historically, racial affinity has been more fundamental than gender affinity in American society. In the political arena, for example, racial hegemony has been consistent. One example is the lack of support from mainstream feminists for Shirley Chisholm's historic 1976 bid for a presidential nomination within the Democratic Party, even though she was the first contemporary woman to seek the post. Instead, support was given to the white males that Ms. Chisholm opposed. In addition, there was no groundswell of support for Lenora Fulani's 1992 New Alliance Party bid for the presidency. She too was opposed by white males. Nor did women's groups rally around Angela Davis during her bids for the vice-presidency under the Communist Party banner. In 1988, however, the National Organization for Women and other women's groups flocked to Geraldine Ferraro's campaign and made the gender gap a major issue in her bid for the vice-presidency on the Democratic ticket.[10] To suggest that "chances" for winning determined the level of support for the respective female candidates is actually an admission that feminist principles are conditional at best.

While white feminists overwhelmingly supported Anita Hill during the Clarence Thomas hearings, it is important to remember that her confrontation was with a black male, and the debate was framed as a gender-only issue. White women also used that situation to voice their outrage at their absence from the Senate. Subsequent to the hearings, white females focused on getting women elected. The Year of the Woman was the outcome of the confrontation.

Feminist scholarship growing out of the mainstream framework effectively marginalizes black female contributions to American feminist theory and practice. Scholars who accord intellectual character to the contributions of "other" women are seen as voices for a subgroup for special populations. Only "they" speak for American women.[11] In effect, white feminists universalize their theories of gender and liberation while particularizing and thereby minimizing the theories of other women. However, a critical divergence exists between mainstream and revolutionary feminism. The search for alternative approaches to oppositional feminist struggle in American society is informed by the theoretical paralysis resulting from the ascendancy of mainstream feminism.

In response to white hegemony, black women have initiated a politics of identity that calls attention to the differences among women, especially differences in women's forms of oppression and access to or denial of privileges. They attribute these differences to interlocking structures of domination, socially defined and constructed down through history in terms of race, class, and sexuality.[12] Too few white feminists understand and acknowledge this difference or the racist and nonrevolutionary nature of their feminism.

Barbara Smith suggests that much of what white women call feminism is actually female self-aggrandizement, because inherent in the definition of feminism are a theory and practice to free all women. Anything less than this vision of total freedom is not feminism.[13]

American revolutionary feminism grows out of the activities and experiences of enslaved African women and creates alternative voices and strategies of struggle. Angela Davis notes that one of the supreme ironies of slavery was that the black woman had to be released from the chains of the myth of femininity in order for the slave master to extract the greatest possible surplus from her labor.[14] She suggests that the revolutionary consciousness of the slave woman was honed in the bestial realities of her daily experience and that her oppression necessarily incorporated open forms of counterinsurgency. Enslaved women became part of overt and covert movements to overthrow oppression. They wanted to destroy the system of slavery and the state that sanctioned it. Women like Sojourner Truth and Harriet Tubman are well known, but countless others provided support and fodder for revolts and radical forms of resistance to various types of oppression. This larger question of human rights, the basis of revolutionary feminism, was a part of their consciousness.

This revolutionary consciousness was also manifested during the civil rights movement. Fannie Lou Hamer and other women like her, guided by the assumption that she was discriminated against because of race, gender, and class, concluded that the system of segregation and the state that supported it had to be transformed.[15] Because Ms. Hamer and other black women have experienced multidimensional oppression, they have sought multidimensional and radical strategies to end that oppression—strategies that go beyond the reformist goals of the civil rights movement and the mainstream feminist movement.

Conceptualizing Africana Feminism

Until feminist struggle is transparently linked with global struggles like the development struggle and the struggle of peoples and states for self-determination, it is unlikely that the fundamental questions and issues in black female liberation and the obstacles to it will be adequately understood and addressed. Development theory, state theory, and feminist theory all touch on aspects of women's lives, but only when the three converge is there clarity about where women of African descent stand in the world order. To lay the foundation for an alternative paradigm for women of African descent, it is necessary to examine and compare global movements and theories that attempt to address the hegemonic model of racist/capitalist patriarchy.

In the 1960s and early 1970s, attention was focused on the role of women in the development process within the nation-state, with emphasis on economic development. Both scholars and policy makers approached the issue from a utilitarian perspective; ethical issues and the rights of women were seldom addressed. The argument, essentially, was that women play critical roles in agricultural and rural development and that failure to provide policies and programs to increase and improve their productivity would be disastrous for development programs.[16] Greater participation by women in the development process and their ultimate integration into the economies of given nation-states were the popular recommendations of the 1960s and 1970s scholars.[17] Only in the 1980s did some of these scholars note that integration and more participation by women in the development of the patriarchal state could make them participants in their own oppression.

It is fortunate that research and debate during the United Nations Decade for Women focused on the question of equity for women in development, not simply participation by women in the development process. For women of African descent, this new focus helped solidify concerns about the relevance of many aspects of Western feminism. Official government delegates to the U.N. Decade Conference, who were interested in integration and participation of women within the nation-state, did not enter into dialogue, which suggested that subverting or undermining the patriarchal state was a legitimate goal of female victims of the state. Nonofficial delegates, however, wanted to examine all available options and to engage in discussions that would clarify their status and roles in the state and would prepare them to discuss revolutionary ideas.

It is within this global context that the question of women within the hegemonic framework was discussed and the role of the nation-state in defining and maintaining cross-national oppression was addressed. The global feminist dialogue that resulted aided the development of Africana feminism.[18]

In this climate, feminist scholars of African descent began to collaborate and corroborate common themes and realities. They discovered that no matter where they were placed on the global battlefield, they were engaged in the same struggle and would likely benefit from combining their knowledge and resources. Out of this dialogue and common journey, the basic tenets of Africana feminism were formed.

Those African American women representatives to the conference who were from the academy were made aware by the dialogue that they should link Africana theory building to black studies and women's studies programs. They were conscious of the internal inconsistencies, contradictions, and biases of these academic programs, and many felt that their interests were not well served by either of them: black studies programs emphasized the needs and concerns of black males, and women's studies programs focused on the needs and concerns of white females. Rather than viewing black women as the common link between them, both groups saw them as appendages. Thus, in response to the failure of white women to confront their racism and the failure of black men to confront their sexism, black women's studies was born. The title of a 1982 publication captures the essence of the struggle: *All the Women Are White, All the Blacks Are Men, But Some of Us Are Brave: Black Women's Studies.*[19] The emergence of black women's studies did not end the concerns about the marginalization of African American women in the academy. A decidedly nationalistic, middle-class bias characterized early black women's studies programs. In fact, the failure of middle-class black women to confront their nationalist orientation and class biases led to the comparative and global approaches found in Africana women's studies. The research, teaching, and discourse in this arena, along with African women's experiences in the economic and political crisis of the 1980s, contributed significantly to Africana feminist theory building in America.

The International Cross-Cultural Black Women's Studies Summer Institute was among the groups that evolved during this period. This group meets annually, in a different nation each year, to examine the state of black women and discuss issues of primary importance to the host group while at the same time doing research and organizing around issues of common concern to all oppressed people. Out of the research and discussion come resolutions that transcend regional and national boundaries.

The women who participate in this work are formulating broad-based strategies to confront the global impact of racist/capitalist patriarchy. They are also suggesting that Africana feminism might be the concept under which a variety of global ideas and strategies may be subsumed. First, Africana feminism seeks to deconstruct the notion of separate and discrete struggles against racial oppression, class oppression, and gender. Second, in addition to eschewing the one-dimensional approach of mainstream feminism, Africana feminism transcends nationalistic, cultural, class, and geographical boundaries. Third, Africana feminism recognizes that women of African descent are stratified and that building a movement that binds this stratified group together and addresses common needs is as difficult as it is important. Fourth, Africana feminism recognizes the need to deconstruct and change the contaminated knowledge base and distorted mirror image that support racist/capitalist patriarchy. Fifth, Africana feminism is not antimale or antiwhite; nor is it opposed to honest and fair accumulation of wealth. It is unconditionally opposed to sexism, racism, and accumulation at the expense of others, especially women of African descent. Finally, and in sum, Africana feminism opposes all of the false assumptions undergirding the hegemonic paradigm.

Thus it should not be difficult to understand how and why Africana feminism emerged and why it attempts to seek out, subvert, and destroy racist/capitalist patriarchy or why it is necessary to situate an analysis of black women in the academy within the Africana feminist paradigm.

Africana Feminism in the Academy

Once black women in the academy situate themselves within the global struggle against racist/capitalist patriarchy, they are positioned to build a bridge for youth and others in the academy and are poised to serve as both catalysts and resource leaders for empowering the community of the oppressed.

How does one begin to deconstruct a self-perpetuating paradigm based on the values, interests, and views of oppressive power holders? Any viable approach to this phenomenon must focus first on deconstructing contrived history, demystifying the false scientific basis of subjective knowledge, uncovering the hypocrisy and special interests that undergird it, and presenting it clearly and forcefully to those who are paralyzed by the controlling paradigm. We begin the deconstruction by seeking an Afrocentric perspective.

By naming ourselves African American women, we acknowledge the African link, and we sanction and reinforce the global connection. This perspective enables us to understand that we should not accept the minority status offered us by the hegemonic paradigm. Using a global approach to facts, we are a majority. The difference in conclusions is based on where one stands when looking at objective reality. Topics chosen for study in the academy; the amount of time, energy, and resources devoted to the research; the context used for framing research questions; methods of analysis; selective emphasis on one set of facts over others; interpretation of those facts, how they are designed, and whose interest they are generated to serve—all depend on perspective within a prevailing paradigm. Justice, logic, equity, and freedom are all defined by, administered by, and sanctioned by the logic of the paradigm.

As African American women in the academy, we must question the placement of the mirrors in the dominant paradigm. We must inform our youth that the instrumental values of American society are set by those who benefit most from them, that the images emanating from those values reflect their strengths while ignoring their weaknesses. In contrast, they reflect poorly on those who are most unlike the self-serving images. We must convince our peers and youth of the need to create our own images and eschew the ones reflected in the mirror. We must take over the commanding heights of our struggle and determine our impact and our status in the world order.

Since the rich industrialized nations of the West are aligning with nonindustrialized and poor European nations, and those nations of the former Soviet Union with majority populations of color are excluded from the new accord, it appears that the realignment taking place and the new world order are based on racial dominance.

It seems obvious that an alternative paradigm is necessary to shape a liberation struggle for those who are exploited by the prevailing framework. It seems equally obvious that the path to that new model is knowledge. Since the academy is the vehicle through which contaminated knowledge is disseminated to our youth and the place where the youth are socialized to perpetuate the paradigm, it is a good place to initiate change, a good place to prepare for a viable alternative to racist/capitalist patriarchy. It must be understood, however, that the struggle within the academy is but part of the larger struggle for liberation, and, while it might (and should) produce versions of facts to undergird the struggle, it must always be guided by the tenets of the larger, global struggle.

As African American scholars, we can research, write, and publish works to be used in deconstructing the prototype. We can teach concepts and approaches that counter the negative thrust of history and liberate African peoples from paradigm paralysis and from never ending, ever changing, and constantly escalating exploitation within the paradigm. Too few of us are engaged in theoretical and/or empirical research that looks seriously at our place in society and in the academy. Without focusing more attention on decontamination of the knowledge base and deconstruction of the hegemonic paradigm, we will never break the mirror that reflects our marginalization. We will never burst loose from the dominant model. We will never free ourselves from white hegemony. But free ourselves we must. No one will, can, or should be expected to do it for us. It is our challenge. African American women in the academy must meet that challenge.

We must also begin to recognize and acknowledge the works and contributions of other women of African descent. Many of us fail to cite them in our publications, place them on our reading lists, and recommend them to our students and friends. This is one way to encourage, acknowledge, and support alternative voices and scholarship. We must not fall into the trap of assuming that only publications in refereed journals or those produced by "reputable" publishing houses are worthy of citation. If we would but consider the hegemonic norms of those publishing houses and the constraints on getting works with alternative messages published, we would realize that much of the information that we seek is excluded from the legitimated knowledge base, and therefore we must make a special effort to locate, critique, and disseminate the best of the ideas that we find elsewhere. Unpublished papers, speeches, guides, flyers, and other forms of expression contain messages that are important to the struggle. We must begin to use them in the academy.

Perhaps the most valuable skill that we can develop and pass on to our youth is critical thinking. Learning to raise questions about facts, relationships, and conclusions is important, but questioning structures, frameworks, and underlying assumptions and goals is basic to ending paradigm paralysis. Critical thinking is also a key element in the proper socialization of our youth.

At this point in history, more African American women than African American men enter the academy; however, too little attention is given to women's socialization. Everyone recognizes that socialization is critical to development and that people can be socialized for enslavement or liberation, but too few of us have begun to create models based on versions of facts that focus on the needs of young African American women.

By confronting and exposing the contaminated knowledge base and the smoke and mirrors that fuel the global hegemonic model, we are empowered to create an alternative, emancipatory paradigm. This is the promise of Africana feminism. This is the challenge to African American women in the academy. How we address the challenge facing us is not yet clear. But address it we must. Not to address it at all is unthinkable.

Notes

1. Dale Spender, ed., *Feminist Theorists: Three Centuries of Key Women Thinkers* (New York: Pantheon, 1983).

2. See Audre Lorde, *Sister Outsider* (New York: Crossing Press, 1984); and Shelby Lewis, "A Liberationist Ideology," in *Women's Rights, Feminism, and Politics in the United States*, edited by Mary Shanley (Washington, D.C.: American Political Science Association, 1988).

3. See Bell Hooks, *Yearning: Race, Gender, and Cultural Politics* (Boston: South End Press, 1990); and Diane Fowlkes, *White Political Women: Paths from Privilege to Empowerment* (Knoxville: University of Tennessee Press, 1992).

4. Susan S. Klein, ed., *Handbook for Achieving Sex Equity Through Education* (Baltimore: Johns Hopkins University Press, 1985).

5. Shelby Lewis et al., "Achieving Sex Equity for Minority Women," in *Handbook for Achieving Sex Equity*, 365.

6. Barbara Sizemore, "The Education Paradigm: Black Schools in America," speech delivered at the annual meeting of the African Heritage Studies Association, New Orleans, 1988.

7. Shelby Lewis, "Africana Feminism: The Ties That Bind," paper delivered to the "Conference on African and African American Women: The Ties That Bind," Baton Rouge, 1990. See also Filomina Steady, "The Black Woman Cross-Culturally: An Overview," in *The Black Woman Cross-Culturally,* edited by Steady (Cambridge: Schenkman, 1981).

8. Mary Lyndon Shanley, *Women's Rights, Feminism, and Politics in the United States* (Washington, D.C.: American Political Science Association, 1988), 7.

9. See Jo Freeman, *The Politics of Women's Liberation* (New York: Longman, 1975).

10. See the *Atlanta Constitution* and the *New York Times,* November 3, 1988, and other major newspapers around the country.

11. See Mae King, "The Political Role of Stereotyped Images of the Black Women in America," in *Black Political Scientists and Black Survival,* edited by Shelby Lewis Smith (Detroit: Balamp, 1977); and Jewel Prestage, "Political Behavior of American Black Women," in *The Black Woman,* edited by La Frances Rodgers-Rose (Beverly Hills: Sage, 1980).

12. Diane Fowlkes, *White Political Women* (Knoxville: University of Tennessee Press, 1992).

13. Barbara Smith, "Racism and Women's Studies," in *All the Women Are White, All the Blacks Are Men, But Some of Us Are Brave: Black Women's Studies,* edited by Gloria T. Hull, Patricia Bell-Scott, and Barbara Smith, (Old Westbury, N.Y.: Feminist Press, 1982).

14. Angela Davis, "Reflections on the Black Woman's Role in the Community of Slaves," *Black Scholar* 3, no. 4 (December 1971): 7.

15. Leslie McLemore, "Fannie Lou Hamer," speech presented at the annual meeting of the National Conference of Black Political Scientists, Baton Rouge, 1989).

16. Ester Boserup, *Woman's Role in Economic Development* (New York: St. Martin's, 1970); Joycelin Massiah, "Indicators of Women in Development: A Preliminary Framework for the Caribbean," in *Women and Work and Development,* research papers, Women in the Caribbean Project (Cave Hill, Barbados: Institute for Social and Economic Research, University of the West Indies, 1984); and Christine Obobo, *African Women: Their Struggle for Economic Independence* (London: Zed, 1989).

17. Andre Nicola McLaughlin, *Report of the International Network of Women of African Descent* (New York: International Resource Network of Women of African Descent, 1985); and Shelby Lewis, "African Women and National Development," in *Comparative Perspectives of Third World Women,* edited by Beverly Lindsay (New York: Praeger, 1979).

18. Shelby Lewis, "African American Women in Their Own Struggle," *African Commentary* (August 1990): 13–15.

19. Gloria T. Hull, Patricia Bell-Scott, and Barbara Smith, eds. *All the Women Are White, All the Blacks Are Men, But Some of Us Are Brave: Black Women's Studies* (Old Westbury, N.Y.: Feminist Press, 1982).

Chapter 4

The African American Female Ontology
Implications for Academe

Beverly M. John

The twenty-first century will create and require totally new configurations. Intellectually, politically, and socially, traditions that have guided and governed will have to be adapted and relinquished as demographic shifts and political upheaval rearrange and redefine power relationships. Social and political rearrangements will precede any paradigmatic shifts in academe much as technological changes precede ideological shifts. Those rearrangements that are discussed in paradigmatic/ideological terms will be carefully selected to insure their reification of traditional models.

Hegemony notwithstanding, programs that illuminate the necessity for redefining human and environmental coexistence receive limited but increased visibility. Recycling is an example of an idea that is more visible now than in times past, but the urgency of its implementation is yet to be truly understood. Western consciousness still does not really perceive human beings as part of the ecosystem. Peaceful coexistence is not a priority; manipulation of natural and constructed contexts is the major goal. The West will now have to learn what the East has always known. Specifically, a holistic analysis is prerequisite to clarity: spirit and matter are one.

Indeed, the philosophy, values, vision, and techniques of the white Western male perspective will be insufficient to address twenty-first century conditions and will be increasingly dependent on the very philosophies and populations that this perspective has systematically marginalized. This exploration will attempt to illuminate the juxtaposition of formal power and a systematically marginalized population: namely, white males and their domination-oriented ontology and African American females and their dominion-oriented ontology. Domination assumes entitlement; dominion assumes responsibility.

This chapter will explore the African American female ontology and its intellectual implications for the academy. The exploration must commence with an examination of the nature and quality of academe. Having clarified the context in which the African American female scholar is placed, the discussion will move to the concept of ontology, its Western and African conceptualizations, the obsolescence of the Western model, and an analysis of an African American female ontology in its own right and within the academy.

The Structure of Academe

The structure of academe, as constructed by a white Western male perspective, includes both theoretical and bureaucratic components. The theoretical structure, rooted in Western philosophical tradition, is constituted of the ideas that undergird the canon and curriculum advanced by this perspective; the bureaucratic structure, born of a commitment to rationalism, provides the framework through which the ideas are operationalized. Both structural components have a primary commitment to exclusivity. This value is manifested theoretically in its ethnocentrism and bureaucratically in the demographics of the academy.

The bureaucratic structure of the academy defines higher education as the major conduit. This conduit facilitates hegemony through the promotion of canon vis-à-vis (1) the definition of certain ontological assumptions and epistemological techniques as prerequisites to consideration as scholarship; (2) the reification of these assumptions and techniques in the scholarly debates/conceptualizations that are accepted by major journals and promoted at national meetings; (3) the access provided to "gatekeepers" in their appointment to policy-making bodies, think tanks, and commissions; and (4) the translation of this gatekeeper critique into the implicit and explicit ideology of textbooks and teacher training manuals.[1]

Hegemonic environments are necessarily stagnant, as their goal is not development but self-perpetuation. Thus, within such contexts, mimicry and memorization are valued over critical thought. Juxtapose this education with cultural values such as "individualism" and "the end justifies the means," and then look at youth behavior. Benjamin R. Barber says, "The illiteracy of the young turns out to be our own reflected back to us with embarrassing force. We honor ambition, we reward greed, we celebrate materialism, we worship acquisitiveness, we cherish success, we commercialize the classroom—and then we bark at the young about the gentle arts of the spirit."[2] American students have been taught the ideal cultural values of inclusion and justice while observing the real cultural values of exclusion and ethnocentrism. America's future is as paradoxical as its past.

The Impact of Western Values on Intellectual Development

No entity, bureaucratic or theoretical, can develop a select few to lead many and define that development in a vacuum. A commitment to exclusivity constructs a narrow and false reality known only to the select few. They will have been trained and socialized to two social facts: first, a God-given entitlement to their status, and second, the antithetical origin and entitlements of the many.[3] Once anointed, the elite have never had to substantiate their position: it is theirs because it is theirs.

The Western academic model has designed a curriculum for failure, and it has been eminently successful. When a model feigning intellectual rigor is, in fact, designed to create clones as opposed to critical thinkers, it may well achieve its stated goals, but the achievement of those goals will insure its ultimate demise; clones merely sanction status quo rhetoric, whereas critical thinkers seek truth and generate new knowledge. The superficiality of race and culture discourse in a period when shifts in these areas abound is a testament to the parameters hegemony imposes on itself.

Case in point: In periods of constant and rapid social change, one would expect to find a multiplicity of new concepts, paradigms, and methodologies. It seems logical that new circumstances would yield new understandings, new ways of viewing the world, new ways of ascertaining information. Yet this is not always true. Certainly some historical and contemporary occurrences have yielded some changes in the disciplines most closely related to the phenomenon. But in a review of the impact of social phenomena on academic discourse, what seems to remain fairly consistent is the relationship between the trajectory of an event and its visibility in mainstream discourse. Specifically, it seems that when social behavior is bottom-up in motivation, there is less of a tendency for it to generate new sensibilities in the discourse. When motivation is top-down, however, it is more likely to appear as an issue explored within the various venues operative in the aforementioned academic parameters. For example, social science textbooks, journals, conferences, and funding will reflect the significance of the post–Soviet Union struggles. Undergraduate and graduate curricula already include elective and nonelective courses on the topic; exchange programs are in place; white women's organizations have already created support groups and training programs to facilitate female consciousness-raising and inclusion from Uzbekistan to Bosnia and Herzegovina. This was a top-down phenomenon, and it will be explored in finite and scientific fashion within the context of mainstream discourse. It will be used for study in its own context and used as a heuristic device to explain or explore the experiences of other top-down phenomena. But what new paradigms, concepts, or methodologies were generated by the civil rights movement or the dismantling of apartheid? What new understandings about oppression and resistance, save an occasional movement-specific tome or concept in the area of social movements, were generated after the nation and the world experienced these major upheavals? These bottom-up phenomena had minimal impact on the study of social change, oppression, or even race relations. The tendency to acknowledge and discuss only those events wherein the will of the powerful obtains is consistent with the behavior that enabled the rise of Western civilization. The central issue is hegemony: the ability of those with power to define their interests as the national interest. This power is buttressed by class, race, and gender designations that enable the human actor to impose his interests and perspectives to the exclusion of all variations. The sterility of the emergent environment is a cultural vacuum.

The ability of the academy to define and control the issues that appear in mainstream discourse, regardless of their national and international visibility and implications, is an awesome power. Such control has simultaneously circumscribed the nature, quality, and scope of what is defined as knowledge and who is capable of generating it. This has created an extremely comfortable pseudointellectual niche for the anointed. The anointing was, for most of American history, a race- and gender-specific ritual. Currently, the race variable remains constant with some acquiescence to same-race females. Demographic shifts in American society make this academic race niche a blatant contradiction in terms. How will academicians, suckled on a top-down understanding of social reality, deal with a social world populated overwhelmingly by people with bottom-up experiences?

Ontology

The basic predisposition of a group, characterized as its "assumptions or beliefs about the nature of existence or the essence of being"[4] or its "perception of ultimate reality,"[5] is referred to as a group's ontology. Mbiti utilizes Tempels's discussion of the Bantu to illuminate ontology when he says that it "will give a special character and local colour to their beliefs and religious practices, to their language, to their institutions and customs, to their psychological reactions and, more generally, to their whole behaviour."[6] Further, Mbiti's discussion of the inextricable relationship between religion, the individual, and the community in the traditional African context illustrates the translation of an Eastern ontology into cultural behavior.[7] Succinctly stated, "I am because we are; we are, therefore, I am."[8] McIntyre's work clarifies the ontological under-pinnings of African and Native American peoples. She utilizes the concept of spirit to distinguish between them with the statements "Everything *has* spirit" and "Everything *is* spirit," indicative of the two respectively.[9] Ontology defines the most intimately significant values of the group as well as rules for interaction with the material and nonmaterial dimension.

Myers isolates five ontological categories and clarifies and distinguishes Eurocentric and Afrocentric manifestations within each as follows: (1) nature of reality: Eurocentric—five senses; Afrocentric—spiritual and material; 2) basis of knowledge: Eurocentric—external; Afrocentric—self-knowledge; 3) epistemological tendency: Eurocentric—counting and measuring; Afrocentric—symbolic imagery and rhythm; 4) nature of logic: Eurocentric—dichotomous; Afrocentric—diunital; 5) techniques for goal attainment: Eurocentric—technological; Afrocentric—ntuology. Myers also says that self-worth is based on external characteristics in the Eurocentric model and intrinsic characteristics in the Afrocentric model.[10]

Mbiti, McIntyre, and Myers reflect the ongoing work of African and African American theorists to isolate and define the ontological foundations that inform philosophical tendencies and cultural behaviors throughout the African Diaspora. These discussions are the foundations of Africa-centered discourse. They have, in large measure, provided an introduction to the literature that redresses the dominant pathological analysis of people of African descent. The need for black theorists to define black reality demanded a return to the afore-mentioned fundamentals. Other nondominant groups—Native Americans and Latinos in particular—have also had to redress the dominant pathological discourse. Proponents of the pathological analysis of African people, however, have also utilized their version of an ontological critique to make their case. They have resorted to the age-old tendencies to characterize differences as deviations from a defined norm and utilize a profile as opposed to a processed characterization of the group that identifies a list of static qualities totally contrary to the human tendency to evolve.

Alternatively, the ontology of the dominant is rarely if ever addressed. This failure implicitly promotes two erroneous ideas: first, that it is either unnecessary or impossible to isolate and critique the ontology of those in power; and second, that the position of the elite is an organic one—that is, their power is a birthright. Implicitly, both suggest that those who were not born with power are not entitled to it. Failure to explore the values of domination and exploitation, which afforded the empowerment of the elite, facilitates the organic explanation.

The African American Female Ontology

History and objective condition converge in the creation of the constructed reality called culture. Ontology, as indivisible from the individual as culture, is a precondition of both. Black women throughout the African diaspora are not identical; though our conditions are similar in type, we each have our own peculiarities. But the same ontology informed the cultural matrix from which we all derive. Thus the African past must be the point of departure for understanding an African American female ontology. The translation of the aforementioned African ontology into an African American cultural matrix facilitated consistency in gender conventions. These conventions, however, are disparate from the Western logic of mainstream feminism that finds it difficult to process the simultaneity of egalitarianism and sex role stratification in precolonial Africa. In her seminal work *The Black Woman Cross-Culturally*, Filomina C. Steady identifies four major characteristics that differentiate the worldview of black women throughout the diaspora from that of white feminists. Since worldview derives from ontology, clarity on the African worldview regarding the role and significance of women will illuminate some fundamental ontological assumptions about womanhood. Specifically: (1) autonomy and cooperation are the appropriate framework for the examination of sex roles vs. the Western feminist framework of competition and opposition; (2) the central significance of the role of mother in African family and society is recognized; (3) the importance of motherhood and the valuation of the childbearing capacity by African women is probably the most fundamental difference between the African woman and her Western counterpart, and this life-giving quality not only endows women with great prestige but also equates them with the life-giving force itself; (4) in the African American female context, power is defined as "control over one's existence and the existence of other" versus the Western feminist conception of formal political power as the most important indicator of power.[11]

The African ontology was reinterpreted by black women in the North American chattel slave context. African ontological characteristics were antithetical to the planter class's definition of womanhood but consistent with their need for strong procreators and laborers. Thus, although in an oppressive fashion, the North American chattel slave context reified the African ontology for black women and facilitated the transition to an African American female ontology. This inclusive, group-oriented interpretation of gender roles, even in an exclusive race- and gender-stratified context, affirms Steady's definition of the African woman's worldview. Female slaves in North America interpreted their power in their unequivocal commitment to the survival of self and loved ones. Much in line with Mbiti's analysis of the immutable relationship between religion and community, black female existence was inextricably linked to family and group survival. From infanticide to the establishment of maroon communities, all their practices demonstrate a group and race commitment to survival and family.[12] Contrary to the white female dilemma, our men were not our enemies.

The analogy of academe and the plantation is not lost. Both structures reify, in content and form, the ideology of the power elite; both stand as seemingly self-sufficient entities yet are, in fact, totally dependent on the labor each exploits. So, as the black woman in the antebellum context facilitated the existence of the planter's family and the survival of her own, so the contemporary black female academic and activist poised between the ideal culture of America's rhetoric and the real culture of her double jeopardy has a pivotal role. Who has an angle of vision that can view social reality from high and low places in the configuration?

Enter the marginal mind and its position-based proclivity for observing and interpreting multiple realities. How uncanny that the very populations who were consciously, consistently, and structurally alienated from academe will be the same groups whose insight is prerequisite to its survival.

The Interface

If a volume on the experiences of black women in academe is to be of any merit, then the issues and questions raised within it must not be bound by the conventions that created our "peculiarity." We must be free to explore and explain our circumstance in ways that flow into and out of our collective memory. For me, that flow is some strange combination of spirit and scholar, of theorist and muse. But these combinations are strange only in the context of academe. Indeed, in our past, the scientist was the healer, the medium, and the midwife. And so, theoretically, we must reach beyond "canon." Methodically, we must not be bound by positivist constraints or the idiocy that separates self and subject. In truth, there is no subject when self is alienated from it. Consistent with its top-down philosophy, Western academe has relegated the experiences of black women to the realm of exemplar. Indeed, there are no mainstream paradigms or concepts born of black female experiences and assumed applicable to the entire human experience. So admittedly, as we critique this conundrum, we are often constrained by its limitations. But our consciousness of its narrowness and flaws is an initial step toward our liberation from it. So we must, as always, assume multiple, even contradictory, postures; we must simultaneously be conversant with the dogma and deconstruct it in search of our own. But what is so important and exceptionally difficult is that, as we move in these arenas, acquire credentials, assume our positions of institutionalized marginality, and even interact amicably with those anointed to act in the interest of antithetical spirits, we *must* remember that what will keep us sane is what keeps us separate; that if we find it quaint, but less than scholarly, to juxtapose Fannie Lou Hamer with Frantz Fanon and motherwit with Marx, we have devalued ourselves. Our task is mammoth, the road is hard, and there is no prototype. We must know, celebrate, and be affirmed by ancestrally sanctified, psychologically safe places to which we can astrotravel while our bodies remain in the boardroom, classroom, and executive suite. We must not compartmentalize ourselves in a fashion so enamored with the contemporary that it is uncomfortable with the past.

Herein I want to ask and explore aloud our joust with *this* millennium's oppression. Nothing new can present itself; we have seen it all. We have critiqued it five ways from Sunday, but have we generated a master plan? *See, we are so intent on survival that we just keep going.* We develop spontaneous techniques for survival—some good, some not—and they become part of who we are without our conscious acknowledgement. So we experience trauma, process it, and continue on. The trauma is both public and private—public as we are perceived and responded to as a monolithic, publicly constructed phenomenon; private because our essence is so antithetical to the Western environment that many times our private selves are reconstructed to survive. This forced reconstruction, this defensive response to systematic alienation, is what we must forestall if we are to pass to our daughters the wonder and worth of our ancestors. Where do we begin in exploring ourselves? How do we reveal to our daughters and sons those dichotomies that we know better than the other side knows itself? How do we make certain that we always, first of all, use the techniques we learned along the way to insure our own survival—not individual but collective?

We have known, used, and worked our duality since the beginning; now we must formalize it. We have known that we had to pick and choose battles that we have had to confront and defer and that none of these ploys defined our essence. They were merely the crazy rules of an unfair game, and if we wanted to play—that is, work and support our families—then we had to temporarily be *down with the madness.*

Now, how do we translate our knowledge as the Queens of Multiple Juxtapositions into the theory and bureaucracy of Western academe; or do we? How do we insure that, as the inevitable reconfiguration occurs, our lives and the lives of our ancestors become a model for the study of the human experience?

The ontology of African American females is a constellation of collective memories, race experiences, and definitions of strength and integrity that stand counter in imagery to the roles we currently hold. My maternal grandmother was simultaneously the embodiment of femininity and strength; though she neither attended college nor joined a support group, she prepared me for my journey. The lessons she learned as one of seventeen children in a family in rural North Carolina facilitated my survival more than half a century later in a premier doctoral program. This spanning of universes, this ability to reduce time and space to a few important understandings, is a blessing bestowed by centuries of women who used the double jeopardy hand they were dealt to guarantee the survival of the group.

Conclusion

What is the master plan? Will we create or find the eye of the storm? Our role in the transformation of academe, or the world, must begin with a critique of ourselves. And the transformation will proceed in two stages: first an analysis and buttressing of ourselves, then a transformation of the intellectual and physical spaces we occupy.

Toward an analysis of ourselves, we must first know ourselves, love ourselves, and define our boundaries and commitments. For sister scholars, we must understand what negative lessons about knowledge and development were part of our miseducation in the ivy halls. What behaviors did we assume to survive in those milieus that we did not relinquish when we completed our studies there and left? Even for those of us who have studied the colonized mind, there is the tendency to try to replicate "The Other." We must acknowledge the impact of hostility and oppression on our psyche and spend our lifetime working to unlearn it, even as we go about our other work. If we call ourselves race women, then we must conduct ourselves as such in interaction and demeanor. If we espouse the rhetoric of sisterhood, we must interact kindly with sisters. How can a reputation be based on so-called feminist scholarship that adulates black women and their wonderfulness and not treat black women with respect in personal and professional encounters? We must make the rhetoric and the behavior consistent.

To transform the intellectual and physical spaces we occupy, we must bring the best of our collective memory to the fore. The position we now hold, and have always held, gives us an angle of norm that only double jeopardy could create. Our commitment to survive hostility and oppression has taught us lessons that the oppressor, in academe and beyond, must now learn. The following race/gender lessons are instructive for academe: to do the cakewalk is to laugh at those who deny our validity and know that self-knowledge must come first—academe must acknowledge the limitations of its ethnocentrism and linearity; to nurse the child who will ultimately be defined as your superior is to know all places in the human equation—academe must acknowledge the inevitability of essential change and relinquish its defensive posture; to feign naïveté when we are actually familiar with precipitating events and potential outcomes is to know the balance between aplomb and humility—academe must acknowledge that to be consistently devalued and ignored is to know invisibility—academe must acknowledge the inevitability of change; to endure circumstances too inhumane to recount is to believe in the unseen and know that spirit governs all—academe must acknowledge that material reality is the least significant component of a far greater scheme.

These are the values we bring to the academy. These are the implications of an African American female ontology for academe. This is the wealth we bring to this waning, lackluster goliath standing on the brink of distinction. And our task, as we stand as testaments to our ancestral strength, is to envision the beauty of human development and design an agenda that insures it. This new agenda must celebrate the wonder of intellect and creativity, with no admonition for uniqueness; it must acknowledge the origin and integrity of each entity and be neither ruled nor defined by race or gender initiatives. This mammoth task completed, we will have found the eye of the storm.

Notes

1. Beverly M. John, "Alternative Paradigms for the Twenty First Century: African American Women in the Academy," paper presented at Eastern Sociological Society Meeting, April 1992.

2. Benjamin R. Barber, "America Skips School. Why We Talk So Much About Education and Do So Little," *Harper's Magazine*, November 1993, 42.

3. John, "Alternative Paradigms," 5.

4. Wade W. Nobles, *Africanity and the Black Family: The Development of a Theoretical Model* (Oakland, Calif.: Black Family Institute, 1985), 106.

5. George A. Theodorson and Achilles G. Theodorson, *A Modern Dictionary of Sociology* (New York: Barnes and Noble, 1979), 283.

6. John S. Mbiti, *African Religions and Philosophy* (Garden City, N.Y.: Anchor Books, 1970), 13–14.

7. Ibid.

8. Ibid.

9. Charshee C. McIntyre, "Three World Views: African, Native American and European," paper presented at the National Council for Black Studies Annual Meeting, Cornell University, 1986.

10. Linda James Myers, "Expanding the Psychology of Knowledge Optimally: The Importance of World View," in *Black Psychology*, edited by Reginald Jones (Berkeley, Calif.: Cobb and Henry, 1991), 19.

11. Filomina Steady, *Black Woman Cross-Culturally* (Cambridge: Schenkman, 1981), 28–30.

12. Dorothy Sterling, ed. *We Are Your Sisters: Black Women in the Nineteenth Century* (New York: Norton, 1984).

Part Three

Black Women Faculty
Issues in Teaching and Research

The American Council on Education reported that the largest number of black women faculty in higher education is employed in the disciplines of education (19.5 percent), health-related fields (16.8 percent), and social sciences (13.9 percent). The other fields include English (9.3 percent), business (7.5 percent), mathematics or statistics (7.2 percent), history or political science (3.8 percent), biological sciences (2.1 percent), physical sciences (0.5 percent), engineering (0.1 percent), agriculture or forestry (0.7), and other technical or nontechnical fields (12.4 percent). Despite the discipline, the Euro-male-centered knowledge base, which generates and disseminates information, discounts and devalues black women's pedagogical styles and strategies and their research paradigms.

Discounting and devaluing black women's perspectives and paradigms affect, for example, the choice of research topic, the selection of research method, the interpretation of data, and the choice of theoretical framework. Since race, gender, and culture orientation impact black women's life chances, black women scholars raise different kinds of questions and concerns. In "Giving Name and Voice: Black Women Scholars, Research, and Knowledge Transformation," Rose M. Brewer notes that as a result of the demographic shift, larger numbers of black women are entering white higher educational institutions, and this pattern has contributed to the current intellectual critiques of Anglo-male paradigms. Brewer argues that we enter this debate from the historical realities of the need for inclusion of race, gender, class, and ethnicity in knowledge transformation and the need to bring them to the center of the field. While Brewer focuses on the discipline of sociology, her critiques and alternative perspectives are applicable to other disciplines as well.

Gwendolyn Etter-Lewis's "Black Women in Academe: Teaching/Administrating Inside the Sacred Grove" points out that black women have a long history of successes in the academy, under the most arduous circumstances, as administrators and teachers. These successes and rich traditions are not, however, found in their written literature but in oral narratives. Who decides how sociohistorical data are collected and preserved in the academy? Western traditions have valued written language while devaluing spoken language. Using oral narratives of black women teachers' and administrators' lived experiences, Etter-Lewis allows the reader to see how oral text can be a valuable paradigm to include in collecting data and preserving the history of black women.

When natural scientists argue that their knowledge is objective, do they include race and gender? To produce objective knowledge of the social world, it is essential to understand the social conditions under which science is produced. As Francine Essien's "Black Women in the Sciences: Challenges along the Pipeline and in the Academy" tells us, the world of science is overwhelmingly male, and it manifests gender and racial biases from elementary school to the higher education academy. The social conditions in which science is produced are reflected in the lack of concern for issues affecting black men and women. There are several good examples of this. According to the director of the Office of Research on Women's Health, National Institutes of Health, black males die earlier and at higher rates from hypertension and cardiovascular disease than white males do. Black women also die from stroke and related disorders more frequently than white women. The incidence of death from complications of pregnancy and childbirth is higher among black women than among white women. Black and Latino women account for 74 percent of all U.S. women with AIDS. Some specific reasons for the current health care crisis include the earlier and continuing lack of concern about health status of people of color as a national priority; inadequate and poor health care; habitual exclusion of black women and men, as well as other people of color, from clinical studies and clinical trials, and the related failure to demonstrate that the efficacy of interventions in one group holds for another; the lack of sensitivity to and respect for cultural diversity on the part of investigators and health care providers; and the failure of educational programs to include participants of color. Essien argues for the inclusion of black women in science, whose perspectives would more likely embrace these issues.

What constitutes aesthetics in the academy? Donna M. Cox's "Eurocentric Hegemony in the College Music Curriculum: The African American Woman Professor Singing the Blues" explains how the Western hegemonic music curriculum devalues and stereotypes some black music forms such as gospel and how such devaluations and stereotypes pigeonhole black music professors as well as how they interface with race and gender inside and outside the classroom, creating a hostile climate.

Changing the academic pedagogy requires not only teaching skills but process as well. Beverly Guy-Sheftall's "Transforming the Academy: A Black Feminist Perspective" shows the reader how to change the academy, incorporating race, class, and gender in the classroom. Using an "oppositional pedagogy," she encourages her students to conduct field studies, for instance, as a way of integrating the cognitive, emotional, and behavioral components of the learning process.

Transforming the academy would also mean the inclusion of African American women's cultural experiences that define the contours of their racial and gendered lives. Linda Williamson Nelson's "Begging the Questions and Switching Codes: Insider and Outsider Discourse of African American Women" explores, through oral life narratives, ways in which black women academicians have "foregrounded their cultural experiences by making those experiences the subject of their critical inquiry." She uses black English vernacular to show how codeswitching is a way of "expressing solidarity and clarifying the significance of personal experience and liberatory struggles."

Finally, a resculptured academy would value the views of those on the margins of the margins. Amina Wadud-Muhsin's "Teaching Afrocentric Islam in the White Christian South" is an experiential account of what life in the academy is like for an African American Muslim woman who teaches religious studies from an Afrocentric perspective in a white university in the South. She calls for a change in the academy that would include imbuing it with spirit and an Afrocentric perspective.

Chapter 5

Giving Name and Voice

Black Women Scholars, Research, and Knowledge Transformation

Rose M. Brewer

By the mid-twentieth century, a full-scale struggle was on for social justice in the United States: the civil rights movement. This movement was embedded in the structural context of post–World War II America. Indeed, economic, political, and social changes in the United States cannot be understood without understanding racial injustice and African American resistance to it.[1] It is in this historical conjuncture of structural shifts and the African American struggle for social justice that I situate and begin my discussion of black women intellectuals in the academy.

For the purposes of this chapter, I focus my lens on black women intellectuals in the contemporary centers of knowledge production in this country: white colleges and universities. With an eye on the particular context of disciplines, I focus on the field of sociology. Although black women have been present historically in white and black colleges, it is their contemporary placement in white-dominated institutions, disciplines, and faculties that I want to problematize. African American women intellectuals increasingly find themselves in new spaces and places where they were formerly denied entry. In these settings, they operate as scholars, researchers, and writers,[2] and this entails a number of contradictions and challenges that I will explore further in this chapter.

Although the political impetus for black women's recent placement in white academe grows out of the racial struggles of the civil rights movement, the struggles for black studies and women's studies in higher education are crucial to understanding African American women's intellectual positioning in the post–civil rights era. The struggles for black studies and women's studies in higher education are central to the critiques that figure strongly in African American women's scholarly analyses. Today, especially in the conceptualizations of black feminist intellectuals regarding the simultaneous issues of race and sex, we find new centers of knowledge production and research by black women scholars.

Black Women Scholars Today

Black women, who are not normally represented as intellectuals,[3] have been entering white universities in relatively greater numbers. The growth in numbers, as well as a shifting self-consciousness around race and gender, positions African American women scholars to challenge their historic erasure in knowledge production and university research.[4] Nonetheless, a poignant reality is how relatively small the increases are; and the pool from which these scholars are drawn—young black college graduates—is declining.

This decline in young black people enrolling in institutions of higher education over the past few years is alarming. College attendance overall peaked for black students in 1976. In that year, 33.5 percent of black high school graduates enrolled in colleges and universities; 33.0 percent of white high school graduates enrolled. By the mid-1980s, the percentages had declined dramatically for black high school graduates. Only 26.1 percent of black graduates were attending college versus 34.4 percent of white high school graduates. Black enrollment in graduate schools was down too; it fell from 6.2 percent of all black college graduates in 1978 to 4.8 percent in 1987.[5]

Most educators agree that the cutbacks in educational funds are strategic to the decline.[6] Furthermore, the downturn in graduate enrollment is quite serious beyond the numbers issue. It foreshadows even fewer black faculty for the 1990s and beyond. Black faculty are already severely underrepresented on white university and college campuses, so any fall in graduate enrollment signals even more trouble ahead.

It is important to note that black women enter into current intellectual critiques in the context of these demographic realities and from a historical place that is embedded in race and gender realities. Lewis makes the case for black women's sex discrimination thus: "The black liberation movement began to generate important structural changes in the relationship between blacks and whites in American society. For black women, these changes served to heighten their perception of sexism, since they experience deep-seated sex discrimination as they engage in increased participation in the public sphere."[7]

Simultaneously, black women's relationship to change, centered in race, culture, and black studies, cannot be ignored. African- and feminist-centered knowledge underpins a good deal of the current thinking in the field of black studies as well as black women's studies. Asante and Asante point out that "all of the African people who participated in the mechanized interaction with Europe, and who colored the character of Europe while being shared themselves, share a commonality."[8]

This commonality is referred to in the analyses of Rodgers-Rose and Collins.[9] The conceptual core of Afrocentricity is an African-centered worldview. In matters of curricula, this means that African experience should be at the center of knowledge in the university. Black studies scholars locate the centrality of Africa in knowledge reconstruction.

Closely related to knowledge reconstruction emerging out of black studies is that occurring in women's studies. Minnich points out that the disciplinary canons in Western knowledge production systematically exclude women, who should be at its center.[10] This parallels the argument in black studies, but both fields have tended to erase black women's history.[11] Black women intellectuals draw from both fields,[12] given the double occlusion of Africanness and femaleness.

Black Women Intellectuals, Research, and Knowledge in Sociology

I would like to make the case for the transformation of knowledge and research in the academy by black women intellectuals through looking more closely at the field of sociology. I begin with two central issues: why has sociological training been so problematic; and why are black women challenging this training?

There is a sociology of knowledge and sociology of science tradition, rooted in the idea that theories about the world do not exist in a vacuum, that informs critical thinking among African American women sociologists.[13] Historical context becomes the basis of what Perdue calls the shaping of "both 'truth' and 'truth maker.'"[14] The key point is that knowledge is a social product.

Thus black women's training and critique of the field of sociology must be understood (1) in the context of training in a dominant paradigm that has been pervasive in nearly all sociology departments in American universities during the last forty years;[15] (2) in the context of three powerful social forces in relation and in interaction—race, class, and gender; (3) in the dialectical tension between mainstream training and a critique of this training; (4) in the positivist imperative in the field; and (5) in the erasure of black women's experiences in the discipline except as problem. In short, I believe that African American women scholars are increasingly calling into question the sociological paradigm central to contemporary knowledge and research in the field. These critiques can be viewed in the context of a broad-based questioning of the field expressed in the work of Vaughan and others.[16] For example, if we locate the dominant paradigm of the past decades, at least through the 1950s, the question of order and the idea of facts, measurable and separable from the researcher, continue to hold sway. Thus I believe this positivist imprint is a basic constitutive element of the field, opening it up to critique and transformation by black women scholars.

Sjoberg and Vaughan go on to argue that the field embraces a natural science model of social research. They point out that "the natural science model is highly entrenched in such well-established specialties as criminology, demography, rural sociology, the family, and social psychology."[17]

Other key problematics in the field are related to the need for attaining scientific legitimacy. Thus, for the gatekeepers of the discipline, those white men who control high-ranking graduate programs and journals in the field, sociology is earmarked by (1) grantspersonship; (2) heavy reliance on the variable approach; (3) statistical and mathematical modeling; (4) techniques and methodology; and (5) traditional graduate training with an emphasis on ethnocentric, Eurocentric, and masculinist perspectives.

I believe that at the center of black women's intellectual agenda in research and knowledge production is the transformation of sociology as a discipline. Even as its specialties include race relations, sex and gender, and social stratification, the field is embedded in a masculinist, Eurocentric context in epistemological assumptions, research practice, and sociological training.[18] Issues of pedagogy, curriculum, and knowledge also enter into this discussion as black women scholars rethink and attempt to transform knowledge and research in the academy.

Yet sociology as a field is problematic because it does not treat African American women as subjects in the world. Black women are too often "the problem," the issue, the pathology.

A Closer Look at Black Women's Sociological Training

Any discussion of black women scholars' knowledge transformation also raises the issue of the sociological training of African American women. Inherent in such an undertaking is the critique given racism and sexism in the university and disciplinary structure. The simultaneity of race and gender inequality for African American women complicates the reality.[19] I contend that sociological training for African American women reflects (1) the larger economic, social, and political forces; (2) the interlocking oppressions of race, gender, and class in training and socialization; and (3) the interplay among biography, oppression, a particular sociohistorical juncture, and sociological training.

Sociological training too embodies knowledge production set in cultural context. Often what is treated as objective embodies the ideologies of racism, classism, and sexism. Stanfield refers to this as treating racial folk knowledge as scientific.[20] Thus theorizing in the field too often does not treat race, class, gender, and ethnicity as deeply embedded social realities. Yet tremendous scholarly activity in the field goes on regarding these inequalities as variables.[21] A variable analysis simply is inadequate for explaining race, class, and gender as central organizing principles of American society, which generates a number of consequences for understanding social life. The current construction of the disciplines, however, establishes a context for a field in crisis and a crisis in training.

A Field in Crisis

I contend that some of the key problematics of sociology today are as follows: (1) *Sociology in a gendered context.* There is a growing emphasis on the sociology of gender without consideration of race. The past twenty years of feminist sociology in the field has engendered a partial transformation of the discipline. The experiences of white Euro-American women are increasingly encoded in the field as universal. Women and men of color remain largely invisible or are misspecified in frameworks that embody the particular experiences of white Euro-American, middle-class women and men. The persistence of an essentialized sociology of gender must be questioned. (2) *Sociology in a racialist, ethnocentric, and Euro-American context.* My major contention here is that the field is rooted in ethnocentric, racialist, and white European prescriptives of the social world. Every specialization, from family to criminology, is predicated on white middle-class normative markers of social life. Racial and ethnic people of color still too often appear as problems or as representatives of pathology. Where is there subjectivity regarding people of color in the field of sociology? How might we understand the complexity of multiethnic political, economic, and societal structures? These social realities are yet to be specified in the field. (3) *The "missing" multicentered representation of social life.* This conceptual issue requires placing at the center of the field the simultaneous, relational, and embedded realities of race, class, gender, and ethnicity. Indeed, while there has been some pluralization of the field, especially regarding the sociology of white middle-class women, any recognition of the intersection of race, class, and gender as powerful social forces in interrelationship is largely absent.

Indeed, graduate education has remained heavily defined in the traditional mode. The recent research of Romero and Margolis supports this assertion and confirms the scarcity of faculty of color in programs granting graduate degrees.

They find in a survey of ninety-two sociology departments that "only 29% of the departments had only one African American faculty; 29% had one Asian American faculty, and 17% had only one Mexican American. Race and ethnicity were not central to course offerings in the discipline. One fifth (20%) of all faculty in graduate programs were listed as conducting research or teaching in the area. Less than a quarter (23%) of the departments had race in the required theory courses. Twenty-six departments did not offer a single graduate course on race, even though six of these departments claimed to offer a specialty in the area."[22]

Kuhn argued in his critical appraisal of science that young social scientists are socialized into the normal science of the day.[23] Their duty is to "learn," internalize, and reproduce the accepted assumptions, theories, methodologies, and working style of science. Once they are trained in this way, it is hard for them to change to any other way of seeing the world. But what if this seamless training web is disrupted or ruptured before it is completed? Kuhn makes his observations in this context of science. I ask my questions in the context of the sociological training of groups on the margin. Surely the multiple disjunctures that black women bring to the academy are potentially challenging to main-stream sociology.

Moreover, dominance in the field by the top few departments continues. These departments are likely not to have either women's studies or ethnic studies in the curriculum or to include the new scholarship on race, ethnicity, class, and gender in interaction. Even today, much of graduate training in sociology is still heavily rooted in a positivist paradigm. Given this reality and the multiple realities of race, class, and gender in the lives of African American women, it is likely that the training of black female sociologists will be marked by conflict or at least not occur in a seamless web of socialization, acceptance, and reproduction of this framework. Of course, not all black women sociologists contest positivism, but my point is that what is presumed to be unproblematic—training into sociology—is touched by the confluence of race, class, and gender in the academy and in black women scholars.

Black Women Intellectuals, Countertendencies, and Knowledge Transformation in the Field of Sociology

Since the 1960s there have been several major efforts to redefine the field. New Left perspectives reintroduced an open critique of capitalism into the field in the late 1960s and the 1970s. This coincided with the struggle to generate a black sociology relevant to the experiences of African Americans.[24] A feminist sociology followed in the wake of the New Left and black sociology critiques. And most recently, a black feminist sociology, predicated on explicating the intersection of race, class, and gender, is emerging.[25]

Although some efforts to reconceptualize the field are going on, the enterprise is fraught with difficulty and contradictions. Yet African American women are raising deeply rooted issues. A long-standing tradition of oppositional cultural representation is central to the resistance to historic and contemporary stereotypes of African American women. Today, as historically, black women are again being blamed for the demise of the black family. The culprits this time are the adolescent mother and the female-led black family.[26] This is not too different from the matriarch ensconced in social science research thirty years ago.[27] Black women scholars are making a different intellectual case for what is going on in African American communities.

It is not surprising that the knowledge claims of African American women have been shaped by the modality of race. A number of the current generation of scholars grew up in segregated America. Restrictions and discrimination were largely played out through the color line. The making of the African American community as a rich fabric of life and culture can also be remembered. This transcends the pathology/problem paradigm that is so central to social science investigations of African Americans. This is captured in Joyce Ladner's *The Death of White Sociology* and the thinking about Afrocentricity by Molefi Asante, who states:

> More damaging still has been the inability of European thinkers, particularly of the neopositivist or empiricist traditions, to see that human actions cannot be understood apart from the emotions, attitudes, and cultural definitions of a given context. The Afrocentric thinker understands that the interrelationship of knowledge with cosmology, society, religion, medicine, and traditions stands alongside the interactive metaphors of discourse as principal means of achieving a measure of knowledge about experience. The Afrocentrists insist on steering the minds of their readers and listeners in the direction of intellectual wholeness.[28]

Black Feminist Intellectuals and the Reconstruction of Sociological Knowledge and Research

Not all black women are feminists, but many are sensitive to gender and race as interlocking realities, and a significant number of black feminist intellectuals are changing the face of research, teaching, and knowledge production in the academy. Although black women's activism and everyday lived experiences have been the spawning ground of black feminist thought,[29] what is notable today is the more systematic incorporation of this knowledge into disciplines, largely the articulation of black feminist framework by black women intellectuals. The arts, history, the social sciences, black studies, and health, among other fields, have been affected.

What is most central about recent black women's feminist thought in sociology is the articulation of multiple realities and oppressions. Their intellectual agenda challenges existing frameworks in sociology, women's studies, ethnic studies, and a range of other disciplines. The ideas of black women scholars in sociology are rooted in the everyday lives of African American women, creatively drawing from a rich African tradition of polyrhythmics,[30] from improvisation, and from issues of institutionalized racism and sexism in the social structure, organization bureaucracies, and political economies. It is important to understand that the analyses are embedded in a cultural dynamic nurtured by African American traditions that spawn at least two possibilities: the transformation of knowledge and the decentering and restructuring of the educational process.

The Critique of the Critique in Sociology

There is a liberal feminist gender problematic in sociology that is troublesome. Williams and Sjoberg point to a dominant wing in feminist sociology that is sensitive neither to race nor to class.[31] This change has not been inclusive of the perspective of women of color or working-class women. Thus, as some enclaves have opened up, including *Gender and Society* under the editorship of Margaret Andersen and new writings by women of color, the field is still dominated by a particular racial and ethnic perspective. Indeed, in core journals such as the *American Sociological Review*, the *American Journal of Sociology*, *Social Forces*, and—most telling—*Social Problems*, the standard conceptualizations are pervasive. Yet with the publication of Patricia Hill Collins's *Black Feminist Thought*, theorizing race, class, and gender has been placed squarely on the agenda. Whether or how much the discipline will shift in a conceptual and curricular sense remains to be seen.

Crucial to both knowledge transformation and reconstruction is the fight for a history of African American women's experiences and the remaking of educational curricula and teaching. Black women enter the academy in the context of historic exclusion. For hundreds of years, African Americans were denied the right to read and write. Since then, especially in recent years, their challenge has emerged and crystallized into a formidable force to be contended with. It has come on the wings of struggle. Even so, their work is often harshly judged as inferior. Bell Hooks puts forth the notion that this absence of a humane critical response has had a tremendous impact on . . . those writers from oppressed, colonized groups who endeavor to speak.[32] For black women scholars, true speaking is an act of resistance, a political gesture that challenges the politics of domination that would render us nameless and voiceless.

Collins, however, identifies the resistance emerging out of exclusion. She notes that "a good deal of the Black female experience has been spent coping with avoiding, subverting, and challenging the workings of this same white male insiderism."[33] In order for inclusiveness to occur, the entire knowledge production process has to be critiqued and transformed. Black feminist intellectuals are an important force behind the recent theorizing, scholarly production, and social commentary about African American women.

Issues of Black Women's Representation and Challenges to Traditional Sociological Knowledge Production

According to Collins, the epistemological assumption that defines the disciplinary liability of dichotomous oppositional thinking is rooted in the categories white over black, male over female, and all other hierarchies of oppression.[34] An intellectual agenda that draws upon the cultural traditions of Africa represents a healthy transformation of Eurocentric epistemologies. King astutely points out that "the relative significance of race, sex, or class in determining the conditions of black women's lives is neither fixed nor absolute but rather, is dependent on the socio-historical context and the social phenomenon under consideration."[35]

Although black women intellectuals generally have not been considered intellectual change agents in the academy, the fact that black women's intellectual energy is rendered invisible in the traditional academy is being challenged. Black women have been change agents in their communities and nationally, and the academy is at the center of this process. They have always linked themselves to the broader black struggle. Today, black women's change energies are more squarely centered on intellectual change, and their explicit intellectual agenda is explicating the complexities and realities of race, class, and gender in multiple locations. Given this, transformation of the field needs to be thought about in the context of faculty reconstruction, pedagogical change, and the reconsidering of sociological research.

Transforming Sociology Faculty

Because the majority of the faculty of nearly all major sociology departments in research universities in the United States is male and white, we need to understand what changes faculty must undergo as we think carefully about disciplinary transformation. Central to the endeavor is getting faculty to rethink what they teach and how they teach. This begins with a self-placement process: how have faculty themselves been socially constructed along race, gender, and class lines? Indeed, a key element is faculty transformation. Faculty cannot do the work of teaching a diverse student body without changing.

Faculty are products of this society. Sociologists must come to grips with the fact that they are embedded in systems of inequality and have internalized racism, classism, homophobia, sexism, the "isms" that are pervasive and systematic in this society.

Different Ways of Knowing and Seeing

Faculty transformation involves an incisive approach based on knowing. Central to this process is coming to grips with the essentialist assumption that white Western male experience represents all that is worth knowing about the world. Getting our professoriate to problematize and question the natural facts of their being and their training is essential to faculty development. This viewpoint is expressed in a recent volume by Andersen and Collins, who point out that

> those who ask us to think more inclusively want to open up the way the world is viewed, making the experience of previously excluded groups more visible and central in the construction of knowledge. Inclusive thinking shifts our perspective from the white, male-centered forms of thinking that have characterized much of Western thought. Thinking inclusively means putting the experiences of those who have been excluded at the center of thought so that we can better understand the intersections of race, class, and gender in the experiences of all groups, including those with privilege and power.[36]

Furthermore, in order to pierce "natural attitudes," recentering knowledge involves understanding the impact of disciplines on our ways of knowing and looking critically and thoroughly at how they have come to know. Ultimately, it entails a radical break and reconstitution of faculty knowledge.

This knowledge-problematizing involves transforming the base of what is worth knowing by use of an amazing new and older scholarship by people of color, which should be moved to the center of the sociology curriculum. Much of this information is introduced through the new scholarship on women of color generally and African American women scholars in particular.

Because a majority of the people in sociology are Euro-Americans, they do not necessarily construct whiteness as a racial category. Whiteness carries privileges, and it is through this phenomenon that internalized domination is acted out. Thus getting sociologists to see whiteness as a racial construction is an important consideration, though these are uncomfortable ideas for many white faculty. Closely aligned with this reality is acquiring a natural attitude embedded in accepting conventional ways of knowing disciplinary perspectives as the norm. These are natural attitudes that need piercing and mystifications that need unearthing.

Getting faculty to think historically and systemically is also key. The historic negative contact and power relationships between Europeans and people of color have been the source of a great deal of tension and conflict. Yet at the same time people of color have not just been victims. There is a rich cultural legacy of resistance and creativity that is not known, or at least not well known. Our sociological work must involve examining resistance as well as oppression, cultural creativity as well as exploitation.

Changing Classroom Process

Faculty also need to think and act on their teaching. Changing sociological content without changing process does not get us very far. Considerations about learning styles, student empowerment, and giving voice to historically silenced and marginalized groups—people of color of both genders, white women, disabled people, older students, gays, lesbians—are key issues to be addressed. The old top-down model of professor as sole authority must be looked at carefully. Faculty should consider more active learning strategies, student responsibility for learning, journals, simulations, and so on. The major idea is that as we must rethink our content, we have to rethink our teaching. This must be an ongoing consideration for sociology faculty. In a corollary fashion, black women are also being challenged to become more than an *authenticating* presence in the classroom.

Conclusions

The difficult assessments that must occur in the field of sociology in particular and all disciplines generally must include reconceptualization of scholarship, training, faculty transformation, and pedagogical change. African American women scholars are increasingly taking on these intellectual challenges. It is important to center our analyses in the multiple articulations of agency and structure, gender, class, race, and culture. These changes are crucial to a deep-level curriculum transformation in higher education in the United States.

Notes

1. Fred Powledge, *Free at Last? The Civil Rights Movement and the People Who Made It* (Boston: Beacon, 1991).

2. For a full discussion of women, see Shirley Malcolm, Paula Hall, and Janet Brown, *The Double Bind: The Price of Being a Minority Woman in Science* (Washington, D.C.: American Association for the Advancement of Science, 1976); Margaret C. Simms and Julianne M. Malveaux, *Slipping Through the Cracks: The Status of Black Women* (New Brunswick: Transaction, 1986).

3. Bell Hooks, *Yearning* (Boston: South End Press, 1990).

4. Gloria T. Hull, Patricia Bell-Scott, and Barbara Smith, eds., *All the Women Are White, All the Men Are Black, But Some Of Us Are Brave* (Old Westbury, N.Y.: Feminist Press, 1982).

5. Solomon Arbeiter, "Black Enrollments: The Case of the Missing Students," *Change* (May/June 1987): 50–54.

6. Ibid., 50–54.

7. Diane Lewis, "A Response to Inequality: Black Women, Racism, and Sexism," *Signs* 3 (1977): 358.

8. Molefi Asante and Kariamu Asante, eds., *African Culture: The Rhythms of Unity* (Trenton: Africa World, 1990), 6.

9. LaFrances Rodgers-Rose, *The Black Woman* (Beverly Hills: Sage, 1980); and Patricia Hill Collins, "Learning from the Outsider Within: The Sociological Significance of Black Feminist Thought," *Social Problems* 33, no. 6 (1986): 14–32.

10. Elizabeth Kamarck Minnich, *Transforming Knowledge* (Philadelphia: Temple University Press, 1990).

11. Hull, Bell-Scott, and Smith, *All the Women Are White.*

12. Collins, "Learning from the Outsider Within."

13. Bonnie Thornton Dill, "The Dialectics of Black Womanhood," *Signs* 4, no. 3 (1979): 553–55; Deborah K. King, "Multiple Jeopardy, Multiple Consciousness: The Context of a Black Feminist Ideology," *Signs* 14, no. 1 (1988): 42–72; Collins, "Learning from the Outsider Within"; Collins, *Black Feminist Thought* (Boston: Unwin Hyman, 1990).

14. William D. Perdue, *Sociological Theory* (Palo Alto: Mayfield, 1986), 9.

15. Ted R. Vaughan, Gideon Sjoberg, and Larry T. Reynolds, eds., *A Critique of Contemporary American Sociology* (New York: General Hall, 1993).

16. Ibid.

17. Gideon Sjoberg and Ted R. Vaughan, "The Bureaucratization of Sociology: Its Impact on Theory and Research," in *A Critique of Contemporary American Sociology*, 80.

18. Joyce Ladner, ed., *The Death of White Sociology* (New York: Random House, 1973).

19. Minnich, *Transforming Knowledge.*

20. John Stanfield, "Epistemological Considerations," in *Research in Race and Ethnicity*, edited by John Stanfield and Routledge Dennis (Beverly Hills: Sage, 1993).

21. Judith Stacey and Barrie Thorne, "The Missing Feminist Revolution in Sociology," *Social Problems* 32 (1985): 301–16.

22. Mary Romero and Eric Margolis, "Race and Sociology," unpublished paper presented at the annual meeting of the Society for the Study of Social Problems, Pittsburgh, August 1992.

23. Thomas Kuhn, *The Structure of Scientific Revolutions*, 2d ed. (Chicago: University of Chicago Press, 1970).

24. Ladner, *The Death of White Sociology*.

25. Collins, "Learning from the Outsider Within" and *Black Feminist Thought*.

26. Rose M. Brewer, "Theorizing Race, Class and Gender," in *Theorizing Black Feminism*, edited by Stanlie James and Abena P. A. Busia (New York: Routledge, 1993), 13–30.

27. Daniel P. Moynihan, *The Negro Family: Case For National Action* (Washington, D.C.: Government Publication Office, 1965).

28. Molefi Asante, *The Afrocentric Idea* (Philadelphia: Temple University Press, 1987), 164.

29. For a discussion of black women's intellectual tradition, see Collins, *Black Feminist Thought*.

30. King, "Multiple Jeopardy, Multiple Consciousness."

31. Norma Williams and Andree Sjoberg, "Ethnicity and Gender: The View from Above vs. the View from Below," in *A Critique of Contemporary Sociology*, 160–202.

32. Hooks, *Yearning*.

33. Collins, "Learning from the Outsider Within," 27.

34. Collins, *Black Feminist Thought*, 4.

35. King, "Multiple Jeopardy, Multiple Consciousness," 49.

36. Margaret Andersen and Patricia Hill Collins, eds., *Race, Class and Gender: An Anthology* (Belmont: Wadsworth, 1992).

Chapter 6

Black Women in Academe
Teaching/Administrating Inside the Sacred Grove

Gwendolyn Etter-Lewis

Black women have been longtime participants in higher education on all levels, from the first black woman to graduate from an American college, Mary Jane Patterson (Oberlin, 1862),[1] to the first black women to earn Ph.D. degrees in 1921 (Georgina Simpson, University of Chicago; Sadie Tanner Mossell, University of Pennsylvania; Eva B. Dykes, Radcliffe).[2] Despite these early successes of outstanding teachers and scholars, the progress of black women in higher ranks of university faculty has been painfully slow. Given these circumstances, as well as the double discrimination black women continually experience, there can be little doubt why we are the "fewest of the few."

In order to fully understand the problem and thereby resolve it, we must examine the academic past from the personal viewpoints of the black women who lived it. Thus this chapter focuses on selected aspects of the private and professional lives of two retired university presidents who held various faculty and administrative positions throughout their respective careers. Their lives, as described in two oral narratives,[3] are both parallel and divergent. Higher education is the dominant thread that binds them together. As these narrative accounts demonstrate (narrators were given fictional names at their request), African American women's experiences in higher education are molded by external factors (for example, a university's history of hiring and retaining faculty of color) and internal factors (such as childhood experiences) specific to "traditional" social roles within and outside of the university.

Crossing Barriers

For black women, earning a college degree was not an easy task, especially in the earliest periods of higher learning. Solomon observed that in the first decades of the twentieth century, "because most of their parents were too poor, and because most schools did not want them, fewer black women gained any higher education."[4] She explained that most of the women who managed to enter college were directed toward home economics and other "domestic" programs. Similarly, even with a college degree in hand, black women found few occupations available to them. According to Noble, "They could teach, they could become home demonstration agents, or they could end up as cooks or cleaning white women's homes."[5] In spite of these dire conditions, black women steadily pressed on and eventually pursued diverse fields of study and worked both inside and outside of the university: "Black women have a history of striving for education beyond what their gender or their color seemed to prescribe."[6]

Although there have been substantial gains in undergraduate degrees over the years, the paucity of black women faculty can be attributed partially to issues related to graduate education (for example, financing, mentoring and support systems, racism and sexism) and to professional concerns within the university (most notably tenure and promotion). While this discussion does not treat these very important issues in depth, it is crucial to note that trends and problems in black women's graduate education have a direct impact on the number of black women available to assume faculty positions.[7]

Missing Pieces

Darlene Clark Hine has said that "the collective experiences, lives and contributions of individual black women in America have been written in small print on the back pages of our historical consciousness. . . . Thousands of faceless female builders and nurturers of black people need and deserve to have their story told."[8]

Information about black women's lives generally has been limited by a variety of factors. Most conventional research tends to incorporate them into the larger, undifferentiated categories of women and/or blacks. Other studies generalize findings, without modification, to all other populations (including black women) regardless of ethnic background. Needless to say, both approaches fail to consider black women as a unique group, and thus they severely restrict the applicability of their findings.

Similarly, studies of black women in higher education tend to be few in number, and aside from statistical reports, most focus on undergraduate education.[9] In those instances in which graduate education has been included, data on black faculty women with terminal degrees are sparse. Again, the emphasis is on black women as students rather than as professors.

A last but equally important factor to consider is the question of privilege in the way we preserve and collect sociohistorical data. Written language, for example, is privileged or valued while spoken language is not regarded as important beyond immediate aspects of personal communication. Consequently, written texts about women's lives are valorized while women's oral texts are frequently overlooked. This Western notion of writing as an exclusive means of empowerment and validation implies that the oral traditions in most ethnic cultures are neglected, unutilized, and unappreciated. Moreover, historical sources that are embodied in the memories and voices of others (people of color and women) are not cultivated because the written record is considered infallible, incorruptible, and the only legitimate means of authenticating the past.

Telling It by Herself

"So once I got there and I had been there for a semester and was going good, and then he saw me in live flesh that I was not perhaps an ignoramus or some strange critter from a black college, he actually suggested that I become a teaching fellow."[10]

Narrative or oral history studies offer scholars and researchers alike an alternative to written texts that have been used as the exclusive means of documenting the past. This development is particularly important to black women whose lives and words have been concealed and/or neglected. According to Gerda Lerner, "It is difficult to find black women in primary sources. . . . The kinds of sources collected depend to a large extent on the predilections, interests, prejudices, and values of the collectors and historians of an earlier day."[11] She remarked that these selections reflect a tendency to marginalize or totally ignore women in general and black women in particular. Therefore, publication of first-person accounts (oral and written) of life experiences and historical events promises to expand the parameters of women's history and women's studies in general. Oral narratives/histories provide a "means of enfranchising and empowering people whose lives have previously been shaped by 'colonized history' written from the standpoint of outsiders."[12] Oral narratives give us insiders' views as well as culturally determined interpretations and values. No other research methodology can furnish such intimate and unique perspectives.

The following excerpts were selected from oral narratives elicited from two retired university presidents who had been among the first women to serve their respective institutions in that capacity.[13] Their experiences as students, faculty, and administrators suggest that the politics of higher education and the process of becoming an academician are informed by issues of race and gender on all levels.

Mavis, born in 1916, former president of a historically black college, told her story in reverse chronological order with emphasis on the most current events in her life. As a narrator, she wanted the audience to know that she was not bragging: "What I'm trying to say is . . . not to just build myself up, but I want you to get the feeling about how I feel about the university, and how I felt about my job." Mavis regarded her job as the university's top administrator a much-loved duty passed down in her family. Her father also had been the university's president almost fifty years before. Having grown up in a campus environment, she considered the university an extension of her community and family rather than an external element unconnected to the personal details of her life.

Mavis first became aware of the politics of gender during her childhood. She vividly recalled the challenge of being female. Her early years were filled with constant reminders that a girl child was not as valuable as a boy:

> So my father said, "Do you still want to be a boy?" And I said, "Yes, more than ever." "Why?" I said, of course by now I knew I couldn't do it by kissing my elbow. But I said, because everybody who comes to the house says to you, "Dr. Brandt [pseudonym], what a shame, you don't have a son." "Dr. Brandt, ooh, well this is all you want? Just one girl, no boy?" "Oh, too bad that you don't have a boy to follow in your footsteps." I'd hear that all the time. . . . And people fill their house up with girls just to get a boy to satisfy that man's ego. So here, I'm hearing this, and I'm thinking there's something bad about being a girl.[14]

The challenge did not go unanswered. Mavis eventually proved to herself and to the community that a girl indeed could follow in her father's footsteps and carry on the family tradition. Perhaps this was the driving force behind her long association with the university. Each of her successes was a way of carrying out some of the work that her father had left undone and simultaneously a defiance of community expectations.

Later, as dean of students, Mavis found that her job responsibilities did not end at the close of the day. Frequently she was called at odd hours. She remembered many sleepless nights: "I kept my jeans and a sweatshirt on my bicycle in my bedroom, and in the middle of the night if a kid O.D.'d, and they will do that, you know. Don't kid yourself. There's dope in all these colleges. Some got sick in the middle of the night. I was in my jeans and over there. We had a tragedy where several girls were severely injured in a car accident. I was the first one there at the hospital. . . . They set up an office for me at the hospital so I could call the parents. And I had to call one and tell him his daughter was dead." Unpleasant tasks did not diminish Mavis's commitment to her job.

She used this as an example to explain the nature of her work as well as the dedication she felt to the students and the university.

Mavis's retirement was less than ideal. After years of working in different capacities at the university, she was dismissed without even a few kind words. Feeling insulted and discarded, she recounted the shock of her first days at home: "I think one of the low points in my life was when I retired. We had come back from an important meeting. We had been successful in our proposal, but they did not know then that the chairman was trying to get rid of me. . . . So I came home from that meeting and the next morning when I woke up, the only decision I had to make was when to get out of bed. And that was trauma."[15]

In spite of difficulties, Mavis survived and was not content to sit by idly. She began work on changing the rules so no one else would have to suffer as she did: "I want a change in the rulings. . . . And that will keep some of this stuff down, because I've known many a college president who has been thrown out just as I. . . . So, that's a bit of that silence, and part of which I believe is a part that is essential to almost every woman's life who has achieved something in a man's world. . . . I am sure there are incidents, they were not all terminal as mine was, but certainly, there were incidents that they [women] had to go through. And the little strings that they had to pull, and the little insults, and little hurts, little big hurts they had to deal with. Ah, as a result, it's not, it ain't no crystal stair." Mavis observed that silence, the habit of not telling, was the plight of all women in a man's world. She implied that incidents of conflict or wrongdoing succeeded because they were kept private or secret. Furthermore, "little big hurts" were painful even though they may have been part of the job.

Unlike many university faculty and administrators, Mavis came to her position from a family history of university service. Part of her professional identity therefore was shaped by this history that bound her to the university over time. When this bond was broken, it was as if family ties had also been broken. Similarly, the question of gender was intertwined in several major events of her life. Just as her community had dismissed her because she was a girl, Mavis felt that the university terminated her because "this man just felt women had no right to be in positions of authority."[16]

Virginia, born in 1924, former president of a predominantly white university, also had an unpleasant retirement experience. In this instance, it was not a man but another woman who made the decision to let Virginia go: "I would have liked to have stayed another year or two but the person in charge in our system decided that people should retire at sixty-five and I was caught in her decision. And then she lied about it and said that it was a board decision as well as hers. And then the board found out after she had said this to me. And that was the final straw that caused them to ask her to leave."[17] Virginia found no consolation in the fact that two women then were out of jobs. She could not determine whether the decision was based on underlying ageism, sexism, racism, or a combination of all three, but the effect was the same—forced retirement.

Virginia grew up in an "academic" family similar to Mavis's. She took pride in the fact that the family tradition of "doctor" had continued for several generations: "My grandfather was a pharmacist, my father was an M.D., I'm a Ph.D., and my son is an M.D. So, there are four generations of doctors in our family. My father was a practicing physician . . . and was quite inspirational and a positive force in my life." It is evident that Virginia is the only female in the family to follow the earlier examples set by males. She makes no mention of this, however, and goes on to explain why she was not attracted to medicine as a profession: "I thought occasionally of being a doctor but . . . I found the pathology very unpleasant and scary. I remember, my father was, as I mentioned, a dermatologist, and he had a book of photographs of skin diseases at home. I made the mistake of looking at them, and I said, 'Never, nope, never, never, never, will I ever do that.'" Even though she rejected medicine as a possible career, Virginia was indeed interested in the sciences. She unfolded the details of her life through the plans that she had made while she was still very young: "My sophomore year in high school, I had a teacher of biology and that's when I decided I wanted to be a biologist. . . . I had a year of biology, actually had five years of science in high school, and then I took an extra semester or two of botany and zoology. Yep, that was when I decided." Virginia always knew that she would go on to college after high school, so it was simply a matter of deciding on a major field of study. Again, she carefully planned her life according to personal goals: "After I graduated from college . . . my goal was to get a master's in biology and . . . teach in high school. . . . And I had a very supportive . . . graduate school experience. . . . I had five years as a teaching fellow. Received my master's which was in original research and my Ph.D. which was also in original research."

As a graduate student, Virginia excelled in her field but decided after the student practicum that teaching on the high school level was not what she wanted. Several years of teaching at the university level led Virginia to administration, in which she held various positions before becoming dean.

Virginia was not surprised to find herself continuously fighting for women's rights to exist autonomously in a campus environment. The threat of dissolution was a common leveler for all those involved in the undergraduate women's college:

> Well, the Dunbar experience is a different kind. We were a campus undergraduate women's college of about thirty-five hundred. We were always battling with the university in general trying to keep our identity as a women's division. 'Cause there were forces that would like us to go disappear. And the plan at the university by the president was to do away with the faculties at each college and merge them into one large faculty of the entire university. So we would lose our faculty as an autonomous group and they would join this larger disciplinary group. And I can understand that from a managerial point of view, but for us and for me and for a lot of us loyal Dunbar people, it was a disaster. So that did happen and that's when I was very happy to . . . leave. I had a tenured professorship at the senior level. I could have stayed here forever.

Regretfully but decisively, Virginia transferred to another university. As a result, this event that appeared to be disastrous on the surface actually propelled her to higher levels of administration.

Once she assumed the college presidency, Virginia discovered the dilemma of being "the only one" (the only black female). She felt that she constantly was being misjudged because of others' inaccurate perceptions:

> I have very high expectations for the faculty and what they ought to be doing, specifically research if they're going to be decent teachers. And . . . at the same time, I had no double standards. All students were expected to achieve the same amount of work and the same amount of evaluation whether they were black or yellow or white or brown. And . . . that often created for some folks, a kind of . . . complicated thinking because they thought as a black person I was going to be easy on black people. . . . At the same time, I was working very hard to get more black students to come to college and aware that they needed support systems in order to function well.

Though there was probably nothing more distressing than being misunderstood by people from the same community, Virginia stood her ground and eventually won the respect of both community and university counterparts.

Embedded in Virginia's success were several instances of covert and blatant racism. She was neither shocked nor disappointed by those experiences:

Well, I . . . had to do the research first [before writing the dissertation], you know, and then you had to write it up and get the discussion and do the background, bibliography, and read the literature and all that. So, it was three years. And . . . I had my advisor correcting my final manuscript eight times. We finally got through it. And then I had my oral defense, which I can remember only vaguely, except there was one man who was known to be prejudiced who was on my defense committee. And my advisor told me we were gonna make this dissertation Slaughter-proof. His name was Slaughter. . . . He taught parasitology and in his class everyone said that he said during some discussion each year, "when round worms were contracted, you could find them under any little nigger's foot in the South." And I never took a class from him. Everybody warned me.

Virginia explained that not only did she avoid the company of such a biased professor, she did not want to be "educated" from a racist perspective. Her strategy was subtle but effective.

Returning to the issue of faculty status, Virginia realized that she was uninformed about crucial details of her employment. Yet once she acquired the relevant information, she acted swiftly:

I was tenured after four years at the college. Then when I went to Dunbar College I didn't ask for tenure. I didn't even know about things like that. I went as dean of the college. I did not have a faculty tenured position. . . . When I got to Dunbar I realized I was never going to move anywhere without having tenure and so I asked for tenure instead of the conditions under which I had come. So I did receive not only tenure but a top professor tenure. And then, of course, here I received tenure after the usual one year evaluation of your, one's dossier, which, of course, had to be very positive 'cause there were people with tenure who had not one fifth of the number of publications I had nor twelve years teaching experience. So I did think of that and knew knowledgeably that I would be eligible for tenure, which I got.

Beneath Virginia's self-assured comments on her qualifications for tenure and promotion was the idea that some unqualified and undeserving faculty members may have received tenure. In other words, she hints at the familiar notion that blacks must do more work and be more qualified than whites in similar positions. As Farmer observed, profiles of black women in higher education (faculty and administrators) confirm the "contention that women and 'minorities' must be better qualified than white men in order to hold comparable positions."[18] Later in her narrative, Virginia made a more explicit statement on this point: "I was voted by the regents unanimously to become dean, but two high ranking officials objected strenuously because they had their own candidate in mind, a Southern white boy. And they proceeded to sabotage the process and they succeeded."[19] In plain and direct language, Virginia assessed the situation that had such a devastating impact on her career. She unashamedly revealed that she indeed was denied the position because of overriding biases.

A last incident from Virginia's narrative revealed the observation that she was constantly being questioned about her ideas, especially when they were made public. Several members of the university community objected to her view on racism and sexism on campus: "Yes, I had a group of faculty from the academic center come to visit me because that [article] was published in the newspaper and in it I talk of course, about sexism and racism. And they said that besmirches the university . . . and I went on to sit with them for an hour to explain to them what I meant. And when I finished, they went out of the room quietly." Again, she stood her ground and diplomatically explained the article without modifying her point of view. Even though the situation was diffused, Virginia resented the fact that she was singled out for cross-examination. She was disturbed by the idea that some colleagues felt that they had a right to infringe upon her freedom to express herself.

Virginia's extraordinary career was shaped by careful planning that began in high school and continued throughout her undergraduate and graduate education. She portrayed herself as fair, deliberate, and a fierce contender who would not back down in spite of the odds of winning. She candidly admitted her vulnerabilities but was not diminished by them.

As university presidents, Mavis and Virginia were rare individuals who found themselves pioneering in uncharted territory (no-woman's land). Although both reported positive experiences in higher education, they were fully aware that racism and sexism existed at the highest levels of university teaching and administration. Their common "academic" family backgrounds suggest that their careers were influenced by the educational achievements of family members, especially fathers. The other comparable theme of both narratives—forced retirement—implies that age may be another factor used to disadvantage women in general and women of color in particular. Both women fought back and otherwise resisted attempts to limit their effectiveness. They would not accept anything less than the respect and cooperation of students and colleagues.

As the history of black women in higher education continues to unfold, it is important to note that unexamined problems and issues will persist until reasonable and effective solutions are implemented. Understanding the past allows us to shape the future from a position of strength. In the words of Darlene Clark Hine, "special kinds of power exist in our history. We cannot accurately comprehend either our hidden potential or the full range of problems that besiege us until we know about the successful struggles that generations of foremothers waged against virtually insurmountable obstacles."[20]

Notes

1. Linda M. Perkins, "The Education of Black Women in the Nineteenth Century," in *Women and Higher Education in American History*, edited by John Mack Faragher and Florence Howe (New York: Norton, 1988), 71.

2. Barbara Miller Solomon, *In the Company of Educated Women* (New York: Yale University Press, 1985), 137.

3. Gwendolyn Etter-Lewis, *My Soul Is My Own: Oral Narratives of African American Women in the Professions* (New York: Routledge, 1993).

4. Solomon, *In the Company of Educated Women*, 76.

5. Jeanne Noble, "The Higher Education of Black Women in the Twentieth Century, in *Women and Higher Education in American History*, 90.

6. Paula Giddings, *When and Where I Enter: The Impact of Black Women on Race and Sex in America* (New York: Bantam Books, 1984), 7.

7. Linda M. Perkins, "Education," in *Black Women in America: An Historical Encyclopedia*, vol 1, edited by Darlene Clark Hine (Brooklyn: Carlson, 1993), 385–86.

8. Darlene Clark Hine, *When the Truth Is Told: A History of Black Women's Culture and Community in Indiana, 1875–1950* (Indianapolis: National Council of Negro Women, 1981), 5.

9. Lucy Slowe, "Higher Education for Negro Women," *Journal of Negro Education* 2 (July 1933): 352–58; Yolanda Moses, "Black Women in Academe: Issues and Strategies" (Washington, D.C.: Project on the Status and Education of Women, Association of American Colleges, 1989).

10. Etter-Lewis, *My Soul Is My Own*, 96.

11. Gerda Lerner, *The Majority Finds Its Past: Placing Women in History* (Oxford: Oxford University Press, 1979), 64.

12. Gary Okihoro, "Oral History and the Writing of Ethnic History," in *Oral History*, edited by David K. Dunaway and Willa K. Baum (Nashville, Tenn.: American Association for State and Local History, 1984), 195.

13. Ruth Farmer, "Place But Not Importance: The Race for Inclusion in Academe," in *Spirit, Space and Survival: African American Women in (White) Academe*, edited by Joy James and Ruth Farmer (New York: Routledge, 1993), 198–99.

14. Etter-Lewis, *My Soul Is My Own*, 60–61.

15. Ibid., 110.

16. Ibid., 59.

17. Ibid., 110.

18. Farmer, "Place But Not Importance," 199.

19. Etter-Lewis, *My Soul Is My Own*, 108.

20. Hine, *Black Women in America*, xxii, xix.

Chapter 7

Black Women in the Sciences

Challenges along the Pipeline and in the Academy

Francine Essien

Black women have achieved as scientists, engineers, and mathematicians in the academy, and they have contributed significantly to our country's progress in technology and medicine, advanced our basic understanding of the physical and life sciences, and influenced the education of subsequent generations in their respective disciplines. Although this chapter will focus on many of the problems that black women encounter in the sciences, what fuels our collective engines is a spirit of survival, of victory on the part of all of the black women who have made it in the sciences and engineering "in spite of."

Black women are invisible and significantly underrepresented in the life and physical sciences, mathematics, and engineering at all levels in the educational pipeline. Of all the bachelor's degrees awarded in the United States in 1990 in the life sciences, for example, only 3 percent went to black women.[1] An article by Dr. Margaret E. Tolbert reports data on doctoral degrees earned by minority women in 1990.[2] In the biological sciences, black women earned only 1.3 percent, and in engineering, 2.0 percent.

This invisibility of black women is perpetuated by the lay media, which provide virtually no images of black women scientists, and other organizations and institutions that may have good intentions but may unwittingly add to the problem. For example, the American Association for the Advancement of Science, the largest scientific society in the world, for several years devoted annual issues of its journal, *Science*, to "Minorities in Science" and "Women in Science." From its 1992 series on women to its 1994 issue titled "Comparisons Across Cultures," not a single black woman was pictured and profiled.[3] This invisibility can also be attributed to sexism. The 1993 *Science* issue on minorities, despite well-meaning editors, illustrates this point.[4] The entire publication featured a picture of only one black woman professional related to the text, although others were mentioned or quoted. Does this sort of treatment transmit positive messages about what diversity in science should be?

The paucity of black women in science disciplines in the academy is a persistent problem that has been discussed at the national level, to a limited extent, over the last twenty years. For example, the 1976 report "The Double Bind: The Price of Being a Minority Woman in the Sciences" illustrates the leadership of some outstanding black women who confronted the issues early on.[5] One of the key organizers of the conference that produced this paper was Dr. Shirley M. Malcom, a physiologist and current head of the directorate for Education and Human Resources Programs (American Association for the Advancement of Science). The chairperson was Dr. Jewel Cobb, a cell biologist who became the first black dean of Douglass College and is now president emeritus of California State University at Fullerton. Unfortunately, a review of that report and similar subsequent ones reveals that significant change has still not occurred to remove the barriers to young black women's participation in science.

The Impact of Family, Community, and Precollege Institutions

Family and community support are vital in helping young black females choose educational and career opportunities in the sciences. This is as true for those representing the "first" in their families to pursue degrees in higher education as it is for those from long lines of college graduates in the family. For example, I recall fondly the times when my mother, who did not go beyond the tenth grade in high school and supported our family by doing "day's work," helped me study for biology and chemistry exams in college simply by letting me "teach" her the material. For those young people who do not have such support in their own families, our churches, fraternities, sororities, and other community organizations must participate with schools in their nurturing and encouragement— from an early age.

Innumerable studies point out the general failure of the American public school system and society to develop and sustain the interest of young people of either gender and all ethnic groups in science and mathematics. This has been devastating to our nation in general, with particularly grave consequences for women and underrepresented minorities. Many observers have noted that before embarking upon the pathway of formal education, virtually all toddlers and young children are "scientists." They are curious and eager, they love exploration, and they have endless questions. However, after several years in our formal school systems, most young people do not like science and may actively hate mathematics. Their test performance in these areas, compared with the performance of students from other industrialized nations, is dismal. When this general national problem is coupled with issues of racism and sexism, the result is the preclusion of the majority of young black girls from the pursuit of careers in the sciences and possible entry into the academy. The 1992 American Association of University Women's report "How Schools Shortchange Girls" provides evidence of the negative impact of teachers' attitudes and the typical classroom environment on black girls' learning.[6]

Our educational systems have denied young blacks access to higher education in all disciplines through inadequate guidance and lack of encouragement at critical precollege stages. Failure to provide black girls and boys with their diverse options with respect to careers in and out of science and technology cheats them and deprives us of their talents in all areas. For instance, while growing up in Philadelphia, I had many very bright neighborhood girlfriends who had the ability to become scientists, lawyers, engineers, teachers, physicians, and so on. Their potential, however, was generally ignored by our local schools, and most of these young women were placed in general education curricula. Later, after entering the workplace, a small number went on to obtain college degrees, and some even pursued professional careers.

Today, more than ever, we must demand that all students in grades K-12 be given adequate and rigorous mathematics and science courses to allow them not only entry into college but success there as well. More dreams from my neighborhood could have been fulfilled if options had not been aborted so early and systematically.

We must be aware not only of the academic factors that affect black girls in school but also of the socialization process. When, as a professor, I gave presentations at local schools on my research in genetics, using mice, the responses of black girls and young black women were strikingly different at various grade levels. The younger ones were right up front, asking and answering questions and insisting on holding baby mice. At high school presentations, the young men dominated discussions and handled the mice, while most of the young women congregated toward the back of the group, reluctant to examine the animals. Some of the young ladies even squealed "appropriately." Numerous studies suggest that one important strategy for locking in black girls' interest in mathematics, science, and technical areas at early stages is providing them opportunities to interact with individuals in these fields and to enjoy "hands-on" experiences.

The Effects of College and Graduate School Experiences

Although their numbers are small, a notable number of young black women do enter college with an expressed interest in science-related careers, particularly medicine. Many excel in their chosen disciplines in schools around the country and should be applauded. Unfortunately, however, too many others are lost during that critical transition period between high school and college.

Ineffective study habits and lack of awareness of the number of hours required to master college level mathematics and science may present problems for some students entering college. When they experience their first unsatisfactory grades, their self-esteem may suffer, they may lose their motivation, and within a semester or so they may change to a nonscience major. Such changes occur among all students in the first two years of college, but among black students this has a disproportionately negative impact. In most institutions, academic support may be available to the general student population; but black students at predominantly white institutions may be less likely to access or utilize such services. It is important to stress that academic difficulties encountered by students do not derive solely from them. Inadequate instructional formats and methodologies in science and mathematics courses can compromise the learning of undergraduates of all backgrounds. Innovations in instruction and cocurricular support systems can greatly enhance student retention and performance.

An especially damaging myth to dispel is that the attrition of black students in science majors is due primarily to lack of potential or ability. Some advisers are rigid in their views about what kinds of students should study science or practice medicine, for example. To improve the educational experiences and success of black students and others, we must encourage greater flexibility with respect to curricula, advising, and related matters. Institutions should also become more aggressive in the training and sensitization of all of their staff and faculty who serve as counselors.

One of the most important nonacademic factors in determining whether or not black students will succeed in college is their financial status. Over the last ten to fifteen years, much concern has been expressed about the effects of reduced levels of financial support for minorities in higher education. Many students have to work long hours, and this, coupled with the stress of worrying about financial matters, can undermine their academic efforts. Although the current political climate is extremely negative, our country cannot ignore the urgent need for increases in financial aid awards, including more scholarships, for black students and others requiring such essential support. One of the most successful intervention strategies to reduce black student attrition in the sciences while simultaneously addressing other issues is awarding stipends for research.[7]

An additional element that influences the retention of black students and optimization of their performance is the nature of the campus environment. At many institutions, the climate may be inhospitable in areas ranging from academic departments and administrative offices to those related to student and residence life. Several studies, such as Fleming's, emphasize how this can affect the retention and success of black students.[8] Indeed, awareness of the importance of a supportive environment and positive sense of community in promoting academic achievement is one of the major reasons for the increased enrollments at historically black colleges and universities (HBCUs) during recent years.[9] This adds to the long list of arguments for enhanced support of our HBCUs and greater recognition of their value as a vital national resource. For example, they continue to be the leaders in producing graduates who go on to professional and graduate schools.

Climates at predominantly white institutions (PWIs) that affect black students adversely may not always result from active racism but may be defined by factors such as the size and organization of the institution and percentage of minority faculty and administrators. At the New Brunswick campus of Rutgers University, for example, thirty thousand undergraduates attend eight colleges with residence units and common academic departments scattered over two cities. The introductory biology and chemistry classes consist, in part, of lecture sessions with more than four hundred undergraduates. Students may never encounter a black professor in their mathematics and science courses. The actual details may vary, but similar situations exist at many PWIs. It does not require great insight to predict the possible effects of such environments on first-year black students. Black women scientists who attended PWIs as undergraduates and graduate students speak often of the sense of isolation they experienced and had to cope with while simultaneously attempting to excel academically.

Other more specific factors also influence the success of black undergraduates in the sciences. Personalized career guidance and exposure to enriching educational experiences are prime examples. Opportunities to connect with individual faculty members constitute one of the more important determinants of student persistence in science disciplines and subsequent entry into graduate or professional programs. One of the most effective means of facilitating such interactions is through the participation of undergraduates on research projects with faculty mentors. All benefit from the association. Students are exposed to new experiences outside of the classroom through which they gain valuable skills and training that will make them more competitive for subsequent opportunities. Moreover, the one-on-one relationship sets up conditions for better, more individualized academic and career counseling and assistance with admission to graduate school. Faculty derive special satisfaction (and an education) from interacting with students in this way.

Mentoring can be accomplished in many different ways, and mentors come in all colors, shapes, and genders. In the foreseeable future, there will not be enough women or blacks to permit the notion that only same-sex and same-race individuals should or can mentor students in the targeted groups. Moreover, mentoring is not philosophically simply about matching by gender/ethnic group; it is about the requirement that any community, such as the scientific one, be held responsible for the nurturing and support of *all* of its young. Thus scientists in the academy and private sector must look upon aspiring young black scientists as part of them, part of their responsibility, and part of their link to the future. White male scientists can effect change at their respective institutions and, because of their positions in the power hierarchy, exert influence in helping blacks, Latinos, and women all along the pipeline persist and obtain grants, positions, and access to other opportunities. Many have indeed played these roles in the education and careers of black women scientists. The chairman of my undergraduate department of biology, where I was one of a handful of black majors, was a white male professor. He noted my interest in genetics, encouraged me to enroll in his graduate course as the only undergraduate, and later recommended me for a summer position in a cytogenetics laboratory at a hospital. At the hospital, I met another significant mentor, who was the director of the unit and a very remarkable woman. She greatly influenced my career interest and my decision to go on to graduate school.

Over the last two decades, many campuses have developed interventions or strategies to retain more black undergraduates in the sciences and promote their pursuit of master's, doctoral, and professional degrees.[10] The programs focus on issues related to academic support, counseling, enrichment, and mentoring. At Rutgers University, we have an Office of Minority Undergraduate Science Program (OMUSP), reporting directly to the provost's office, which serves underrepresented minority students campus-wide. OMUSP administers several academic-year and summer programs for students in the life sciences, physical sciences, mathematics, and engineering.[11] One program proves that such efforts can reap positive results: the Biomedical Careers Program (BCP), cosponsored with Robert Wood Johnson Medical School (University of Medicine and Dentistry of New Jersey), provides summer enrichment for students from a broad range of academic backgrounds. Of the past student participants, 90 percent earned their bachelor's degrees. Of these, over 50 percent went on to graduate or professional schools, and the majority of the others secured science-related positions in educational institutions, the government, or the private sector. (Black women comprise 40 percent of all students who enrolled in BCP). We must still do better, of course, particularly with respect to the total number of students served and with respect to encouraging more to pursue the Ph.D. degree. For our programs and others to do so will require significant increases in resources and commitments from both inside and outside the academy.

Graduate school represents the final critical challenge for aspiring black women scientists; they must earn the Ph.D. degree to join the ranks of today's professorate. Black undergraduates are strongly encouraged to aim for direct entry into doctoral programs whenever possible. Since initial master's level study can provide a vital bridge to the doctorate for students whose undergraduate academic records or Graduate Record Examination scores may not meet the often stringent criteria for many fellowships, greater numbers of stipends and grants should be made available for this stage. Successful students can then transfer easily to doctoral tracks at their institutions after one or two years, with full support and no significant compromise of academic progress. Individual institutions, national agencies, and educational organizations are developing creative approaches to strengthening the link between undergraduate and graduate training prior to the doctoral phase. This will be of significant benefit to underrepresented minorities, with the long-term effect of increasing the number of black women scientists in the academy.

In graduate school, the most crucial issues for black women in sciences—as in other disciplines—relate to the selection of appropriate advisors and mentors. Critical faculty members are those who assist students initially in meeting curriculum requirements in a timely fashion and those who later sponsor their thesis research. The latter individuals serve as especially significant mentors, not only with respect to the quality of the students' training in research but also as key links to positions and opportunities for many years after students earn the Ph.D. degree. They should also play a role in the socialization of students with regard to the political and other nonscience aspects of survival in the scientific community. In my genetics graduate program, the chairperson of the department at that time served as my academic and research adviser. Although she was strict in the laboratory setting, she was extremely supportive of me in all areas. For example, she found ways to help me meet financial needs not covered by the training grant, provided many opportunities for travel to meetings, and counseled me wisely on personal and family problems.

Black women must also depend upon other mentors at their institutions, however, who may provide backup when problems arise with a thesis advisor, for example, or just give general moral and emotional support. My other faculty mentors included a white male chair and a black male, both in the Department of Biochemistry. I collaborated with the latter on a research project in subsequent years, attesting to the potential long-term value of such relationships. In view of our focus in this chapter, I must make note of Dr. Marie Daly, a tenured professor and the only black woman then in the basic sciences (biochemistry) where I was studying. She was interested in my progress in the doctoral program. We worked together on special projects to have more black students admitted to the medical school, and she provided, in the current jargon, a "safe place" for me. Dr. Daly represents a prime example of the special black women scientists who survived under conditions of racism and sexism more extreme than current ones and made important contributions but still remained invisible.

Black women in graduate science programs have many experiences that are similar to those of virtually all black women at the graduate level and, subsequently, in the academy or private sector. Others express doubts about their credentials and abilities—overtly and covertly. They may have to prove themselves constantly, and even at these stages, their commitment to careers in research and teaching may be questioned. Under such conditions, many endure and prosper. This requires great self-confidence and self-esteem and the unflagging support of family, friends, and community institutions such as the church.

In most of the biological sciences today, earning the Ph.D. degree is not sufficient for gaining faculty positions in research institutions. Postdoctoral training of one to three years may also be required. Without discussion at this point, it is clear that this sets up another situation with which black women scientists must cope, with all of the implications related to the research environment and mentors and the probable expression of those "isms." The importance of the postdoctoral experience cannot be ignored, for it is during this period that the job search is initiated and faculty positions are generally obtained.

Finally—Employed in the Academy!

Black women scientists make contributions in a range of academic positions from coadjutant to full professor, dean, and president. Unfortunately, they are affected adversely by disparities that impact both women and minorities in the academy. For example, data represented by Ottinger and Sikula show that with respect to women, this includes discrepancies related to salaries (women's are 80 percent of men's), tenure status (only 58 percent of the women have tenure, compared to 75 percent of men), and promotion (for example, only 14 percent of full professors are women).[12] Women of color lag even further behind in all of these areas (for instance, they comprise less than 1 percent of all full professors.) Data on the ethnic/racial status of members of the academy also show negative trends for blacks as a whole. The specific experiences of black women in science departments vary greatly, depending on a number of factors, such as the time it took them to earn the Ph.D. and the type of employing institutions—four-year or two-year, public or private, research or teaching, large or small, PWIs or HBCUs.

Some perspective can be gained by looking at the kinds of challenges black women face in academic positions at predominately white research institutions, where they are subjected to significant differences in departmental and campus climates, availability of mentors and research support, and general equity compared to their colleagues. In the typical science departments, black women must participate in activities such as teaching, research, and publishing. Additional professional obligations may include participation in professional societies and organizations and in national meetings. They may also be expected to take on service roles in their institutions, both as token women and as minorities. Although the young faculty members must be urged to "just say no" to most of the latter, chairs of their departments and other senior faculty must be held ultimately accountable for their protection.

There is great concern not only about the initial retention of black women in the academy but also about their upward mobility. Junior black faculty must stay constantly informed about the current rules with respect to tenure and promotion—in spite of what may be printed in a faculty handbook.

Support systems for black women scientists in academia can be extensive and quite diverse. Informal networks that include women and men in and out of one's department are essential for survival. These networks may include faculty members, staff, administrators, and, often among the most important, students and maintenance workers. In addition, some women benefit from interactions through organizations with membership comprised primarily of women (for example, the Association of Women in Science), minorities (such as the National Technical Association and Beta Kappa Chi), or both (the National Network of Minority Women in Science, for example).

Blacks in science do not face the same degree of difficulty as some in other disciplines may in having their research considered "scholarly" or relevant enough to mainstream interests or ideology. There are, however, related concerns with respect to whether their work will be deemed "cutting-edge." As graduate students and faculty members, black women must be aware of the dominant cultural patterns that characterize the scientific community, some of which may differ from those related to their backgrounds. Different cultural perspectives may cause misunderstandings at times, but they may also lead to insights.

While devoting much time and commitment to their academic careers, black women scientists must also cope with issues relevant to their personal lives. Young women must not think that those in the field must make a choice between professional success and a fulfilling life that extends beyond the academy—however defined or structured. The challenge is to find balance. Questions are raised most often about pursuing a career in science and simultaneously raising a family. Until just a few years ago, the male-dominated science establishment viewed women's commitment to family (though not men's) as somehow interfering with productivity and dedication to science. Black women are especially suspect in this regard. Earlier achievers either elected not to marry and have families or delayed doing so for several reasons, among which were the negative signals from the scientific community. The environment in science departments in the academy is slowly beginning to change as the larger society adopts more flexible attitudes about families and parenting. Thus women can progress more easily today without the unspoken restrictions on their personal status and choices. If they decide to have children, there are challenges, as there are throughout society, but they can be met. Most important, a supportive family makes it possible to survive on the job and on the home front.

With all of the problems and challenges indicated, one might ask why black women choose to stay in the sciences in academia. The answer comes quickly: because we enjoy science and teaching young people. In my research, I consider many exciting questions concerning how genes control development, and the experiments are like stimulating puzzles. I approach my work with the idea that it may add to our store of basic knowledge and possibly be relevant to our understanding and/or prevention of birth defects. Great satisfaction comes also from working with students. I am delighted when, for example, students "pump up" when they earn those As and Bs; learn of their acceptance to graduate or medical school; or later, as established professionals, return to encourage my new group of undergraduates. All young black women should have the option of achieving similar kinds of fulfillment in careers in academia.

Conclusions

Leadership in science and technology in the next century will play the dominant role in determining world economic power and the resolution of problems related to health and the environment. It is well acknowledged that in order for the United States to sustain its leadership in these areas, it must take advantage of the skills and talents of all of its people. Yet our country underutilizes major components of its human resources: women and minorities. Black women in particular are underrepresented in all areas of science, especially in the academy, the center for both the discovery of scientific knowledge and its transmission to future generations. The relatively few who have endured in science disciplines have demonstrated their value in both research and education. The country must respond more aggressively and with true commitment to the recommendations that have been presented repeatedly for the last twenty years, indicating strategies to increase the participation of black women and men in the sciences.

This is clearly about equal access and equal opportunity for all of America's citizens. It is also about the self-realization of disenfranchised individuals and the affirmation of their group. Black children and youth will not feel that careers in science are relevant to them without adequate reflections of themselves throughout the scientific enterprise. The current situation robs black people of a sense of their history, contributions, and future potential. In addition, it prevents the education and true socialization of whites and others in our society, depriving them of opportunities to experience and understand the diversity of this country on levels that go beyond a few announcements during Black History Month.

The responsibility for bringing about the major required changes "with all deliberate speed" lies at the doors of our educational institutions at all levels, the governmental and other agencies that control their resources and accreditation, and private sector science and technology. The ball has been, and remains, in their court. Leadership, commitment, and accountability are demanded.

It is fitting that we conclude not by focusing on problems but in proud acknowledgement of our successes and triumphs. Several outstanding black women have been noted in preceding sections. I wish that space and time would allow me the opportunity to chronicle the hundreds of others who have made achievements in technology and science. Other resources, however, can be consulted for examples of their contributions.[13] Such women, models of excellence, have opened doors in academia. Now it is time for swells of bright, talented young black women to rush in.

Notes

1. Deborah J. Carter and Reginald Wilson, *12th Annual Report on the Status of Blacks in Higher Education* (Washington, D.C.: American Council on Education, 1993).

2. Margaret E. Tolbert, "Minority Women in Science and Engineering: A Review of Progress," *Journal of the National Technology Association* (Spring 1993): 4–14.

3. See John Benditt, ed., "Women in Science: Pieces of a Puzzle," *Science* 255 (March 13, 1992): 1365–88; Benditt, ed., "Women in Science '93: Gender and the Culture of Science," *Science* 260 (April 19, 1993): 383–430; Benditt, ed., "Women in Science '94: Comparisons Across Cultures," *Science* 263 (March 11, 1994): 1467–96.

4. Elizabeth Culotta et al., "Minorities in Science '93: Trying to Change the Face of Science," *Science* 262 (November 12, 1993): 1089–1134.

5. Shirley M. Malcom, Paula Q. Hall, and Janet W. Brown, "The Double Bind: The Price of Being a Minority Woman in Science," in *The American Association of Science Publication 76-R-3* (Washington, D.C.: American Association of Science, 1976).

6. American Association of University Women, "How Schools Shortchange Girls," in *The AAUW Report* (Washington, D.C.: American Association of University Women Foundation, 1992).

7. "Minorities in Science"; Willie Pearson Jr. and H. Kenneth Bechtel, *Blacks, Science and American Education* (New Brunswick, N.J.: Rutgers University Press, 1989).

8. Jacqueline Fleming, *Blacks in College* (San Francisco: Jossey-Bass, 1984).

9. Special issue, "Focus on Historically Black Colleges and Universities," *Black Issues in Higher Education* 9, no. 13 (1992).

10. "Minorities in Science"; Pearson and Bechtel, *Blacks, Science and American Education*.

11. Francine Essien and Richard Nurse, "Promoting Persistence and Excellence in the Sciences," paper presented at the Noel/Levitz Student Retention Conference, San Francisco, 1992.

12. C. Ottinger and Robin Sikula, "Women in Higher Education: Where Do We Stand?" *Research Briefs* 4:2 (Washington, D.C.: American Council on Education, 1993).

13. Vivian O. Sammons, *Blacks in Science and Medicine* (New York: Hemisphere, 1990); Kathleen J. Prestwidge, "Bibliography of African Americans, Native Americans, and Hispanics in Engineering, Science, and the Health Professions," and "Women in Science, Engineering, and the Health Professions: A Bibliography" (South Oberlin, Ohio: NASA Central Operation of Resources for Educators, 1991); James Kessler, J. S. Kidd, Renee A. Kidd, and A. Morin, *Distinguished African American Scientists of the 20th Century* (Phoenix: Onyx, 1996).

Chapter 8

Eurocentric Hegemony in the College Music Curriculum

The African-American Woman Professor Singing the Blues

Donna M. Cox

When reading the text to the well-known spiritual "I Been 'Buked and I Been Scorned," a white male student asked what "I Been *Bucked*" meant. His ignorance of the spiritual is understandable considering the permeation of Eurocentric values in college music programs. The absence of African American music in college music curricula is readily apparent from even a cursory glance at the offerings and is directly attributable to the corresponding dearth of African Americans teaching music at predominantly white institutions. Preparation for this chapter reinforced my belief that there is a tremendous need for detailed research and analysis of existing conditions. Neither the Center for Black Music Research, the College Music Society, nor the National Black Music Caucus keeps data on the numbers of black professors teaching at either predominantly white or black colleges. Eileen Southern, professor emeritus at Harvard University, prepared a partial report on black women in college music teaching in the early 1970s.[1] Her findings were based primarily on her extensive travels and her experiences as an African American female music professor. Although universities profess to be seeking diverse faculties, Southern's experiences and study, as well as my own, suggest that there remains a yawning gap between the high ideals espoused and actual occurrences.

Southern indicates that a vast majority of black college music teachers are employed at predominantly black colleges.[2] White colleges, which in recent years have been increasing the numbers of black professors, have primarily hired black males, generally to teach some aspect of African American music. Often the African Americans hired, male or female, are employed solely in black studies programs or have joint appointments with the music department. One professor, after earning both the Master of Music in Performing Practices: Choral Conducting and the Ph.D., was discouraged to find that the only schools interested in her application were those with some component of black music for which they needed an instructor. The exceptions were predominantly black universities. This experience fully supports Southern's findings, which also revealed that during the interviewing process the most successful applicant was one who could be "black" enough to satisfy the need for diversity and "white" enough to conform easily to the white academic environment. In short, the successful applicant was not the stereotypical African American.

The evidence documented in this article is based on three primary sources. First, I drew upon a survey of Midwestern colleges and universities that I conducted in the fall of 1993. Second, I used personal interviews with several African American women professors who were teaching music in various positions at predominantly white colleges throughout the country. Third, I have drawn from my own experiences.

Curriculum

The significance of African American music has been corroborated by the very people whom American institutions revere. The respected Bohemian composer Antonín Dvořák concluded that the Negro spiritual was the only genuine music in America upon which a national music could be developed. Because he found the Negro melodies so beautiful, he chose a spiritual as thematic material for his *New World Symphony*. Dvořák's belief in the slave music was echoed a century later by the Impressionist composer Frederick Delius, who had an intimate knowledge of the spiritual, which he later used as the basis for his renowned work *Appalachia*. Yet highly respected music programs neglect this body of knowledge as a matter of course. At most, college choirs will perform one or two arrangements of spirituals during the year. Some may even venture to sing a gospel song. The fact that many consider this sufficient training is a sad commentary on just how little has been accomplished in diversifying curricular offerings, notwithstanding the multicultural musings of administrators and educators alike.

How is it possible for a student in today's music program to study four or more years and graduate without having studied the spiritual? Music curricula are inherently and admittedly biased toward European music. Students in all facets of the music program—music history, applied music, ensembles, theory, and pedagogy—study the works of the "masters." With few exceptions, these are limited to European composers such as Mozart and Bach. Any exposure to African American composers in the white academy is gained through participation in musical organizations or by way of elective courses that are not included in the core curriculum. Having been trained in similar institutions, professors have little knowledge of works by African American composers and are often not willing to change the way they view, and therefore teach, their subjects.

One of my first battles in the academy occurred over the use of the terms "major" and "minor." "Major" ensembles are interpreted as those that take their basic repertoire from classical literature. In practically every music program, participation in these ensembles is required of all music majors. Conversely, "minor" ensembles typically include the gospel choir, the jazz choir, the jazz band, and other similar organizations. Music majors frequently participate in these ensembles, but their degree requirements are not usually linked to participation. It is interesting that in many instances, these "minor" ensembles provide more performance opportunities. Although I was reminded that these terms are acceptable and used throughout the country, I insisted that "core" be used for the 400-level ensembles if the intent was to describe their centrality to the curriculum and not denote their value.

There is also a notion that jazz is the "true classical music" of North America. According to Philip Bohlman, the classicization of jazz suggests "that music in the intensely ethnic matrix of North America has the power to subvert some cultural values." He further states that "jazz has, therefore, succeeded in forging a position for African Americans in the larger society that centuries of social struggle had not completely effected by the end of the twentieth century."[3] His statement contains a modicum of truth in the concert arena but is not representative of the college curriculum.

Beauty and worth in the white academy are measured solely by European classical music standards. Ethnomusicologist Japp Kunst writes that there is an inclination to regard any non-Western music as nothing more than "expressions of inferior, more primitive" cultures.[4] This benchmark is based on certain criteria: complexity, structural logic, harmony, and counterpoint, whereby several simultaneous melodies are both independent and united; the composer's ability to write music particularly suited to voices, instruments, and orchestra; and the ability to relate words and music. Bruno Nettl states that to use these criteria to judge other music would lead to the quick conclusion that "Western music is the best and greatest."[5] From the viewpoint of the musician whose task is to improvise within a melodic and rhythmic framework, reproducing an existing work from written notation to keep it from deviating is unnatural as well as lacking in creativity. Making comparisons the basis for qualitative judgments is the root of the problem in American music programs as they stand.

Filtering all music through the illiberal purview often brainwashes people in the process. Even black students, and some black professors, at white universities derogate the experience of singing indigenous black music, such as gospel. They, like critics of gospel music in general, believe it to be devoid of a rational system because "the predominant sound quality of gospel violates virtually every ideal associated with the Euro-American vocal production."[6] Furthermore, students have been taught that it can damage their vocal cords and ruin any chance they have of learning proper tonal production. Yet they are encouraged to audition for school musicals and positions at amusement parks, which foster "belting," a singing technique used in both gospel and popular music. In 1932, when Mahalia Jackson decided to enhance her career by studying voice with concert tenor "Professor Kendricks," he told her that she had "possibilities" but needed to "stop that hollering," which he indicated was no way to "develop a voice" and was "no credit to the Negro race." "White people," he continued, "would never understand you."[7]

This preoccupation with European musical forms can be seen at most schools, which have little, if any, information on black music within their bindings. Even discussions of African American composers writing in classical genres, if presented at all, are relegated to the final week of the semester. For example, a widely used text, *A History of Western Music* by Donald Grout, has only three pages on black music in the United States and one reference to a black composer, William Grant Still (1895–1978). Unfortunately, Grout's book is typical of texts across the music discipline. Understanding firsthand the value of being musically bilingual propels African Americans to fill this void by supplementing materials from their own tradition, adding yet another responsibility to their already heavy load.

Midwestern College Survey

I recently sent a questionnaire to the music departments of several Midwestern colleges and universities. The purpose was to ascertain what role, if any, gospel music has in the college music curriculum, to determine the attitudes toward gospel music as a serious art form, and to assess the potential for its inclusion in the curriculum of the future. Additionally, schools were asked if they have courses dealing with black music and whether these courses are required for music majors. Several schools admitted that their curriculum is limited to classical music. Out of fifty-seven responses to the survey, not one included any course dealing specifically with African American music in its core curriculum. Courses dealing with African music forms are, with few exceptions, general education courses designed for students in other disciplines who need arts credits. Not only are these courses not required for music majors, but heavy course loads usually preclude their even taking them as electives.

The issue of the inclusion and acceptance of gospel music in the curriculum is symptomatic of the greater issue of the absence of the study of any form of black music in the core curriculum. Because gospel music is a repository of black culture, offering a gospel choir is one simple way in which virtually all music programs could expand their offerings to include some aspect of black music in an authentic cultural environment. Yet results of my survey clearly reveal an unwillingness to take even this step in impacting the college curriculum. Among respondents to the survey, 56 percent acknowledge that there are gospel choirs on campus, with half now offering some credit for participation. However, 41 percent of gospel choirs are based *outside* the music department, usually in student services. Based on the survey, 43 percent of Ohio colleges have gospel choirs, yet only 18 percent give credit for participation in them.

Even though many schools have gospel choirs and offer some academic credit for participation in them, these organizations are still not considered necessary. A black professor at a North Carolina university directs a gospel choir that is a part of two programs—music and the Black Students Association. Survey results show similar trends suggesting that this is not unusual.

An Ohio Lutheran school responded that gospel music is not a part of its music or culture, while a large conservatory stated that gospel music is not a part of its basic mission. This same school was not even aware that an active gospel choir already exists on its campus and answered that lack of student interest prevented the school from considering a gospel choir for its program. Some schools felt gospel music to be of "low priority" and "too limited" in its scope. Its low priority has already been established, but considering it limited is unacceptable when schools have choirs that perform only sixteenth-century madrigals. These postures continue to fuel the idea that African Americans have had no impact on American culture. It is the separatist attitudes expressed that allow music programs to be content with maintaining the study of African American music outside the music department. By choosing not to validate activities such as the gospel music workshop, white faculty leave the entire responsibility of diversifying curricula to the African American professor.

African American Female Music Professors in the Academy

Being black and female creates dual role expectations in the academy. First, the black woman has her own expectations about what is required; and, second, the university has expectations that influence teaching assignments, scholarly and creative activities, and service that directly relate to promotion and tenure.

It is suggested that institutions of higher education have an ideological function designed to transform African American women into "university persons" by stripping them of their identity and giving them a new role tied directly to that of the university. In the university setting, this assimilation of individual and collective self is most frequently split, with one being forced to ignore or sever one of the components of self while affirming the other. "When the collective component of self is affirmed, black women are implicitly and explicitly expected to pursue only those academic interests related to race, gender, or both, and to be experts on these issues regardless of academic training, expertise or interest."[8] Because she may feel as if her credibility will be questioned, the nontenured woman often deems it imperative to find answers to questions outside her normal sphere. An Arkansas professor who teaches American and world music is often asked by students and other faculty to speak specifically about black music. When doing so, she is careful to move away from the monolithic ideals of black culture and music and to point instead to the diversity inherent in it. She stresses the extreme importance of people's understanding the wide range of ideas, thoughts, and philosophies inherent in black culture.

Regardless of the degree of affirmation, being one of so few black people on campus brings an added stress and responsibility. African Americans at every level report feeling as if they represent the entire black race. Prior to teaching at a predominantly white university, I seldom gave issues of race and gender much thought. The academy, however, does not lend itself to ignoring these issues. Because the African American woman is an anomaly, she is constantly open to public scrutiny. This exacerbates her feelings. Fannie Jackson Coppin, a former slave who went on to study at Oberlin College in 1860 and later became a teacher, wrote in her autobiography that she never rose to recite in classes at Oberlin without feeling that she had the honor of the whole African race on her shoulders. She explained, "I felt that if I should fail, it would be ascribed to the fact that I was colored."[9] From my own experiences, I conclude that the black woman must be not only the "voice" but the "thought police" as well. Among the many challenges are to be sensitive to microinequities that happen to African American students and to communicate this to sensitize other faculty members. A college opera workshop presented opera scenes in which a talented black student, who was also a large, dark woman, was dressed in a "mammy" outfit while the other ladies were dressed in frilly pastels. Although this was not an intentional attempt to demean the young singer, it clearly demonstrates the tremendous impact of insensitivity to race and gender.

When the academy affirms the individual component of self, black women are expected not to be actively engaged in research or policies related to ethnicity or gender. Affirming a black woman's individual self to the exclusion of her collective self is to ask her to adopt the perspectives, attitudes, and beliefs that have been historically white-male-oriented. The black woman who willingly accepts this denial of race and gender risks losing touch with her own identity. Furthermore, the academy that affirms the individual self to the exclusion of the collective self of its black women faculty is speaking proverbially "out of both sides of its mouth." While the African American woman may be discouraged from research related to race and gender, the system is designed to exploit these very same characteristics. There is a perception, sometimes voiced and oftentimes not, that black faculty are role models and are used to attract and recruit minority students, faculty, and staff. A professor at a large conservatory of music who is also a vocal artist actually programs few works from the African American tradition, and it is not expected of her. There is, however, a perception that her presence and high profile will attract a certain type of audience.

Being an African American female music professor is a double-edged sword; most are hired to work with or administer one of the black student programs. As long as such a teacher remains in her narrowly defined sphere, few conflicts arise. Yet she becomes defined by her activities in this particular area, often exacerbating already existing stereotypes. For instance, a professor says that although she holds a Ph.D., people assume that her formal training is in gospel music since she teaches that subject. To her knowledge, there are no advanced programs and very few undergraduate programs specializing in gospel. If the black woman professor chooses to move beyond this limited domain and attempts to utilize other aspects of her training, skills, or interest, conflict may result.

Once a person has been pigeonholed into an area such as gospel music, she can be ignored for activities and opportunities in other areas. A patronizing attitude is experienced by African American women professors whose colleagues appear most comfortable when she remains in her pigeonhole. If her primary responsibilities are in African American genres, she may not be included in discussions and policy decisions that affect the classical areas; thus she becomes further entrenched in the less respected areas. Correcting these slights puts her in the position of seeming to be whining about things best left unsaid. Yet not to correct them allows the injustice to deepen.

Stereotypes and the tendency to slot African Americans into one ambit impact all aspects of the academy. One professor recalls her experiences as a graduate student at a large white institution. Although she had been advised to study all areas of choral music history for her oral exams, she was shocked to discover that her examiners wanted to know about the spiritual and whether she thought only black people could sing gospel. Neither of these topics had been a part of her course of study. In fact, not one course in the graduate program touched on the spiritual or the gospel song. Yet these were the topics selected for her. Another professor said she taught musicianship and theory courses before assuming responsibility for the gospel choir. She believes that her colleagues' prior exposure to her as a classical musician helped smooth the way for the acceptance of the gospel choir. Also, she has always made a conscious effort to separate her classical world from her gospel world, rarely showing colleagues both sides of her training at once. These are examples of the role dilemma facing African American female music professors. Professors must know both black and white music forms to work with credibility in the white academy, regardless of personal desire or training.

African American female music professors are also often engaged in a dual battle—as artists and as an African Americans. University administrators often view music as adjunct, as a support to university functions, and not as academically sound. The prevailing attitude is that music is something almost anybody can do. Thus, in this battle, colleagues stand firmly alongside the African American female professor, fighting for the right of music to be viewed as a respected discipline. Into this conflict go resources, time, and energy. In the other engagement, the African American most often stands alone, with little respect for the necessity of the battle, little empathy or understanding, and certainly little assistance.

Student Relationships

African American women professors have the opportunity to impact the lives of students who have had little or no experience with African Americans. At my university, there are fourteen black faculty (eight males and six females) out of six hundred faculty members (increased from six since 1990). It is not difficult to see that in a student body of nearly six thousand students, most never have an opportunity even to see an African American faculty member, let alone study with one. McCombs asserts that students' perceptions are greatly affected by a university's having a small or nonexistent black faculty and staff. White students, since they have such little experience with black professors, may mistakenly conclude that blacks, and particularly black women, are not qualified to be professors.[10]

For instance, I assumed responsibility for a show choir in my first year at the university. The students resented department "interference" in what had once been an all-white, student-run organization. I battled with members who openly questioned and challenged every decision and suggestion I made, while insisting that I be called by my first name. They had no clue they were being insulting when insisting they be allowed to continue interviewing and auditioning prospective members to insure that they be "like them." They were confused when asked to define "like them" and could not see the inherent problem with a group of white students making that statement to a black director.

Research, Scholarship, and Service

Aside from the issues related to curriculum and teaching, research and scholarship in music are inherently perplexing. In areas such as musicology (the scientific and historical study of music), scholarship is clearly defined by written contributions to the field. In many programs, creative activities take the place of traditional, written scholarship. Thus, for concert artists, major recitals and performance with organizations such as an orchestra or opera company are defined as creative pursuits and therefore acceptable as scholarship. There are other areas, however, in which scholarship is more ambiguously defined. It is in this nebulous category that many African American women find themselves. I and the majority of the women I interviewed are solo performers, direct gospel choirs, and engage in scholarly research. A great deal of the writing we do is to secure grants to continue the study of African American music. All the women I interviewed feel that they do not have the liberty to concentrate in one area and often struggle to balance the many demands of scholarship and creative pursuits with teaching and service. This assumption that they need to be active in all areas is further exacerbated by colleagues and committee members who are unsure themselves of what the African American faculty member should be doing and cannot adequately articulate the requirements. I sponsor the annual gospel music workshop. This is clearly a scholarly activity, yet how can it be properly evaluated as such by the people who need to support my candidacy for tenure if they do not attend?

Overlapping duties and expectations obfuscate the line between scholarship and teaching as well as the line between scholarship and service. A principal difference is the manner in which directors choose and teach music. There are three primary sources of literature for the gospel choir. First, recent years have yielded an increasing number of gospel scores. Because gospel music remains fundamentally an aural/oral tradition, it is nearly impossible to teach a gospel song as written. As a result, what is found in written form is a mere guide for the director. The second source of literature is actual recordings. Directors listen very carefully to existing works, learn entire songs, and teach them aurally to choirs. This is the standard manner of learning and teaching gospel music, regardless of the difficulty of a song. The last source is original compositions and arrangements of existing works. Most directors of gospel choirs find themselves arrangers of gospel music regardless of their formal training. Even when a person finds sheet music or listens carefully to a recording for parts, a certain amount of arranging is an integral part of working with gospel choirs. Thus directing a gospel choir involves those aspects ordinarily expected of choir directors as well as a great many creative activities beyond. These activities do not yield publications and do not conform to traditional research methodology.

Further, scholarship and service become blurred when the professor is used as a community and university resource. All of the women I interviewed spoke about the tremendous preparation required for speaking at area schools and churches on some aspect of African American music. In addition, they are often asked to guest-lecture in colleagues' classes. In fact, the entire concept of service is triadic and can be a catch-22 for the black professor. First, the black community needs the expertise and mentors the black professional can bring, particularly the black church, which often perceives a tremendous gap between its music program and that of the college. Second, the university needs to have its African American professors visible in the community if it expects to diversify the student body and develop a good relationship with the community. Often the demographics of the community are not reflected in the faculty and student body. Consequently, maintaining credibility and lessening the perception that it is a racist university may be a constant battle. Third, and perhaps most important, the faculty member needs to be in the community if for no other reason than to establish a history of service. More likely, the African American needs to be visible in the community because it provides a much needed chance to be "black" in a comfortable environment. These opportunities, however necessary, are not accepted as "real" scholarship and are relegated to the lesser category of the three required for successful tenure in the academy—teaching, scholarship, and service.

The centric perspective holds that all experience is culturally grounded but that one is most centered psychologically when experiences are viewed from one's own cultural and psychological center. Molefi Asante asserts that we cannot create apart from our tradition, however positive our achievements. When we forget this truth, we regress as a people.[11] For the African American woman music professor, these qualitative standards are clearly expressed in the research and scholarship arenas.

The seriousness with which the African American professor views documenting her culture finds expression in two primary ways. First, if she chooses (again of necessity because of the paucity of works in the academy) to concentrate on performing the works of African Americans, her performances, in all likelihood, will be judged as marginal or even substandard. A part of this rests in the simple differences in performance practices between indigenous African American music forms and classical genres.

The second way the African American female shows her seriousness in documenting her culture is in choosing to research some aspect of African American music. Women and minorities who reject the masculine mold, defined by white males, often find that their scholarship is suspect and less valued. Research in women's studies and ethnic studies often results in denial of tenure and promotion and loss of job. Ethnic studies is still viewed as more marginal than women's studies.[12] Getting articles published often means publishing in journals and magazines that are not considered "acceptable." An African American in the communications department who researches rap music finds that he is always defending the arena in which his findings are published.

Conclusion

What must the African American woman do to facilitate change in the curriculum in the white academy? The first step in the change is to break through the old consciousness. McCombs asserts that even the decision for an African American woman to enter and remain in an environment that is often hostile to her very nature is an individual and collective one.[13] It is her continued presence that, even to a small degree, encourages the university to take an honest approach to its claim to desire true diversity. Furthermore, history has shown that if she is not present to offer an Afrocentric perspective to the study of music at American universities, the role African Americans have played in developing indigenous American music will continue to be relegated to the periphery.

There are three ways the African American female can break through the old consciousness: (1) she must diligently seek to raise the awareness of the administration on the need for diversity; (2) she can break through the old consciousness and stand firm in her resolve to research African American music;

(3) she must constantly seek ways to challenge old paradigms and bring new, refreshing methods to her research, teaching, and service. It is only through these paths that she can best impact the attitudes of the university and the world while remaining true to her culture.

Notes

1. Eileen Southern, *A Partial Report on Black Women in College Music Teaching*, Status of Women Preliminary Studies (1974), 22–25.

2. Ibid.

3. Philip Bohlman, *Excursions in World Music* (Englewood Cliffs, N.J.: Prentice-Hall, 1992).

4. Japp Kunst, as quoted in Alan P. Merriam, *Anthropology of Music* (Evanston: Northwestern University Press, 1964), 8.

5. Bruno Nettl, *Folk and Traditional Music of the Western Continents* (Englewood Cliffs, N.J.: Prentice-Hall, 1990).

6. Melonee Burnim, "The Black Gospel Tradition: A Complex of Ideology, Aesthetic, and Behavior," in *More Than Dancing: Essays on Afro-American Music and Musicians*, edited by Irene V. Jackson (Westport, Conn.: Greenwood Press, 1985), 147–67.

7. Laurraine Goreau, *Just Mahalia, Baby* (Waco, Tex.: Word Books, 1975).

8. Harriet McCombs, "The Dynamics and Impact of Affirmative Action Processes on Higher Education, the Curriculum and Black Women," *Sex Roles* 21, nos. 1–2 (1989): 127–44.

9. Portions reprinted in Gerda Lerner, ed., *Black Women in White America: A Documentary History* (New York: Vintage, 1992).

10. McCombs, "The Dynamics and Impact of Affirmative Action," 131.

11. Molefi Asante, ed., "Afrocentricity, Women, and Gender," in *Malcolm X As Cultural Hero and Other Afrocentric Essays* (Trenton, N.J.: African World Press, 1993), 7–15.

12. Reginald Wilson, "Women of Color in Academic Administration: Trends, Progress, and Barriers," *Sex Roles* 21, nos. 1–2 (1989): 85–97.

13. McCombs, "The Dynamics and Impact of Affirmative Action," 136–37.

Chapter 9

Transforming the Academy
A Black Feminist Perspective

Beverly Guy-Sheftall

This chapter challenges the normative Eurocentric pedagogical assumptions undergirding the American academy while subscribing to a black feminist revolutionary pedagogy that promises to transform the academy from "cultural literacy" to "multicultural literacy." In a compelling essay describing her own revolutionary pedagogy, feminist theorist and professor Bell Hooks invokes Miss Annie Mae Moore, her favorite high school teacher, whom Hooks calls her "pedagogical guardian" and who embodies the idea of the teacher as subversive. Miss Moore was

> passionate in her teaching, confident that her work in life was a pedagogy of liberation, one that would address and confront our realities as black children growing up within a white supremacist culture. Miss Moore knew that if we were to be fully self-realized, then her work, and the work of all our progressive teachers, was not to teach us solely the knowledge in books, but to teach us an oppositional world view—different from that of our exploiters and oppressors, a world view that would enable us to see ourselves not through lens of racism or racist stereotypes, but one that would enable us to focus clearly and succinctly, to look at ourselves, at the world around us, critically, analytically.[1]

Hooks reminds us that in his introduction to Paulo Freire's *Pedagogy of the Oppressed,* which delineates the concept of "education as the practice of freedom," Richard Shaull offers a concise definition of revolutionary pedagogy to which Miss Moore might have exclaimed, "Amen!" "Education either functions as an instrument which is used to facilitate the integration of the younger generation into the logic of the present system and bring about conformity to it, or it becomes the practice of freedom, the means by which men and women deal critically and creatively with reality and discover how to participate in the transformation of their world."[2]

There have been two major problems in the American academy that my own teaching over the past twenty-one years has struggled against. The first is that much of what goes on reinforces the problematic and erroneous notion that the normative human experience is Western, Euro-American, white, male, Christian, middle-class, and heterosexual. A deep sense of alienation is likely to plague students whose identities are different from what they have been led to believe is the norm by the texts they are required to read and the Eurocentric values they are encouraged to embrace. Students who represent this norm—and they are fast becoming a minority in many educational settings—have difficulty seeing the world and their place in it differently. Second, because students have not been encouraged to feel connected to what they are required to learn—they are led to believe that education is an objective, purely rational endeavor—it is no surprise that they feel unattached to the world of real human beings and therefore disinclined to want to change the conditions under which many people live throughout the world.[3]

As I was thinking about our dilemmas as progressive educators and reflecting upon my own professional career as scholar/activist, certain questions kept intruding: (1) Can the university be a site for serious, transformative work? (2) Can one be truly "oppositional" or "subversive" as a university professor within one of the most hierarchical institutions in our society? (3) Can we teach in ways that don't reinforce structures of domination, racism, sexism, or class exploitation? (4) How can we use our power as teachers in ways that are not coercive, punitive, controlling? (5) Can we undo the "miseducation" that most students have been subjected to by the time we get them in our college classes?[4] (6) Can we undo our own "miseducation" since most of us are also victims of patriarchal, racist, sexist ways of knowing and teaching?

Are we willing to endure the anger and frustration and even hostility, at times, of students and other faculty when we challenge their most cherished ways of seeing the world and themselves? For example, despite what most students have been taught since the beginning of their formal schooling in the United States, Christopher Columbus did not "discover" this country in 1492; in fact, from the American Indian point of view, he invaded indigenous peoples' land and set in motion the process of decimation and even genocide. How radical it would be for all of us to teach in such a way that all of our children would know who the real criminals and thieves have been throughout history. One can get a hint at such answers by going to museums and seeing artifacts that belong to someone else. How refreshing it would be to know who the real victims have been and, most important, what has been stolen and by whom. How radical it would be simply to tell the truth, which would of course begin with admissions in our own country about the annihilation of native peoples, their culture, their ways of life.

What I attempt to do in my classes at Spelman College, where I have been teaching since 1971, can be seen as an illustration of how we might begin to think about transforming our classrooms and our pedagogues and thus the academy itself. On the first day of class I am very open and explicit about what I am trying to accomplish. I don't present myself as politically neutral, void of a value system and biases. I indicate that much of what I think and believe and value is not consistent with the dominant culture's belief system, especially as it relates to race and gender. I acknowledge that I don't know everything—that I am always, hopefully, in the process of growth and self-evaluation. I indicate that I'm not the same teacher that I was ten or fifteen years ago, thank goodness! I also indicate that I am not the ultimate authority in the class.

On the first day of Introduction to Women's Studies, which I presently coteach with Johnnetta Cole, Spelman's president, we assign a group of autobiographical texts by non-Western women or women within our own culture who would be considered "other" and indicate that the students will become "experts" on the cultures from which these texts emerge; in subsequent classroom discussions on the varieties of female experiences, they will provide insights they've gleaned from their assigned texts and their reading (histories, ethnographic studies, sociological literature, and so on) about these cultures as we are discussing race, class, ethnicity, and gender questions. We choose autobiographies or autobiographical novels, in some cases, because these genres place women at the center of their own experience and provide "an occasion for viewing the individual in relation to those others with whom she shares emotional, philosophical, and spiritual affinities, as well as political realities."[5] These texts, which are supplemented by secondary material on the culture from which these life stories emerge, include Beverly Hungry Wolf (Blackfoot), *The Ways of My Grandmothers*; Helen Sekaquaptewa (Hopi), *Me and Mine: The Story of Helen Sekaquaptewa*; Winnie Mandela (South Africa), *Part of My Soul Went with Him*; I Rigoberta Menchu, *An Indian Woman in Guatemala*; Tsitsi Dangaremba (Zimbabwe), *Nervous Conditions*; Kamala Markandaya (India), *Nectar in a Sieve*; Narissatou Diallo (Senegal), *A Dakar Childhood*; Ellen Kuzwayo (South Africa), *Call Me Woman*; and Maxine Hong Kingston (Chinese American), *The Woman Warrior*.

On the first day, I also introduce myself to the class and have the students introduce themselves so that they will know that who they are as particular human beings is significant in terms of what transpires in the classroom. I say to them, the majority of whom are black women, that what they have experienced already is more representative of the lived experience of the world's population (people of color and women) than what they've read about in most of their classes—the experiences of a small group of Western white men. A significant component of my "oppositional" pedagogy is to decenter Eurocentric, male models and experience and to critique the process by which we come to believe that whiteness and maleness are the most valuable commodities that humans can possess.[6]

Where one begins is very important. I would begin, for example, in world literature classes where human civilization began—not with the Greek classics the *Iliad* and the *Odyssey* but with texts such as *Sundiata*, an epic from Mali, and the *Book of the Dead* (Egypt) from ancient Africa.[7] Spelman students are frequently shocked to learn that the cultural and intellectual heritage of the West is traceable to ancient African civilizations. Writing assignments would include comparisons of the epic tradition in different cultural contexts.[8]

In the Introduction to Women's Studies class, I begin with the experiences not of middle-class Western white men but with the experiences of many Third World women of color who are still agricultural workers, food producers, hard workers, and whose very survival and that of their families and kin groups depends on something so basic as their ability to locate water and find firewood. During the first two class periods I show filmstrips on women in cross-cultural perspective, specifically women in sub-Saharan Africa, India, and China.

A second major pedagogical strategy is making central to my students' learning the idea that knowledge is also experiential. We learn not just by reading books and doing library research but by getting outside the parameters of conventional classroom instruction. A major assignment is for students to choose a site where gender, race, and class issues are played out; students are required to visit their chosen sites not just as objective, unconnected observers but as workers—volunteers, if you will—and to do a final paper and oral report. It is hoped that what students have learned about the complexity of the human experience from their reading of the autobiographies and autobiographical novels will be useful as they embark upon the "real world" evident in their chosen sites outside the university.

What follows is the poignant introduction to a student's final paper on her experience at a battered women's shelter. This report underscores in a profound manner the connections students are able to make between themselves and the persons being "studied":

The shelter is an enormous gray Victorian house. I entered cautiously, unsure of what awaited me. I looked for cots lined up against a wall. There were none. After I sat there a while watching the women milling about, entering and exiting their bedrooms, tidying the living rooms, cooking food, talking, laughing, and watching television, I realized that I had slipped into a tiny community unaware. "Are you new here?" asked a little boy who could not have seen more than six birthdays. "No, stupid," returned a little woman of eleven. "She works here." The little boy in his faded overalls and runover shoes voiced the most startling of all of the observations I made during the hours I spent volunteering at the Council on Battered Women: there are no obvious distinctions between me and the women who ran for their lives to the safety of the shelter. I often traveled unnoticed among these women about whom there are so many societal assumptions.

The papers should also demonstrate a synthesis of students' reading of secondary sources about particular issues (domestic violence if a student is visiting a battered women's shelter; alternative education if the site is a private school for African Americans); the insights they have gained at their chosen places; and analyses (from history, sociology, anthropology, and psychology, for example) of the concepts and theories (such as the relationship between patriarchy and male violence against women) they've learned in class and from reading assignments about culture, race, and gender. What I and my coteacher hoped, as well, was that students would be able to see something of themselves within the communities they experienced. The conclusion to the paper above demonstrated just that:

> On the corner of the street I visited, there is a large house filled with women and children who have everything in common with any other women and children you might know. The kids like to play Nintendo and eat cookies just like my nieces and nephews. The women are sometimes in good moods, sometimes in bad moods, like all other women. Like the rest of the world, they want to be happy and want their children to be happy, and safe. And just like all of us, they have felt the sting of patriarchy. The only difference is that for them, it is not just a figure of speech.

I am convinced, from what students tell us and from what they write, that teaching in these new ways (being very conscious about what we teach and why we teach what we teach)—which Bell Hooks describes for herself as adopting a revolutionary feminist pedagogy—has the potential for facilitating real change in our students. Some concrete examples from my own classroom can illustrate this point. The class I cotaught with President Cole in 1989 was an unusual one for Spelman College. There was a lone white student from Agnes Scott, a predominantly white women's college on the other side of Atlanta, who admitted on the first day that she was very nervous and had not had the experience of being a racial minority in a classroom; there were two students from Morehouse, a historically black men's college across the street from Spelman, with whom we share a history, who were also nervous and huddled close to Cole and me on the first day, feeling somewhat more safe, I presume. Within three weeks, one of the Morehouse men (who later in the course of the class died tragically following a fraternity hazing incident) was talking openly about his new ideas about being a good father, especially as it related to raising a daughter, which he admitted he now preferred to raising a son. His friend talked honestly about violent behavior in his relations with his sister and why it was necessary to reconceptualize notions of masculinity. He chose as his site Men Against Violence, a self-help, all-male group organized for the purpose of understanding and struggling against their own patterns of violent behavior. The student from Agnes Scott decided to spend a semester as an intern in Washington, D.C., working on minority issues. She wrote back to us, after the last governor's election in Georgia, that her grandfather had voted for Andrew Young! This was astounding, she asserted, because he was the person who had literally, in his role as jailer, locked up Martin Luther King Jr. during his early imprisonment in Georgia.

I am convinced that what happens in this women's studies class is suitable, even critical, for students everywhere irrespective of their race, ethnicity, or gender. Students leave this Afrocentric, women-centered class not only knowing more about themselves and the world in which they live but also feeling connected to the people about whom they studied and among whom they worked. At the end of her paper about a homeless shelter, a student mused:

What separates me from a homeless pregnant girl in the street? What is the fundamental difference between my mother and the women addicted to crack standing in line everyday between 10:00 A.M. and noon for food? Is the difference money? Education? While I do this study and go back and forth to my warm room, looking forward to Christmas at home, I ask myself what makes me different. I realize I am asking the wrong question. What makes us all the same? We look at these statistics and we try to isolate these people from society, but we can't do that. Everyone is part of society; you cannot exclude according to circumstance.

Another student alluded to feelings of hopelessness and the difficulty of "letting go:"

> One day I walked into the shelter and felt like crying. I saw Levinda, Karen's little girl, and she was in the corner crying. I asked her what she was crying about and she said that in school that day the kids were making fun of her, saying that she lived in the homeless place. She also said that they made fun of her because she didn't have barrettes in her hair like the other girls. Levinda said that she asked Karen for some barrettes, and she told her that she couldn't afford them. After I left the shelter that evening, I went to the drugstore and I bought Levinda barrettes. . . . I felt so good about myself once I gave her the barrettes and I braided her hair and put them on her. That night I went home and I thought about it, and it all seemed so insignificant. Buying Levinda barrettes couldn't make her situation go away and it really bothered me. . . . I don't think anything has ever affected me the way Cascade House did, because it made the problem real for me. Initially, I saw the homeless as statistics, and really thought of it as drunk men on the side of the street corner, who I felt should get their "act" together. I think I could relate better when I saw that it was women and children, along with men, who were suffering. . . . It was the first time that I researched something and felt as if I couldn't let go. . . . I stopped by to say good-bye to Levinda and her mother and I felt as if I was abandoning them. . . . When I left Cascade House that day, I left a part of me there.

Finally, we have tremendous power as teachers and administrators to help students rethink and challenge their own socialization with respect to racism, sexism, heterosexism, to name only a few "isms" that hurt all of us. Despite our sense of powerlessness when it comes to overcoming the awesome problems that confront us, we can help to influence the direction in which this country will move as we approach the twenty-first century. At the end of a feminist theory class I taught at Spelman this academic year, a male student from Morehouse commented upon how the course had "changed" him in some ways:

> I can definitely say that some of my attitudes on gender were stereotypical and therefore problematic. I think this was due primarily to my lack of knowledge . . . as well as to some underlying misconceptions I had

about what it means to be male and what it means to be female. . . . Though female oppression exists, I hadn't recognized its importance in the struggle of African people. Moreover, my readings of the various texts have made a considerable impact on the way I view myself, females in general, and my relationships with females. If nothing else, the texts have prompted intense introspection and forced me to ask very challenging questions, including (1) Is marriage a viable option? (2) Must the African female's struggle be separate from that of the total liberation of African people? and (3) Must I now reevaluate what it means to be male in order to understand female sexuality?

White students certainly need an inclusive curriculum and "oppositional" pedagogy as much as "ethnic" students do. We must not lose sight of the ultimate purpose of "revolutionary" pedagogues, which is educating students who will work to make this planet a better place for all humans to live. Working with an advocacy agency for women of color with AIDS (Sisterlove), a student of ours confronted her homophobia and the need to embrace differences:

While at the office working, I had the opportunity to speak with feminists, lesbians, homosexuals, and other men involved in the fight against AIDS. At first I was nervous about being in the room, but soon after, I loosened up. We had interesting discussions about our differing sexualities and practices. . . . At the conference on December 1, 1990, World AIDS day, I no longer concerned myself with who was or wasn't straight. As the Rev. Jesse Jackson said, "We all were bonded by the common thread, making up one large quilt."

We must prepare students for a world in which non-Western peoples of color and women are the world's majority. Our collective human survival and the freedom and dignity in which some of us can live will depend, in large part, on our commitment, as educators, to helping eradicate poverty, racism, sexism, and other forms of domination that various groups continue to experience globally. We must not continue to teach only "the canon," which has consistently excluded or devalued the experiences of many groups of people. We must discontinue the harmful practice of educating many students away from themselves. We must disrupt the practice of "miseducating" the majority of our students. Sensitivity to issues of race, ethnicity, gender, and class would begin the process of achieving "multicultural literacy" and rid us of the ignorance in which we have basked so blissfully and arrogantly for decades. In opposition to E. D. Hirsch's call for "cultural literacy," we must create educational environments that will produce multicultural literates. "Multicultural literacy is the ability to function effectively in a nation and world made up of peoples from diverse cultures, races, and groups. . . . [It] helps individuals to respond effectively to diversity by recognizing the interconnected nature of our society."[9] We must also heed the words of Bell Hooks, who makes a compelling argument for the need to transform ourselves into different teachers armed with "radical and subversive" feminist strategies capable of forging a new world desperately in need of emerging: "We must learn from one another, sharing ideas and pedagogical strategies. . . . We must be willing to . . . challenge, change, and create new approaches. We must be willing to restore the spirit of risk—to be fast, wild, to be able to take hold, turn around, transform."[10]

Notes

1. Bell Hooks, *Talking Back: Thinking Feminist, Thinking Black* (Boston: South End Press, 1989), 49.

2. Ibid., 50.

3. Margaret Andersen, "Denying Difference: The Continuing Basis for Exclusion in the Classroom," Research Clearinghouse and Curriculum Integration Project (Memphis: Center for Research on Women, Memphis State University, 1987).

4. Carter G. Woodson, *The Mis-Education of the Negro* (Washington: Associated Publishers, 1933). See also Elizabeth Kamarck Minnich, *Transforming Knowledge* (Philadelphia: Temple University Press, 1990).

5. Joanne M. Braxton, *Black Women Writing Autobiography* (Philadelphia: Temple University Press, 1989), 9.

6. Elsa Barkley Brown, "African-American Women's Quilting: A Framework for Conceptualizing and Teaching African-American Women's History," *Signs* 14 (Summer 1989). Also see Bell Hooks, *Feminist Theory, from Margin to Center* (Boston: South End Press, 1984); Chela Sandoval, "U S. Third World Feminism: The Theory and Method of Oppositional Consciousness in the Postmodern World," *Genders* 10 (Spring 1991): 1–24.

7. Molefi Kete Asante, *Kemet, Afrocentricity and Knowledge* (Trenton, N.J.: Africa World Press, 1990). See also Onwuchekwa Jemi Chinweizu and Ihechukwu Madubuike, *Toward the Decolonization of African Literature,* vol. 1, (Washington, D.C.: Howard University Press, 1983); Martin Bernal, *Black Athena: The Afroasiatic Roots of Classical Civilization,* vol. 1 (New Brunswick: Rutgers University Press, 1987).

8. Beverly Guy-Sheftall, "Women's Studies at Spelman College: Reminiscences from the Director," *Women's Studies International Forum* 9 (1986): 151–55.

9. Cherry A. McGee Banks and James A. Banks, "Teaching For Multicultural Literacy," *Louisiana Social Studies Journal* 16 (Fall 1989): 5.

10. Hooks, *Talking Back,* 54.

Chapter 10

Begging the Questions and Switching Codes

Insider and Outsider Discourse of African American Women

Linda Williamson Nelson

> The internal politics of style (how the elements are put together) is
> determined by its external politics (its relationship to alien dis-
> course). Discourse lives, as it were, on the boundary between its
> own context and another alien context.
>
> Mikhail Bakhtin, *The Dialogic Imagination*[1]

I believe with Bakhtin that we grasp the significance of the form and content of
a people's language by moving from the outside in. That is to say, inherent in
the discourse of any group is the codified manifestation of the dynamics of
political tension that reside in the larger society in which the group is located.
The broad concern of this discussion is the hierarchical arrangement of discourses and the manner in which the linguistic negotiations of individual writers and speakers affirm their affiliation within high- and low-prestige speech
communities. The juxtaposition of discourses from different domains, in the
form of codeswitching, affirms the user's marginal group affiliation at the same
time that it represents the speaker's or writer's resistance to exclusion from the
arenas of power and prestige, represented by the high-prestige discourses or
linguistic codes. A discourse, as a representation of sociocultural meaning that
is encoded in writing and in speaking, articulates the values, beliefs, and points
of view of a particular segment of society regarding societal structures and processes. It is taken for granted that the discourses of some communities of speakers, who have historic and ongoing political, economic, and social power, dominate in the hierarchy of discourses. In its acrolectal or high-prestige position,
the mainstream culture's discourse and all that it represents are continually

sedimented and reinforced by public institutions such as educational systems. In this way, cultural and linguistic hegemony holds sway, though rarely without challenge.

I am particularly interested in the ways in which African American women in the academy have foregrounded their cultural experiences by making those experiences the subject of their critical inquiry. By so doing, they interrogate the historical practice of erasure of the complexity of our lived experience. Moreover, to challenge the totalizing authority of the mainstream discourse and the cultural matrix it represents, these scholars have often self-consciously employed particular black vernacular rhetorical strategies in their works that lack institutional validation. Inasmuch as the spoken language logically occurs prior to the written, it should be no surprise that in the spoken discourse as well there are signs of solidarity with other members of the African American vernacular community.

This chapter will look at two black vernacular rhetorical forms found in the written discourse and the spoken language of African American women working in the academy. I begin with an examination of morphological code-switching—that is, the juxtaposition of grammatical forms from two languages or, in this case, two dialects (standard English and black English) within the same language context. Second, the culturally derived discourse strategy—personal narrative as premise validation—stands in contrast to the discursive, linear reasoning and the bifurcation of emotion and reason that predominate in mainstream scholarly discourse. I argue from these illustrations that such code-switching—that is, the employment of nonstandard discourse forms and strategies and the assumed foregrounding of points of view that are routinely erased— provokes a shift in object and subject position so that what we normally experience as peripheral or "other" becomes "unmarked" or normalized. The marginalized discourse thereby shares focality with the belief system and ways of expression of the powerful.

This manner of challenge to the prevailing domination of symbols is the focus of anthropologist Susan Gal's discussion as it pertains to Pierre Bourdieu's treatment of cultural hegemony.[2] Bourdieu maintains that the status of a particular linguistic variety correlates positively with its ability to provide access to earning power in the marketplace. Moreover, this high status is facilitated, as I have already stated, by a process of legitimation through social institutions, primarily the education system, which accomplishes a hierarchical ordering of language varieties by not only enforcing the language of the powerful but also avoiding recognition of the absence of intrinsic superiority of that variety. Individuals who are enculturated in such a system thereby come to accept the position of the acrolect (as opposed to other varieties) as a given, wholly due its status because of its supposed inherent properties.

Gal contends, however, that emotional as well as material gains to users of nonauthorized varieties, emanating from social networks, often mitigate against such hegemony.[3] As Gal suggests elsewhere, codeswitching, which "usually involves the use of a state-supported and powerfully legitimated language in opposition to a stigmatized minority language that has considerably less institutional support,"[4] speaks to a symbolic representation of the tension between the two codes and the way in which users of the minority discourse challenge the complete authority of the language of public power.

Moreover, codeswitching seems to suggest that speakers and writers have some measure of positive regard for both varieties, and it is just this affiliation with more than one discourse community that calls attention to a paradox inherent in codeswitching. As Heller indicates, while an analysis of codeswitching must begin with an understanding of the separation of domains, we find that "codeswitching itself is a direct contradiction of the separation."[5] It appears as if the act of moving from one linguistic strategy to another, when the *other* or *marked* variety is low-prestige, is a way of scrutinizing the unarticulated assumptions, as implied in my title, "Begging the Questions." That is to say that someone is challenged and accused of "begging the question" when he or she is, in fact, assuming a premise to be true prior to substantiation of the premise. The juxtaposition of codes or discourses, in effect, interrogates the assumptions of the legitimacy of one code alone.

Morphological Codeswitching

In collecting and analyzing the oral life narrative discourse of African American women, a project conducted over the course of several years, I discovered through a verification process (by which I solicited from informants their own valuation of their use of the vernacular) that, in spite of advanced degrees and positions in the academic arena, African American women found in codeswitching from their standard English (SE) to black English vernacular (BEV) a way of expressing solidarity, intensifying meaning, and bringing multivalence to their utterances.

The narrator of the following excerpt was thirty-five at the time of the recording. She was then and remains an assistant professor of health science at a state college. In the following life narrative excerpt, she reminds the investigator of the source of the most fundamental beliefs that guide her life. While the excerpt does not in itself provide an example of conversational codeswitching, it offers a philosophical context that informs our understanding of the informant's relationship to vernacular culture.

The informant, whom I shall call Agnes, said, "A lot of values, attitudes, and beliefs that I have are generated from generations of black folks that came from the South . . . meaning the family is important, education is important, relationships are important, faith . . . religion is important, and identity is very important. So those are all aspects of the core culture or that if you talk with people who consider themselves black people from generations [ago], family folks, you will hear those kinds of things come through all the time. So, I believe a lot of values from the core culture." As we shall see, this informant assigned a positive valuation to her morphological codeswitching from SE to BEV. In the case of all thirty informants for the initial study that produced these narratives, more than 50 percent of all codeswitches of four types — morphological, prosodic, lexical, and makings (as signification) — were assessed by the speaker herself as having positive value.

In another segment, Agnes talks about her mother's active involvement in her education. "I still tell the story about when they were talking about bussing and she [her mother] used to tell us she got up and told this white woman, 'I don't necessarily want my children next to yours either.' She says, 'But if that's what's necessary, then we'll do it.' Yeah. I expound on the story and I said my mother said, 'because you'll bring them down" or something, but she *didn't* never really say that, but you know, as you tell the story you have to [embellish]. . . . That's what she meant. So we had a good education."

Then she speaks of her mischief making with young friends as they came to an awareness of the racial separation in their community: "Sabrina and Urcellette were older and they were, like my mother called, the 'fast' girls and they had all the little boys and you never knew what they were doing, but you had an idea what they were doing, and I hung out with them. And they would always get into mischief so we would run around; we would ring white peoples' bells. . . . *It wasn't* a lot of white people in the neighborhood, but *we be* ringing the bells and run or we would pick *they* flowers because they didn't want us little kids coming through the neighborhood."

The part of my methodology that I formally identify as the verification process was the process during which I returned to the informants, asked them to listen to the point at which they codeswitched, and then to listen to my SE translation. I then proceeded to ask them a range of questions such as "Could you have said it this way [SE]?" and "Is this the same?" in order to allow them to offer me their assessment of their own use of BEV. My questions to Agnes identified the following BEV forms:

- *didn't never*—double negation
- *it wasn't*—*it* as expletive
- *we be*—invariant or durative *be*
- *they flowers*—unmarked possessive pronoun

In response to my questions regarding the multiple negation, the informant said, "I had to bring in another negative for emphasis." Regarding the expletive, she said that it "seemed more specific to the situation." Similarly, regarding the invariant or durative, *be*, and the use of *they* as a possessive pronoun, the informant remarked, "It was us against them." In short, Agnes's responses to the validation process represent the tendency among all my informants, across age and economic strata: BEV marked their utterances with emphasis, represented solidarity or ethnic identity, and, in other cases, brought a polysemous quality to the otherwise limited range of meaning (from the point of view of some speakers) of the same utterances approximated in standard English.

As I mentioned from the outset, the juxtaposition of discourse domains is not restricted to speech. Writers as well can be seen to challenge received notions of correctness in their academic work by moving in and out of culturally derived rhetorical strategies and smaller contextualization cues such as morphologies and lexicals.

Bell Hooks offers a forthright illustration of the intersection of discourse domains and, in a very real sense, the way in which individuals who negotiate in more than one discourse community come to understand their own necessary duality. In *Talking Back*, Hooks tells of her consternation at the assumption of the white poetry professor who, after hearing Hooks's poem written in black English vernacular, encouraged the young writer to continue to develop her "true or authentic voice."[6]

> The insistence on finding one voice, one definitive style of writing and reading one's poetry, fit all too neatly with a static notion of self and identity that was pervasive in university settings. It seemed that many black students found our situations problematic precisely because our sense of self, and by definition, our voice, was not unilateral, monologist, or static, but rather multi-dimensional. We were as at home in [black] dialect as we were in standard English. Individuals who speak languages other than English, who speak patois as well as standard English, find it a necessary aspect of self-affirmation not to feel compelled to choose one voice over another, not to claim one as more authentic, but rather to construct social realities that celebrate, acknowledge, and affirm differences, variety.[7]

Inasmuch as writers as well as speakers are socially constructed through each discourse act, we are reconstituting our concepts of selfhood within each production. As I have argued elsewhere, particular discourse strategies such as codeswitching, especially as it involves movement in speech or in writing from the authorized codes and strategies to the language of the marginalized, represents the dialogic that is inherent in discourse even when only one universe of meaning is seemingly articulated. The deliberate juxtaposition of the two discourse forms, moreover, is where we can locate the inevitable multivocality in every utterance and the point at which we must "seriously question any assumptions of the uncontested acquiescence of the peripheral group members to discourse hegemony."[8]

When Geneva Smitherman published *Talkin and Testifyin* in 1977, those of us interested in issues relating to black vernacular were vociferous in our praise for her courage as well as her accuracy. In this comprehensive discussion, which ranges from the historical connection between BEV and West African languages and worldview to present-day stylistic propensities and related educational issues, the author moves eloquently from standard academic discourse to the vernacular and back again. That is to say that the vernacular forms that appear in this text are not merely examples of what the author seeks to identify as BEV morphological features, as is usually the practice among scholars writing for an academic audience. In addition to the varied and rich illustrations, she uses the vernacular grammatical features herself as she makes her way through explication of the issues. An example of this can be found in the author's discussion of the ways in which servitude and oppression contributed to black semantics, particularly the practice of codifying meaning so that words and phrases could be understood only by members of the black speech community.[9] She explains:

> Due to the work of Du Bois and others, we now know that the Old Testament–based Negro spirituals *wasn't bout no "after here," but "dis heah"* [my emphasis]. The slaves used other-worldly lyrics, yes, but the spirituals had for them this-world meanings. They moaned "steal away to Jesus" to mean stealing away FROM the plantation and TO freedom (that is, "Jesus"). . . . The Biblical analogues hit a responsive chord in the black slave community, and the Old Testament, with its themes of oppression, flight, and the tormented wanderings of God's chosen people, became a rich and easily adaptable resource for black songs and sermons of freedom.[10]

The highlighted words above are classic examples of black English morphology or grammar. The verb *was* in the subject- verb core *spirituals wasn't* and represents the nonobligatory inflection of the past tense verb *to be*. The effect of this codeswitching is that even the reader who is unaccustomed to reading a vernacular in an academic discussion is compelled to consider its possibility. Moreover, with a small amount of curiosity and a conscious suspension of ethnocentricity, the willing reader might discover the ways in which the vernacular embellishes the discussion and how it is even capable of communicative possibilities heretofore denied it.

Lest the point of this illustration be misinterpreted, it is important to say that while linguists (such as the writer of this essay) do not privilege one dialect over another for factors supposedly intrinsic to a particular dialect, we readily acknowledge that indeed, some discourses are associated with access to public power and opportunity while others are not.

Nonauthorized Discourse Strategies

Aside from morphological switches, what is found more frequently in critical texts is the introduction of nonauthorized discourse strategies such as the personal narrative in explication and validation of a point. To explain the significance of this strategy and its salience in the discourse style of African Americans, I return to Smitherman, particularly the chapter entitled "The Forms of Things Unknown: Black Modes of Discourse," in which Smitherman writes,

> The story element is so strong in black communicative dynamics that it pervades general everyday conversation. An ordinary inquiry is likely to elicit an extended narrative response where the abstract point or general message will be couched in concrete story form. The reporting of events is never simply objectively reported, but dramatically acted out and narrated. The Black English speaker thus simultaneously conveys the facts and his or her personal sociopsychological perspective on the facts. . . . Unaware of the black cultural matrix in which narrative sequencing is grounded, whites . . . often become genuinely irritated at what they regard as "belabored verbosity" and narration in an "inappropriate" context.[11]

Perhaps one of the most compelling examples of narration put to service in the explication of empirically derived data as well as abstract concepts is in Bell Hooks's study of feminism, articulatory power, and self-recovery—*Talking Back: Thinking Feminist, Thinking Black*. To my mind, this essay best exemplifies the manner of codeswitching that I am attempting to describe, for the author's process is reflexive. That is, Hooks uses *metadiscourse* to comment on the process of challenging received academic discourse strategies. Namely, she examines the form and content of her work and its relationship to the ways in which various forms of oppression reinforce each other and are identifiable in the lived experience of ordinary women. Early in this text, for example, she comments on the ways the book *Talking Back* represents a departure in discourse strategies from her earlier works:

> Since *Feminist Theory: From Margin to Center,* I have had more time to think even more critically about this split between public and private; time to experience, and time to examine what I have experienced. In reflection, I see how deeply connected that split is to ongoing domination (especially thinking about intimate relationships, ways racism, sexism, and class exploitation work in our daily lives, in those private spaces that is there that we are often most wounded, hurt, dehumanized; there that ourselves are most taken away, terrorized and broken). The public reality and the institutional structures of domination make the private space for oppression and exploitation concrete — real.[12]

One of the author's major intentions in this text is to clarify the significance of personal experience in all liberatory struggles. Hooks responds to critics who are concerned that a focality of personal experience will eclipse the larger issues, the structural inequalities on the macro or societal and institutional levels. She argues that "confession and memory" have the ability to clarify experience that is contextualized theoretically. That is to suggest that we need not fear narration will glorify personal consciousness as the end-all measure toward social change. On the contrary, the author maintains, "Theorizing experience as we tell personal narrative, we have a sharper, keener sense of the end that is desired by the telling. . . . Story telling becomes a process of historicization. It does not remove women from history but enables us to see ourselves as part of history. . . . Used constructively, confession and memory are tools that heighten self-awareness; they need not make us solely inward-looking."[13]

It was quite some time ago that I recognized the potential in individual life stories to inform the larger cultural and historical experiences of the group to which the narrator belongs. It was this wonder at women's stories, heard in the warmth of the kitchen while friends and I sat absorbed in good talk, in doing hair, and in other caretaking rituals, that prompted me to undertake an analysis of the cultural meaning encoded in the life narrative discourse of African American women. In those moments of female community, I heard repeated allusions to what seemed to be a common matrix of cultural beliefs and values. As listeners, we consistently testified with words, gestures, and intonational contours to our recognition of shared experience. In these informal gatherings of black women, I was witnessing the construction of ethnic and gender identity through communicative acts in much the same way that the discourse of the speaker and the writers cited above have communicated, in form and in content, their cultural affiliation.

Conclusion

This discussion set out to examine specific ways in which black female academics, a state college teacher and two well-known scholars from the black vernacular tradition, have entered into speech and academic discourse, unauthorized culturally derived morphology, and rhetorical strategy. While I maintain that such use of these nontraditional forms necessarily challenges discourse hierarchy or linguistic hegemony, it should also be apparent that this discussion is not meant as an either/or advocacy. The tension and the challenge, I maintain, lie in the juxtaposition of voices, of discourses. The very proximity of codes in which we speak and write reminds us that we are always "begging the question," foregrounding hegemonic assumptions. The discourses mentioned here—a formal, discursive received tradition in the academy and the narrative, personal voice and vernacular morphological forms—are only two discourses among many others that are not mentioned in this context. African American discourse tradition is only one that we typically encounter on the margin. In addition, either/or advocacy is misguided as it denies the obvious overlap of discourse forms. There is overlap, I would suggest, because African Americans share much of the same geographic terrain and some of the same ideological terrain of those whom we associate with the language of the public and the powerful. Finally, because of the very marginality of African Americans and our movement within the borders, as a matter of survival, even those who come from outside the mainstream discourse community (and this is by no means all African Americans) have, to a certain extent, juxtaposed and even melded the two universes of meaning.

Throughout this chapter, I have been inescapably reminded of my first attendance at the annual meetings of the American Anthropological Association. As a newly trained anthropologist and an African American, I gravitated to the business meeting of the caucus of black anthropologists. Before the budget discussion and other business began, a leader of the body took the podium and led us in tribute to the ancestors long gone, to whom we were still unmistakably connected. The purpose of this closing anecdote is to illustrate in my own lived experiences the way in which two distinct discourse communities can stand side by side without one's obliterating the other.

Notes

1. Mikhail Bakhtin, "Discourse in the Novel," in *The Dialogic Imagination*, edited by Michael Holquist (Austin: University of Texas Press, 1981), 284.

2. Susan Gal, "Language and Political Economy," in *Annual Review of Anthropology* 18 (1989): 345–67.

3. Ibid., 354.

4. Susan Gal, "The Political Economy of Code Choice," in *Codeswitching: Anthropological Perspectives*, edited by Monica Heller (Hawthorne: Mouton De Gruyter, 1988).

5. Monica Heller, "Introduction," in *Codeswitching: Anthropological Perspectives*, 7.

6. Hooks, *Talking Back: Thinking Feminist, Thinking Black* (Boston: South End Press, 1989), 11.

7. Ibid., 12.

8. Linda Williamson Nelson, "Codeswitching in the Oral Life Narratives of African American Women: Challenges to Linguistic Hegemony," *Boston University Journal of Education* 172, no. 3 (1990): 154.

9. Geneva Smitherman, *Talkin and Testifyin* (Boston: Houghton-Mifflin, 1977).

10. Ibid., 48.

11. Ibid., 161.

12. Hooks, *Talking Back*, 2.

13. Ibid., 109–10.

Chapter 11

Teaching Afrocentric Islam in the White Christian South

Amina Wadud-Muhsin

Even as African American women make various paths in the academy by walking them, it is important to remember that the academy is an institution that has as great a potential to enhance the quality of our soulful lives as it has to destroy our souls. Part of our present dilemma is the contradiction between the stated goals of American educational institutions and the nature of the experience of many African American women within the walls of the academy.

Although the academy often establishes criteria of evaluation from outside the center of the experience of African American women, we continue to participate successfully within these criteria. Our success means we are accepting these criteria. When the paradigm of our oppressor is used as a measure of our own self-worth, we risk potential self-destruction. To participate within the institution without letting it lead us to our own demise, we must implement an invulnerable change through the dynamic and unique nature of our participation in it.

Our very survival is the basis of our unique contribution, for it bears the secrets that can heal the heart of our learning, teaching, and academic institution making. To reveal these secrets, we need to examine the varieties of African American women's self-actualization within the academy. We have demonstrated our potential to excel in the system as it presently exists. In its early stages, however, education in America was intended to destroy the spirit of African American people. Proper education for the African slave was that which taught him or her to accept being less than human.

As my title indicates, I will discuss my experiences teaching Islam in an academy in the South and the efforts I continue to make to effect a change in its infrastructure. The American South remains dedicated to its own brand of

Christianity. It is related to the Christianity that was used to justify the enslavement of people on the grounds of race. I have analyzed my experiences in a manner that was influenced by my activities before I accepted the position of assistant professor in the Department of Philosophy and Religious Studies in Virginia Commonwealth University.

The Background I Brought to Academia

I came to Virginia from Malaysia, a small country in the Asian-Pacific region that is blessed with luxurious tropical gardens, white sandy beaches, economic prosperity, political stability, but alas, no African Americans. Black people don't usually go east. In addition to there being virtually no African Americans and few Africans in Malaysia, there are none of the characteristics there of white-black hegemonic oppression common in the United States. There are certainly ethnocentrism and prejudice. The effects of colonialism are so lingering that some Asians surgically reduce their puffy eyelids to acquire a more European look, and some Indians favor fairer skin and straighter hair. These contemptible variants are typical responses of humans who have experienced domination; the African American community manifests them even today. Such recurrent responses to social-cultural contexts hinder true inner harmony and spiritual wholeness.

Because these are dynamics of relationships between peoples possessing more or less the same amount of power—or powerlessness—within society, however, they do not result in hegemonic social and political constructs. I believe that Malcolm X expressed it best when he said after his international experiences, "Over there, when someone says 'I'm white,' they are referring to the color of their skin. Here, when someone says 'I'm white,' they mean 'I'm boss.'"

As part of collective identification, people generally prefer their own ethnic group over others. Similarities are familiar and therefore comfortable. Differences are foreign and therefore suspect. Such primal prejudicial attitudes lead to extreme negative consequences that exploit the rights of others only when the power dynamics allow one group to violate the human rights of others. When any person or group becomes a *means* toward another person's or group's end rather than being an end in and of itself, then basic human rights are denied.

I worked with nongovernment organizations primarily run by women but all dedicated to attaining social justice for the people. In these forums, it was evident that people needed to identify with their own people and to work collectively for the wellbeing of each member of the group. Even the opportunity to teach at the International Islamic University in Malaysia was intended as an effort to demonstrate the necessary autonomy of a particular worldview in its own development. I saw that learning was about social change and development of a higher consciousness, not just the acquisition of random bytes of information. This was attempted under the banner of an Islamic worldview that enveloped more than one racial-ethnic group. Although members of a group might have felt more inclined toward their own group than toward others, this ethnocentrism did not preclude the participation of other groups for larger social-spiritual concerns.

In the United States, the white-black dichotomy has moved beyond mere ethnocentrism toward personal and systemic exploitation of blacks by whites so extreme that most blacks respond to white supremacy as if it were original. Although we reject it, to react indicates that something outside our own spiritual-cultural center generates the definition of our humanity. We do not operate from ground zero, the point at which no arbitrary inequity exists.

To protect our African American children against having their sensibilities affronted in this country, we prepare them to *respond* to racism; but when we impart the message "You must be prepared to respond to the inferior status in which you are held by society," the child perceives the message as "You *are* inferior."

I returned to this glaring climate of inferiority with my children, who had lived among Asians—Indians, Chinese, and Malays—with various ethnocentric tendencies. They had witnessed or participated in various customary and religious practices of Buddhists, Hindus, Muslims, Confucianists, Taoists, Christians, and Sikhs. Most people, irrespective of class, educational level, or age, spoke more than one language: Malay, Mandarin or Cantonese Chinese, Tamil, English.

Although there is nothing particularly Afrocentric about Malaysia, neither did the place imply that there was anything inherently inferior about one's African roots. We were part of a variety of diverse possibilities, a natural part of life on the planet. When we returned to the United States, we had to adapt ourselves to the presumption of white supremacy and its inverse—the inferiority of African American people. This was a tremendous culture shock for my younger children, who had spent most of their "memory shaping" in Malaysia. Not only did they fail to identify with the presumption of racial inferiority, but also they are Muslims. They were no longer privileged to have the positive mirrors for the two most essential aspects of their identity. Positive mirrors significantly help toward the development of self-esteem and spiritual wellness.[1]

What I witnessed concerning my children's growth and development was further expressed in my own experiences as an African American female in a nontraditional department, teaching Islam. The percentage of African Americans in theology and religion is already disproportionately low. It is even more isolating to teach a marginalized subject within a nontraditional department. Being on the margins of the margins was the very characteristic that inspired my strategies for survival within the institution. I would not be a willing lamb to the slaughter of mainstream thought. I would challenge the destructive aspects at the very core of academic experience.

Afrocentrism

This leads me to define in precise terms what I mean by Afrocentrism. It involves an ongoing process that begins with surrounding our children with images, ideas, dialogue, artifacts, and practical elements from our African and African American past and present. It is a concerted effort to provide them with mirrors for self-affirmation and cultural identity. Without some semblance of positive reinforcement and self-enhancing mirroring from one's immediate environment, various dysfunctional responses can develop and become deeply rooted and volatile; these include frustration, despondency, low self-esteem, despair, anger, and violence.[2]

Like other parents, I realized that my children must be prepared to meet racial inequities or they might suffer continuous emotional bruises, which could lead to irreparable spiritual damage. I labored, however, to make these mirrors a part of our original culture and contributions rather than a reaction to white racism.

Afrocentrism includes more than the minor artifacts. It also incorporates the cultural events that include black thought. It is a concerted effort to demonstrate the presence of black people in activities other than those handed down to us by our slave masters and now portrayed for us through commercials. Consequently we do not frequent the malls and other places of consumerism. We go to see African dancers, hear African storytellers, and visit Africana exhibits—aesthetic and cultural events that focus on the dignity of a people with a history and a culture, not just a skin color. Warith Deen Muhammad, a national spokesperson for the African American Muslim community, once pointed out that *black* is neither culture nor race: it is a color. This leads to dichotomy and fragmentation. My goal is to teach synthesis and harmony since Afrocentric enhancement of our environment is not a response to what white people do.

This personal experience with my children emphasized for me the role I must play within the academy. To participate further in meaningful teaching, I had to challenge the limitations and presumptions of racist systems. I began by including examples of diverse skin hues and cultural backgrounds in *all* discussions. I positively affirm examples of African descendants within "everyday-or-dinary" contexts.

Such "racialism" has now come under attack as reverse discrimination (as if what it is called mattered in the slightest). I continue to recognize African Ameri-can presence and contributions and to insert the significance of racial dimen-sions into discourse. I even compare arbitrary things on the basis of race. I em-phasize things *for* their potential to preserve black beauty and enhance its natural significance.

Virginia Commonwealth University as a Reflection of the White Male Christian South

Because of the uphill battle in the Department of Philosophy and Religious Studies at Virginia Commonwealth University (VCU), I am still ambivalent about my position there. While VCU promotes all the dialogue currently in vogue about pluralism, diversity, and interdisciplinary academic structures and prides itself on being an urban-based academy, it is still selective about its "di-versity."

While the measures of positive affirmations I use with my children may seem remedial, in my role as a university professor I also consciously employ examples from diverse races, economic classes, and gender to highlight abstract ideas in my teaching, especially in depicting elements of the transcendent or other com-mon religious paradigms. For example, in my class on Islam, I discuss the three components in the paradigm of forgiveness in Islam: (1) recognition that an error has been committed, which means accepting the responsibility for com-mitting it; (2) conscious intention not to return to the error, or repentance (there is no penitence, as in Catholicism); then, and only after these first two compo-nents, (3) supplication to the divine for forgiveness. If the error committed was an offense against another person, however, the first part involves seeking the pardon or forgiveness of the person who was wronged. Without this, divine forgiveness cannot proceed. That is why I said American racism cannot be for-given. Americans have yet to acknowledge their error, accept responsibility for it, and seek forgiveness from those whom they have affronted.

This discussion has led a few white males to insist that they are exempt from being racists and therefore from accepting responsibility for racism since they neither held slaves nor created the system in which they now enjoy so many undue privileges. (This sounds somewhat like our brothers, who say that since they have no power in the construction of this white male system, they cannot be held responsible for the sexism they practice against our sisters in it.)

Such attitudes and statements are a regular part of my teaching experiences in the South. In early American pluralism, various forms of Christianity were tolerated and incorporated under the banner of ecumenicalism. I challenged my students to explain why Native American and African religions were not included, and one student replied that it was because they were "primitive."

I always discuss the historical context of the Declaration of Independence and its statement that "all men are created equal." There is a double bind of potential for meaning in the terms juxtaposed to the applied meaning of the context in which it was constructed, which included only white male property holders. We continue to overcome this contextual limitation and arrive at ter- minological potential, but one student said to me, "Let's face it, a Muslim or a Buddhist is not going to be president." In other words, "all men" still does not include non-Christians, de facto if not de jure.

In response to an examination question on the variant meanings of human worth and single systems of evaluation, one student wrote, "These two black bitches (excuse me, but that's what they were) said they acted that way because of their African roots, but I have an African friend and she doesn't act like that." On the one hand, we could say these are students, and they are expected to exhibit some immaturity and ignorance. After all, they are in the university to learn. But on the other hand, it is true that even the staff maintains similar presumptions.

My department includes the disciplines of both religion and philosophy. These two have become further divided as younger white male philosophers define for themselves exclusive priority in the vision they have of their disci- pline. Sometimes this priority must be maintained by sheer political strategies that elevate some over others. One of the members in the religious studies pro- gram shares his position in the university with the Department of History. He has done so for twenty-two years and has held full voting rights throughout. Recently the philosophers decided that he deserved only one-half a vote to re- flect his one-half status. Although this is clearly against the university policy regarding half-time positions, the department exercised its right to decide on the matter autonomously. I argued against this decision since it went against the twenty-year precedent of his having full voting rights. The department chair countered my argument by saying, "Despite precedent, the slaves were set free."

I later responded that this statement was inappropriate and insensitive and could be misconstrued as racist. He defended his example as racially neutral. I said, "Let's face it, if I weren't black, you wouldn't have used that example." In addition, it implies that for him, African slaves never held the original prece- dent of being free people.

Later in a private conversation he told me that I seemed to have some feelings of animosity but that "we have a way of doing things around here." That *we* consists of all white males, for I am the only female and African American full-time staff person who also happens to be Muslim. This must mean that I am expected to adopt *their* manner of doing things around there, or I will not be considered appropriate and legitimate.

An African American female will be more readily reproached for her racial attitude than will her African American male colleagues, who narrow the permissible arena of exchange with whites by the mere threat of black male virility. This is, of course, a sensitive point of dispute between us and our brothers. On the one hand, Africana women are viewed as less threatening than they are and may have greater access to some positions. On the other hand, when we are in those positions, we are further exploited on the basis of race *and* gender in such matters as legitimacy, salary, tenure, and authority.

In addition to racial and gender presumptions, I must deal with widespread ignorance about Islam, which further exacerbates my position as illegitimate. A major presumption still lingers that all women who observe traditional Islamic dress are ignorant and oppressed. It is believed that I could not possibly cover my head unless I were a victim of a gravely unjust system and therefore incapable of holding and presenting my own ideas. The actual impetus behind my dress was in contradistinction to the experiences of African slave women who were stripped of their garments of piety before the lecherous eyes of slave auctioneers and masters. In fact, I covered my hair and wore long dresses before I accepted Islam.

In any place in American academia other than the historically black colleges, what complicates teaching from an Afrocentric perspective is most obviously that I am a black female. However, because I am a Muslim teaching religious studies in the Christian South, my obvious abandonment of the religious expression white America considers standard further excludes me from any category with which it identifies, and thus it threatens my legitimacy.

Anything I say that does not reflect the status quo—and I say such things often—will be challenged as inappropriate, illegitimate, or accusatory. This goes beyond healthy discourse of differences; the presumptions are that I do not know what I'm talking about and that I intentionally insult my coworkers' fundamental beliefs or insult them personally. Meanwhile, as an instructor, I must remain professionally neutral while they continually make denigrating statements.

It goes without saying that white male professors are standard makers. Substantial research on the attrition rates of women and minorities in the academy indicates that what white male professors do is considered the standard by which women and minorities are judged. We must respond to or reflect their standard or we are considered inappropriate, illegitimate educators. Because I am a black female Muslim teaching religion in the Christian South, it is presumed that I could not even possibly *know* what that standard is.

Because my dress distinguishes me as a Muslim, when I teach general religious studies courses it is fairly frequently presumed that I could not know anything about Christianity. Students explain the rudiments of Christianity to me as if I had recently landed from another planet. I have to mention early on in almost every public lecture, television interview, and classroom setting that my father was a Christian minister, so I have personal and professional knowledge of the complexities of Christian history, development, ideology, and practice. Once this first presumption is removed, we can begin to explore some of these complexities that indicate that Christianity is not monolithic.

Attempts to drum this same point home in courses related to Islam is often to little avail. Most Americans cannot be convinced that Islam is not an Arabic religion, that not all Arabs are Muslims. There are more Muslims in Indonesia than in all of the Arabic-speaking countries combined (some of which are on the continent of Africa). With regard to the diversity of Islam in America, everyone who is black and a Muslim is not necessarily a follower of Louis Farrakhan or part of the Nation of Islam movement. However distinct, the Nation of Islam does not teach a brand of Islam so radically distinct from mainstream Islam that it is impossible to consider it among other variants of Islam that have existed through Muslim history.

Students get their ideas about religion from the larger context of the South. The presumption of Christianity extends quite far. The food provided at a gathering for the College of Humanities and Sciences included a few cheeses but mainly centered on ham sandwiches and shellfish (oysters, to be precise). I had quite a laugh with a Jewish colleague over the blatant disregard for our dietary restrictions. Other than this, we actually have nothing in common. On this occasion we were thrown together by our exclusion from the meal. Yet even he had more beverage choices than I because there was only one nonalcoholic choice, and Muslims do not drink alcohol.

My last professional example of the presumption of Christianity in the South crosses into my own racial and gender territory. At the annual meeting of the Southeastern Regional American Academy of Religion, I asked a presenter from the African American religion section about overcoming retrospective historical reading—inserting ideas from our historical or cultural present as criteria by which to judge other times and places. In her response she included the phrase "and I'm as Christian as anybody." I told her that was quite funny considering she was talking to me. Who are these "anybodies" she compared her-self with but white bodies who are Christian?

Critical Afrocentric Presence of Women in the Academy

What does all of this have to do with Afrocentric teaching? In its narrowmind-edness, the presumption of Christianity in the South reflects a lack of familiar-ity with the complexities of the world in which we live. It helps in self-preserva-tion but does not yield very readily to even the slightest disparity between that self and others. As an African American Muslim woman academician, I am a clear other.

Despite such assaults, I continue to plug away at my teaching and commu-nity participation under what I describe as spiritual activism. I feel disinclined to teach without including some elements of my concern over social justice in the process, which I specifically relate to the Islamic paradigm. Since Ameri-can academia has not systematically researched this phenomenon and the media cannot adequately characterize it, spiritual activism among African Americans converts to Islam needs some elaboration.

Religion in America is often characterized by passivity and tolerance, even against glaring injustice. The Christian soldier stands firm and proud in the face of taunting racists, barking dogs, and exploding fire hoses—a martyr to the cause of goodness, made virtuous by nonviolent resistance. Juxtaposed to this is spiritual activism as expressed by the most famous convert in America, El-Hajj Malik El-Shabbazz (Malcolm X): "I do not advocate violence, nor do I stand on the sidelines and watch innocent women, children, and old people being beaten while I overcome their oppressors with my capacity to love."

The Islamic code of justice *requires* the true believer to use "any means nec-essary" or possible to get rid of injustice and oppression. Fourteen centuries ago the Prophet Muhammad said, "If you see a wrong, you should stop it with your hand; if you cannot, then you should speak out against it; if not that, then at least, condemn it in your heart, that being the weakest form of faith."

In Islam, faith is linked with conscious action against injustice. The ten-dency to translate this into random and arbitrary violence is a technique per-petuated in the media by the oppressors to overshadow the fundamental hu-man right to act for justice. Since teaching is a conscious action, it too must include this element of justice. Actions for justice are part of faith in Islam.

Faith in Christian America is often characterized by passive resistance. When the two worldviews come into collision, Islam must be made to seem abhor-rent. Hence, to sustain the element of fear, the media reiterate only the actions of terrorists and the most radical statements of Louis Farrakhan. Those who are well aware of such media tactics—the same ones used in the past that kept black activists from becoming more mainstream—search beyond media projections to find the *Truth*.

Faith in Islam is always faith in the *Truth*. It is not true that white America deserves a larger share of the productivity of black labor and sacrifice just because of its whiteness. It is not true that the black man should have to camouflage his virility in order to be accepted for jobs so he can provide for the family. It is not true that the black mother who survives without the benefits of that provider is the cause of the downfall of the community. It is not true that the complex predicament that we find ourselves in as a community is the result of our inadequacy as a people. It is not true that we can do nothing against the racially biased oppression of the American academy.

What are we to do? We adopt a position of strength. For an increasing number of African Americans, Islam provides that position of strength because the criteria for judging the worth of an individual are fixed on two factors—faith and good deeds. Anyone from any circumstance can possess these two characteristics and achieve *taqwa,* or moral excellence. It matters not from what context: rich or poor, city or rural, educated or illiterate, mother or father, child or adult, black or white. Each individual who strives with faith as the center of spiritual being will bring about positive change in the immediate environment and achieve excellence.

The moment each member of the community begins this participation, he or she continues to be elevated until the final judgment. Our experiences in the Diaspora, however—especially slavery—have affronted and attempted to destroy the very element of our well-being that is the key to this participation: the element of spirit. Without it, we do not attain to human excellence because we are no more than empty shells. Without it, we do not possess the courage necessary to fight injustice but instead perpetuate random acts of violence through fear, even against our own people. Without it, we cannot know ourselves but are forever reacting to the white master's definition of us as inferior.

So the attraction that Islam has for so many African Americans is at the very core of our survival and movement into excellence—spiritual activism. One who possesses the inner spirit does not accept injustice but strives through any means necessary to establish justice and honor on the earth. This is the attitude behind my participation in the academy.

Spiritual activism is not sensational. It is a process that aims for human excellence and implements whatever actions lead toward gaining human dignity. Yet the stamina required to participate in an alternative worldview that offers relief from self-perpetuated oppression—the oppression of false thinking—is the stamina needed to choose to maintain a life imbued with spirit in American academe. We need to learn how to tap into this source for soulful growth to lead radical and comprehensive change in the way we construct our world, educate others, and participate in our environment.

Imbuing It with Spirit

Our efforts as African American women in the academy must prevent the loss of the stamina from our souls that occurs when we buy into the white male capitalist paradigms of development, education, and learning. The goal of education is to transform behavior, attitudes, and ideas about self, others, environment, and the cosmos. We willfully engage in this process of education as a means for positive change—improvement in behavior, attitudes, ideas, and environment.

The difference between surviving in the academy the way that it is and raising critical responses to the information presented, historical accounts, and evaluation of the education process is crucial. To do the latter requires a self-constructed definition of being and worth that could be used as a criterion for evaluating the results of successful completion of the institution's goals. Discrepancies that arise need to be evaluated along the lines of a self-projected black female image. The goals of the establishment are to produce results as close to the white male model as possible.

This process of self-evaluation and systems criticism is ongoing. My situation as an African American female theologian teaching Islam in the white male Christian South allows a precise demonstration from which general principles can be summarized.

In spite of the greater systemic, personal, and environmental oppressions experienced by the African American woman for the duration of her sojourn in the Diaspora, she has remained centrally focused on her inner voice for spiritual well-being and personal stamina. Such a voice needs to be a persistent part of the academy now.

Notes

1. Gloria Wade-Gayles, *Pushed Back to Strength* (Boston: Beacon Press, 1993).
2. Heinz Kohut, *Self Psychology and the Humanities* (New York: Norton, 1985), 124–60.

Part Four

Black Women Administrators in the Academy

During the 1980s, black women administrators increased their share of positions in higher education. In 1979, according to the American Council on Education, black women made up 2.9 percent of full-time administrators; in 1989 the percentage increased to 4.2 percent, which represents an 87 percent change. Black women administrators in higher education hold a larger percentage of positions than black women faculty. Nevertheless, they are still underrepresented in administrative positions, and usually these positions are mid-management level, such as financial aid officers and affirmative action officers. They are also primarily concentrated in predominantly black institutions.

These administrators in both black and white milieus are challenging, as their numbers increase, the institutional culture of the academy that perpetuates racism and sexism. In addition, they offer their insights to guide others through its cultural maze.

In the opening article, "Rites of Passage and Rights of Way: A Woman Administrator's Experiences" by Phyllis Strong Green, the reader is given an insightful personal account of racial and sexual barriers that Green encountered in white academe and how she challenged and resisted the academy's culture that guides the norms, values, practices, beliefs, and assumptions that shape the behavior of individuals and groups.

While black women administrators were excluded from white academe until the late 1960s, Brunetta Reid Wolfman, in "'Light as from a Beacon': African American Women Administrators in the Academy," notes that in the black community, the black woman educator/administrator is part of a historic tradition. She places African American women administrators in historical perspective in both African American and white majority settings and recounts the management positions they have occupied in both types of institutions. Wolfman also examines the ambiguous status of African American women, the social class origins and family backgrounds of black women administrators, and the barriers they have encountered in higher education as well as ways in which black women cope.

In addition to teaching/administering, nursing has been a traditional occupation open to black women. Elnora D. Daniel's "African American Nursing Administrators in the Academy: Breaking the Glass Ceiling" states that life has not been a crystal stair. Black women nursing administrators face not only barriers of sex and race but also biases because of the low status of nursing in the academy and the stereotypes about nursing. These triple jeopardies intertwine to affect the life chances of nursing administrators. Daniel provides strategies for overcoming these barriers.

Racial and sexual struggles are the Achilles' heel for black women. Julia R. Miller and Gladys Gary Vaughn, in "African American Women Executives: Themes That Bind," write that issues faced by female African American administrators in higher education are consistent with historical struggles to render effective leadership in American education. The twin disguises of racism and sexism, as framed by legal precedent, still impose great restraints on the utilization of the competence and talents of African American women in both predominantly black and predominantly white institutions. Miller and Vaughn surveyed executives in business, law, medicine, and education and found overarching themes that bind them, such as "countering race and gender discrimination; constant challenges to, and questions of, competence and educational credentials; family support; personal determination; development of self-preservation techniques; the value of extensive educational preparedness; and the importance of mentors and role models."

Martha E. Dawson's "Climbing the Administrative Ladder in the Academy: An Experiential Case History," vividly illustrates the themes that bind women executives and contribute to their success. Dawson shares with the reader the hard lessons she has learned in a career that has spanned more than fifty years of working in both black and white institutions.

Finally, M. Colleen Jones continues Miller and Vaughn's theme in "Does Leadership Ability Transcend Gender and Race? The Case of African American Women College Presidents." Jones shows us that power is more than domination and control. It is empowering others. In her study of African American women college presidents, comparing selective views on leadership attributes, Jones found that black women college presidents are more likely to recognize human needs, to emphasize both process and outcome, and to create team players who transcend self-interest. Such transformational leadership attributes are necessary to shape the changing culture of the academy and to manage its diversity.

Chapter 12

Rites of Passage and Rights of Way
A Woman Administrator's Experiences

Phyllis Strong Green

Gender, race, power, and identity are inexorably intertwined in academia. The experiences of black women administrators and faculty attest to this fact. Women in higher education look to new challenges but find countless frustrations in actions and decisions that are treated as painful rites of passage rather than as painless rights of way. Yet as much as we know that an institution that is dominated by white males is filled with promises and perils, we do not always know how to navigate the perilous waters. We must depend on the experiences of others for guidance. Because so few women occupy high- or mid-level administrative positions in most universities, and because these positions are often isolated from one another, knowledge of potential roadblocks often comes too late if at all.

Subjective experiential accounts can provide knowledge of the challenging opportunities in higher education as well as the potential pitfalls. Yet we are acutely aware that their value is limited by the fact that they are based on anecdotal evidence, small numbers of interviews, and observed patterns of behavior that may or may not be generally applicable. Consequently, those of us who were educated to believe in the value of scientific evidence based on empirical data are not altogether comfortable with ethnographic studies based on the experience of individuals. In fact, we find it hard to use the word "I" with any frequency, knowing that it may be followed by idiosyncratic information. In the real world, however, we find ourselves wishing that there were case studies or experiential accounts to provide insights on the complex world of which women in academia must try to make sense.

This chapter describes my experiences in three leading public universities over a period of fifteen years in which I served as an assistant professor, a university administrator, and an associate dean of a graduate school. It discusses the significance and implications of the following factors in organizational change: (1) formal power and authority, (2) the political environment, (3) the organizational culture and its values, (4) external support in building allies, and 5) negotiating skills in deal making. It then suggests coping mechanisms and strategies that young women administrators and faculty may find helpful in an economic climate in which reorganization and cutbacks are commonplace. The conclusion offers recommendations for becoming an effective change agent.

Background I Brought to Academia

I had entered academia with a nontraditional career path, having received my doctorate when I was over forty. Then, after teaching political science for five years at a major Eastern university, I spent one year in college administration at a Western university and almost a year as a chief legislative aide for a state legislator in an Eastern state. When I applied for the position of associate dean, I was a true outsider, and my experience in university administration was limited. On the one hand, the position that I sought had strong appeal for me. On the other hand, the downside was hard to decipher at the time. A female Ph.D. candidate on the search committee alluded to the "difficulty of the environment," stating that it "had more than its share of prima donnas" and that my predecessor had experienced personality problems with the head of the program. There were also some problems, she said, that were associated with being a full-time administrator in a nominal faculty position. Nevertheless, my interview went surprisingly well. Before I returned to the East Coast, I received a telephone call informing me that I was the first choice of the search committee. The search committee, I was told, had selected me because my "maturity, outgoing personality, and experience" made me "the best person for the job" and would help me "to cope with our very bright and engaging but sometimes fractious and demanding graduate students."

Political Environment

The political environment that I had entered was beset by problems. Although I was unaware of it at the time, the dean was also contemplating retirement. Two acting deans and a permanent dean were to follow within a three-year period. The school was receiving criticism from alumni, students, and campus officials for having no full-time women or minority faculty. It had the reputation of being insulated, as well as isolated, and generally inhospitable to women and minorities. The full-time faculty was not only all male but heavily Jewish, senior in age, and relatively conservative. The perception of clannishness was

so pervasive that a black professor on campus was motivated to stop by my office for a visit to determine for himself whether or not I was black, as someone
had suggested, or Jewish, as my light skin color and appearance had suggested
to someone else.

Organizational Environment

As I discovered more about the political environment, it became apparent to
me that the formal powers and authority of the office that I held provided the
breadth and flexibility to make some needed changes in the status quo. I also
recognized that there was much to learn from the organizational culture—that
is, its "basic assumptions, cognitive patterns, values, myths, and unspoken beliefs" that distinguish it from others. Organizations, it has been said, become
institutions only after they are infused with values.[1] Knowledge of the organizational culture helped me to understand how the values of collegiality, institutional memory, merit, and a "good fit" can be used to help some organizations
and to undermine others.

Formal Power and Authority

Within the formally prescribed areas, I had significant power and authority to
influence outcomes as well as the flexibility and autonomy to make creative
choices. Given my areas of responsibility, I realized that I could become a change
agent in the school, making it more inclusive of minorities and women. While
there were a number of openings for new staff, the first cut had already been
done and included no minorities. As new positions opened up with turnover,
the staff became more ethnically diverse. Utilizing the formal powers that I
had, I decided I would work to achieve the following objectives:

First, I made the placement office more professional by computerizing and
streamlining its operations. I worked to increase the number of on-site recruit-
ers and to promote equity by ending the practice of favoritism in the selection
of students for jobs and internships. Second, I attracted more minority students
to the graduate program through fellowship grants, recruitment, and creating a
more hospitable social environment. Third, I frequently did student advising
that not only generated goodwill among minority students but also produced
graduate school and summer institute applicants. Fourth, I participated in key
campus committees and accepted invitations to serve on panels at events such
as an annual black managers' campus-wide meeting. Fifth, I spearheaded activities to promote the recruitment of women and minority faculty. Sixth, I initiated action to derail a planned protest meeting and march that could have
endangered the progress we were making in affirmative action.

Many aspects of my work were rewarding and stimulating, enhancing my self-esteem and experience, while others left me with feelings of powerlessness and social isolation. There were no other blacks in positions analogous to mine on campus, but I made an effort to get to know other minority and women officials to reduce my periodic discomfiture.

Organizational Culture: Four Values

In my organization, certain values emerged over time. I soon understood how these values and underlying assumptions served to help or hinder women administrators, depending on how they were used.

Collegiality. For example, the value of collegiality can facilitate a sense of identity or belonging somewhat akin to the "professional courtesy" that physicians extend to one another. Similarly, some professors share resources and experience, while administrators act as mentors, serve on committees, and participate in special projects.

One unspoken assumption of collegiality is loyalty to the group. At one faculty gathering, I mentioned my empathy for Derrick Bell, the former black law professor at Harvard, who undertook an unpaid leave of absence to protest the law school's unwillingness to consider tenure for a black woman professor.[2] Seated at our long table was a professor who immediately challenged my comment. He angrily argued that Professor Bell's act of conscience had violated the rule of collegiality. A discussion ensued between us. The professor was unwavering in his censure of Bell. Not a single faculty member supported my point of view. No other women or minorities were present.

A friend of mine, a white woman professor in a predominantly black university, gave a different spin to definitions of collegiality. She confided to me that collegiality in her college meant favoritism based on affiliation with black fraternities. In a situation analogous to British school ties, these men, she claimed, sided with fraternity brothers in committee meetings and supported one another in other ways. She observed that faculty members who were associated through sororities showed no similar proclivities. Males held positions of power in that university, while few women were in the position to help other women colleagues gain upward mobility.

Institutional memory. The "institutional memory" is another value that can be used to retain the status quo. The term refers to the historical knowledge of the institution: its customs, mores, folkways, and special knowledge, such as "where the bodies are buried." The institutional memory can be analogous to war stories or organizational anecdotes about sequences of events in an organization's history. Since it is shared by old-timers in the organization, it is selectively used to communicate core messages implicitly, metaphorically, or symbolically in order to socialize newcomers. Newcomers can then pass on the torch of continuity and tradition.

The institutional memory can be an excuse for rigidity, selectively invoked to discredit innovative ideas. For example, I suggested to a dean that guest lecturers be used occasionally in a weekly faculty lunch forum. He rejected the idea, commenting that the forum had been used traditionally as an outlet to unwind and enjoy the company of colleagues. Ironically, a later dean, who came from outside the school, offered many nontraditional ideas. One was to have guest lecturers at the weekly faculty lunch forum. Another time I proposed that minority alumni be consulted about the possible formation of a working group to mentor minority students in the program. The dean said that separatism was not countenanced in the institutional memory. In response to students' concerns, I suggested to another dean that he consider incorporating into his core course case studies that portrayed women and minority managers as leaders. He dismissed the proposal. Several years later, under new faculty, students were able to institute both proposals.

Ironically, the institutional memory can be used for change if a new idea is embedded in a traditional value. A women's studies chair reported that she learned to use the institutional memory for her own ends. She legitimated a nontraditional curriculum by placing it squarely in support of high quality research, which is considered a central mission of the university. The chair sought and was awarded a sizable research grant from a prestigious mainstream national foundation. The grant brought favorable publicity to the university and helped to validate not only the research but also the women's studies program.

Merit. If there is a single value that academics honor in word, if not in deed, it is merit. Excellence, high standards of performance, and achievement are taken as the sine qua non in the selection of faculty and administrators. Unfortunately, merit and standards have been used more than any other values to exclude women and minorities from positions and promotions. The problem, however, is that merit is not always easy to determine once a certain level of proficiency has been met. At that point, variables such as "ascriptive traits, personal qualities of style and manner, conforming behavior, mentors, and sponsors" come into play in academic appointments and tenure decisions.[3] Or, as one scholar stated, in some situations, standards are "nothing more than standardized preferences."[4]

Employment and tenure decisions are frequently based on consensus. Sometimes a few negative words by a key faculty member or an outside referee are used to reject a candidate, while positive words of support by the right sponsor can lead to an appointment. Even with the subjectivity in the faculty recruitment process, some faculty believe that merit and standards are unduly undermined in the quest for student body diversity. For example, one chair of the student admissions committee expressed vehement opposition to affirmative action "when a minority student with very good, but not outstanding, credentials takes the place of a more qualified white student." Several committee members argued that the student in question exemplified standards of "relative excellence" enhanced by interesting work and community experience and a unique background that would enrich the class. The student was admitted and successfully completed the graduate program.

"A *good fit*." The term "a good fit" has frequently been used by the leadership of an organization to eliminate prospective or current members. Prospective members can also use the term to decline offers to join an organization that, upon closer scrutiny, does not fit their interests or needs. As a form of "anticipatory socialization," it serves to "reduce risk by selecting those who share similar goals and values, employing the same methods and agreed-upon ends, and who can be trusted with the maintenance of institutional values."[5] To the extent that women and minorities are trained by the validating organization, they will be "a good fit" unless they rock the boat by challenging its values.

Organizational values change with leadership. When a new leader was selected in my organization, he told me that I was not a good fit. He then expressed his desire to bring in a staff of "young hotshots." As I mentioned earlier, I had been hired to complement the qualities of a former dean who had told me that my background made me a "particularly good fit" for the program. When changes in leadership occur, however, it is difficult to determine to what extent personality differences or other variables explain decisions, or whether race, gender, and age play a role. I do know that with a change in leadership, the term "a good fit" assumed a new and painful meaning for me.

Male camaraderie helped new faculty and visiting faculty to fit in. The tendency of male faculty members to go to lunch, have a drink after work, or play squash or basketball with other males diminishes the ability of women to gain access and information, which, in turn, may lead to occupational mobility or immobility. A number of men readily admit that they are reluctant to go out with female colleagues singly or in groups because of "the sexual connotations attached." They buttress this concern by pointing to their desire to avoid any rumors or sexual harassment allegations. Regardless of the validity or invalidity of these concerns, what is clear is that informal social exchanges and networks make a difference in information access that, when used judiciously, can lead to even greater access.[6]

Communication Styles of Men and Women

Men and women have different communication styles that can determine the level of comfort in which they function and can affect their sense of identity and self-esteem. Since language exerts a powerful influence over thought and perceptions of reality, communication style can mean that one's ideas are heard and the other's ignored.[7] For example, the weekly faculty lunch in our organization, which was open to colleagues on campus, was a forum not only for pleasant informal exchanges but also for grandstanding and posturing speeches that I sometimes found intimidating. Women guests and the women who eventually joined the faculty generally preferred one-on-one exchanges. They rarely took center stage. To my knowledge, the men never noticed.

Women who lead organizations also express feelings of frustration over male communication styles. A woman dean on another campus, whose reputation was hardly one of reticence, remarked that she had attended deans' meetings in which her relatively soft voice could not be heard over the aggressive exchanges of her fellow deans. Since these men interrupted one another without pause, she felt that she had been reduced to an invisible and silent presence.[8]

Women in diverse administrative positions voice similar frustration over not being heard by male colleagues. One administrator referred to a common pattern in meetings in which the woman states her idea only to have no one follow up with a comment that confirms its validity. Later in the meeting, a man will state the same or similar ideas in different words, apparently believing that the idea was his own. Then male colleagues will voice agreement. This administrator speculated that men seem to understand the language of other men, independent of their status. Validation in these circumstances appears to be associated with the gender of the speaker rather than the idea itself.

The values of collegiality, institutional memory, merit, and a good fit do indeed work in the organizational culture to exclude women and minorities. As women become more aware of the bias embedded in these values and practices, they can begin to develop more inclusive strategies for change.

Building External Support

The importance of cultivating supporters outside of your organizational unit to embrace the wider campus cannot be underestimated. This strongly permits women administrators and faculty to establish allies and networks at all levels, including secretaries and other staff members who may prove helpful. One administrator reported that she had worked with a vice-chancellor on a special projects committee and had built credibility with him. When her building was demolished, she sought a favorable site for her department. Her division chief rejected her request and criticized her for "not being cooperative." She decided to fight the decision and take her case to the vice-chancellor. Her strategy was to present the issue clearly and effectively with facts and figures that justified her choice of one site over the other. The vice-chancellor approved her request.

Affirmative Action

Two issue areas, affirmative action and pay equity, directly address opportunities for minority women in academia. Several trends in regard to affirmative action are noteworthy. One trend that women have observed is that in many departments, a token number of women and defined minority groups—African American, Latino, Asian American, and American Indian—are being appointed. After that, there seems to be an absence of commitment to continue this inclusive practice or to encourage minorities to expand the supply by entering the Ph.D. pipeline. Consequently, white males are appointed to any other positions that become available. Or, as one professor stated impatiently after an affirmative action search, "Let's just make the appointment and get it over with and move on to more serious business."

There is another trend, however, that holds more promise. Age discrimination is being challenged as more older women, faculty, and students enter the academy. In one department, for example, a female candidate who was over sixty years old was appointed in a multiple department search. I was present when a male faculty member raised the issue of her "seasoned" age and was reprimanded by a younger male colleague for violation of federal legislation. It is often the younger male faculty who hold promise for change.

Although present trends make it difficult to predict the course and consequences of affirmative action in academia, women and minorities need to be alert to practices that undermine it and supportive of activities that promote equity and fairness.

Pay Equity for Men and Women

One issue in which gender appears to be more important than race is pay equity in administrative and faculty salaries. My attention was first called to the pay gap problem faced by women in 1985 when I was asked to develop and chair a national conference on comparable worth. In some universities, the assumption persists that women are not the primary breadwinners and, consequently, men deserve to make more money. Women whom I know in academia have not been willing to make salary compromises. One highly placed student services official said that when she accepted a new job and was negotiating her salary, she was told that as a professor's wife, she "didn't need a higher salary." The woman took a tough stand, insisting that her pay be equal to that of her male colleagues. Her demand was approved.

Deal making has recently emerged as a pay equity issue. A woman psychology professor who brought a sex discrimination lawsuit argued that deals are cut for men that are not cut for women.[9] I found this to be true when I was hired as an assistant professor and later as an associate dean. I was not as sophisticated as many young faculty are now about deal making. Over time, however, I observed the deals cut by new minority faculty in universities that were seeking greater faculty diversity. When periodic merit pay increases were an issue, I made sure that my performance evaluations were well documented and that the increases were subsequently approved.

Black women would be wise to follow the advice of Janet McKay [Janet Holgren], president of Mills College, who argued that women will have to negotiate as aggressively as men for higher salaries. She asserted, "Women are not going to break the glass ceiling in academia if we don't address these differences. The only way things improve is when an institution takes this seriously and puts into place affirmative remedies."[10]

Gender or Race?

In dealing with equity or discrimination issues, black women sometimes find themselves in the double bind of not being clearly able to separate race from gender. Black women with whom I spoke generally agreed that they had experienced more gender discrimination than racial discrimination. They felt that women were usually supportive on diverse issues, while on some occasions "men didn't take me seriously." Many of these women found little difference in the support they received from minority and white male colleagues. In contrast, I found that minority males, including Latinos and Asian Americans, were for the most part my valued allies, serving as mentors, advisers, and advocates.

Several senior women faculty and administrators explained why they believed that "bonding along gender lines supersedes race." They reported having had a number of negative experiences over the years with minority men of their generation. One woman asserted that some male colleagues "had trouble with women in authority" and "were so seduced by power that they were jealous of women in leadership roles." Another added, "They are fearful of the independent critique that women bring to the table." She advised junior women colleagues not to be intimidated by male colleagues.

Economic Environment

Academia in the 1990s reflects a national economy in which structural changes make budgetary cutbacks and reorganization commonplace. Even the most prestigious public universities are vulnerable to the demand by state legislators that they reduce costs by downsizing and economizing on the one hand and raising student tuition and fees on the other. In such a volatile environment, women and minorities who are not protected by tenure safeguards may find it hard to survive. Black women administrators are particularly vulnerable to university-wide attrition incentives and cutbacks. Those who hold "soft money" positions may go first, while others who lack seniority or other nonexpendable attributes may soon follow.

Structural changes also create a fluid environment in which leadership changes are steady and relentless. As new leaders emerge, women and minority administrators may find themselves in the precarious position of being out of favor with the new guard. As reported earlier, I had served under three deans (including two acting deans) over a four-year period when a new permanent dean was selected. The new dean initiated efforts to recruit a younger, more diverse faculty in the wake of faculty retirements and other organizational changes. An "out with the old, in with the new" attitude prevailed. I was considered part of the "old structure" whose major allies were retiring. My strategy at that point became to survive and move on, move out, or move over.

Coping Mechanisms

Moving on was not a viable option at the time, so I learned to cope by building on my strengths and creating options to deal with change. In order to meet the need of the new campus-wide American Cultures curriculum, I developed a course for undergraduate majors that was a joy to teach. I also assisted the new dean in ways that I thought would be helpful to him. This was my way of defining the situation rather than being defined by it. I hoped to take advantage of untapped opportunities and challenges.[11]

Conclusion

Many women in academia find themselves in the role of, or seeking to be, change agents who make a difference. They strive to overcome inequities and make their organization more inclusive and hospitable to minorities and women. To this end, I present the following recommendations for becoming an effective change agent, which are based on my experiences: First, think about what you want to change and prioritize your objectives. Then use the formal power and authority that you have to reach these objectives. Second, learn about the culture of your organization, its values (for example, collegiality, the institutional memory, merit, and a good fit), and gender-related modes of communication. Then use this knowledge to your advantage—for example, to legitimize an initiative or course of action. Third, build external support outside your unit or department to embrace the wider campus or, if necessary, other campuses or organizations. This may be viewed as an investment in political capital that can be drawn on when needed. Fourth, develop strong negotiating skills and use them aggressively to cut the best deal you can. Apply them to win higher salaries and merit pay, promotions, and other benefits. Fifth, take care of your own interests. Define the situation rather than being defined by it. Create options and explore opportunities for professional development and personal fulfillment that enhance your sense of identity and self-esteem. *Finally*, make plans to leave when changes in leadership or organizational structure dictate. Don't burn your bridges while you use the external support and options you have developed to move out and move on to something better.

Notes

Author's note: I am grateful to Elizabeth Morgan for her helpful comments.

1. J. Steven Ott, *The Organizational Culture Perspective* (Chicago: Dorsey, 1989), 8.

2. See Anthony Flint, "Bell At Harvard: A Unique Activism," *Boston Globe*, 7 May 1990, 1.

3. William Exum, "Climbing the Crystal Stair: Values, Affirmative Action, and Minority Faculty, *Social Problems* 30, no. 4 (April 1983): 393.

4. Patricia J. Williams, *The Alchemy of Race and Rights* (Cambridge, Mass.: Harvard University Press, 1991).

5. Ott, *The Organizational Culture Perspective*, 88–89.

6. Winston A. Van Horne and Toni-Michelle C. Travis, "Introduction," in *Ethnicity and Women*, ed. Winston A. Van Horne and Thomas V. Tonnesen (Madison: University of Wisconsin System AESCC, 1986), 14–15.

7. Ott, *The Organizational Culture Perspective*, 20; Judy C. Pearson, *Gender and Communication*, 2d ed. (Dubuque, Iowa: William C. Brown, 1991), 4–18 and 218–22.

8. Carole Edelsky, "Who's Got the Floor?" Deborah James and Sandra Clarke, "Women, Men, and Interruptions: A Critical Review," Deborah Tannen, "The Relativity of Linguistic Strategies: Rethinking Power and Solidarity in Gender and Dominance," all in *Gender and Conversational Interaction*,edited by Deborah Tannen (New York: Oxford University Press, 1993).

9. Louis Freedberg and Ramon G. McLeod, "Pay Gap Between Sexes Extends Across Academia," *San Francisco Chronicle*, 5 November 1993, A1 and A19.

10. Ibid.

11. See Lois Benjamin, *The Black Elite: Facing the Color Line in the Twilight of the Twentieth Century* (Chicago: Nelson-Hall, 1991), 211.

Chapter 13

"Light as from a Beacon"

African American Women Administrators in the Academy

Brunetta Reid Wolfman

"Be yourself and not the white man's image of you. Let the world catch your light as from a beacon rather than from a mirror's pale reflection."[1] This seemingly simple yet complex advice from W. E. B. Du Bois to American blacks has been an unconscious guide for African American women who have been administrative leaders in American higher education institutions. These women have an ambiguous status, particularly those working in predominantly white colleges and universities, where they are given minimal recognition and respect because they are newcomers to administrative positions in the academy. While black women administrators remain virtually invisible in white academia, they are accorded high status and respect in the African American community. This chapter will discuss the dimension of high in-group status and historical position and explore some of the characteristics of black women managers in white higher education institutions. It will also review the stresses and strains in their professional lives and examples of the ways in which they alleviate those tensions and adjust to the barriers of the duality of race and gender.

Pioneering African American Educators

African American women's involvement in education began during slavery with reports of slave women who managed to learn to read and then conducted secret classes or schools, teaching other slaves to read.[2] This educational work was carried out with the women's full knowledge that apprehension carried severe penalties, including death. After the Civil War, many of those formerly enslaved teachers were joined by educated northern free black women who went south to teach the newly freed men and women there. Many of the northern teachers originally planned to journey to Africa as missionaries but felt a stronger call to work in the South. The schools in which the women taught were established to impart basic academic skills, and many later evolved into colleges. From their inception, those institutions were coeducational because the need for teachers and missionaries was so great, and the painful memories of bondage and restrictions on education so recent, that gender segregation was never a possibility.

The number of female African American founders of institutions is so small that most historians do not recognize them, and their contributions have gone unacknowledged by both the black community and the majority community. Historical records indicate, however, that Haines Normal School in Atlanta (founded in 1866), Bethune-Cookman College in Daytona Beach, Florida (1904), and Frelinghuysen University in Washington, D.C. (1906), were founded by black women. The names of these pioneers are not often mentioned today. Lucy Laney of Haines and Anna Cooper and Rosetta Lawson of Frelinghuysen have faded into oblivion, while Mary McLeod Bethune is recognized more for her political connections to Eleanor Roosevelt than for founding a college.

Most of the early African American female educators and administrators were educated in southern black colleges, though some of their counterparts were educated in northern colleges including Oberlin, Smith, and Wellesley. Even though few of these women were titular heads of institutions, as wives of college presidents or faculty they often assumed important administrative responsibilities in the colleges in which their husbands worked. Many of these women taught in addition to acting as deans, supervisors of maintenance work, buyers of provisions, chaperons, fund-raisers, and liaisons to the churches and women's associations. One need only read histories of the individual colleges to discover the major roles played by such spouses in the development of African American higher education. One of the primary purposes of the colleges was to prepare teachers to staff rural schools being established to quickly ready the black population to be self-supporting. In a very real sense, the obligation of black women to enter the educational field has a historical basis rooted in racial concern.

As the higher education institutions for blacks became more structured, one of the entry points for women was as heads of the more specialized nurse training schools for blacks, first in the racially segregated facilities affiliated with hospitals, where they assumed leadership positions, and later when these units became affiliated with higher educational institutions. The black women who became leaders of the higher education nursing groups fought for recognition not only for themselves but also for their profession, striving to provide opportunities for nursing education outside the South, targeting segregated settings.

Their initiatives were instrumental in transforming their sphere from nurse training to the more credentialed nurse education, and they upgraded the profession in the process.[3]

Another point of entry for black women in the academy was as dean of
women. One of the most revered deans was Lucy Diggs Slowe, first dean of
women at Howard University; a founder of Alpha Kappa Alpha, the first black
sorority; and one of the first black members of the National Association of Deans
of Women.[4] Her situation perhaps exemplified the professional category and
problems of the dean of women, a now defunct position, in that she was hired
for her professional experience as an educator and her strong organizational
affiliations. Her argument with the Howard administration was for compensa-
tion and status equal to that of the Howard's male deans. Her organizational
affiliations were an expression of her concern for women students and their
needs, so the positive results of both Alpha Kappa Alpha and the National Association of Women in Education are the fulfillment of the aspirations of Lucy
Diggs Slowe.

Black female educators developed academic programs that blended the ideas
of W. E. B. Du Bois, which emphasized classical academic preparation for a
leadership group, and those of Booker T. Washington, who proposed vocational
education and preparation for work, self-support, and racial interdependence.
These women took from each of the philosophies as they created a vision of the
future, for they realized that the black community needed cultural and social
organizations to improve living conditions, strengthen families, and provide
direction for the future. They founded church and women's groups to carry out
programs that would benefit the race. "Uplift" was the word most commonly
used to describe the goal of those groups. Most of their organizations are still
functioning. The founders established a pattern for community involvement
that educated black women have followed since that time. The contributions
of these early black women educators have not been fully acknowledged by the
black higher educational community or by their heirs. African American women
administrators owe their foremothers a debt of thanks for their pioneering efforts in opening up the professional ranks and establishing an intragroup image
of the black professional woman and competent administrator.

The social structure of the black community and the stratification of that
community are quite different from the social structure and stratification of
mainstream American society. These differences are important in the circumstances surrounding the evolution of black female leadership. The black social
structure is more loosely configured than that of the larger society; this can be
attributed to the constraints of prejudice and discrimination. Thus social status

among blacks has traditionally been less determined by income and occupation than that among whites, although this is changing as the black middle-class grows and becomes more differential. In black society, in contrast to white society, the behaviors and aspirations of families were often used as the key to acceptance into the middle-class. Congruent with this were the aspirations for daughters. The expectation that black women must work has been a constant in the black community. It has always been important that girls be prepared to be self-sufficient, preferably to be professional women in respected service-oriented professions. Their alternatives would be to work as domestic servants or in unskilled jobs, subject to the harshest and most degrading aspects of bigotry. This explains historically why more African American women generally have been enrolled in colleges than African American men.

From the 1940s until the 1970s,[5] black men were able to obtain relatively high-paying jobs without college degrees. Even more important, the black tradition has valued the notion of egalitarian relationships between the sexes and opportunities for achievement by both sexes. Race and survival have overridden concepts of superiority of one gender over the other. Though black popular culture would give the impression that African American women are subjugated in the same fashion as white women, history and empirical evidence contradict this.

The social-class origins of African American women administrators have not been studied as much as the type of family environment that nurtured them. As noted above, these women are middle-class, as defined within the black community, by aspiration and behavior. They were encouraged by working mothers and other women in their families. Early in their lives, they joined organizations, churches, and youth groups in which they were given leadership roles.[6] It is likely that black women administrators share social-class origins in that their families valued education, had high aspirations for their daughters, and tied those aspirations to conformance to certain social behaviors in school and community. These women were taught to value self-reliance, expected to work hard, held to high standards for performance and outcomes, taught to value family and friends, and expected to be well-rounded but grounded in the realities of the socioeconomic environment. They developed an inner drive that propelled them through school and a series of achievements to fulfill their obligation to succeed. Though they may have gravitated toward occupational roles in the "female sector" of the economic system, they have been socialized to have self-esteem higher than that of other sex-race groups, probably as a means of self-protection.[7]

African American women administrators recognize their responsibility to transmit their economic African American value systems to their daughters. As one of my interviewees noted, "I think that we have to help them learn the most that they can learn. We have to promote self-dignity and self-esteem, but we have to help them learn to compete. . . . I want them to have an education that teaches facts and skills, but even an education is not enough. . . . I think we have to teach children reality."[8]

One respondent in a study of women administrators was an independent African American woman who came out of the black tradition but embraced the valued characteristics of women managers at large, including a concern for others; a need to connect and share with others; a need to exemplify values and morality; a need to show compassion and empathy; a need to inspire and model behaviors that create and strengthen organizations so that those working within the organizations are empowered to carry out their responsibilities in imaginative and joyful ways while assessing their strengths and weaknesses.[9] These characteristics are often described by whites as marginal in relation to leadership qualities.

In the larger society, African American women administrators are negligible, hardly noticeable, since they are such a small proportion of the managerial class. They are certainly marginal in the context of American higher education, where they constitute less than 5 percent of the administrative group. On the whole, they are unseen by the general population, though many public institutions are now headed by black women, perhaps more than by African American men. Although they are an integral part of American society, African Americans are perceived by the majority population as marginal.

Marginality implies a type of lonely existence, functioning at the edge of the group, a status that can lead to many dysfunctional behaviors. However marginal African American women are to the larger society, they are centered in their own group and families. Even those at the margin of one group may be at the core of another.

These administrative women are leaders in their own milieu, their institutions and communities; they may not be leaders in the public sense, but they are intragroup experts in their fields. In fact, they are held in high regard and accorded high status in the African American community. The fact that they are perceived in such diametrically opposed views by the majority and minority groups does not appear to create emotional problems for them, perhaps because of their own high self-esteem and sense of tradition. When the women in Bean and Wolfman's study, undertaken in the 1970s, were asked to define and describe a Superwoman, a black woman administrator described all black women as super: "You are asked to do so many things in your role as an employee and then so many roles at home; this is what makes you the super person. I think that trying to perform all these roles, and how well [you perform them, causes] you to integrate all of these things. Whether or not you feel you have to be the best in what you do, I think, comes from our own background and upbringing. In order to get the positions that we have, oftentimes, you have to be better prepared for that job than some other woman who is not a minority. You come to the position at a different level. You have had your background bring you to this point. I think we've been superwomen from the time we started out in America; its just that other people can't know that."[10]

Even with the strengths that develop out of struggle, the challenges black women administrators must confront are enormous. It is not easy administering an organization or a unit and supervising people working in it; there is stress associated with management responsibilities. It is often described as a normal part of the life of an administrator, but the strains experienced by white female and male managers are far different from those minority managers must endure. The debilitating effects of conscious and unconscious bigoted acts tend to sap the intellectual potency and undermine the professional expertise of minority managers. Too little is known about the ways in which institutional racism finds expression; much of the discussion is anecdotal rather than analytical. Perhaps this is an area for serious research that could provide the basis for better understanding and training to facilitate positive attitudes about race relations.

Often black women experience stress because of their efforts to do twice as much, to accomplish tasks better than expected, in addition to the external and societal forces they wrestle with. The stress may be self-induced internal pressure or endemic in the particular work setting. In white institutions, black women administrators often are ghettoized in low-status positions; they may be squeezed between white institutional power and black students to whom they provide services and who often place heavy emotional and unrealistic demands on them. In many primarily white institutions, black women administrators are left on their own, without mentors, having to learn the institutional culture through observation, guile, and intelligence. Sometimes they are ignored or find themselves trying to understand the puzzles of the more esoteric and subtle aspects of polite racial hostility. They are, however, less threatening to white men than black men are and less often viewed as sexual objects than are white women. As a result, they may be less distracted from their work.

It may be that African American women demand much of themselves, setting their own standards of excellence, which they then must meet. This often creates problems with coworkers, who may not share these standards or understand the necessity for them. Many African American women also experience tension because of their multiple roles: professional, personal, and in the community. Given the extended family ethic, they often have responsibilities spanning three generations. In addition, they often belong to a church or women's group and fulfill duties necessary for the operation of the group and for their own satisfaction. As one woman said in an interview:

> An ordinary black woman is a very complicated conglomerate of many roles, probably first as a daughter. I think that most black women have been shaped by their mothers. She is a sister, both as an actual sibling, and also part of the black sisterhood. Then, you add all the other sorts of external roles that we normally achieve in society. I think there is a bond, even in black women you don't know, because you know that if they have made any kind of achievement externally, you know the price that has been paid. You know all the other roles that most of us, by and large, are doing, as opposed to people with housekeepers and all of that.[11]

Just as family, church, and community responsibilities contribute to the stress of these women's lives, however, these same affiliations help relieve that stress by providing creative outlets and sources of renewal. It is the family that provides a continuity of identity and a reality base for black women; it is supportive, nurturing, and corrective. Family chores help frame the workday, adding another dimension to the lives of these black women administrators that mitigates their deep immersion in work responsibilities. Many black women create surrogate families when their jobs are distant from home, thus easing the pangs of loneliness and becoming part of a second accepting group within which they can relax. One woman explained: "I would be very lonely here if I didn't have some people to turn to. I guess that it has been difficult for me, because I am single, and I am expected by the other people in my office to do more since I don't have a family. I have created a family. I cling to my black friends here who do have families. I have become very close to them, because I find that it makes life more bearable."[12]

Children and husbands also contribute to the emotional stability of black women administrators as they share home responsibilities, through which the children also learn. Cooperation is an important part of African American home life and helps fortify the members of the family to meet the adversities produced by prejudice in the outside world.

Relationship to the church is another way in which African Americans find relief from stress. Church is a place where leadership skills are first taught and tested and a place where women have long found meaningful relationships.

They have run the prayer circles, the avocational clubs, the Sunday schools, the fund-raising activities, and the social events. The church has long served as the center of black family life, a place for respectable social programs. For many African American women administrators, the church is a restful haven and a source of spiritual and emotional energy. Similarly, many black women find another outlet for tensions in their involvement in black secular organizations ranging from informal social clubs to structured national affiliates.

Some black women administrators are adamant about the separation of the workplace from their personal lives. An administrator stated in an interview: "I don't ever want my personal integrated with my professional life. I've found that, in working, the two seldom mix. It's a good idea to keep what you do when you go home among you and your friends, and not share it with your colleagues. It makes things easier. Working is work, and I don't find any pleasure in being chummy with my co-workers. I realize that they are not my friends. I realize that I am there to perform a function, to do a job, and it goes no further."[13]

Another black women administrator placed the need for social separation in a cultural context:

I need to have some separation. I would not want to leave my office and continue a discussion of all the stressful situations when I get home. I need to feel that I'm going to be able to relax in some way. Besides, I feel we have to make some kinds of cultural distinctions because black people, particularly black women, socializing with whites is a relatively recent phenomenon. Black people and white people, as a rule, socialize differently, and when we do integrate the two, the form is not the average black person's primary form of socialization. It is seen as a necessary evil. When black people really want to socialize, they go to other black people.[14]

African American women maintain a realistic, objective attitude toward work even as they devote themselves to meeting standards of excellence. They have grown up with the understanding that work is a necessity but that employment may be precarious because of labor market and economic fluctuations and the ever-present problem of racial discrimination. Since higher education institutions have hired African American women in small numbers and often as an afterthought, the objective attitude and lessened emotional investment appear to be protection from the grief that can accompany loss of employment, a means of retaining good mental health, and a way of coping with racial discrimination. This separation of work from emotional involvement explains the importance of family, friends, and organizational involvements, all based in the African American community and within the African American tradition. These social units are buffers against a hostile world and a means of maintaining a sense of equilibrium. In spite of their tenuous economic status, African American women place work in a healthy perspective. Work is a part of life; it is not all of life. Work is precious though precarious.

Though black women are marginal to mainstream institutions of higher education, Moore and Wagstaff have noted that black women's contributions to the historically black colleges have provided "backbone" to those colleges.[15] In the nineteenth century, it was those women who responded to the academic needs of students new to higher education. It was African American women who loved learning, who creatively developed methods to help poorly prepared students master the curriculum. At the end of the twentieth century, many white higher education institutions are faced with some of the same challenges that confronted the historically black colleges in the nineteenth century. White administrators would benefit from studying many of the methods black women developed to help students learn. More attention needs to be given to these methods and to the women who developed them. The expertise that has been developed can be used on a color-blind basis.

African American women administrators are in a unique position to bridge the gulf between the races by helping white institutions understand the changing demographic character of their student bodies. This group of women stands in the historical tradition of its community and is accorded respect and high status in that community; thus it can interpret for whites and blacks and for other minorities of color. By undertaking such initiatives, white institutions could lessen the marginal status of African American women administrators and benefit from their coping and mentoring strategies. Their talent and potential contributions to American higher education are still to be tapped. The skills and expertise of African American women can light the way for academia.

Notes

1. W. E. B. Du Bois, "Being Oneself," in *W. E. B. Du Bois: A Reader*, edited by Meyer Weinberg (New York: Harper and Row, 1970).

2. Milla Granson, "A Slave Woman Runs a Midnight School," in *Black Women in White America: A Documentary History*, edited by Gerda Lerner (New York: Vintage/Random House, 1973).

3. Darlene Clark Hine, "From Hospital to College: Black Nurse Leaders and the Rise of Collegiate Nursing Schools," in *Black Women in United States History*, edited by Hine et al. (Brooklyn: Carlson, 1990).

4. Patricia Bell-Scott, "The Business of Being Dean of Women: A Letter from Lucy Diggs Slowe to Howard University Trustees," *Initiatives* 54, no. 2 (1991): 35–42.

5. William Julius Wilson, *The Truly Disadvantaged* (Chicago: University of Chicago Press, 1987).

6. Mae Colleen Thompson Jones, *Learning to Lead: A Study of the Developmental Paths of African American Women College Presidents* (Ph.D. dissertation, George Washington University, 1992).

7. Walter R. Allen, "Family Roles, Occupational Statuses, and Achievement Orientations Among Black Women in the United Sates," in *Black Women in America: Social Science Perspectives,* edited by Micheline Malson et al. (Chicago: University of Chicago Press, 1990), 79–95.

8. Brunetta Wolfman, *Roles* (Philadelphia: Westminster, 1983), 81.

9. Sally Helgesen, *The Female Advantage: Women's Ways of Leadership* (New York: Doubleday/Currency, 1990).

10. Joan P. Bean and Brunetta R. Wolfman, *Superwoman: Ms. or Myth: A Study of Role Overload* (Washington, D.C.: National Institute of Education, 1979), 23.

11. Wolfman, *Roles,* 48.

12. Ibid., 88.

13. Ibid., 95.

14. Ibid., 96.

15. William Moore Jr. and Lonnie H. Wagstaff, *Black Educators in White Colleges* (San Francisco: Jossey-Bass, 1974).

Chapter 14

African American Nursing Administrators in the Academy

Breaking the Glass Ceiling

Elnora D. Daniel

African American nursing administrators in academe are predominantly women.[1] They face many uphill battles daily as they struggle valiantly against the triple jeopardy of race, gender, and status in the nursing professions. Their efforts to break the glass ceiling are often thwarted as they strive to ascend to higher rungs on the administrative ladder of the academy in a discipline whose status as a professional school in the university setting gained acceptance only during the early part of this century.

This chapter will (1) extrapolate basic propositions of Freire's theory of oppression as the framework for exploring the dilemma of the African American nursing administrator in higher education; (2) provide a brief historical overview of the ascendancy of nursing education in the academy; (3) explore the emergence of nursing education in the university for African American women; and (4) present specific strategies that they may use to confront oppression based on race, gender, and profession and to facilitate their success in the academy.

Basic Propositions of Freire's Theory of Oppression

Race, gender, and the professional status of the nursing discipline converge to complicate the lives of African American female nursing administrators in the academy. Freire's theoretical framework of oppression provides a distinctive context for analyzing how this triad affects their position in the university setting.

The following basic paraphrased propositions of Freire's theory of oppression are especially applicable to the condition of African American nursing administrators in higher education:

(1) Realization of full human potential is a basic vocation for human individuals and groups. (2) Negation of humanization occurs by acts of injustice, exploitation, and dominance and leads to a yearning for freedom and justice. Such negation is a tacit acknowledgment of the human potential of the dominated group. (3) The oppressed state creates a distortion of reality for both the oppressed group and the oppressor group, in that the consciousness of the more powerful and privileged oppressor group is absorbed and taken to represent reality in the world. (4) Only the group that is negated or oppressed can liberate itself and its oppressors, a process that begins with perceiving the state of oppression and becoming committed to action and thoughtful reflection (praxis) aimed toward becoming more fully human. Liberation will not be initiated or supported by the dominant group. (5) The barriers to liberation or to achieving freedom and justice are primarily rooted in the consciousness of the oppressed. (6) Because it is in the perceived best interest of the powerful group to maintain its privileges, and its privileges depend on the continued domination of the less powerful group, the oppressed use various devices to assure continued domination. These devices include limiting the quality and extent of education granted the oppressed group, keeping the oppressed group divided among themselves, and granting periodic acts of false generosity for the oppressed group. (7) Actions to achieve liberation usually begin with acts that appear to be violent to the oppressor group but are essential to initiate control by the oppressed group of their own destiny and to claim their right to be liberated.[2]

When the decanal role of the African American woman in the nursing discipline is viewed through Freire's theoretical framework of oppression, one finds that nursing leaders are particularly vulnerable, and this vulnerability has existed since modern nursing first entered the hallowed halls of academe.

The Ascendancy of Nursing in the Academy

Class and gender have historically stood as oppressive barriers between the academy and the nursing discipline. Even though there were opportunities for women to attend colleges at the turn of this century in the United States, few colleges admitted them, and it was very unlikely that these colleges would establish nursing programs.[3] Indeed, women's colleges, which one might have expected to be more receptive, evaded vocational and professional training programs and concentrated on the liberal arts. These institutions catered to female students who were perceived as potential wives and mothers rather than to women who needed preparation to work for the long term. Students who were accepted into early women's colleges were from middle-and upper-middle-class families, while those entering nursing training were more often from lower-middle-class families.

From its inception, members of the medical profession have been perceived as "men recognized for their unusual abilities to assuage the hurts and calm the fears of others by mediating among them and between them and the powers of the universe."[4] Thus, from a historical perspective, physicians have been visualized almost as gods, and the position of dominance they have assumed over other health care professions is thus not illogical. The perceptions of gender and race dominance, primarily male and white, have continued to perpetuate this view.

Medical education entered the private academy during the early part of the 1800s, and physicians found it advantageous to exploit nurses by keeping them almost dehumanized and shackled to an apprenticeship type of education in hospital settings.[5] For example, when a California law included nursing students in a bill that outlawed women from working in sweatshops for more than eight hours, it was violently opposed by physicians, who frequently complained about the overtrained nurses.[6] It was not until 1909 that the first nursing course was taught; this happened at the University of Minnesota. The first degree program, however, was not established until 1916, when the University of Cincinnati initiated a five-year program leading to a bachelor's degree in nursing.[7] Since the inception of this program, the professional schools of nursing in university settings have made great strides, but the struggle for administrative advancement for its female academic leaders is still evolving.

Nursing Education for African American Women

In early nursing training programs, some charters in nursing schools restricted the admission of minority students to only one Jew and one Negro in each class. This restriction prevented African American women from entering early nursing training programs in hospitals; thus they could not realize their potential as the modern era of nursing developed.[8]

During the early part of the twentieth century, rigid systems of segregation and discrimination were in force in the United States. These patterns of separatism affected all levels of education, and African American educators began to take action to correct the injustice and exploitation that were occurring in the profession of nursing. Further, as African American males began to return home from World War I, the need to provide nursing care for the segregated hospital facilities became more acute, prompting the establishment of segregated hospital schools of nursing to educate African American female nurses to provide care to African Americans at little or no cost to the hospitals.[9]

The first hospital school of nursing for African American students had been established in 1886 at Mac Vicar Hospital, located on the campus of Spelman College for women (formerly Atlanta Baptist Female Seminary). It was not until 1922, however, that the first baccalaureate program for African American females was established when Howard University instituted a five-year program that led to a bachelor of science degree in nursing. This program was taught in collaboration with Freedman's Hospital, which was operating a hospital-based nursing program. The baccalaureate program required students to spend two years taking liberal arts courses from Howard and three years of nursing at Freedman's Hospital. The program was discontinued in 1925 because it did not attract enough applicants to maintain viability.

Eighteen additional baccalaureate nursing programs were established in historically black colleges and universities, including Hampton University, from the 1930s through the 1980s. These programs continue today to educate the largest number of African American nurses in America, but their administrative leaders, for the most part, are still waging a war against oppression and inequities in academe, perpetuated by the male-dominated hierarchy of the academy and the health care delivery system, which itself is perpetuated by the male-dominated medical profession.

African American Nursing Administrators in Higher Education

The dual and systematic discrimination of racism and sexism is still pervasive today, and, for African American nursing administrators, exclusion based on their particular academic profession further compounds these oppressions. The resultant devaluing of women and the loss of the valuable contributions they could make can no longer be afforded or tolerated in view of the recent findings of researchers who have forecast that by the year 2000, the majority of the workforce will be women and minorities.[10]

Currently there are more than 1,500 nurses holding top-level administrative positions at the university level. In 1993 there were 750 deans and directors of schools or departments of nursing in senior colleges and universities in the United States;[11] approximately 98 percent of these individuals were women. Although this number represents a large percentage of female deans in higher education, the number of nursing program heads who are promoted to higher-level administrative positions is extremely small, and even smaller for African American nursing leaders.[12] In 1990 only 5 women with nursing preparation were college or university presidents, and only 3 were vice-chancellors of academic affairs. Of this number, 2 presidents, 2 vice-chancellors for academic affairs, and 1 special assistant to the president for academic affairs were African American women with nursing backgrounds.[13] These statistics validate Freire's propositions that oppressed groups are limited in terms of the quality and extent of opportunities available to them.

Also consistent with Freire's theoretical framework, female African American nursing administrators—and, in some instances, all women—face many special barriers that prevent them from achieving equity in the academic marketplace. Those barriers, which are particularly problematic to African American female nursing administrators in the academy, are related to socialization, image and stereotypes, loneliness and isolation, and tokenism. Each of those barriers warrants further elaboration.

Socialization

The socialization of women in general and African American women in particular acts as one of the special oppressive barriers to their ascendancy in the academy. Historically, females have been socialized to be subservient to males and to play a less significant role in most societies. This has relegated women to second-class citizenship in the world of work.

Further, the oppression of women is perpetuated through the communication process. For instance, men are socialized to dominate women by using different communication styles. French and French, among several researchers who have come up with similar findings, say that "male communication is perceived as associated with professionalism and power, while female communication is associated with powerlessness. An analysis of the male style of speech revealed a communication pattern with features such as (1) assertiveness; (2) impersonal and abstract speech with limited self-disclosure; (3) competitive, devil's advocate interchanges; (4) disruptive comments, especially used when women are speaking; (5) speech that controls the topic of conversation; and (6) physical gestures that express dominance and control."[14] In contrast, they state, "Female communication styles revealed features such as: (1) less assertive speech; (2) more personal and cooperative speech; (3) inappropriate smiling; (4) gestures that express attentiveness or give encouragement to others; and (5) averting eyes, especially when dealing with men and with those in positions of authority."[15]

Loden asserts that while some male members of a work group or team compete for control, female members are more likely to aim for compromise or consensus building. In contrast, males tend to control, dominate, and maneuver the group in order to satisfy their own interests, whereas females demonstrate less vested interest in proving that they are right and are more concerned with maximizing the chances for an outcome that is satisfying to everyone in the group.[16] These diametrically opposed socialized and controlling behaviors reflect differences in socialization between men and women and further document Freire's theory of oppression.

The first nurses were trained by religious orders and military groups, which were highly controlling and required strict obedience and adherence to higher religious and/or military authorities. Training consisted of a hospital apprenticeship for nurses, and the educational process was dominated by physicians. Those who survived this training were somewhat docile, vulnerable, and obedient.

Historically, the nursing discipline, which is mainly female, has been repressed by the physician-dominated health care delivery system. Although some vestiges of male-physician dominance have been eliminated, the perception of nurses as subservient to physicians still exists. Recently, however, nurses with advanced degrees have become more militant, as described by Freire, and are using health care policy and other legal strategies to acquire some degree of parity in salary and position.

Image and Stereotypes

Freire's theory postulates that when the oppressed group has internalized the image of the oppressor as "right," "powerful," or "good," this constitutes a barrier to the realization of full human potential. The oppressed group may also have internalized the oppressor's views to represent reality in the world. It is not surprising, therefore, that in this country research confirms that when people think of leaders, the images are of white males. Many people have not had an opportunity to work with a woman leader and may experience anxiety or even fear at the prospect. Many individuals find it so difficult to perceive women in leadership roles that when a man and a woman enter a room at the same time, very often those present assume that the man is the one with higher status.[17]

The variable of race, added to the scarcity of women in leadership positions, creates indisputable confusion and mistrust around the African American woman. Extensive research has found that people tend to cluster around other individuals who share their appearance. Advantages accrue to the familiar, from a small degree of likeness to a mirror image.

An additional image barrier to the African American nurse administrator's movement into higher administrative levels of the academy is related to the perception of the nursing discipline itself. Only since 1913 has nursing been able partially to release itself from the shackles of a hospital-based apprentice-ship education to enter the academy. In the years since, dominant male physi-cians have frequently been replaced by dominant male administrators. As a newcomer, the nursing profession has been viewed with some degree of suspi-cion and disdain. Many academicians feel that nursing is not a genuine science but merely a vocation requiring manual skill and dexterity but little mental prowess; therefore they question the appropriateness of its being in the acad-emy. The resulting low esteem accorded the nursing profession and its poor intellectual image render it tremendously difficult for the African American female nursing administrator to make advances in the university setting beyond the confines of their discipline.

These women are especially likely to be stereotyped in terms of their sexual-ity, and this often leads to increased sexual harassment. The stereotypes are prevalent because of the sexy image of nurses portrayed in the media during the 1960s and 1970s.[18] Accordingly, some males view the female nurse admin-istrator as loose and an easy prey for sexual favors. Other people, both male and female, believe that the only way she could have acquired her administrative position was by providing sexual favors to someone in authority. Seldom are skills, abilities, hard work, ambition, political savvy, and tenacity recognized for their central contributions to a nursing administrator's achieving prominence in academia. Consequently, oppressive stereotypical interpretations of African American nursing administrators' behaviors may also often interfere with their upward mobility in the academic marketplace.

Loneliness and Isolation

African American nursing administrators who dare to accept the challenge of executive administrative positions face numerous risks. Two of the most pain-ful are loneliness and isolation. African American women are isolated both from male power groups and from other women in the university. They may have less access to communication and feedback about their job performance or to informal channels of information about university-wide issues, problems, challenges, directions, and politics. Isolation may lead to greater feelings of loneliness, to the persistent awareness of "not fitting in," to always being on guard, and to the fatigue that comes from always having to be one's own sup-port system. Consistent with Freire's theory of oppression, African American nursing administrators are seldom appointed to prestigious and influential com-mittees and are excluded from the most important decision-making groups.

When they do finally increase their influence and participation in decision making, they are vulnerable to a significant backlash.[19]

These administrators are more likely to be excluded from the informal social gatherings in their departments and institutions, sometimes by white women, but mostly by white men who are usually their colleagues at the executive level of administration.[20] Their male counterparts tend to gather in locker rooms, in clubs, and on the golf course to the exclusion of not only white females but particularly African American women. Such "male bonding" provides situations in which significant decisions are made, thus bypassing the board room and further isolating the African American female nursing administrator.

Tokenism

According to Freire's theory of oppression, tokenism is a device frequently used to control and perpetuate the loyalty of the oppressed. Thus the African American nursing administrator is recruited, appointed, and placed in highly visible showcases. She is shown off like a trophy even before she has familiarized herself with the institution and her newly acquired position. Because there are so few women in this position, they are overused to such an extent that they become overwhelmed before they are allowed to acquire sufficient knowledge of the nuances and intricacies of their administrative positions to function efficiently. Often these female administrators are given more responsibility than power, with little support from their superiors. An African American female nursing administrator is seldom regarded simply as a competent executive; she is an African American woman who is a nurse. If she does not meet the established standards, many observers will take this failure as evidence that an African American female nurse could not do the job. If she succeeds, she is often seen as an exception to her race, gender, and discipline.

The dilemma of too much visibility versus too little visibility, which is encountered by women generally, is often intensified among African American female nursing administrators. For example, "their comments may be ignored in seminars or departmental meetings; on the other hand, they may be continually called upon to present the 'minority view,' 'the woman's view,' or 'the minority woman's view,' or the 'health care provider's view,' rather than their own views."[21] Yet if their own research deals with issues concerning women and/or minorities, it may be seen as "not really scholarly" and consequently devalued in the promotion and tenure process. According to Freire's postulates, these are mechanisms used by oppressors to maintain the status quo and continue their dominance over oppressed groups.

Strategies for Breaking the Glass Ceiling

Despite the barriers outlined above, which operate in various combinations and in varying patterns of ascendancy and descendancy, many African American women do succeed as nursing administrators in the academy. A review of selected literature reveals strategies to facilitate breaking the glass ceiling in academe. Dickens and Dickens classify selected strategies as internal, external, and environmental. Internal strategies proposed include those that are based on the African American woman administrator's intrapsychic understanding of herself. The external strategies include those that relate to the outside stimuli that influence her and the interpersonal relationships in which she is involved. Finally, the environmental strategies are those used to affect the setting in which she operates.[22] Nursing literature would characterize those divisions as intrapersonal, interpersonal, and extrapersonal elements of the academic hierarchical social system.

Internal (intrapersonal) strategies can be described as self-help and coping mechanisms, which include (1) clarifying goals and values; (2) developing a strong sense of self; (3) establishing realistic career development plans; (4) cultivating good health habits and high energy levels; (5) learning to present oneself in the best perspective; (6) becoming assertive when participating in many forums; and (7) acquiring formal and informal education.

External (interpersonal) strategies emphasize peer development and relationships with others that serve to limit professional isolation. They include (1) becoming a member of national nursing networks; (2) joining support groups for women administrators; (3) participating in workshops related to administration; (4) participating in forums with top-level administrators; (5) joining professional organizations that include professionals other than nurses; (6) acquiring broad and varied administrative experiences; (7) giving women candidates an equal opportunity to be interviewed and recommended for administrative positions; (8) examining selection criteria; and (9) supporting research.

Environmental (extrapersonal) strategies include (1) joining groups on the university campus that are influential in changing university politics and practices to prevent discrimination and oppression; (2) participating on permanent committees formed to explore and report on professional climate issues and to make campus-wide recommendations; (3) lobbying for the designation of a particular person (such as an ombudsperson) or office to be responsible for institution-wide efforts to insure an equitable professional climate; and (4) providing that person with direct access to top administrators, preferably the president.

Conclusions

It would appear that a paradigm shift in the academy must be achieved if African American nursing administrators there are to effectively combat the triple jeopardy of race, gender, and profession and reap the fruits of equality with their male and white colleagues. This paradigm shift must encompass the expulsion of old myths and stereotypes, the development of strong and consistent support systems, and the confrontation of the reality that African American nursing administrators have the right to control their own destiny. "In other words, clearly, we must create a multipronged effort to alter the opportunity structure in American society if race, gender, and professional inequities are to be reduced. There are no short cuts to equal opportunities in American society."[23]

The strategies suggested in this chapter can help in changing the unjust social order, transforming the nursing profession, and reinventing the world in which nurses live and work. They are offered "as a fortification for those on their way, including those who toil in difficult inner landscapes, as well as those who toil in and for the world."[24]

Notes

1. A. E. Johnson and Jerry E. Hutchinson, "Executive Order 11246 and the Demographics of Academic Administrators," *College and University Personnel Association Journal* (Spring 1990): 20.

2. Paulo Freire, *Pedagogy of the Oppressed* (New York: Seabury, 1970).

3. Mary Elizabeth Carnegie, *The Path We Tread: Blacks in Nursing 1854–1984* (New York: Lippincott, 1986), 17.

4. William J. McGlothlin, *The Professional Schools* (New York: Center for Applied Research in Education, 1964), 2.

5. Carnegie, *The Path We Tread*, 17; see also *Dimensions of Professional Nursing*, edited by Bonnie Bullough and Vern Bullough (New York: Macmillan, 1966), 5.

6. Lucie Young Kelly, *Dimensions of Professional Nursing* (New York: Macmillan, 1985), 41.

7. Bonnie Bullough and Vern Bullough, eds., *History, Trends, and Politics in Nursing* (New York: Macmillan, 1984).

8. Carnegie, *The Path We Tread*, 17.

9. Ibid., 20.

10. Alvin Toffler, *The Third Wave* (New York: Bantam, 1990).

11. Olga Andruskiw, "Women in Higher Education," in *Administrative Theory and Practice: Issues in Higher Education in Nursing*, edited by Mary Conway and Andruskiw (Norwalk, Conn.: Appleton-Century-Crofts, 1989), 249.

12. Susan Russell, "The Status of Women and Minorities in Higher Education: Findings from the 1988 National Survey of Postsecondary Faculty," *College and University Personnel Association Journal* (1991): 3.

13. Johnnetta Cole, *Conversations: Straight Talk With America's Sister Presidents* (New York: Doubleday, 1993).

14. Jane French and Peter French, "Sociolinguistics and Gender Divisions," in *Women and Education: World Yearbook of Education 1984*, edited by Sandra Acker et al. (New York: Nichols, 1984), 83. See also Stanley Eitzen and Maxine Zinn, *The Conflict and Order: Understanding Society* (Boston: Allyn and Bacon, 1993), 338–50; and Carol Gilligan, *In a Different Voice* (Cambridge: Harvard University Press, 1982).

15. French and French, "Sociolinguistics," 53. See also Casey Miller and Kate Swift, *Words and Women* (New York: Garden City Press, 1976).

16. Marilyn Loden, *The Case for Feminine Leadership* (New York: Time Books, 1985) 65–68.

17. Bernice R. Sandler, "The Campus Climate Revisited: Chilly for Women Faculty, Administrators and Graduate Students," in *Project on the Status and Education of Women* (Washington, D.C.: American Association of Colleges, 1986) 13, 14.

18. Floyd Dickens Jr. and Jacqueline B. Dickens, *The Black Manager* (New York: AMACOM, 1982), 221, 252, 274.

19. Sandler, "The Campus Climate Revisited," 14.

20. Ibid.

21. Ibid.

22. Dickens and Dickens, *The Black Manager*, 221, 252, 274.

23. Deborah K. King, "Multiple Jeopardy, Multiple Consciousness: The Context of a Black Feminist Ideology," in *Black Women in America*, edited by Micheline Malson et al. (Chicago: University of Chicago Press, 1988), 129.

24. Clarissa Pinkola Estés, *Women Who Run with the Wolves: Myths and Stories of the Wild Woman Archetype* (New York: Ballantine, 1992), 21.

Chapter 15

African American Women Executives
Themes That Bind

Julia R. Miller and Gladys Gary Vaughn

The issues faced by African American female administrators in higher education today are consistent with those they have faced in their historical struggles to assume effective leadership roles in American education. The twin disguises of racism and sexism, as framed by both tradition and legal precedents, still impose great restraints on the utilization of the competence and talents of African American women at both predominantly black and predominantly white institutions.

Continued examination of these current issues is needed. In this chapter, the authors present a developmental contextual model of multilevels of organization as a framework for analyzing the workplace experiences of African American female executives. To further substantiate pertinent research related to the various parameters of the model, a qualitative analysis was undertaken of the contextual and ecological milieu in which African American women experience success and confront barriers in the institutional cultures in which they find themselves. Overarching themes were formulated across the experiences of women in executive management positions in business, law, medicine, and education that exemplify endemically ingrained discrimination and other issues present in certain professional cultures.

Developmental Contextualism and the African-American Female Executive in Higher Education

The study of African American women as a unit of analysis has received limited emphasis in the literature. In fact, reported research has been scant and narrowly focused on such variables as race, ethnicity, class, age, and leadership; when data are gathered, they are collected in a manner that poses difficulty for disaggregation.[1] More specifically, when African American women in management and leadership positions have been studied, they have often been statistically categorized under the customary broad headings *women, black,* or *minority*; thus relevant data were frequently lost.[2]

Theoretical frameworks used in the study of African Americans have been limited, more often than not because of a focus primarily on families rather than solely on females. A major fallacy of these models is the comparison of African American families with middle-class European families. Two recently developed models that appear to have great promise in examining African American women and their families have been the cultural model (emphasizing that a woman's behavior can be understood within the context of cultural traditions, values, and norms of nuclear and extended families) and the interactive model (suggesting ways to examine racism and sexism across gender-race groups, with independent effects of experiences uniquely defined).[3]

In this chapter the authors suggest a theoretical model to analyze African American females in roles of leadership, particularly in higher education; this model is developmental contextualism. The model emerged during the 1970s. It focuses on the reciprocal and dynamic interactive influences of biological and psychological processes and environmental conditions. In short, there is dynamic reciprocity between individuals and their context.[4] As Blank suggested, "Contextualism goes beyond the point of acceptance of both personal and contextual influences to emphasize the co-extensive nature of personal context and fundamental inadequacy of separating person from environment (alienating the two)."[5]

Lerner and Miller cited several developmentalists whose work emphasized that dynamic interactions exist among variables within multiple levels of organization (biology, psychology, social groups, professional cultures, and families).[6] These dynamic relationships have a significant impact on human behavior. Further, history and temporality provide elements of change in the multiple integrative levels of organization, thus influencing the behavior and development of the individual.[7]

Developmental contextualism is most pertinent to the authors' purposes here. In our view, it provides a holistic perspective of the immediate and tangential environments in which African American women function. The contexts within which they interact at multiple levels of analysis greatly influence their capacity to contribute and develop professionally and personally. According to Washington, "Studying Black women is a formidable and challenging task. The task draws on many fields. . . . Understanding Black women is further complicated by the fact that our existence in the United States has been under conditions of social instability, societal discontinuity, and rapid social change. . . . Black women are not a monolithic group. While there is considerable evidence for common personality patterns and world views based on history, culture, and social circumstances, it is time to move toward an ecological and liberating perspective on Black women."[8]

In further establishing use of developmental contextualism principles, Bronfenbrenner's four structural levels of the ecological environment provide a pertinent relational perspective. These are (1) the *microsystem*—the interaction between the individual and the immediate setting or context; (2) the *mesosystem*—the relationship among various contexts in which the individual finds herself or himself; (3) the *exosystem*—the primary social structure that influences the individual; and (4) the *macrosystem*—the overarching institutional patterns of the culture, of which the micro-, meso-, and exosystems are specific and concrete manifestations.[9] The macrosystem serves as a basis for a proposed framework for analyzing the workplace experiences of African American executives in higher education.

A Proposed Developmental Contextual Model

African American female executives are interconnected with multilevels of organization, all of which potentially impact on personal and professional development. These levels are exclusively interactive and/or dynamically transacted as the female addresses various components of the macrosystem's person-environment dynamics. Figure 1 illustrates some of these levels; among them are family and community interactions, informal and formal professional networks, and the higher education workplace.

Family and Community Interactions

The family is one of the strongest and most influential forces in the African American community and is vital for its survival. Moreover, the female has historically played a significant role in African American families and remains a major thread in the fabric of solidarity. Thus females function more from a partnership, or egalitarian, role.[10]

Within the contextual dynamics involving the African American female, family and community are interwoven with such entities as religion, culture, racial identity, rituals, beliefs, and values. These social-cultural-environmental components provide ongoing support that simultaneously serves as a basis for nurturance and a framework for establishing and maintaining a positive sense of self and identity. Also, this nurturance is embedded within a broad definition of the family, which includes the family of origin, extended family of kin, and fictive kin.[11] Thus family is a culture vested in support of and responsibility to its members and its kin networks, of which women are the primary movers.[12] Perennial factors of family networks have been *expectations of accomplishments and success as a means of racial uplift and generational transmission*.[13]

Historically, as African American women have succeeded in fulfilling family, individual, and community expectations while pursuing higher education and charting careers leading to executive management positions, they have been faced with social and intellectual environments steeped in racism and sexism.[14]

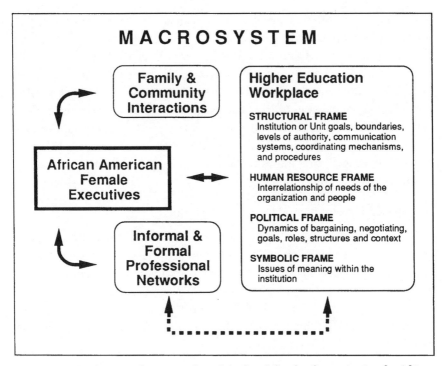

Figure 1. A developmental contextual model of multilevels of organization for African American female executives in higher education (adapted from Bolman and Deal, *Reframing Organizations*, 1991).

These manifestations are more often than not played out in behaviors that result in "chilly" environments for African Americans. The family and community serve as havens for emotional support, protection, and stability as one transcends the challenges and meets the opportunities of the workplace culture. For example, an ethnographic study of black female achievers in academe conducted by Smith cited the overwhelming importance of family members and other members of the community in playing supportive roles and in providing guidance and understanding as these women ascended the ladder to executive positions.[15]

Informal and Formal Professional Networks

Informal and formal professional support networks of African American female executives in higher education are critical to them in making both personal and professional decisions as they move through the workplace culture. Such networks are vital to African American women's survival and success because these women tend not to be in the mainstream of the university milieu. Harvard substantiated the position of relating support networks to survival in administration.[16] Inarguably, if there is a feeling of distrust and isolation from involvement in decisions, one is constantly exerting undue energies trying to determine what criteria and rules are centrally implicit or explicit to discussions, negotiations, and decisions. To be sure, knowledge of and adherence to the rules of the workplace provide no guarantee of survival or advancement, even when strong support networks are in place.

Some researchers have found that mentors serve mentees best when they are more like them. While acknowledging that cross-gender and cross-cultural mentoring are not necessarily destined to be unsuccessful because of gender and cultural differences, by and large Eurocentric male mentoring models have not proven to be productive for females in general and particularly not for African American females. Thus African American and other minority women potentially benefit from those relationships in which greater assessment and selectivity have been used to insure more similarities than differences in values, philosophy, and "like self" dynamics.

Professional meetings, symposia, and other fora are vehicles for establishing both formal and informal networking linkages. Such platforms can be reality checks for "state of the art" issues and directions that may be central to providing continued leadership in one's home institution. Fundamentally, the psychological and physiological release can chart a course for one to continue providing effective leadership.

Higher Education Workplace

The developmental contextual model, which proposes a framework to analyze the workplace within four organizational frames, can be used to explain the reality of African American females in leadership roles. Bolman and Deal termed these frames (shown in figure 1) *structural, human resource, political, and symbolic*, as follows:[17] (1) *Structural Frame:* The development of an organization's structure in response to its environment and tasks. It represents the goals, boundaries, levels of authority, communication systems, coordinating mechanisms, and procedures of an institution or organization. *Division of labor and coordination of responsibilities are central issues of structural design.* (2) *Human Resource Frame:* The interrelationships between organization and individual needs. It addresses management strategies that best meet the dual needs of the organization and those of the employee. *The skills, insights, ideas, energy, and commitment of the employees are the organizations most critical resources.* (3) *Political Frame:* The political behavior of the organization and the complex variety of interests of individuals and groups. It is characterized by coalitions, enduring differences, scarce resources, conflict, power, bargaining, and negotiations. *Organizational life is viewed as a political arena; organizational goals arise from an ongoing process of negotiation and interaction among key players.* (4) *Symbolic Frame:* The symbols and rituals that organizations create to form their identity and to build an organization's culture. This centers on the concepts of meaning, belief, and faith. It interprets and illuminates the reasons symbolism is a powerful dimension of the human experience. *Organizational life is viewed as more fluid than linear.*

Since organizations such as universities have undergone changes and multiple realities, leaders may operate within these frames differently. It is suggested here that African American females integrate the four frames in meeting the challenges and opportunities of the workplace. Integrating the frames, as opposed to operating frame by frame, is important because of the difference between "perceived" and "real" positions of women in higher education leadership. Because African American females are at the margin of organizational power, they often view the organizational lenses from several perspectives. Dumas felt that although black women are beginning to assume positions of authority and prestige, there are forces now, as in the past, that are demanding on their emotional stamina. Further, in her view, they experience situations in which their authority is undermined, their competence compromised, and their power limited.[18] Such experiences place African American females in the position to view the integrative nature of organizational parameters related to the frames *differently* from their counterparts in administration.

Black women face an incongruence between status and role. Society attempts to assign inferior status to their sex and race, insisting that they perform as leaders while at the same time taking care not to seem threatening. This phenomenon simply adds to racial and gender stereotyping, causing the black female leader's dilemma to intensify. Additionally, if one is to effectively conceptualize the role of African American females within their environmental context (that is, higher education leadership), the challenges of the workplace have to undergo ongoing analysis.

To further examine the developmental contextual model proposed for African American females in executive positions, the authors conducted a small, informal national study of forty professionals in higher education, business, law, and medicine. Common themes were identified and constructs developed to encapsulate and categorize the career experiences of these executives. The authors took the position that regardless of context, *African American female executives encounter universal experiences that are institutionalized in America's workplaces.* The section that follows summarizes the survey results and is a testament to the perennial and emerging experiences to which the African American female is a firsthand witness.

Career Experiences of African American Women in Executive Positions

The purpose of the study was to collect qualitative information related to (1) paths women have taken to achieve career objectives and their impetus for assuming current positions; (2) supports, stereotypes, and obstacles they have encountered; (3) adequacy of educational preparation; (4) perceptions of freedom to achieve personally and professionally; (5) definitions of success; (6) political and symbolic dimensions associated with employment; and (7) mentoring experiences. A twelve-item free-response questionnaire was mailed to the subjects in December 1993. Of those forty professionals surveyed, 43 percent either returned the completed questionnaire or responded to the survey by telephone.

Although the backgrounds of the individuals surveyed varied widely, each was a professional of merit in her chosen field, none lacked educational credentials, and there was no conflicting ideology among their responses. When the developmental contextual model—which includes family and community interactions and informal and formal professional networks—is juxtaposed with the four organizational lenses existent in the workplace, the responses of these female executives substantiate previous research.

Educational preparation was an important dimension of their professional dreams and goals, and appropriate educational credentials were crucial for performance and career advancement. An administrator emphasized, "Since my academic background is very specialized and science-based, I found a need early in my career to obtain formal preparation in administration and leadership. Most importantly, skills in networking, negotiating and 'educational politics' were developed. Also, it became important for me to diversify my experience base in the type and size of the organization." Although each possessed more than adequate educational preparation for her position, the women's competence and expertise were often questioned and challenged. One stressed, "During the early stages of my current administrative position, I found myself constantly justifying my existence. There was much resentment from white males of my holding the position and being their supervisor. Many innuendos were apparent which reflected questioning my credentials and preparedness."

Being the target of race and gender biases was a common experience among the professionals; these biases were the major obstacles they encountered. These twin problems were manifested in a variety of ways, including assumptions on the part of others that the women were inferior, incapable intellectually, and unprepared.

One respondent confided that "the greatest obstacle to my advancement was the organization into which I transitioned. . . . The hiring organization was a stable, conventional, male-dominated body whose culture promoted white male leadership. The fact that I was female, Afro-American, and not one of their own resulted in significant discomfort for organizational members and for me, though to a lesser degree for me." Another interesting dimension reported by several respondents can best be described as expectations of gratitude. Even when these individuals earned promotions, salary increments, and other symbols of success, employers expected behaviors that demonstrated gratitude.

Family members, including parents, siblings, children, and spouses, were considered first-line support by these women. Other sources of support that are traditional in the African American community were also indicated, including mentors (retired professors), colleagues in the historically black college system and network, and longtime friends.

Meeting time demands and balancing the demands of work, family, and community commitments were other challenges; these were countermanded, however, by coping behaviors, lessons from mentors, and support networks.

The survey requested a definition of personal and professional success. Some of the views reported by the respondents included freedom to grow and develop, the quality of time they spent with family and friends, participation in community service, the ability to balance work and other dimensions of their lives, enjoying their employment positions, and faith and adherence to personal standards. Assuming a leadership position in their profession was not an early career objective of most of the respondents, although each had arrived at a position of leadership.

Political and symbolic expertise was acquired largely through on-the-job training and carefully analyzing the realities of the workplace. Experiences they encountered within the frames of politics and symbols that could have been traumatic were buffered for some by family life experiences, careful observations of others, advice and counsel of mentors, a willingness to prepare continuously for the competition of the workplace, and standing up for justice.

The value and presence of mentors within the lives of most of these women were particularly significant. Most had mentors who helped clarify career goals; provided moral support, advice and counsel; and simply "listened." Those who did not report mentors and peers at the same level of their current positions expressed the value that such relationships could have for them.

This survey of contemporary professionals revealed several themes in the lives of African American women in executive positions that are not unlike those of their counterparts in earlier eras: countering race and gender discrimination; constant challenges to and questions of their competence and educational credentials; family support; personal determination; development of self-preservation techniques; the value of extensive educational preparedness; and the importance of mentors and role models. Thus the practical experiences of these professional women mirrored those experiences reported in research studies previously cited in this chapter.

The last survey question asked for "wisdoms" that could be used by emerging African American females aspiring to executive-level positions. An interesting but not unexpected array of responses was obtained: (1) take risks; (2) pursue life-long learning; (3) visualize yourself in positions of authority and leadership; (4) exercise freedom to make decisions on the basis of personal experiences and principles; (5) "know thyself" and do not allow others to erode the self concept; (6) understand the role of educational preparation in career advancement and success; (7) mentor and be mentored; (8) develop strong personal and professional networks; (9) give back to the community; and (10) know that discrimination exists and that nothing is guaranteed.

Conclusions

For the African American female who aspires to be successful at the highest levels of the academic arena, a working knowledge of the institutional culture— that is, the structural, human resource, political, and symbolic frames—is an absolute necessity. Likewise, a knowledge of the rules and the politics under which one has to work, such as the university's formal and informal policies and applicable laws, is of utmost importance.[19] Furthermore, one must have acquired the appropriate skills and competencies necessary for administrative positions and must assume a posture of personal security based on that competence.

Persons committed to social justice must insure that the workplaces of America eradicate race and gender currents and cross-currents that are debilitating to the progress of those who are not accepted into the mainstream of institutional and organizational cultures. Finally, African American females functioning in and aspiring to administrative or executive positions in higher education and other sectors must learn from the past while dealing with the present and future; build on their historical strengths of endurance in spite of the odds; value and capitalize on the support of the family and the community; and collectively embrace that which is shared by and given to others through mentoring, friendship, and collegiality.

Notes

1. Audrey Williams, "Research on Black Women College Administrators: Descriptive Interview Data," *Sex Roles* 21 (1989): 109; Karen F. Wyche, "Psychology and African-American Women: Findings for Applied Research," *Applied and Preventative Psychology* 2 (1993): 116–18.

2. Patricia A. Harvard, "Successful Behaviors of Black Women Administrators in Higher Education: Implications for Leadership," paper presented at the annual meeting of the American Research Association, San Francisco, April 1986.

3. Wyche, "Psychology and African American Women," 116–18.

4. Donald H. Ford and Richard M. Lerner, *Developmental Systems Theory: An Integrative Approach* (Newbury Park, Calif.: Sage, 1992).

5. Thomas O. Blank, "Contextual and Relational Perspectives on Adult Psychology," in *Contextualism and Understanding in Behavioral Sciences: Implications for Research and Theory,* edited by Ralph L. Rosnow and Marianthi Georgoudi (New York: Praeger, 1986), 108.

6. Richard M. Lerner and Julia R. Miller, "Interpreting Human Development Research and Intervention for America's Children: The Michigan State University Model," *Journal of Applied Developmental Psychology* 14, no. 3 (July-September 1993): 352.

7. Richard M. Lerner and Celia B. Fisher, "From Applied Developmental Psychology to Applied Developmental Science: Community Coalition and Collaborative Careers," in *Applied Developmental Psychology,* edited by Celia B. Fisher and Richard M. Lerner (New York: McGraw-Hill, 1994), 512.

8. Valora Washington, "The Power of Black Women: Progress, Predicaments, and Possibilities," keynote address, tenth anniversary conference of the Association of Black Women in Higher Education, Albany, New York, May 5, 1988, 3.

9. See Lawrence B. Schiamberg, *Child and Adolescent Development* (New York: Macmillan, 1988), 54–55.

10. Harriette Pipes McAdoo, "A Portrait of African American Families in the United States," in *The American Woman 1990–91: A Status Report,* edited by Sara E. Rix, (New York: Norton, 1990), 90.

11. Harriette Pipes McAdoo, "The Social Cultural Contexts of Ecological Developmental Family Models, in *Sourcebook of Family Theories and Methods: A Contextual Approach,* edited by Pauline G. Boss et al. (New York: Plenum, 1993), 299.

12. Shirley J. Hatchett and James S. Jackson, "African American Extended Kin Systems: An Assessment," in *Family Ethnicity: Strength in Diversity,* edited by Harriette Pipes McAdoo (Newbury Park, Calif.: Sage, 1993), 105.

13. Gwendolyn Etter-Lewis, *My Soul Is My Own: Oral Narratives of African American Women in the Professions* (New York: Routledge, 1993), 68–69.

14. Ibid., 79.

15. Carol Hobson Smith, "Black Female Achievers in Academe, *Journal of Negro Education* 51, no. 3 (1982): 318–41.

16. Harvard, "Successful Behaviors," 11.

17. Lee G. Bolman and Terrence E. Deal, *Reframing Organizations: Artistry, Choice, and Leadership* (San Francisco: Jossey-Bass, 1991), 9–16.

18. Rhetaugh G. Dumas, "Dilemmas of Black Females in Leadership," *Journal of Personality and Social Systems* 2, no. 1 (1979–80): 5.

19. Karen Bogart, "Toward Equity in Academe: An Overview of Strategies for Action," in *Educating the Majority: Women Challenge Tradition in Higher Education,* edited by Carol S. Pearson, Donna L. Shavlik, and Judith G. Touchton (New York: Macmillan, 1989), 390.

Chapter 16

Climbing the Administrative Ladder in the Academy
An Experiential Case History

Martha E. Dawson

In an era when women of all races seem to develop a career blueprint, I would describe my administrative journey as one that was directed by providence. When I was preparing for graduation from Virginia State College, I received a call from Sister Pancraus, a nun, inviting me to accept a position as a lay teacher at Van de Vyver Institute in Virginia. Although my salary was to be only fifty dollars a month, I was delighted and felt honored that one of my former elementary school teachers, a white European nun of the Franciscan Order, had invited me to become a colleague. I knew that I would have to be a good teacher. My critics would be pupils who were in attendance when I was a pupil and nuns who had guided me between the ages of five and seventeen. Thus I accepted my first professional position with some fear. I had no long-range plans to become an administrator; my goal was simply to be as good as the nuns who had taught me.

When I was midway through my third year as an elementary teacher at Van de Vyver, a stern educator visited my classroom. She was looking for a teacher. My college roommate, an art teacher at her school, had informed her that she might want to observe me.

Following her observation, Miss Katherine Johnson offered me a contract to teach at Baker Street School in Richmond, Virginia. To move from the parochial school to the public school was a difficult decision. I went to Sister Pancraus for guidance and was shocked when she encouraged me to leave, pointing out that I would have increased professional opportunities. Miss Johnson, the principal at Baker Street School, was demanding, innovative, and well trained; above all, she insisted that the teachers in the school provide the best education possible for the poor children in attendance. I soon realized that if I wanted to keep my position in "Miss Johnson's school," I would have to engage in further study.

The Academic Advisor Who Changed My Life

When I went back to Virginia State College for graduate study, I did not have a study plan. All I knew was that, if possible, I did not want to enroll in a class with my former undergraduate instructors. Thus I went to the unknown young professor Dr. W. Bruce Welch, who was advising students, to get assistance in arranging my summer schedule. He advised me to enroll in educational research with Dr. P. C. Johnson, who had a reputation for toughness that was known up and down the East Coast. He suggested that I also take Problems in Elementary Education, a course that was taught by Dr. Alma Stegall, who, by all students' accounts, was literally insane in her demands and her philosophy of education. My third course was Teaching Elementary Social Studies, taught by Dr. Welch, who took charge and put my feet on the path to higher education.

Welch became the mentor who refused to let me be comfortable with where I was in life. It was he who said to me that my world was too narrow and I needed to have multicultural experiences, and that having two young children and a husband was no excuse for not doing so. My pursuing a master's degree and doctorate, he said, would make their lives better. It was he who insisted that I consider Indiana University.

When my husband and I returned to Virginia State College in the fall for a homecoming football game, Dr. Welch encouraged us to consider a family move to the Hoosier State. This meeting was followed by a return visit to Virginia State College a few weeks later, when Welch introduced me to Dr. Merrill T. Eaton, a professor from Indiana University, who made an annual visit to his former black students in the South to recruit promising students to pursue graduate study at his university. This was in the heyday of segregation, and the Commonwealth of Virginia awarded out-of-state grants to black students for graduate study rather than have them matriculate at the University of Virginia. Eaton encouraged me to consider Indiana University for graduate work.

The family move to Indiana was never consummated. When my husband, a graduate of the Virginia Trade School, traveled to Indiana to scout job possibilities, he found that blacks were not allowed to work in the trade unions as skilled craftsmen. While he looked for a job in Bloomington, Dr. Eaton convinced him that I should come to Indiana University. Thus he returned to Richmond to inform me of their decision. I appreciated the interest that Welch and Eaton had in my professional development, but I really didn't want to make the sacrifice of leaving my young son and daughter to get an advanced degree. Dr. Welch persisted, however, and finally arrangements were made for me to attend Indiana University.

Another Professor Takes Over

During my first summer at Indiana University, I enrolled in a course called Social Foundations of Education, which was taught by a young German American professor, Dr. Leo Fay. I became Dr. Fay's graduate assistant during my second semester. This appointment led to my extended relationship with the Fay family.

When I completed my master's degree at the end of the first year, Dr. Fay and Dr. Eaton directed me to spend an additional year and complete the course work for the doctorate. Dr. Fay became my doctoral and dissertation advisor. At his insistence, I left Indiana in the fall of 1955 to collect data and resume my teaching duties at Baker School. I returned to Indiana University in the summer of 1956 and was directed by Dr. Fay to report to him on a daily basis on the writing of the dissertation. Fay's pressure led to my writing and defending the dissertation within a six-week summer session. In August 1956 I returned to Richmond as Dr. Dawson, a first for a black female in the Richmond public school system.

An Anchor for the Future

The early years of my career may appear irrelevant, but they formed the anchor for my later success in the academy. It is a mistake for one to assume that success in the academy can be accomplished by a "quick fix." I learned lessons and coping skills during the early years that continue to be invaluable resources. I would make the following points: (1) I learned the importance of stability and understanding when one is charting new ground. (2) In spite of segregation, racism, and sexism, there will always be someone out there who cares. I learned not to judge people by the color of their skin. (3) The early encounters with Dr. Bruce Welch gave me the confidence needed to survive in spite of adversity. (4) The confidence those early supporters had in me has enabled me to undertake each professional position with the assurance that I can make a difference.

Black females aspiring to top administrative positions would do well to find leaders who will give them the needed push. In looking for such individuals, one should not overlook the fact that there might just be some black or white men, as well as other women, who can help. Just don't overlook the guardian angel who might be in your midst.

Coping with Massive Resistance

Racism and sexism in the 1990s are often institutionalized. You can't see them; you can't touch them; you can't feel them. For black professionals striving to launch a career in the 1950s, racism was alive and clearly evident. At that period in American history, affirmative action was not the order of the day.

While the acquisition of a doctorate might have been a significant accomplishment in the black community, it was of little consequence to the white community. In fact, it became another factor that the political system had to reckon with since the philosophy behind segregation was that blacks were inferior, especially those who were of chocolate shades.

My family had overprepared and insulated me for the black "inferiority game." My mother had washed and ironed white people's clothes so that she and my father would have funds to pay tuition to send us to a Catholic school so that, as my mother said, we would not have to attend the two-room county school where she didn't learn much. She also had the farsightedness to purchase attractive white dolls and ask a neighbor to paint them brown. She said to us, "I don't want you to ever have to push [nurse] white people's children like I had to." She had programmed us to believe that the symbols of inferiority in society were challenges in the face of which we would demonstrate that we as a family were by no means inferior, but rather superior.

Thus I was not shocked or hurt when the *Richmond Times-Dispatch* called the principal at Baker Street School to check out a press release the paper had received from the news bureau at Indiana University stating that I had been awarded the doctorate of education degree. The reporter questioned the principal in disbelief and placed the announcement in the rear of the newspaper with the classified ads. Had I committed a crime, I would have made headlines on the front page. This experience was typical of the period in Virginia's history, and it was one that made me more determined to help black students.

Through the interception of Mrs. Willie Segar, the primary supervisor for Negro schools, I was given an appointment as a consultant teacher in the central administration of the Richmond public schools. The position gave me a chance to work with new black primary teachers. In addition, I gained insight into the strengths and weaknesses of precollege teacher-training programs. As a member of the public schools' central administrative staff, I became painfully aware of the inequities of public education as well as the institutional racism that was prevalent throughout the system.

As consultant teacher, I had an office on the segregated suite of the central office building. I drank from "colored" water fountains and used "colored" bathrooms. I endured the joint meetings with the white supervisors, where it was common practice to pay little or no attention to black participants.

Having one's ideas and contributions ignored also happens in a predominantly black or male professional setting. While such behavior is frustrating, there is little value in fussing and shouting about the gender and racial inequities that currently exist. We must be smarter. We need to become more self-assured and, as a consequence, direct our goals toward developing a professional reputation that is outstanding and unique.

On to Higher Education to Replace a Legend

There is no one model for climbing the administrative ladder in higher education. My climb was certainly not the model that one would find in the higher education literature. In fact, it was not my intention, in pursuing the doctorate, to seek a career in higher education. However, in keeping with the pattern through which I had attained previous positions, in the late 1950s I was called and asked whether I would accept a full-time position at Hampton Institute (currently Hampton University). I had to make a career change.

Upon arrival at Hampton, I discovered that I was being groomed to assume the position of one of Virginia's top educators. Dr. Eva C. Mitchell was a legend in her own right, widely known throughout the United States for her work in adult literacy and for Hampton's elementary education teacher preparation model. Elementary education majors who had come through Dr. Mitchell's program were widely sought. Dr. Mitchell was slated to retire in a year, and there were a number of Hamptonians waiting in the wings, hoping to assume her mantle. Taking over her position as chair of the Department of Elementary Education in 1959 was indeed one of the significant administrative events of my entire professional career. Even today it is my opinion that my greatest contribution to higher education was in the position of department chair.

Department Leadership

When I approached the president of Hampton Institute in the early 1960s with the idea of establishing a nongraded elementary laboratory school, he researched the idea and found money from an anonymous donor to fund the innovation. The laboratory school brought recognition to the institution and also enhanced my career.

Recognition Among Peers

In serving as chair of a department, it took a great deal of human engineering for me to gain the cooperation of other administrators, faculty within the unit, and the support of central and upper level administrators (who are often ruthless in their jealousy and competitive spirit). I made it my business to ignore detractors and to maintain a professional attitude even when I was annoyed. Remaining focused despite certain people's attempts to create problems was a skill I honed during my tenure in the lower-level administrative position.

Serving in a lower-level administrative position became a vehicle for me to gain the respect of my colleagues. For my contributions to the profession as a department chair, I was honored with the Lindbach Teaching Award, the highest award given to faculty at Hampton University. It carries with it a monetary stipend for professional growth.

It is in the lower-management level that one should gain a national reputation in his or her field. A distinguished track record as a teacher and scholar is invaluable for moving into competition for a position as dean, vice president, or president in higher education. While it might be true that some males reach the executive office without distinguished teaching and research careers, it is not likely that women will do so. Hence it is at the lower academic levels that females who aspire to climb to a higher rung on the ladder should fine-tune their administrative skills. I would suggest the following: (1) Increase your leadership skills and knowledge base. (2) Learn to be politically astute in open meetings; never take on the boss. (3) Develop collegial, nonthreatening relationships with a diverse group of professionals at all levels. (4) Develop cordial relationships with staff and faculty. (5) Work on self-concept. Drop the little-girl syndrome of expecting everyone to praise you. (6) Seek to understand rather than to be understood (Saint Francis). (7) Utilize conciliatory skills when necessary. (8) Become a critical listener. (9) Accept both just and unwarranted criticism. Never let the other person know you are upset. (10) Commit yourself to putting in overtime to gain new knowledge and skills. (11) Develop a sense of humor. (12) Expand your horizons through family, social, and community activities.

Challenges and Decisions

While I was enjoying a successful career at Hampton, I was faced with personal challenges of a sort that often get in the way of females who are on the fast track. My youngest daughter was born while her sister was a senior in college and her brother was a junior; I was faced with an unexpected divorce after more than twenty-five years of marriage. These events placed me in the position of being a single mother, which, with faith and determination, I managed to balance with the career.

I was invited by Dr. David Clark to return to Indiana University as a tenured professor. I decided that I wanted to have the opportunity to compete in a large research institution. While my career had been successful, I had not played in the major league, and Indiana University would provide that opportunity.

Taking on the Burden of Sex and Race

I joined the faculty of the School of Education in August 1970. While I had attended the university, I was not completely prepared for the subtleties of sexism and racism. There were a few black students who, for some reason, felt that I was there to save them, a role I refused to accept. There were white students who were in awe that I walked, talked, and lived in the same manner as their middle-class parents. If a black female makes a decision to take a position at a historically white institution, she has to decide how she intends to cope.

I was determined that I would not become so consumed with racism and sexism that I failed to enhance my career and to make a difference. When an individual walked into my office and made the assumption that my secretary was the professor, I made certain that mistake would not be made again. When I was asked to respond to a question relative to a race or gender issue, I found a way to inform the inquirer that I was not an expert on racial and gender issues, that I couldn't speak for the group. My reactions helped many to learn that there are no simple responses to complex issues. It was important for me to establish the fact that I was not at the university to be the affirmative action officer.

Development of a Multicultural Teacher Education Model

I was fortunate to arrive at Indiana University during a period when the School of Education was in the process of reforming the teacher education program. There was an air of excitement in which I found encouragement to design new approaches to training teachers. Up to this point, few institutions had given attention to the diversity that existed in states such as Indiana. I was struck by the pockets of poor whites in Southern Indiana, the concentration of inner-city blacks in Indianapolis, the Latino enclaves in East Chicago, and the concentration of black working-class people in Gary. The state's system of higher education needed to serve its diverse citizens. The faculty and students at Indiana University were, for the most part, middle- and upper-class. The dominant group was white. Diversity was of little interest.

I went to Indiana University prepared to be competitive within the system. Thus I chose to develop an innovative teacher education model and subject the model to peers for approval and implementation. I chose to work with colleagues who were of diverse backgrounds. As a result, I received approval to implement a multicultural teacher education model.

The multicultural teacher education program caught the attention of diverse students, the majority of whom were white. Once the program caught the attention of the media, institutional racism, similar to that which I had observed in my early career in the Richmond public schools, raised its ugly head. Fierce competition ensued; a white male colleague was allowed to establish a Native American field experience model for student teaching, which was in direct competition with the experimental multicultural living component of the teacher education model I had developed. I had demonstrated that a black female could not only develop a viable teacher model but could also attract interdisciplinary faculty members and predominantly white students. In allowing the white male to introduce a competing program and to move his office next-door, the university provided yet another example of institutional racism.

Had I been a white male, I doubt that I would have had to endure such frustration. While I was annoyed, I realized that I couldn't single-handedly wipe out institutional racism and sexism. I chose to accept the competition more as an annoyance than a frustration. I vowed that I would extend my presence in the university beyond the School of Education. I learned early in my career that, in spite of adversity, one must keep moving up. I had enough positive experiences with diverse faculty members to help me stay focused on my personal agenda.

Serving the Larger Academic Community

Even while I was busy with a new teacher education program at Indiana University, I became involved with the university at large through committee work and social interactions, and I became a member of the faculty club. As I review my career, I would identify my committee work at Indiana University as the major factor that prepared me to assume middle and upper administrative positions. I was elected to both the school and the university faculty councils. These positions gave me insight into the infrastructure of a large research institution and brought me into personal contact with key decision makers.

While at Indiana University, I also served a three-year term on the all-university promotion and tenure committee. This powerful assignment was time-consuming, but it was one of the best means of gaining insight into a range of disciplines. As a member of the tenure and promotion committee, I had the opportunity to study and make decisions on dossiers submitted from faculty in all disciplines at the university as well as professional schools. The knowledge I gained was invaluable when I later assumed the position of vice president of academic affairs at Hampton University

Serving on key university committees provided me with the opportunity to interact and be recognized by top university administrators. When I left Indiana to assume the deanship at Virginia State University in 1977, I brought with me support from chief administrative officers in a Big Ten university.

On the Move Again

In the fall of 1977 I was invited to assume the position of dean of education at Virginia State University. I returned to Virginia and moved into middle-level administration. When I assumed the position, I had no way of knowing that my tenure as dean of the School of Education was to be limited to less than two years. This appointment was short but productive. Among my achievements was bringing together an interdisciplinary team to develop a generic teacher education model. There are three other initiatives I took there of which I am proud. First, there was the establishment of the School of Education Leadership Team. Its membership included chairs and coordinators from those disciplines offering programs in teacher education. The dividends were in administrative team building. Second, I procured a National Institute of Education Research Grant for Faculty Development. Consultants from research institutions were brought in to provide professional development training for faculty in writing articles for publication and conducting research activities. Third, I procured a Teacher Corps Grant in which Virginia State implemented a linkage program with the Surry County public schools. This project provided us with the resources to offer technical assistance to public school educators in a rural community.

Tapped for an Upper-Level Position

I was happily settled in Petersburg, at Virginia State University, when I learned that my name had been submitted for consideration for the position of vice president for academic affairs at Hampton Institute. In later offering me the position, President William Harvey pointed out that he was attempting to assemble a team representing diversity. He was seeking experienced and young professionals, black and white, male and female, and most important, people who could bring insight to the university as a result of having served in a wide range of leadership positions. I returned to Hampton in the fall of 1979.

The position of vice president for academic affairs/provost is unique in the hierarchy of higher education administration. It is a complex administrative position requiring bonding with the chief executive officer. There are conflicting pressures that infringe upon the administrator holding this position. In spite of these demands and distractions, the provost has to find a way to make a difference at the university. While serving as vice president for academic affairs, I made the decision to facilitate the professional skills of administrators and faculty.

Special Administrative Leadership Training Institutes (SALT) were implemented to improve the professional skills of academic administrators. The first SALT Institute was introduced in July 1980. The professional development activities it offered addressed contemporary issues in higher education, with leading authorities serving as consultants.

The SALT Institutes had a significant impact on the growth and development of administrators and students. President Harvey was most supportive. As a result of the university's initiatives through SALT, we received funds from the Bush Foundation for the implementation of what we called the Center for Teaching Excellence. This professional development center became a significant factor in improving the teaching and research skills of faculty. The SALT Institutes and the Center for Teaching Excellence were invaluable resources in the development of the successful turnaround model implemented at Hampton University during my tenure as vice president for academic affairs.

A New Assignment

After twelve years as vice president for academic affairs, I made the decision to join the ranks of those who had the distinction of having the title *emeritus*. This would give me an opportunity to write.

President Harvey had asked whether I would continue to serve Hampton University by documenting the turnaround model that had been developed during his tenure as president and mine as vice president for academic affairs. I would remain on the payroll, have a secretary, and enjoy the full support of the president in pursuing my research and writing interests.

This new appointment in 1991 was another example of the support I enjoyed throughout my career. I believed that being the director of the Living History Research Project was indeed to be my last full-time appointment in higher education. I was positive that I had realized all of my impossible dreams in the spring of 1993 when I had completed the documentary history of Hampton University and was in the process of seeking a potential publisher. As had been true throughout my career, however, there were other plans in the making.

God's Not Finished with Me Yet

Contrary to my wildest imagination, the new president of Virginia State University, Dr. Eddie N. Moore Jr. visited with me in the spring of 1993 to ascertain whether I would join his team as provost and vice president for academic affairs. Today I find myself in still another position that I did not seek and one in which I still have an opportunity to lead and to serve. I owe a debt to Virginia State University, and I am grateful to God for giving me a strong body and sound mind, which enable me in some small way to serve my alma mater. My "days are filled from start to finish." As this case history reveals, there are always new steps to climb on the academic administrative ladder.

Reflections and Recommendations

The case history that I have presented summarizes significant professional events in one individuals's career. It is certainly not a blueprint for others who aspire to become administrators. In fact, I doubt that there is any one model that guarantees success for black females in the academy. As a result of my experiences as a black female administrator, I learned several invaluable lessons, and I share them.

First, an administrator has to recognize that the desire to be appointed to a position does not mean that she should have or will receive the position. There is limited room at the top. If she is not offered the position, she must vow to make a difference where she is. Second, it is essential for one to recognize that the very structure of the university is built on a hierarchy—a pecking order. This is evident in the classification of students, the ranking of faculty, and the titles of administrators. In such an environment, only a select few will occupy top positions. Third, success and mobility are based on diverse networking. One cannot expect to move into and assume leadership in the broad arena of society or a university when her contacts have been confined to a limited sphere of the larger world. Each of us can do something about expanding her own professional network. Fourth, there is no substitute for excelling at the lower step on the ladder before giving consideration to the next step. One must develop a track record that attracts the attention of others. Fifth, while preparing for that desired top administrative post, an administrator must give the same attention to her current appointment as she would give to the presidency or vice-presidency if such became available.

Excellence rarely goes unnoticed, even in a lower position, as is exemplified in the following poem, which reflects the attitude of a white female toward a black female who was performing menial tasks for her family during the segregation era. Sarah's contributions to the family were recognized.

It was November, nineteen thirty-nine
Sarah came one morning about half-past nine,
To see if we had some work for her to do;
Saying that she would be honest, upright and true.

She finds her way to our house every single day;
Cooks the meals, sweeps the floor, and helps our baby play.
In her cooking she excels; her rolls are pure delight,
'Cept for gain of weight, we'd eat 'em morning, noon and night.

She's a staunch Baptist in her belief, you see.
If you'd be just right, a Baptist you must be.
That's Sarah's real philosophy of life.
Well, why shouldn't it be? She's a Baptist preacher's wife.
Eva Akers Amos, February 13, 1940

In summary, I would like to respond to a question I am often asked: "To what one single person or condition would you credit your success?" The answer is simple. If my case history reflects any contributions I have made to higher education, I credit that success to Sarah. She was good in her profession and expected no less of me in mine. Sarah was my widowed mother. The poem was written five months after I entered Virginia State.

Chapter 17

Does Leadership Transcend Gender and Race?
The Case of African American Women College Presidents

M. Colleen Jones

This chapter is grounded in a research study of leadership development of African American women college presidents. When the data were collected in spring 1991, twenty-eight collegiate chief executive officers were African American women. To put that number into perspective, it is necessary to note that there are approximately 3,000 colleges and universities, and 328 of them have women presidents.[1] A comprehensive search of the literature revealed that very few studies of women college presidents of any racial or ethnic background have been conducted. Generally these women chief executives are included in broader studies of college presidents, but their comparatively small numbers (about 10 percent)[2] impeded any insightful or meaningful analysis. Those studies that have focused on women presidents have concentrated on general demographic information and patterns and on personal career histories. To date, no other study has focused on leadership styles of women college presidents by looking at background information to determine the antecedent factors that helped them cultivate the skills, talents, and abilities that they bring to and utilize in their daily activities and that may characterize their approach to leadership. This chapter focuses on the differences and similarities between the African American women college presidents and their executive cohort.

This study utilized two instruments: (1) the Multifactor Leadership Questionnaire (MLQ), an instrument designed to measure the behaviors constituting transformational leadership (characterized by the leader's recognition of subordinates' existing needs and by the ability to arouse and satisfy higher needs), transactional leadership (characterized by the leader's pursuit of a cost-benefit, economic exchange to meet subordinates' current material and psychic needs), and laissez-faire leadership (indicated by the absence of leadership, the avoidance of intervention, or both);[3] and (2) the Myers-Briggs Type Indicator (MBTI), an instrument designed to illustrate psychological type with a profile of selected aspects of personality or cognitive style.

As the conceptual framework was developed for the research, it became apparent that the theoretical grounding was an interdisciplinary one. Nevertheless, it was important to characterize the college presidency as analogous to the essence of leadership found in government and the private sector. Only after the acceptance of that premise were meaningful comparisons facilitated. A body of management literature asserts that executives and high level managers possess some general personality, background, and experience attributes. Some of those postulates are presented here to elucidate the significance of those theories and perspectives in explaining the leadership development and style of African American women college presidents.

Personality and Cognitive Attributes

The cognitive orientation of African American women presidents does not generally resemble the cognitive orientation of corporate executives or other high-level academic administrators. Contrary to this postulate, findings from this research indicate that the cognitive attributes of African American women college presidents *do* resemble those of other administrators, exhibiting high levels of extroversion, thinking, and judgment. Kotter's research found more extroverts than introverts among his study group.[4] Weddle, who studied middle-level women academic administrators, also found a sample preference for extroversion.[5] Research confirms the general tendency for executives, administrators, and managers to show preference for extroversion. Again, Weddle, Birnbaum,[6] and Kotter, in separate studies, found executives to be more intuitive than sensing. Weddle's research focused on women, and Birnbaum's and Kotter's studies contained predominantly male samples. The African American women college presidents are more often intuitive than sensing. These findings contradict previous findings by Myers that executives show stronger preference for sensing.[7]

Life Experiences

Maccoby and Gardner postulated that *role models and mentors (male and female) had attributable influence in the formation of an approach to leadership.*[8] Familial influences were found to be very strong for the African American women college presidents. The messages they derived as children from interactions with parents and significant adult others were quite powerful ("Always push the system"; "Be unwilling to settle for less"; "Set the standard; don't follow the crowd"; "Destiny is choice, not chance") and illuminated their paths throughout adolescence and adulthood. The influence of these persons on the leadership approach of the African American college presidents is positive but indirect. As youths, these women were surrounded by environments that nurtured their intellectual, interpersonal, and spiritual development. Even though most were not obviously set on a trail directed toward leading others, they were encouraged to be altruistic in service to others. That dimension of their upbringing is manifested in the exhibition of higher levels of transformational leadership behaviors.

There is a parallel pattern of life experiences among the African American women college presidents. Even with the diversity provided by lifestyles, geographic dispersion, socioeconomic status, and specific adults, the African American women college presidents have very similar life maps.

Parental Influences

Chase and Kotter provided evidence to support the assertion that the African American women college presidents who are fifty years old or older are *not* "first generation" college graduates.[9] That is, one or both of their parents attended college or graduated from college. Results of this study substantiated that pattern. Six of the African American women college presidents who are over fifty years old have at least one college-educated parent.

The converse of this finding contends that the African American women college presidents who are *younger* than fifty *are* first generation college graduates. The rationale for that assertion was that the greater participation of women and enhanced educational access following World War II allowed more African Americans from working-class, noncollege families to obtain a college education. Of the seven women who are younger than fifty, the parents of four of them never attended college; consequently, that proposition was weakly confirmed.

Participation in childhood and adolescent activities was marked by an ethic of accomplishment stimulated by parents or significant adults.[10] It is quite evident that the African American women college presidents' youthful engagements were promoted by the adults in their lives. None of the women recalled being "pushed" into participating in any activity, but their involvement was encouraged by parents and other adults.

Other Adult Influences

The significant spiritual role model for African American women college presidents was another woman (or other women). These role models provided ego strokes, "reality checks," emotional centering, network access, and the like. A pivotal finding was that women (both familial and "public") were very significant to the African American women college presidents as they were growing up and persisted as influences throughout their adult lives. This finding is consistent with findings of Hennig and Jardim.[11]

The respondents did not indicate that their significant technical (or professional) *role model* was a man (or men). Often the African American women college presidents commented that their paradigm for a "professional" was another woman, and they emulated a variety of behaviors that she displayed. However, because of the dearth of women in their academic and professional milieu, their *mentors* were mostly male. These persons (by example or instruction) provided orientation to political skills, structured opportunities for the women's work to be seen, nominated them for new ventures, and were the gauge they used to measure their accomplishment or guide their behavior in unfamiliar situations. Hennig and Jardim proposed that for women entering administrative venues, their primary technical referent would be male. The African American women college presidents have found meaningful influence in both male and female role models and mentors.

Professional Opportunities

Those with adolescent or collegiate office-holding experiences (either elected or appointed) made the switch from faculty to administration within five years and decided to pursue an administrative track during or immediately following the receipt of their terminal degree. Kotter advanced the perspective that the decision to follow an administrative or executive track is made relatively early in one's career. Eight of the seventeen African American women college presidents had no collegiate teaching experience at all and therefore have always been in the administrative pipeline (even though some were external to higher education). In general, the African American women college presidents who were in academe did not consciously decide to enter administration; more were tapped for the positions.

All of the respondents identified or recalled the person(s), incident(s), or series of events that put them on the path to a college presidency. Generally the decision to enter administration was precipitated by a personal condition of frustration, anger, or challenge. In their interviews, the respondents revealed situations of burnout, incompetent supervision, and professional stagnation as being significant antecedents to their initial "switch" to an administrative position. Others were "drafted" for administrative assignments by colleagues and mentors or encouraged by spouses or family members to step into a larger arena and use their latent managerial abilities.

The perspective offered by the literature that *the African American women college presidents younger than fifty had fewer traditional professional experiences than their older counterparts (that is, they had less time as faculty, entered administration earlier, or had initial career positions outside of academia)* was not substantiated by this study. In fact, the younger subset of African American women college presidents had three *more* years of administrative experience than the older women in the sample, even though both subgroups averaged five administrative positions prior to their presidential appointment.

Leadership-Developing Activities

In his research of corporate general managers, Kotter discovered that *they had very similar sets of personal and career experiences prior to their acceptance of a high visibility leadership role.* It was thought that this population of women leaders would have the same properties. Results from this research indicated a similar chronicle of leadership-developing activities during childhood and adolescence, but there is some divergence in the paths that preceded these women's decisions to seek a college presidency. The avenues taken can be summarized as "teacher-administrator," "practitioner-teacher," "researcher-teacher-administrator," "administrator-teacher-administrator," and "practitioner-administrator," but no particular route predominates.

Even though the data do not reveal a consistent pattern of activities that preceded the consideration of presidential appointment, *there are specific experiences and challenges that African American women college presidents recognize as being essential to the acquisition of skills necessary to be a college president.* So while their paths vary widely, the following experiences and skills were mentioned by more than half of the African American women college presidents interviewed and identified as the most salient background factors: acquisition of a terminal degree; comprehension of budgets and budgetary processes; involvement and recognition in national organizations; understanding group dynamics and political behavior; expertise in persuasive communication conflict resolution and consensus building; knowledge of the instructional mission of an institution; insight into the "faculty mind" and shared governance. These skills were identified as being the most salient background factors.

Opportunities to Observe Leadership Behaviors

Following the findings of Bass and Gibbons,[12] one would posit that *as the number and diversity of leadership-developing activities increased, the approach to leadership in the presidential role would become more transformational.* To determine the veracity of this assertion, the study participants' means on the Multifactor Leadership Questionnaire were examined. Generally, higher means on the transformational factors translate to more transformational behaviors by the leader. Research reveals that African American women college presidents were involved in numerous extracurricular activities through which they learned the rudimentary skills for leadership. As youths (ten through eighteen) they were involved in a variety of activities that afforded them the chance to directly observe and be guided by and/or work for persons in positions of leadership whom they admired or emulated. This finding supports the work of Maccoby and suggests that exposure to and participation in a variety of formal organizational structures instills the values and behaviors that may be manifested in mission management, referent power, creative problem solving, and appreciation of individual strengths and talents.[13] Kotter and Maccoby each presented data to indicate that *participation in childhood and adolescent activities was marked by an ethic of accomplishment stimulated by parents or significant adults.*[14] One of the strongest messages from this research has been the influence of parents (especially mothers or female family members) and other adults on the early lives of the African American women college presidents. These were strong progenitors who guided the lives of their children with vivid examples and poignant messages. In their interviews during this research, the African American women college presidents consistently shared childhood memories of conversations, admonitions, and lovingly veiled threats that helped them understand, negotiate, and achieve in climates that might have been otherwise hostile and confining for competent, intelligent, and active black girls. A distinct message from this research is that parents provide a context that figures prominently in their children's development. By encouraging participation in structured projects, modeling responsible behaviors, and advocating values of honesty, hard work, tenacity, discipline, altruism, self-esteem, and community, parents lay the foundation for their children to operate in and from which to discern the world around them.

Gibbons's study on leadership development found that *transformational leaders' engagement in selected activities as adolescents and new professionals were conscious decisions to develop a particular skill or overcome a perceived weakness.*[15] This did not hold true for the African American women college presidents. It was only later in their careers (for example, during their terminal degree program, under the influence of a strong mentor, or when they entered a mid-level administrative position) that they started to purposefully select and/ or accept challenges, training opportunities, assignments, or educational pursuits that would augment their skills.

Leadership Approach

African American women presidents *perceive themselves and are identified (by working colleagues, peers, and associates) as possessing an approach to leadership that is more transformational than transactional.* The findings of this research build upon the studies conducted by Gardner, Birnbaum, and Bass.[16] In the interviews, the respondents were asked to describe their leadership style or their approach to leadership. Universally they used concepts and terms that raised images of participative management, empowerment, team building, vision creation, and hands-on supervision.

Contrary to the findings of Gibbons,[17] the African American women college presidents *do not perceive their leadership philosophy and approach as being the result of conscious decisions and purposeful objectives throughout their lives.* Most interviewees said that they could have just as easily been a classroom teacher, a nurse, or a secretary as a collegiate CEO. As reported previously, none of the African American women college presidents started their professional careers with the objective of becoming a college president. The idea of becoming a college president most often came at the time when a woman was nominated for a specific position. The African American women college presidents can reconstruct, in retrospect, where and how they learned to lead, but while they were in the process of evolving and maturing, they were unaware that it was *leadership* they were developing—most were simply "having fun" or "just doing a job."

Summary

This study of leadership development surveyed a sample of seventeen African American women who as college presidents responded to the Multifactor Leadership Questionnaire, the Myers-Briggs Type Indicator, and a personal interview. The research examined the relationships between cognitive attributes, extracurricular activities, and interpersonal networks and the influence of those catalysts on the degree of transactional and transformational leadership behaviors exhibited by the study participants.

This endeavor, which was built upon Lewin's framework that behavior is a function of a person and the environment,[18] was undertaken to describe a segment of the population of leaders that is virtually absent from the literature and to develop a model for how leadership is learned. In that context, the exploratory and descriptive objectives have been achieved. This kind of research, however (which combines qualitative and quantitative measures of selected characteristics of populations virtually absent from the literature), is only the beginning.

With this research as a starting point, the following kinds of empirical ventures will advance the knowledge bases in leadership studies and other aspects of the behavioral sciences: first, since the cohort of African American women college presidents is growing, continuing the study to fill in the missing data by replication of this design with the new members of the population will strengthen the relationships and implications derived from the data as well as adjust the components of the model. Second, this study design can also be used with other populations (for example, women college presidents of all races, male or female corporate managers, military personnel, political leaders, and men of color who hold positions of leadership and authority). Because of the scarcity of research with significant cohorts of women and people of color, emphasis should be focused on these emerging executive cohorts. Third, the components of the model can be isolated and utilized to respond to various questions. Norms for the MLQ were developed without large samples of women and people of color. Nor have there been many samples from higher education, manufacturing, or customer-service industries. Oversampling of women and people of color will push the norms to be more representative of general populations and recognize the changing demographics of the managerial and working populations. With the findings from this and another recent study by Bass and Avolio that indicate that women have higher transformational means than men,[19] additional study would determine if these two samples represent a statement of fact or simply report anomalies. The MBTI has a much broader research base, but it too has not fully utilized the increasing numbers of managerial and executive women to reevaluate its norms. This study joins others in finding that executive women show preferences for thinking above feeling, but the normative data still assert a feminine preference for feeling. The preeminence of thinking among women may be a prevailing trend that warrants examination.

Finally, leadership is the most studied and least understood topic in the behavioral sciences. The presence of an emerging cohort (a "new population") of high-profile leaders that is "different" from the typical executive profile on gender and racial dimensions symbolizes an unexplored research reservoir to be tapped. This study has examined cognitive attributes, life experiences, and leadership-developing activities to establish their relationship and contribution to the leadership approach of African American women college presidents. We must continue to search for the antecedents of leadership so we can better prepare for our future and understand how we learn to lead.

Notes

1. American Council on Education, *Fact Book on Women* (Washington, D.C.: American Council on Education, 1990).

2. American Council on Education, *Annual Study of American Colleges and Universities* (Washington, D.C.: American Council on Education, 1987).

3. Bernard M. Bass, *Leadership and Performance Beyond Expectations* (New York: Free Press, 1985), 14, 20.

4. John P. Kotter, *The General Managers* (New York: Free Press, 1982).

5. Catherine J. Weddle, "Leadership Styles of Successful Women Administrators in Higher Education," in *Impact of Leadership*, edited by Kenneth E. Clark, Miriam B. Clark, and David Campbell (Greensboro, N.C.: Center for Creative Leadership, 1992).

6. Robert Birnbaum, *Responsibility Without Authority: The Impossible Job of the College President* (College Park, Md: National Center for Postsecondary Governance and Finance, 1988).

7. Isabel Baggs Myers and Mary H. McCauley, *Manual: A Guide to the Development and Use of the Myers-Briggs Type Indicator* (Palo Alto, Calif.: Consulting Psychologists Press, 1985).

8. Michael Maccoby, *The Leader—A New Face for American Management* (New York: Simon and Schuster, 1981); John W. Gardner, *On Leadership* (New York: Free Press, 1990).

9. Pearline Chase, *Black Women College Presidents: Perceptions of the Major Job Roles, Problems, Expectations and Experiences.* (Ph.D. dissertation, Harvard University, 1987); Kotter, *The General Managers.*

10. Kotter, *The General Managers.*

11. Margaret Hennig and Anne Jardim, *The Managerial Woman* (New York: Anchor Press, 1976).

12. Bass, *Leadership and Performance Beyond Expectations*; Tracy Gibbons, "Revisiting the Question of Born vs. Made: Toward A Theory of Development of Transformational Leaders" (Ph.D. dissertation, Fielding Institute, 1976; abstract in *Dissertation Abstracts International*, 11554).

13. Maccoby, *The Leader.*

14. Kotter, *The General Managers*; Maccoby, *The Leader.*

15. Gibbons, "Revisiting the Question of Born vs. Made."

16. Gardner, *On Leadership*; Robert Birnbaum, *How Colleges Work—The Cybernetics of Academic Organization and Leadership* (San Francisco: Jossey-Bass, 1988); Bass, *Leadership and Performance Beyond Expectations.*

17. Gibbons, "Revisiting the Question of Born vs. Made."

18. Kurt Lewin, *Field Theory in Social Science* (New York: Harper and Brothers, 1951).

19. Bernard M. Bass and Bruce J. Avolio, *The Transformational and Transactional Leadership Behavior of Management Women and Men as Described by the Men and Women Who Directly Report to Them*, Center for Leadership Studies Report 91-3 (Binghamton, N.Y.: State University of New York, 1991).

Part Five

The Social Dynamics of Academic Life

Black women's voices are finally being heard, but it is still difficult to listen to them amid the clang of racism and sexism. In the ivory tower, the voices are shrouded beneath a racist and sexist cloud that is often chilly at white institutions and lukewarm, at best, in black ones. African American women, particularly those in white milieus, encounter isolation and nonnurturing environs that affect the promotion, retention, and tenure process. Tenure is by far the major concern among black women and other people of color, particularly on white campuses. These faculty, who are already underrepresented on campus, are concerned about their job security. And it is a valid concern, especially since the tenure rate in 1989, as reported by the American Council on Education, was 58.6 percent for black women, 62.9 percent for black men, 59.5 percent for white women, and 76.2 percent for white men.

In their poignant, vivid voices, Vernellia R. Randall and Vincene Verdun, in "Two Black Women Talking About the Promotion, Retention, and Tenure Process in Law Schools," reconstruct dialogue of their own experiences with these processes. Norma J. Burgess's "Tenure and Promotion Among African American Women in the Academy: Issues and Strategies" underscores Randall and Verdun's personal accounts. Burgess focuses on issues associated with promotion and tenure among African American women such as lack of sponsorship, double-duty service, insufficient research opportunities, and quality of teaching.

J. Nefta Baraka's "Collegiality in the Academy: Where Does the Black Woman Fit?" argues that different cultural orientations intertwine with racism and sexism, making it difficult for black women to fit into (white) academe. Employing an intercultural communication perspective, Baraka poses important questions and dilemmas about these differences that impede collegiality. She places the onus of responsibility for change in the academy on whites.

Saliwe M. Kawewe's "The Dynamics of Patriarchal Meritocracy in the Academy: A Case Study" confronts experientially the issues of recruitment, promotion, retention, tenure, and collegiality as these factors interface with gender, race, and ethnicity in both black and white institutions.

Other issues such as gender and sexual harassment affect the academic climate for black women. Jacqueline Pope and Janice Joseph's "Student Harassment of Female Faculty of African Descent in the Academy" documents, through a survey, some faculty-student problems and challenges black women encounter. Pope and Joseph note that sexual and gender harassment is embedded in campus life, but few studies have documented the general problems women faculty encounter with students, particularly African American women, who experience widespread harassment.

Chapter 18

Two Black Women Talking About the Promotion, Retention, and Tenure Process in Law Schools

Vernellia R. Randall and Vincene Verdun

We offer each other the best that we have, and what we have is often the best there is. African American women are peculiarly alone in legal academia. Because of the race barrier, our interests are often drastically different from those of our white women colleagues, and if we are lucky enough to have a black male around, we still face the gender barrier. Sometimes African American women are lucky to find nearby support among each other—as we have done. We are two women from two separate campuses. We bridge the seventy miles between the University of Dayton and Ohio State University by telephone, by fax, by next-day delivery mail, and by automobile. By whatever means available, we talk, we share, we support each other in the pursuit of our professional and personal goals.

Promotion and tenure are significant events in every law professor's career. For African American women, who are particularly susceptible to the silent, unconscious biases that accompany gender and/or race, the process can be fraught with peculiarities. The conversations below typify the kinds of discussions two African American women law professors would have when one of them is being evaluated for a promotion. Though the events described are based upon the cumulative experiences of many African American women, we offer an intimate look into the kind of sharing that takes place when there are two black women talking.

Part 1: The Office Visit, October 7

Vernellia: Hi, Vincene. I've been trying to reach you all day. This promotion review has me worried.

Vincene: That's natural, Vernellia; just don't let it get to you. You've done everything you are supposed to do. You've written all those health care articles, and they only get you on the teaching if the scholarship isn't right. Besides, your teaching was satisfactory in that retention review last spring, so you are going to get the promotion. But it is okay to worry.

Vernellia: I know. I know. It's just that all the uncertainty creates so much pressure. And you know women have had a shaky track record at the law school. In eighty-three years, the school has never tenured a woman, and just a year ago two women were let go at their retention reviews. But I guess what really started me worrying is a conversation I had with the dean. Last summer I wrote and received a summer research grant to write an article on fetal alcohol syndrome. But you know how things go. At the very beginning of the summer I got involved in the health care reform issue. So I went to the dean and told him that I wanted to change the topic for my summer research. He agreed to the switch. Now he comes into my office, sits down, and says, "I want to talk to you about scholarship." Then he qualifies, "But this isn't P&T business." So he proceeds to ask me when I think I'll be through with the fetal alcohol syndrome article.

Vincene: The dean comes in making a disclaimer, which I imagine really put you at ease, huh? [sarcastically]. Did you ask him why he was asking you about the fetal alcohol syndrome article?

Vernellia: I didn't ask him anything. I just answered his questions. I was stunned. I didn't want to say too much, and I didn't know what I could say.

Vincene: You could have said, "I am totally uninterested in fetal alcohol syndrome now and I may never pick it up again." I mean, that is one appropriate response.

Vernellia: I just feel so uncertain. Part of the problem is not knowing what the guidelines are. What are the limits of my academic freedom? What is my responsibility in relationship to the summer research grant? You know, the school did give me a grant, and I did say I was going to do it. Does that mean that now if I don't do it, somehow that impacts how I am viewed as a person? A scholar? That I have taken on a topic and then just dropped it without following through?

Vincene: But that happens all the time! [emphatically]. You have an idea, a research idea. You say, "OK, this is what I want to research." You get in the middle of the research and discover you are totally uninterested in it, and you drop it. Or you get sidetracked by a new, urgent idea, like the Clinton Health Care Plan, drop everything, and pursue the new topic. Maybe you get back to the first topic; maybe you don't. I have never heard of a law school that binds its professors to their summer research grant proposals. The expectation is that you should be productive, not that you must have a paper on a particular topic!

[emphatically]. You shouldn't be yoked with a topic merely because you proposed it in a summer research grant.

Vernellia: Yes, that's what you say; but how is a new person, any new person, supposed to know what the guidelines are? And as an African American I often feel as if I don't know the informal, unwritten rules. Sometimes I feel that the rules are being changed right before my eyes. Whether white male faculty are held to the same standard seems almost irrelevant. The promotion and tenure committee can easily legitimize something as an appropriate evaluative standard.

Vincene: So you think this is one of the issues in the P&T committee meetings? "She said she was going to do this fetal alcohol syndrome paper. She stopped before the summer began. She doesn't follow through on the topics she chooses." Stranger things than that have happened to African American faculty. The rules have been known to change suddenly just when one of "us" comes along. Since the dean came to your office to ask you about the article, and he sits on the P&T committee, I guess we shouldn't discount that possibility. What did you tell him?

Vernellia: I told him that I am working on the health care reform piece and that I definitely would not have the fetal alcohol syndrome piece done in the spring. To which he responded, "Well, how about the end of the summer?" I said that it was quite possible that by the end of the summer I would have it done. He said, "Well, what form is it going to take?"

Vincene: He asked, "What form is it gonna take?" [amazement]. Duh-uh, well, it's going to be English, typed, double-spaced [mockingly, with laughter].

Vernellia: I said, "I'm not sure what you mean." He then asked if it were going to be a typical law review article and added, laughing nervously, "Not that anything you do is typical."

Vincene: That's a loaded comment. Is atypical good or bad? That is a troubling comment. Did you ask him why he thinks your scholarship is atypical?

Vernellia: No. All I did was answer questions. I was stunned. He was totally uninterested in the progress of my current work. Naturally I got defensive about my work. I pointed out that my other two articles were law review articles. And the fetal alcohol syndrome article would take the form that they had taken [sarcastically, with laughter].

Vincene: So you basically said to him, "If you think that my other work is atypical, this is going to be equally atypical." Good for you, Vernellia [laughter].

Vernellia: Right. He then asked me what length I thought the article would be.

Vincene: Amazing! Let me get this straight. The dean is asking about a piece that never got any further than the proposal for the research grant, and he wants you to commit to a page length. You must have been really nervous not to point this out to him.

Vernellia: I was very nervous. I told him that it probably would be about the same length as my other law review articles, which are fairly long.

Vincene: But he didn't say whether what you had done was enough or not. Okay, Vernellia, what was his angle?

Vernellia: That is just what I am trying to figure out. He asked those questions about the abandoned article. He didn't ask me anything about my health care reform article, even after I mentioned that it has already been accepted for publication.

Vincene: Let's regroup. The dean comes to your office while you are under review for promotion, disclaims that his visit has anything to do with P&T, asks you when you will complete a project and the page length of the project, and calls your work atypical with no indication of what that means. Vernellia, that is just plain mean. Anyone with half an ounce of sensitivity would have to know that a seemingly purposeless conversation with a faculty member under promotion review would drive that person crazy with anxiety. The dean owes you an explanation. I think you need to go right in and ask him why he asked you about a project that he knows you are not working on currently. But don't let him snow you about your obligations, Vernellia. Law faculty have a lot of flexibility in changing gears on research topics. Productivity is most important, and a lot of people get grants summer after summer and publish nothing.

Vernellia: I understand what you are saying, Vincene, with my head; with my heart, I'm not so sure. I always feel as if I were walking a tightrope—any wrong step seems enough to declare me incompetent, and I will fall to my death. I feel that I have only as much flexibility as they allow me, and that is never as much as my white male colleagues have. I don't get good guidance on the nonwritten rules. I am the first African American woman on the tenure track, and although the school does have an African American man who started with me, he is just as "in the dark" as I am. I do not have sufficient information about the promotion process to judge what's happening.

Vincene: It should not be that way, Vernellia, but that is our reality. They let us in the club, but we never get all of our membership rights. The painful truth is that not only do we not learn the unwritten rules, but they change once we come along. Before you know it, there are new rules, and coincidentally, the first time they are ever applied, an African American or a woman is the target. Even as I tell you what is usually the case, I cannot fathom the dean's telling you that the rules are different, starting right now. And he will have very race- and gender-neutral reasons for the change. He'll argue that a school has the right, even the responsibility, to increase its standards. The fact that you get caught by a rule is evidence of your incompetence, while your colleagues' competence is presumed, even though none of your white male predecessors were subject to the rule. In fact, I would be willing to bet that a number of your faculty judging your scholarship may not have written as many articles as you have in their entire academic careers, but they will not hesitate to judge you based on the higher standards and not flinch when they determine that you have not lived up to them.

Vernellia: It's so tiring. I feel so alone, so isolated. I feel that there is no one here to speak up for me and plead my case, that I have no real ally on the faculty. Sure, I'm social enough with my colleagues. But there is no one on this faculty in whom I have enough confidence. I know that some of the faculty see me as an affirmative action hire, even though I have outstanding credentials. I have no idea who is fair and who is not.

Vincene: You know, Vernellia, I have been on this faculty for five years now, and I have not developed a personal relationship with a single white colleague. I am blessed to have had two African American men on the faculty when I came, so I was not a pathfinder; I definitely had someone to show me the way. But I still relate to how you feel. I have felt alone and uncertain of whom to trust before. I have even experienced the severe consequences that come from misplaced trust. That taught me whom not to trust, but it is harder to learn whom *to* trust.

Vernellia: Yes, and it is not safe to rely on the faculty with liberal ideas to support you. One "liberal" faculty member refused to interview me when I came to visit and has let it be known generally that he does not support the law school's efforts to specifically recruit minorities. He maintains that he believes in race-neutral recruitment. Another "liberal" faculty member has done several things to undermine me as a faculty member, not the least of which was asking my students specifically about how things were going in my classes.

Vincene: That's a real problem. If you get any twenty-five white people together with any twenty-five African Americans and let them get to know each other, then poll each group on who in the white group could be relied upon to be fair in the evaluation of an African American colleague, I guarantee you the white group will pick different people than the African American group will. African Americans have learned to look at what people do rather than what they say in determining whom we can depend upon. Liberals frequently lose their idealism and show their stripes when race is an issue. I cannot believe it,

Vernellia. You should be a shoo-in for a promotion with all of your scholarship, but I think you'd better gear up for a fight. I don't want you to panic or anything. You may have to pull out all the stakes. Fill me in on the promotion and tenure process there. What is expected of you for promotion and for tenure, and what is the process?

Vernellia: It's a pretty complicated process. We are reviewed six out of eight semesters, and we are videotaped every semester. The third-year review is more than just a retention decision. It is a decision on whether the P&T committee thinks the untenured faculty is making the progress needed to warrant tenure.

Vincene: You have to be kidding. You have been under constant review ever since you set foot in that place. They review you every semester. My goodness, do you ever get a reprieve? Who thought up this policy?

Vernellia: Now remember, they had never tried this policy on any white male. They implemented it, at least in part, to protect women and minorities from the arbitrariness of faculty decision making. The policy was adopted right before the first women were hired. They hired three women and then fired two of them at the third-year review.

Vincene: Wait a minute. The law school implemented this policy in order to protect women that they were hiring to join this previously all-white male faculty—which had never given tenure to a woman—and then they used the policy to fire two of them? Then I believe we can declare this policy a documented success [laughter]. So anyway, you passed through all of the reviews, including the third-year review. What scholarship does the policy require?

Vernellia: According to the policy, scholarship includes not only typical law review articles but also books, articles for nonlawyers, practitioner work, pro bono work, and everything in between. But the expectation for promotion, I have been told, is one law review article. Both of the women who were not retained had published works in the nontraditional categories. You know, it is interesting, Vincene: during the interview stage, I tried to size up the school's readiness for African American faculty. I even took my name out of the running at a school that was having obvious problems. One of the things I liked about this school was its comprehensive P&T policy. I was particularly impressed with the policy's expansive definition of scholarship.

Vincene: Even with an expansive policy, there is always the old "it ain't analytical enough" trap. This policy is a real-live snare. It includes nontraditional scholarship, much of which by it nature is more descriptive than analytical, but the committee can still deny promotion, retention, and tenure based on analytical content. So both of these women had good reason to believe that they had met the scholarship requirement sufficiently to be retained, yet both of them were dismissed. But you went through the process and were retained?

Vernellia: I was retained. I had one major law review article at the time and had started on a second. I had also written a book review. I had a couple of continuing legal education outlines, and I had two annotated bibliographies done for CLEs. So I had completed one traditional law review article, one book review, and four CLE items, and I was retained. Since the last evaluation, I've completed an additional law review article, a chapter in a book, and a journal article.

Vincene: All of that since April. The volume alone is impressive, which means you shouldn't even have to worry. You passed a teaching and scholarship review in April, and you have these additional articles, so you shouldn't have to worry. I just don't see how they can get away with anything except approving your promotion. It makes me so mad sometimes, Vernellia. We have been told all of our lives that we have to do twice as much to get half as far as a white person. Then we do it—twice as much—and we still have to worry about getting our due. Sometimes I just get sick of this damn yoke we have to bear [angrily]. Wouldn't it be nice if you could relax and say, "I've bagged this promotion."

Vernellia: Yes. That was my plan all along. I wanted to make sure at every step of the way that I had much more than what was required by the faculty rules.

Vincene: You know that strategy could have bugged the committee. They never want us to feel confident, competent, assured of our capabilities. Your obvious self-confidence may have unnerved them. We will have to watch and evaluate every move of the committee very carefully.

Vernellia: I'm afraid you're right [in a depressed tone]. Shit! We seemed to be damned if we do excellent work and damned if we don't.

Vincene: Don't be too disheartened. You will make it. It's good that you are having an outside review of your scholarship. Outside reviews can really help when the committee is biased, although I have heard of determined committees finding something negative in even the most favorable review. Let me know when you get that draft report from the P&T committee.

Part 2: The Draft Report, November 11

Vernellia: Vincene . . . [sob].

Vincene: My goodness, Vernellia. What is it? Did something happen to Tshaka or Issa [Vernellia's children]?

Vernellia: It's the draft report from the P&T committee. I got it back today and it's demeaning! [teary].

Vincene: You have to be kidding. How could it be? You have all that scholarship and a great outside review; you've served on university committees and law school committees, given speeches all over the country, and testified at presidential hearings on health care. Oh, no! Don't tell me they came down on your teaching?

Vernellia: They did [crying]. They said terrible, demeaning things about my teaching. They said I couldn't teach and made doctrinal errors and came to class unprepared. It was so condescending. They lectured me on how important teaching was and how it was my first responsibility. The report just goes on and on, page after page, tearing my tort classes apart.

Vincene: Alright, let's start with the important business. Vernellia, you know that you are a good classroom teacher, right? You know that you have lively class discussions with lots of student participation; you know that you know your subject matter; and furthermore, you know that you conscientiously prepare for your classes. Let's start with all of that as a given. Now you cannot let the committee, their draft report, or the dean define who you are or what you are capable of. Vernellia, you have to decide who you are, accept your own evaluation of what you can do, and proceed from there. We cannot afford to let others define us.

Vernellia: I know you're right. You'd think that after twenty-five years of working, I'd be used to it. It's just that it hurts to have them say those horrible things about me, especially since I work . . .

Vincene: Stop it, Vernellia! Just add it to all of the other hurts that have been heaped on you all of your life and keep on pushing. You cannot afford to let them get you down now. This is not the first time your effectiveness has been challenged by white people. It won't be the last. You know that many white people start out with a presumption that African Americans are inadequate, and any little evidence is used to support their preconceived idea. I know it hurts, but you cannot internalize the things they said about you in the report. You have to decide what kind of teacher you are and how you stack up relative to other teachers in your school and to live with that evaluation. Don't forget, this is the same committee that said your teaching was satisfactory in April when they considered you for retention. Now it's November and you've received an outstanding outside review on your scholarship, which takes it beyond reproach, and all of a sudden your teaching is the issue and a reason to deny you a promotion. That is not logical, Vernellia, and when erratic things happen to us, we have to start thinking about motives. It is not time for you to wallow in self-pity and doubt. You are being persecuted by this committee; it is race-based, and it is time for you to get mad and fight back.

Vernellia: You know, my African American colleague's report was terrible too. They challenged his scholarship.

Vincene: Excuse me, but do I detect a pattern here or what? Two African Americans—one with impeccable teaching credentials who is challenged on scholarship despite great reviews; one with outstanding scholarship who is challenged on teaching despite good reports in previous reviews. Seems to me they are determined to get both of you one way or the other. Are you mad yet?

Vernellia: It's so tiring. Why can't they treat me with respect? I'm so damn tired of it all. You know, the faculty rules say that they don't expect any change in teaching between the third-year retention decision and the promotion decision. So I thought my job was to produce more scholarship over the summer and everything would be okay. The P&T committee had criticized my teaching in previous reports, but the criticisms have gone to teaching technique, proofreading, grammar, and pronunciation. The criticisms were not related to substance in teaching or scholarship. Since they retained me, I never thought teaching would be the issue on promotion. They gave me no hint. I took steps to correct issues they identified, and I focused on scholarship. And then they pulled the rug right out from under me. They interpreted the rule to say that it didn't mean that they wouldn't revisit teaching, just that they ordinarily wouldn't expect any change, but that it is possible that change could occur.

Vincene: In other words, unlike the usual curve we would expect in which teachers grow better with time, it appears that you could have grown worse between April and November. Incredible!

Vernellia: I know. I think that P&T committee tried to cover its basic argument because it went back and reevaluated some of my spring teaching tapes.

Vincene: Let me get this straight. Once they decided that your scholarship was adequate, the P&T committee just didn't evaluate your fall teaching. Instead they went back to the spring tapes and looked at those, which had already been evaluated and found satisfactory. I know that you get really good student reviews in your upper-division classes. You get mixed reviews in your first-year classes, but it is so typical for a law professor, especially African American women, to have mixed reviews—great reviews in your specialty areas and O.K. reviews in other areas. It's the devil/angel syndrome. White students often either love you or hate you. So what's the deal about your teaching? Three years of saying that you are a satisfactory teacher—how did they attack it?

Vernellia: That's the irony here. For three years the P&T committee report said that I was satisfactory in teaching, and they said that the students' complaints related to my level of knowledge and my ability to teach were unfounded. But you know, the committee changed in September. I suppose this is one of the flaws of having a P&T process conducted by less than a full faculty. You never know when a changing committee will introduce someone into the process who has been harboring a bias.

Vincene: The P&T process can certainly be influenced by individuals who have a strong racial or gender bias.

Vernellia: I think that's what happened to me. When the committee changed, a new committee member went back and picked my tapes apart. He essentially said, "Wait a minute, fellows, I don't know how the other committees missed this, but this person is not qualified," and then wrote a memo to that effect. Vincene, he never gave me the benefit of the doubt on anything. He construed every slip of the tongue and every difference in doctrine or presentation as evidence of my incompetence. Then the bias for the rest of the committee came into play because they did not recognize what was going on, or they were fearful that the other committees may have allowed an African American into the academy who was not qualified. The committee didn't immediately accept the memo. I think they were troubled. Some of the committee members had been on the spring P&T committee. To accept the professor's memo must certainly have called into question their competence in evaluating me. On the other hand, to ignore it might mean that the horrors of horror would occur. An unworthy African American female would be allowed into the academy.

Vincene: Boy, do we live under the burden of the presumption of incompetency. They really are fearful of not picking a "good one," an African American who is different from the rest—the aberrational "smart one." It doesn't take much to feed their doubts about their choices.

Vernellia: Exactly, and they are so willing to accept "evidence" from the most reliable sources. At any rate, the committee gave the memo to one of the other law professors who teaches torts. He concluded that "what we have here is just teaching within the normal range of teaching. I don't think that this is evidence of any serious problems."

Vincene: Vernellia, this is borderline hilarious. One torts professor writes a memo saying that you are an incompetent teacher because you make errors that would confuse the students. Mind you, he had to rewind the tapes over and over to pick the specific points of law in your class tapes and take issue with them. One of the other professors, at least 50 percent of the time, disagreed with one or the other of you. So there are three torts professors here, one of them saying, "Here are five things that Vernellia Randall did wrong," and another professor who says, "I agree with Vernellia in two cases, and I agree with my other colleague in three." In other words, we have five issues on which reasonable minds might differ, as is noted by the fact that we have three torts professors on one faculty that disagree on these points.

Vernellia: Exactly! How can I be incompetent if "reasonable minds" could disagree? Why isn't the professor who wrote the memo incompetent for being wrong at least half the time according to the opinion of my other colleague?

Vincene: That kind of disagreement over doctrinal points seems pretty normal for law school faculty. So something went wrong on this committee when they failed to see it that way.

Vernellia: Yes. What went wrong? Is the bias—the willingness to construe my opinions, slips of tongue, and minor errors made in the heat of classroom discussion—used as evidence of incompetency rather than normal?

Vincene: Your P&T rule provides you an opportunity to respond to the draft report, doesn't it? The good news is that the draft report didn't actually deny you promotion. Your response has to be a dynamite one. This committee needs a wake-up call. We have to bring the rest of the world into their meeting. That committee cannot feel so insulated that it can screw its African American faculty and not be held accountable for it. You said your torts classes were taped. That means you can make copies of the tapes and send them to torts professors outside your school and ask them to review your classes for you. Also, you should solicit outside reviews of those articles. Your response has to be tight enough to make the committee sit up and take notice. Let them know that they are accountable to a larger community when they make their decision, and maybe they will consider whether their actions will cause embarrassment to themselves and the school. Maybe we can force them into some objectivity. Also, the kind of file you will build is the same as you'd build if you were preparing for a lawsuit. I'm not suggesting that you ever waste your time suing them, but it ought to be very clear that the evidence you present from some heavy hitters in your area establishes the basis for a good discrimination lawsuit. By the way, why don't you fax me a copy of that draft report and those memos in your file? And if you want me to, I'll proofread your response for you.

Part 3: The Response, November 25

Vernellia: Vincene, I got back all of the class reviews. I'm so glad I did this. No matter what the committee decides, the reviewers confirmed my confidence in my teaching and the fact that this committee is persecuting me. You know how distraught I was. I felt betrayed by the P&T process—raped.

Vincene: Rape! That is a strong accusation.

Vernellia: Yes, intellectually raped. I'm vulnerable in this process. Yet these six white guys, under the guise of some kind of responsibility to the school, tear me apart and then stand back and say, "We are sorry none of this was noted before, but we are duty-bound to note it now." Furthermore, just as in sexual rape, afterward they stood back self-satisfied, pointing to minute details in my behavior as justification for their intellectual violence. Emotionally I wasn't prepared to accept anything they had to say, but I realized that if I had a problem, I needed to know it. So I thought your suggestion to have outsiders critique my teaching could help me to accept the P&T committee's evaluation and move on to constructive action.

Vincene: This is killing me, Vernellia. What did they say?

Vernellia: All three of the reviews essentially said that I was more than qualified, more than satisfactory in my teaching. Add that to the great outside reviews on my scholarship, and I feel like I could fly if I set my mind to it.

Vincene: Nothing like a little confirmation from people with impressive credentials. Hard to believe that they were looking at the same videotapes as the P&T committee.

Vernellia: Yes, even though they were very busy people, they were very willing to help. Even though they didn't really know me.

Vincene: This is wonderful, Vernellia. Isn't it self-assuring to get some positive feedback when you are under attack? I am so glad you got this affirmation. No matter what this committee decides on your promotion, life is so much bigger than a promotion decision. You do know there are no guarantees you will get promoted. The committee may be offended that you have gone to outsiders on your own over an internal matter. They may refuse to consider all of your outside reviews because they were solicited by you, not the committee. But you have lost nothing. There was no doubt in my mind that the committee that wrote that draft report was not about to change its mind based upon a personal response from you. So we are playing the long shot. Maybe a well-documented response, which includes outside challenges to their conclusions, will sway them. We have given the committee a solid road map to use to do the right thing if it is so inclined, but the committee members could be so entrenched in their bigotry by now that they fail to see the path. Prepare yourself now for denial of the promotion, Vernellia, because that is a real possibility.

Vernellia: Believe me, I did this more for myself than because I really thought I could change the committee's position. It has been reassuring to have some of the most respected law professors in my field approve of my teaching and my scholarship. It was worth the effort, no matter what the committee says.

Vincene: You know, Vernellia, it is not too soon to start planting seeds with our colleagues around the country that you are in the market for a new home. Anyway, don't forget to fax me your draft response before you leave tonight.

Part 4: The Final Report, December 7

Vernellia: I got the final report of the P&T committee today [depressed tone]. They did not change their draft report, except on the issue of Doctrine of Transferred Intent, which was the example they used to say that my writing was confusing to students.

    Vincene: Oh, really? Did they delete that issue? That was a big one.

    Vernellia: No, they didn't. Of all the things I submitted in my response, everything was ignored except for my analysis of transferred intent and the Prosser and Keaton article supporting my analysis. And they commented only to say that I hadn't read the article right.

    Vincene: So let me get this straight. First they say you are incompetent because you don't know enough law. Then when you get support for your analysis, they ignore it. And their only change in the final report was an "Oh, by the way, not only don't you know the law, but you can't read either" [laughter]. Now, what happens next?

    Vernellia: The committee recommended to the dean that I not be promoted, based on teaching. The dean has a choice. He can ignore or accept the committee recommendation. Oh, by the way, the committee also recommended that my African American male colleague not be promoted.

    Vincene: No surprise in that. Since the dean sat on the committee, I don't guess there is much chance that he is going to recommend against the committee. If he were on your side, he would have used his influence to sway the committee's decision. I know of a similar situation that happened to another African American woman. One of her colleagues taped her class, then wrote a damaging memo to the dean. The dean buried the damaging memo and transferred her out of the biased colleague's teaching area. That dean took steps to protect her from bias. Your dean has made little effort to protect you. It's not likely now that he's going to step out.

    Vernellia: There is one little happy scene in this tragedy. One of the members dissented from the committee's recommendation and wrote a two-and-a-half page report. He concluded that my teaching was adequate and justified my being promoted. Furthermore, he thought my scholarship and service were exemplary and—these were his words—"standard-setting for the law school."

    Vincene: A voice of sanity on the committee. A voice that adhered to the age-old unwritten rule that if the scholarship is excellent, the standard for teaching is that you show up for class regularly with class notes and a clue. Prolific scholars, like yourself, just are not denied promotion or tenure because they aren't great teachers. Your next move is with the provost, Vernellia. It is still not time to give up this fight. You do all that committee work on main campus, so I know you have developed a good reputation. Have you developed any relationships in the provost's office?

Vernellia: As a matter of fact, I have.

Epilogue

Unlike what happens in fairy tales or other stories, these battles never end. If we are not fighting our own battles against bias, discrimination, sexism, and racism, we are helping others fight theirs. We hope that this story might help you in your passage through the academic battlefield called the promotion, retention, and tenure process.

Chapter 19

Tenure and Promotion Among African American Women in the Academy

Issues and Strategies

Norma J. Burgess

Tenure brings power, privilege, and prestige. Thus the single most important goal most faculty members have upon entering the academy is the attainment of this status, which is often difficult and sometimes impossible but always highly desirable because it insures job security, more money, eligibility for sabbatical leaves, and institutional support for research.

After a notorious case in which a faculty member was dismissed because his research offended a major donor to his institution, the American Association of University Professors felt the need in 1915 to create a vehicle to provide more job security for its colleagues.[1] After a probationary period on the job (typically seven years), a faculty member is subjected to a rigorous review by a committee of peers to assess his or her achievement in the areas of research, teaching, and service. Successful completion of this process, which results in the granting of tenure, appears to distinguish membership in the academic community from the common definition of employment because it assures academic freedom to teach and do research without fear of dismissal or other reprisal.[2]

In predominantly white institutions, the white male power structure controls the tenure process. Not only has its hegemony resulted in its being the body to establish guidelines for the achievement of tenure, but also it is not uncommon for these guidelines to be changed in midstream to preclude some populations from attaining the grand prize of academia. Hence being awarded tenure is by far the major concern for men and women of color in institutions where they are already underrepresented. A survey by Moore and Wagstaff of African American faculty found that as many as 50 percent of African Americans in senior institutions are not only nontenured but also in nontenure-track positions. They also found that only 10 percent of the African American faculty in white institutions taught graduate students (a necessity for tenure and promotion in some institutions).[3]

For African American women in academe, then, it can come as no surprise that gaining tenure in a predominantly white institution is often difficult. The confounding issues of race and gender render African American women defenseless against rules and regulations that have been written to preclude their access to these hallowed grounds.

This chapter provides insight into some problems that affect the tenure and promotion process for African American women in the areas of sponsorship and networking, double-duty service, research and publication, and teaching. It concludes with suggestions on how black women in the academy can cope with these issues.

Sponsorship and Networking

Sponsorship has always been an important part of the white male's success in academia. It is as important a component in upward mobility and acceptance as are competition and competence. Senior faculty acting as mentors assist untenured junior faculty in locating and acquiring research funds and developing research proposals; provide technical assistance and counsel; and generally help younger males enter into the "old boys' network." The white male senior faculty member seldom sponsors women and almost never serves as a mentor to African American women. The stereotype of the strong, independent individual works with overt and covert prejudice and hostility to exclude African American female faculty members from sponsorship, aid, and formal and informal avenues of professional communication. Valverde's research indicates that a mentor chooses a protégé who is most similar to him in physical attributes, values, and personal characteristics.[4] African American women, who are physically and culturally different from white males, stand little chance of gaining significantly from sponsorship in academia. During the tenure review process, the tendency of predominantly white male review committees to replicate the social and ethnic makeup of their departments is likely to affect African American women disproportionately.[5]

Similarly, African American females suffer from a restricted communication network, and this has a negative impact on their productivity. Like sponsorship, communication with one's peers is necessary for success in academia. A National Institute of Mental Health study concluded that poor productivity is, in many instances, a result of a disadvantaged position in the communication system of one's discipline rather than the result of a lack of ability or motivation. African American women in academe often operate on the periphery of established networks. Inability to gain access to timely and pertinent information handicaps them in acquiring research funds, presenting papers, publishing, consulting, and gaining visibility among their peers—activities necessary for tenure and promotion in the academy.[6]

Lack of sponsorship, exclusion from networks and other means of professional communication, discrimination, and isolation have made it difficult for African American females in the academy to pursue research successfully. Without research, they are caught in higher education's notorious revolving door, through which African American faculty gain admission but are seldom retained.

Double-Duty Service

In addition to lack of sponsorship and related problems, women in general and African American women in particular face special problems because, in many cases, their assigned tasks (which are for the most part service-oriented) make it almost impossible for them to give sufficient time to the type of scholarly activities that would afford them success in the tenure and promotion process. Women's institutional and community service is often evaluated differently than men's. African American women are frequently asked to serve on faculty committees but are given no reward for this service.[7] Meetings can put a significant drain on their already overloaded schedules.

Nevertheless, these women continue to take on even more work because they are aware that their voices need to be heard. Because they cannot be present on all committees, it is important for them, when given a choice, to select and work through the committees by which the most important decisions are made— those that directly impact the quality of life on campus—and to choose committee assignments with the same care.

The burden of numerous committee assignments on top of excessive teaching loads and requisite community service is further exacerbated by the academic environment in which the rules for attaining academic success are not explicitly delineated. For example, African American women are expected to assume the responsibility for mentoring all African American students in an effort to contribute to their social and emotional adjustment on a hostile, predominantly white campus while at the same time trying to cope with their own professional isolation. Obscurity of rules makes their socialization and adjustment to their campus environment difficult and greatly diminishes their effectiveness in achieving their established goals, and at the same time helping others.

Furthermore, in evaluating faculty for tenure and promotion, most universities assess candidates on research and publication, teaching effectiveness, and service to the academic department and the college community at large. The latter is much less valued by those institutions that grant large numbers of doctorates or by those receiving a significant proportion of their external research funding from federal sources. In such situations, African American women are at once placed at a definite disadvantage for tenure and promotion.

Research and Publication

Despite their lack of sponsorship and the double-duty service that is forced upon them, African American women do engage in research, one of the most important areas they must be judged effective in to gain tenure and promotion. This area is a major concern, however, for the African American woman, particularly on the predominantly white campus, because their research and publication records are scrutinized more severely than their white counterparts. Their research is often described as having no substance or theoretical value, and publication is deemed acceptable only when it is in a mainstream journal. Thus much of what African American women publish is negated because their colleagues often do not recognize their publication in minority journals or simply discredit any research on minority issues.[8] Research on women's issues and interdisciplinary areas such as women's studies and ethnic studies is often especially discounted during tenure review, with the result that African American women, who tend to participate more in both of these areas than their white colleagues, are doubly disadvantaged.[9]

In an effort to satisfy tenure and promotion requirements, the African American woman faculty member is often placed in the position of choosing a research topic that will reflect Eurocentric hegemonic thinking about the "race" and "gender" questions, which negates the position of blacks generally, black women, and other underrepresented groups in the United States. How does one remain true to oneself and simultaneously gain respect for the work that is being conducted outside the dominant paradigm?

If the work being conducted produces findings contrary to popular thinking, major journal editors, considering their readership, may have little interest in its focus and thus reject the manuscript that describes it, causing the writer to question her ability to write, conduct research, or communicate premises. Few African Americans publish works in "top" journals. Does this negate their scholarly capabilities? The attitude that deters African American scholars from conducting research on their own groups has far-reaching effects for them. However, the volume of African American women's voices is gradually being raised to reflect information and experiences that are not captured in the literature on African Americans or that on women generally in American society.

Another concern is that the majority of research on African Americans reflects the lower socioeconomic class of individuals, and thus the generalizations are made from that group. The challenge, then, is to select a research agenda that does not negate self but adds to the collective knowledge in the field and gains recognition for one's approach to intellectual development. The bind is double for the African American woman.

The quality and validity of research methods and theories are challenged as a result of the race/gender overlap. Any challenges to current thinking are viewed negatively because standard descriptions and designations of African Americans are often under attack. In the evaluation process, it is essential to acknowledge the hostilities and controversies associated with the research topic in order to avoid self-doubt. One possibility is that the mainstream journal editors do not wish to engage in an intellectual discussion that challenges traditional thinking about the issues of race and gender, or perhaps they do not consider their journals the proper fora for the work for which the African American female scholar wishes to be known.

This realization raises the question of peer identification. If you are an African American female academic trying to do the research and publication that will help you gain tenure, you must ask yourself what are the characteristics of the audience you are targeting? Does it read the journal to which you have submitted? Whose opinion do you value? Is the editorial board familiar with the orientation of the research you are conducting or with the theoretical assumptions you are questioning? At this juncture, it is important to educate your colleagues about new trends that may involve alternative approaches to research, including qualitative techniques, historical perspectives, or other avenues that may be race- and gender-specific. Increasingly also, African Americans' scholarship is becoming more interdisciplinary.

In addition to the type of research problem and methodology, institutions of higher education have used research funding to deny African American women tenure and promotion. The amount and kind of research they can do are related to the funds available. The amount of funding and the nature of the research problem selected depend on the willingness of private and public agencies to fund them.

For African American women who have developed grant-writing skills, it is essential that proposal reviewers be familiar with their research area. Frequently granting agencies will request a list of recommended reviewers for the researcher's work as well as a list of persons who are hostile to the research agenda or whose perspective may be on the opposite end of the spectrum. The lack of knowledge of such strategies may well account for the fact that grant submission rates are lower among African Americans and lower still for African American women. Grant writing was once perceived as a strictly meritorious means of getting awards, with the submissions of the highest quality being accepted for publication or the best ideas being recommended for funding. This formula works in ideal settings where the playing field is both equal and level. Writing grants that get projects funded takes some measure of ingenuity and political awareness. Political awareness in this case translates into having colleagues pass information along in a timely fashion with suggestions as well as having the ability to get the content of one's work recognized during the blind review.

Teaching

Even in the face of an irrefutably excellent record in grantsmanship and publishing, "poor teaching" is sometimes cited as a reason for denying tenure and promotion to African American women. Can one receive tenure and promotion for teaching excellence? Are the rewards of recognition and higher pay greater for teaching or for research? Communicating one's expertise in the classroom is an essential part of an academic career in higher education. As important as the teaching role is in the academy, however, it has only been in recent years that assessment techniques have been developed to assist the faculty member in developing teaching strategies that work. The debate continues on whether or not the academy will recognize and reward good teaching or will it redefine teaching as a scholarly endeavor.

As the controversy continues over teaching versus research, many innovations are on the horizon for helping teachers develop excellence in teaching. Documenting good teaching is essential in the tenure portfolio. Recommendations from students, classroom climate, and motivation of students are criteria that are sometimes used to determine the level of quality being generated in the classroom by teacher-scholars. For African American women who are employed in tenure-track positions in predominantly white institutions, the difficulties will often arise in the unspoken questioning of authority or perceived lack of knowledge. Many college students are encountering an African American female in the classroom for the first time. Biases among these students often result in negative teacher evaluations.

Women are often assigned heavier teaching loads and more introductory courses than are their male counterparts. They also tend to use more participatory classroom teaching techniques, which are often evaluated unfavorably by male faculty as lacking rigor and by students of both sexes as weak if they have been socialized to interpret nurturant behavior in this way.[10]

African American teachers are often expected to take on the additional responsibility of mentoring students who otherwise would not be likely to receive support in the academy. This added burden is not always acknowledged and accounted for in the tenure and promotion review. Documentation is essential to provide proof of this addition to the role of teaching.

In the era of downsizing and smaller student enrollment, higher education is focusing on its role in educating the student, which is defined primarily as teaching. If African American women become increasingly engaged in the teaching function, will the necessary voices committed to alternative research perspectives and scholarly publications become silent? Can the professor's time continue to be balanced between teaching and writing? If the time is not available to African American women to provide intellectual discussion and dissemination of the issues affecting their well-being in the academy, who provides the medium through which they are viewed and reviewed for tenure?

Conclusion

Since institutions of higher education have many unwritten rules, various approaches to granting tenure and promotion are used, including guidelines that range from very vague to very specific rituals, mechanisms, and strategies. To help African American women cope with the obscurity of guidelines and navigate the rough waters of the tenure and promotion review process, I offer these suggestions: (1) Develop a ten-year career plan, including research and networking. Doing good work is not enough; an excellent research portfolio must be supported by faculty allies for the review process. (2) Make research a top priority. Seek facilities and outside funding. (3) Work with other faculty members on your campus through a faculty women's association or related organization. (4) Explore options for making the tenure system more flexible, such as stopping the tenure clock for a year for the birth or adoption of a child and for medical and family emergencies. (5) Evaluate research that uses interdisciplinary approaches and examines nontraditional topics on a par with more conventional work. Often scholarship by African Americans about other African Americans is not made available because it is not published in mainstream journals that are assigned in graduate school.

These suggestions will not solve all problems, but at the very least they should help African American women begin to think about how to claim a place within the academy through tenure and promotion.

Notes

1. American Association of University Women, *Women and Tenure: The Opportunity of a Century* (Washington, D.C.: American Association of University Women, 1989).

2. Athena Theodore, *The Campus Troublemakers: Academic Women in Protest* (Houston: Cap and Gown, 1986).

3. William Moore Jr. and Lonnie H. Wagstaff, *Black Educators in White Colleges* (San Francisco: Jossey-Bass, 1974).

4. L. A. Valverde, "Promotion Socialization: The Informal Process in Large Urban Districts and Its Adverse Effects on Nonwhites and Women," paper presented at the American Educational Research Association Convention, Boston, April 8, 1980.

5. American Association of University Women, *Women and Tenure*.

6. Nadya Aisenberg and Mona Harrington, *Women of Academe: Outsiders in the Sacred Grove* (Amherst: University of Massachusetts Press, 1988).

7. American Association of University Women, *Women and Tenure*.

8. Michelle Howard-Vital, "African American Women in Higher Education: Struggling to Gain Identity," *Journal of Black Studies* 20, no. 2 (December 1989): 180–91.

9. J. J. Irvine, "The Black Female Academic: Doubly Burdened or Doubly Blessed?" in *Stepping off the Pedestal: Academic Women in the South,* edited by Patricia Stringer and Irene Thompson (New York: Modern Language Association, 1982), 109–19; see also American Association of University Women, *Women and Tenure*.

10. Aisenberg and Harrington, *Women of Academe*.

Chapter 20

Collegiality in the Academy
Where Does the Black Woman Fit?

J. Nefta Baraka

In this chapter I employ an intercultural communication framework to explain how racial and sexual stereotypes and behaviors hinder the collegial experiences of African American women in higher education. In the ideal culture of the academy, collegiality can, according to Yolanda Moses, "foster a sense of community as well as an atmosphere of creativity where people can share ideas, collaborate, and generally benefit from working together."[1] Racial and sexual stereotypes, however, particularly on white campuses, create a missing link in their collegial experiences. So where does the black woman fit in institutions of higher learning that are finishing schools for notions of European superiority? Since the values and procedures of other cultures are met with resistance and negative judgments, African American women's contributions to the academy are not always appreciated. Consequently they experience tension between participation practices of the academy and understanding the destructiveness of the hegemonic cultural values to the African American community. Cultural hegemony in the United States has rendered the meaning of "American" as synonymous to "whites of European descent."

Hence I turn to intercultural communication theory to illustrate how collegiality for the African American woman in the academy sits precariously within the context of racial and cultural assumptions, values, philosophies, and behaviors of members of the dominant culture. *Intercultural Communication* is an interaction process between people from different cultural backgrounds. The discipline of intercultural communication focuses on cultural factors that impede communication among or between persons or groups of different cultures. Intercultural communication theorists believe that "the core difficulty in cross-cultural interaction is a failure to recognize relevant cultural differences."[2]

After centuries of denial by both blacks and whites, the United States is coming to grips with the reality that Americans of African descent represent a cultural entity that is distinct from the white majority in worldview, values, assumptions, and behaviors. In American society, "culture," "ethnicity," and "race" are used interchangeably to describe African Americans and other ethnic groups distinctive from the white majority. Being born black does not automatically make one share Afrocentric culture, but it *does* make one subject to socially significant attitudes toward differences in appearance, speech, and behavior, some of which are culturally distinct from those of the white majority.

While acknowledging a continuum of adaptive stages of African culture that has been extensively influenced by an alien culture, I also acknowledge that individuals so influenced vary in the extent to which they retain the core values of their own culture or become assimilated into another culture. This discussion, however, is focused on actual Afrocentric culture rather than violations of it or adaptations of it, which either create the illusion of a third culture or confuse people into believing in the melting-pot myth that makes us "all Americans" — or white. Excluding those marginal experiences, the persistent schism between the majority of blacks and white America reveals differences in *procedural culture* rooted in different deep culture values, assumptions, and philosophies. These differences provide built-in conflict between the dominant culture in America and all others. *Espoused cultural values* and what is actually practiced represent *deep culture* values in dominant American cultural patterns. *Procedural culture* is "a complex [social] pattern with a goal orientation that combines surface behavior and *deep culture* in a specific context of application."[3] Deep culture is "knowing what," and procedural culture is "knowing how." Intercultural communication, therefore, is made difficult between blacks and whites in the academy by differences in communication styles, in the role of emotion in human behavior, in beliefs about equality and progress, and in practices around beliefs about affiliation versus individuality. Additionally, misunderstanding is caused by white confusion of collegiality and friendship and by the imposition of standards affected by peculiarities of Euro-American ethnocentrism.

I. Deep Culture Differences

African and African American values are located on the "group/being" end of the procedural culture continuum in contrast to values evident in the opposite Euro-American "individual/doing" end of the continuum. African Americans value group orientation, cooperation, time to serve the purpose of living, indirectness in communication, hierarchical relationships, and the value of a person in simply "being." Euro-American deep culture values include individualism, competition, time as equal to money, directness in communication; egalitarian relationships between people, and a "doing" orientation toward human activity.[4] African Americans value interdependence and mutual aid, spiritualism, and reverence for elders. Conversely, the white majority values independence, materialism, and youth worship.[5] Racism and sexism are exacerbated by these important differences in procedural culture and become problematic in interactions between the African American woman and her white colleagues. I shall turn to these differences in cultural styles.

Differences in Communication Styles

In American culture, a premium is placed on facts, logical analysis, and practical results. These depend upon a style of conversation known as *linear*. Speakers come to the point by moving in a straight line of logical thought to an explicitly stated conclusion with no digressions and few contextual comments. Americans deeply believe in this sparse communication as a way to quantify the world. It is difficult for them to understand the reactions of others to this style of communication, in which the message is based more on what is stated than on what is not.[6] This is *low context* communication, which is more or less independent of the circumstances in which it takes place and is problematic to most of the rest of the world population, which bases communication on an entirely different set of assumptions.

Non-Western cultures and countries assume that communication supports relationships, that the listener will be actively engaged in taking responsibility to understand the speaker, and that meaning is drawn from the circumstances surrounding the words that are spoken as well as the words themselves. Most of the rest of the world therefore engages in what is called *phatic communication*, which includes small talk, rituals of communication, and other practices aimed at maintaining or developing human relations for the purpose of social processing.[7] It is a communication style that is *contextual* in that speakers establish the context in which a conclusion can be reached, but materials need not be presented in any particular order. It is the listener's responsibility to divine the conclusion implied by the context, and, in some cases, listeners are expected to discern the theme rather than to prod for the main point or the problem.

Cultural differences are aggravated by ethnocentric communications that seem to evaluate African American views and expressions negatively. The likely defensive reaction that follows an ethnocentric message from a white person results in a *mutual negative evaluation* between that person and someone of a different culture. Often in black-white dialogue, attempts to overcome the negative reactions of blacks to a white ethnocentric comment further exacerbate tension as ethnocentric procedures are used. The communication event deteriorates even further into a *regressive spiral*, in which negative evaluations are intensified. The white person accuses the African American woman of "ambiguity," then "evasiveness," "deviousness," "deception," and finally spirals down to "dishonesty." On the other side, the African American woman finds her white colleague "immature," then "impolite," "brash," "impertinent," and finally "offensive." In this pattern, the actions of each person intensify the reactions of the other.[8]

Different Attitudes Toward Emotion

Sophisticated new forms of racism are every bit as crippling to the professional advancement of the African American woman as was the old. For example, the African American woman is subtly penalized if she expresses emotion in the same way with whites as she does within the safety of her own cultural group. One colleague, a woman serving on a curriculum committee, was outraged to hear a white male colleague say, "If there is a black culture, and I am not convinced that there is one . . ." Her justifiable anger at his rudeness and arrogance was met with "hurt feelings" by some white colleagues. They believed the existence of African American culture could be reduced to a subject of discussion using the "scientific method" and that she was being unreasonable to accept such a premise as insulting. Her feelings about the dismissive rudeness of the remark were of no consequence to them.

Stewart and Bennett, in *American Cultural Patterns*, noted that "a strong convention to preserve surface cordiality renders emotion and social feelings into undercurrents in American human affairs. Americans consider emotions to be essentially outside the range of willful control, distrusted as guides for behavior, and essentially neglected in communication. African-Americans are more likely to believe that high levels of emotion can be controlled and thus are more comfortable with relatively intense emotional expression."[9] In dialogue, deep culture fears that whites have of blacks cause them to overreact to any emotion, real or imagined, displayed by blacks. Stewart and Bennett also observed that "in arguments between American blacks and whites, whites commonly react to the raised voice and facial set of blacks, but they may fail to perceive the presence or absence of change in personal distance accompanying the vocal and facial cues. For blacks, change in distance is the crucial cue that indicates whether or not the confrontation is physically threatening."[10]

Distinctions in confrontation styles are problematic to whites who are uncomfortable with those different from themselves. They strain for common ground; "searching for the familiar and failing to recognize cultural differences, they may interpret clashing styles of thinking as social conflict."[11]

Differences in Beliefs About Equality

To African Americans, whites often appear schizophrenic in their practice of their stated values—particularly in their notions of how to practice the value of equality. Cose describes a climate of silence regarding the white norm of inequality toward African Americans in saying, "Even more damaging than self-imposed silence [of African Americans] are the lies that seem an integral part of America's approach to race. From simple self-deception as claiming 'colorblindness' to unwillingness to acknowledge the existence of racial bias, untruthfulness masks solutions to America's enduring racial problems."[12] The American assumption that "all men are created equal" delineates sharply divergent experiences between whites and African Americans. Frequent American violations of the assumptions of equality, while continuing to insist upon it as an ideal, illustrate an American inclination to perpetuate a value through a social norm that is part illusion and part reality. African American cultural differences have been stigmatized by the white majority and dealt with by different social norms. Whites consider it impolite to discuss minority-group differences in public. "The effect of this conspiracy of silence is to perpetuate the stigma attached to the different cultural patterns of some Americans."[13]

Affiliation Versus Individuality

A major contributor to black-white tension is the clash in procedural cultures expressing the Eurocentric value of individualism and the Afrocentric value of affiliation.[14] Euro-Americans are unlikely to suspend judgment about differences in behavior because they assume, unconsciously, that their own ways are normal, natural, and right. Those of other cultures, therefore, must be abnormal, unnatural, and wrong. For example, African American assumptions are based upon *relational thinking*, which involves a high degree of sensitivity to context, relationships, and status.[15] Relational thinking is oriented to the past and turns for guidance to tradition and to those who have gone before. African American women value harmony in relationships as prerequisites for group accomplishment; accommodating differences to bring harmony between opposites is one of their consummate relationship skills. It is the African American woman who attunes herself to the needs of others.

African American women work in a climate of embedded notions of individualism and white supremacy that tinges every practice from performance evaluation to organizational mission statements to budget priorities. Individualism intrudes into each domain of activity. The American self, dependent on external evidence of "doing" rather than functioning as an expression of internal integration, encourages notions of supremacy of the individual in his or her activities. People who do not locate the self within the individual are bewildering to most Americans. That the self can be centered in a role or in a grouping of some sort is to them a culturally preposterous idea.[16]

American individualism and self-centeredness are problematic to the African American woman, who strives to balance her many roles and responsibilities in both her personal and professional life. She is not only a professional educator with identifiable rank and position; she is also someone's daughter, granddaughter, mother, sister, niece, and so on. For her, family status and responsibility must be upheld. Deferential address to elders, concern for all children in the family and community, and formal address to those outside the family circle mark personal boundaries to identify status differences between those within the extended family and community and those who are not.

Self-centered individualism, accompanied by the values of competition, and achievement for self-glorification pervade the academic climate and cripple chances for collegiality. Language expressing concern for the good of the total society is missing in dialogue about realities of cultural pluralism versus individual rights and equality.

Friendship and Collegiality

Collegiality is confused with friendship in a climate dominated by a broad definition of friendship. "An American friend may refer to any one from a passing acquaintance to a lifetime intimate."[17] Tension is created when varying views of friendship come together in the academy. Whites, lacking understanding or respect for boundaries of the African American woman's personal, cultural, and professional space, exhibit behaviors that exacerbate alienation between both cultures. For example, some white colleagues were unable to comprehend why a young African American woman became upset when they took sips from her drink, helped themselves to a taste of food from her plate, or touched her hair. They then behaved as if *she* was the one whose behavior was a violation of the norm and felt hurt and bewildered at what they perceived to be a rejection of their "friendship" — never concerning themselves with the legitimacy of the African American woman's viewpoint.

Euro-American Ethnocentrism

Under circumstances of contrasting values, assumptions, and worldviews in the academy, the African American woman must constantly handle the tension between dominant group misconceptions about her and her knowledge of her true self as tremendously capable and resourceful. American feelings of superiority are derived not only from their negative conditioning about dark skin color but also from ethnocentrism. From an ethnocentric vantage point, her white colleagues consider the African American woman a polar opposite of the privileged white male. Black, woman, and competent professional are paradoxes in the eyes of white society, conditioned by stereotypical expectations of servitude from African women. According to K. Sue Jewell, "African American women have the least common physical attributes compared to white men who belong to the privileged class."[18] The African American woman is neither white nor male. She brings to the academy her values and the ability to express them in powerful ways that are not understood by the white majority and those black men who have totally adapted to a Eurocentric worldview. What results is a climate of tension that mostly affects the African American woman.

II. The Clash of Culture, Race, and Gender in the Academy

African American women must cope with tensions arising from the values of achievement and competition as a mode of social interaction. The competitive American way, which has also been adopted by some black men, creates a setting in which "participants may perceive themselves as adversaries, each striving to achieve his or her own personal goals in relationships . . . such actions can assume the proportions of coercion to foreigners [and ethnic American minorities] with more affiliative tendencies."[19] This coercive and competitive climate yields little empathy for the needs of the African American woman.

Combined with racism, a competitive climate makes the African American woman an easy target for stress. These forces are what Tatum calls "mundane extreme environmental stress" (MEES), in which "the many forms of racism and oppression are an ever present part of daily living rather than occasional hazards." For the African American professional, these "chronic, unpredictable acts of racism . . . and MEES, which is anticipated, ongoing and pervasive" result in what she calls "assimilation blues."[20] All adjustment to the newly "diverse" environment is expected to take place through the conforming behavior of the newcomers, as was the case with European immigrants whose similar racial characteristics allowed easier assimilation.

The Eurocentric academy most readily embraces those African Americans who divest themselves of their culture and heritage to become more acceptably European and limit their interests to "black" or "gender" issues. Cose reported that "many blacks who have made huge efforts to get the right education, master the right accent, and dress in the proper clothes still find that certain doors never seem to open, that there are private clubs—in both a real and a symbolic sense—they cannot join . . . regardless of talent, hard work, and outstanding accomplishments."[21]

Institutions appear incapable of envisioning black talent put to use in any area other than service to blacks or other minorities. Paradoxically, if from those positions one advocates for the elimination of racism or addresses "the fear of being forced to shed one's identity in order to prosper,"[22] the African American risks being labeled a "troublemaker" and "undesirable," or "not a team player." Whites become focused on externals in avoidance of the *cause* of the advocacy as they react to *how* the advocacy is expressed. As a result, "many blacks find their voices stilled when sensitive racial issues are raised."[23]

In predominantly white institutions, the paradox of underattention and overattention is experienced by black women. On one hand, black women and their comments may be ignored in some classes and in seminars while, on the other hand, they may be called upon to represent their race."[24] The visible/invisible paradox experienced by the African American woman is reflected in the results of my comparative study of African American and white women in a sample of 576 successful women. A third of the African American women in the study reported the experience of having their contributions to a discussion ignored by whites who would talk only to each other.[25]

While she is managing a disproportionate work load, the African American woman's understanding of a broad range of academic concerns is relegated to a supportive rather than leadership role in the minds of whites and some black men. One African American woman member of a committee on multicultural education expressed her views in a meeting and was told by her white colleague chairing the committee that she would have to withhold her views and wait for the rest of the committee to catch up with her level of understanding of the issue.

The recurrence of such incidents and the pressure to conform or to be invisible contribute to a climate of MEES within and outside of the academy, rendering collegiality for the African American difficult to achieve and maintain.

III. The Solutions: Bicultural Competence and White Responsibility

As the African American woman in the Eurocentric academy works to develop expertise and authority in her chosen field, she balances her cultural values, beliefs, philosophies, and behaviors with those that are fundamentally different from her own in interpersonal interactions. She is challenged to balance her perception of herself as derived from her own cultural reality with that of the contrived image of her held by the dominant culture. She negotiates success around the unexamined conditioning of whites who think of blacks in stereotypical terms ranging between indifference and hostility to a more "benign" expectation that the African American woman will somehow apply herself to meeting the nurturing needs and expectations of whites.

Most conscious African American women have no choice but to develop coping skills to deal with the misperceptions of the majority. Part of the coping mechanism is the development or strengthening of an Afrocentric worldview and advocacy for whites to claim responsibility for reducing conflict in the academy rather than pressuring everyone else to conform to their ways.

According to Asante and Davis,

> although it is generally acceded that blacks are more likely to possess "bicultural competence," little research has been done on the effect of the lack of such bicultural competence on the part of white employers, supervisors, and managers on intercultural and interracial communication. . . . A true picture of the interracial encounter in the workplace cannot be separated from all the other aspects of society. If we are talking about communication between people of different cultural and racial backgrounds, we are also talking about historical, functional, and structural differences in the way they approach interaction.[26]

In the academy, the diminished capacity of whites to accept expressions of ethnic, racial, and cultural differences severely limits their recognition of the authority of African American colleagues. At odds is the African American belief in education as a vehicle for uplift and enrichment of both one's self and one's community, on the one hand, and the Euro-American view that "education improves the individual who is then transformed by experience into a rational manipulator and controller of the environment,"[27] on the other.

The parasitical nature of white freedom complicates collegiality in the academy. Whenever the two races and cultures come in contact, the black woman faces challenges arising from racial attitudes of her white peers, both male and female. The African American woman has become a part of white America's avoidance and denial mechanism as African Americans are used as a metaphor in the struggles of white women and other groups. Blacks are continually cast as "the other" as we have been diluted and expanded from "colored" to "minority" to "multicultural" to "diverse" to accommodate the white conceptual framework. Once again, the unfinished African American agenda is pushed into the background of a collective white psyche suddenly preoccupied with championing the cause of new "others." The African American woman academic attempting to illuminate and communicate any reality of black life is often responded to *by Whites*, heretofore silent but now quick to defend inclusion, with the statement "It's not *just* a black-white thing; what about _____?" Fill in Hispanic, Asian, Native American, or whatever group the white speaker would rather think about than African Americans. The African American woman in such a setting strives for collegiality with people who view her as an outsider coming to fulfill a specific, narrow purpose.

Advocacy and support for training and development of a majority in areas of intercultural sensitivity should be the responsibility of everyone in the academy and accompanied by calls for whites to recognize, claim, and correct their own racial conditioning, unconscious acts of racial bias, and lack of multicultural competence. Only through a more central role of the white majority will the academy recognize the regressive spirals that seem to emanate from dominant group behavior and become institutions of higher learning where the African American woman can truly fit with shared authority among colleagues who recognize her as a person of equal rank, position, or background—as peer—and where intercultural communication skills are modeled by all colleagues in the academy for generations to come.

Notes

1. Yolanda T. Moses, *Black Women in Academe: Issues and Strategies* (Washington, D.C.: Project on the Status and Education of Women, Association of American Colleges, August 1989), 18.

2. Marshall Singer, *Intercultural Communication: A Perceptual Approach* (Englewood Cliffs, N.J.: Prentice-Hall, 1987), 68.

3. Edward C. Stewart and Milton J. Bennett, *American Cultural Patterns: A Cross-Cultural Perspective* (Yarmouth, Maine: Intercultural Press, 1991), 149.

4. Janet Bennett and Milton Bennett, *Communication Perspectives: Diversity in Values* (Portland, Oreg.: Intercultural Communication Institute, 1990).

5. Nsenga Warfield-Coppock, "The Rites of Passage Movement: A Resurgence of African-Centered Practices for Socializing African American Youth," *Journal of Negro Education* 61, no. 4 (1992): 471.

6. Stewart and Bennett, *American Cultural Patterns*, 126.

7. Ibid., 154.

8. Ibid., 165.

9. Ibid., 150.

10. Ibid., 59.

11. Ibid., 29.

12. Ellis Cose, *The Rage of the Privileged Class* (New York: Harper Collins, 1993), 56–68.

13. Stewart and Bennett, *American Cultural Patterns*, 93.

14. Linda J. Myers, *Understanding an Afrocentric World View: Introduction to an Optimal Psychology* (Dubuque, Iowa: Kendall/Hunt, 1988), 44.

15. Stewart and Bennett, *American Cultural Patterns*, 3, 42.

16. Ibid., 129, 132, 142–43.

17. Ibid., 101

18. K. Sue Jewell, *From Mammy to Miss America and Beyond: Cultural Images and the Shaping of U.S. Social Policy* (New York: Routledge, 1993), 7.

19. Anne Wilson Schaef, *Women's Reality: An Emerging Female System in a White Male Society* (New York: Harper and Row, 1985), 105.

20. Beverly D. Tatum, *Assimilation Blues: Black Families in a White Community* (Northampton, Mass: Hazel-Maxwell, 1992), 9.

21. Cose, *The Rage of the Privileged Class*, 56–68.

22. Ibid.

23. Ibid.

24. Moses, *Black Women in Academe*, 2–3.

25. Jeanne Baraka-Love, "Successful Women: A Racial Comparison of Variables Contributing to Socialization and Leadership Development" (Ph.D. dissertation, Western Michigan University, Kalamazoo, 1986), 194.

26. Molefi K. Asante, William B. Gudykunst, and Eileen Newmark, *Handbook of International and Intercultural Communication* (Newbury Park, Calif.: Sage, 1989), 386.

27. Stewart and Bennett, *American Cultural Patterns*, 114.

Chapter 21

The Dynamics of Patriarchal Meritocracy in the Academy

A Case Study

Saliwe M. Kawewe

American colleges and universities claim that they pursue excellence in academia, which is reflected by meritocracy and is measured in the categories of teaching, research, and service. The reality is that universities reflect a universal patriarchal model of administration, education, research, evaluation, and distribution of power. Molded on the pattern of Western male dominance, American institutions of higher education mirror the values of racism and sexism inherent in Western traditions. What this implies is that the processes of employment, retention, and tenure are shaped by the racist and sexist choices and preferences of the most dominant and powerful group in academia.

The case study that follows is my own experiences as an international black woman on a journey that has covered one historically black and three predominantly white undergraduate public universities, all of which supposedly emphasized teaching over research and service.

Because they purport to seek the truth about the universe, universities claim to have a motto of academic freedom. The practical truth is that no such academic freedom exists except in relative terms. The lack of academic freedom and my concern for the consequences will limit the information to be divulged or shared here. Because of the controversial nature of some of the subject matter, no specific institutions or persons will be identified by name.

I have both an international and American academic and employment background. I got my elementary, secondary, and undergraduate education in Zimbabwe, Tanzania, and Zambia respectively. I earned a master's degree in social work and a doctorate from two private universities in Missouri. I sought employment in academia with ten years of work experience in the United States and abroad.

As I began my academic job search, I responded to a few advertisements in the National Association of Social Work's newsletter. At the invitation of the director of a social work department, I flew to my first interview, only to find upon landing that there was no one to meet me. The director, a white male, showed up about an hour later and offered no explanation or apology for his tardiness. This is a well-respected professional in my field, and he displayed such ill feelings toward me that I knew by the time I interviewed that I could not work in that setting.

My next interview was at a Southern university, where the enthusiasm and eagerness of the chair to hire me complemented my desperation to become a professor. I was offered, and accepted, an entry-level position at a corresponding salary. One white female and two white males, all Ph.D.s, joined me as new faculty members in the department, and the commonality of our experiences brought us together to seek mutual support. I was the only black person in the department, which consisted of three women and nine white men. At the outset, I overheard the chair telling the new white female faculty member not to divulge the fact that she had been given transportation and moving expenses by the university, because I had been denied these emoluments.

The department housed four disciplines—sociology, geography, social welfare, and criminal justice. The social welfare program, in which I was employed, also included two tenured white faculty members, a female and a male, the latter of whom was the social work program director. They were both cold toward me, and I learned later that they had opposed my appointment.

At the end of my first two semesters, I was told that if my students' evaluations of my teaching did not improve, my employment at the university would be at stake. I had no previous experience in undergraduate instruction, so I accepted some advice from a female faculty member and solicited verbal and written comments from students on how to improve my teaching. By the end of my third semester, I had earned the highest evaluations in the department.

Sexual and racial discrimination, as well as xenophobia, then began to surface. One white male faculty in the geography wing of the department told me that I, an African woman, had nothing to offer to Americans, and therefore I should not be teaching in the United States.

At the end of two-and-a-half years, I returned to Zimbabwe for what I intended to be a one-month visit. I had visa problems, however, and was delayed for eight months pending the receipt of a new visa. The chair of my department sent an ultimatum that if I were not back on the job by a certain date, I would be given a year's notice of termination, under the terms of my contract. I failed to meet his deadline, and, true to his word, the chair terminated my employment.

With a year's grace period, I began to search for a job elsewhere and was pleased to receive an offer from a historically black university in the Midwest. I readily accepted, feeling that I would not be confronted there with the racism and xenophobia that had prevailed at the predominantly white institution in the South. I joined an unaccredited undergraduate social welfare program with one faculty member, a black female, who was also chair. Here I became the victim of exploitation. The chair, supposedly engaged in seeking program accreditation, assigned me to teach all of the courses offered, which meant that I taught three classes daily on a quarter system. I felt clearly discriminated against in a historically black university on the basis of nationality.

With the permission of the chair, I had my mail forwarded to her home address while I was trying to get settled, but I did not always receive my letters. I had flooded the market with letters of application when I was searching for employment, and strangely enough, the only responses the chair gave me were those that indicated that there were no jobs available.

I established good rapport with my students and enjoyed the teaching experience. The chair, however, seemed to have a need to be in control and began to act in a manner that was very disrespectful to me. When I told her that I was concerned that I had not been receiving my mail, she became very angry. She visited my classes and became engaged in an argument with the students and was very disruptive. I determined that I would have to leave the university.

I began my job search and went for an interview during a school break. When I did not receive any responses in a reasonable amount of time, I called the university and was told that a letter offering me a position had been sent to the chair's address the week before. I was told, further, that the chair and the dean had contacted them in an effort to discourage them from hiring me, but to no avail.

I accepted a new position at a prestigious predominantly white undergraduate public university in the Southeast. The social work program was well focused, though it was program driven because of the preference of the two senior faculty members. Sometimes I felt that academic freedom was undermined. Yet I found the university's atmosphere congenial, and I quickly gained visibility. I was again, however, the only black woman on a social work faculty of two white men and one white woman, the chair. I shared office space with a white male, who was also a new appointee. We experienced a few problems based on racism and politics, and I was finally given office space in a new location.

I enjoyed a very rewarding teaching experience in this university and was given good evaluations by my students. But I realized after a year that if I wanted to gain tenure, I would have to do more than just excel in teaching. My teaching load was heavy, and with other assigned duties, I had little time left for research and publication. I felt that in order to fulfill this necessary requirement, I would have to move on to a university that offered more research opportunities. I was content with my income; the department, however, had limited resources, lacked flexibility, distributed work loads unfairly, promoted sexual and racial stereotypes, and lacked departmental support for research and scholarship. My prospects of tenure thus appeared bleak. I decided to seek other employment.

I have been working in my current setting for more than three years. Although gender and racial discrimination and xenophobic attitudes exist here too, I have research opportunities. In addition, the university gives tangible incentives in the form of its allocation of teaching loads to nontenured faculty.

The first two years of work here were a challenge. For example, my authority was undermined by a senior faculty member, who took over one of my classes as a result of my absence because of family illness. I had just returned test results to my students at the previous class meeting, and the senior faculty member spent the whole class session facilitating and entertaining student complaints about me in this human behavior class. After three weeks, I just happened to hear what had transpired from a student who had attempted to defend me during the class. When I confronted the senior faculty member, he attempted to simplify matters with the response that students were just venting their anger because they had not done well on their first test.

On one occasion I had to make arrangements for a student to take a make-up examination on a Saturday because she had been involved in an automobile accident and had no transportation during the week except after 4:00 in the afternoon. This same student bought an airline ticket to visit her parents and was scheduled to depart before the exam. I told her she would have to change her departure time to accommodate the final exam schedule. Because her parents had connections with some senior university officials, I was attacked by the department head, who told me that I didn't deserve what I was being paid. He also claimed that many students had come to him to complain about me. When my program director asked him later how many complaints he had received, he said three. I had a phone call from a senior administrator who accused me of being "a stumbling block." He told me to fax the exam to the student, which I did. On the day the exam was scheduled, efforts to contact the university where the student was to take the exam were in vain because that university was closed. The student took the exam unmonitored. As a nontenured, black international faculty member, I felt that this incident was a misuse and abuse of power. I later learned that the department head had opposed my appointment and had mobilized groups of students to subvert my authority.

The environment has been less than accepting of me. Racism, sexism, and xenophobic attitudes of students and faculty are key factors in creating a hostile climate. The climate is further complicated by faculty politics. Although competition is keen among faculty, black women are not expected to compete successfully. The discrimination and low expectations seem more intense if the black woman has no American roots. Seemingly, when those expectations are contradicted, desperation appears to infiltrate the other faculty and lead them to use students against the black woman.

When I moved from the previous institutions, teaching had been my greatest strength. When I came to the current setting, the teaching evaluations were low, but the students' comments were generally worded similarly, reflecting a bias. I have since earned improved teaching evaluations, but overall evaluations by those in positions of power reflect the past. I received an excellence in teaching award from the Mortar Board Society; I have letters from students who have graduated and from current students who are appreciative of my teaching skills; and I had high teaching evaluations in summer classes. None of the above were incorporated in the annual tenure and promotion evaluations. The tenured faculty excluded this information in forwarding my reappointment and tenure review documents to the higher levels of the university. I have not pursued this for fear of being called a troublemaker.

I have also volunteered at an elementary school since I began working, and at the end of my fifth semester, I was told that volunteering at a school is "good citizenship but does not count for community service in tenure and promotion considerations," although it counted during the other four semesters. The rules were changed in the middle of the game. The splitting of hairs does not stop here; now I am asked to prove that I have submitted chapters and manuscripts for publication by giving copies to the tenure and promotion committee. I am required to publish during the third year of employment, although I have not been given a clearly stated number of publications for tenure eligibility. Depending on the source, it ranges from three to six.

The path to tenure is further complicated by other departmental duties, which place a strain on untenured faculty. For example, our department was once a program in a different department and has now earned full departmental status in another school. We are, however, preparing for reaccreditation, which is a major undertaking for faculty. The department is understaffed, and I am assigned equal work with tenured faculty but am expected to find time to accommodate the efforts described above. I recently turned down an extra teaching load to cover for a vacant position. This negatively affects tenure. I must be cooperative or there will be no job for me.

Many racist, sexist, and xenophobic discriminatory actions have been displayed in my present academic milieu, but I cannot point them out because I fear reprisal. Overall I have lived up to the terms of my contract. Yet discriminatory remarks have been made about my inability to understand the American way because I am from a different culture. I have been blamed for problems of a dysfunctional department. White colleges can simply imply that you cannot get along, regardless of how good you are in teaching, research, service, and collegiality. It appears easier to blame a black female than to attempt to find a remedy for the situation. I can only hope that my colleagues recognize my efforts and view me as an asset rather than a threat.

Three common themes and assumptions have infiltrated my employment experiences in the academy: (1) that I should appreciate whatever treatment I get because I come from a Third World country; (2) that I am subjected to the Western supremacist view that demeans the role of women; and (3) that I am not worthy as a human being and do not deserve respect and dignity.

Even with my experience, I consider the pursuit of excellence in academe a worthy aspiration, but recognition and reward for such a pursuit are saved for a privileged few, based on certain racial, gender, and relational attributes.

Like other black professional women, I had to earn the necessary credentials to enter the academy, but we have usually been denied credit or recognition. For instance, when I have been accorded rewards, it has been because my performance was at least twice as good as that of my colleagues. I have worked at developing courses, revamping curricula, and developing criteria for professional gatekeeping. I have contributed innovations. But senior faculty usually claim all the credit by taking over just before a project is completed. In fact, if the idea is too clearly mine, the faculty will water it down and, in a few weeks, reword it and implement it with credit that it can claim.

In an era in which gender and racial discrimination is rampant, the only way to have gender and racial equality is to instill equity not only in hiring but in promotions and retention as well.

Chapter 22

Student Harassment of Female Faculty of African Descent in the Academy

Jacqueline Pope and Janice Joseph

> After reading his grade, the student lunged out of his seat, threw the chair on its side, and shouted very loudly, "I don't want that grade. You can't teach. You black women are not qualified; you are here because of affirmative action. I'm going to see that you don't get tenure." He then stormed out of the room. I was terrified, embarrassed, scared, and shaken. This was my first semester at the institution. The matter was reported to the dean, who simply shook his head, implying that boys will be boys. Although it has been several years since the incident, it still vividly haunts me as if it were yesterday. This was a horrible experience for me.

The description above, given by a female professor of African descent, illustrates the nature, responses, and effects of acts of harassment black females experience on college campuses. In sharing the episode with other African American female faculty, this teacher was surprised to learn that they too had personal horror stories or had heard similar ones. The need for information concerning this form of harassment was apparent. Thus, with our institution's support, we began to document such incidents that black women encounter in college and university classrooms across the nation.

Student harassment of female faculty of African ancestry runs the gamut from subtle statements to physical attacks. Though these women, who vary widely in age, physical appearance, marital status, and discipline, are subjected to this victimization, there are very few studies that document this kind of harassment among all faculty women, despite the fact that numerous studies have been published concerning campus sexual harassment generally. The wide-ranging and basically inclusive research addresses student problems (female and male) and workplace violence women faculty sometimes face.[1]

It is interesting to note that women's perceptions, definitions, and responses to sexual harassment are varied. As DeFour and Paludi state, "Definitions in the perceptions of and reactions to sexual harassment by white women and women of color suggest that further research needs to be done in this area."[2] While such definition is a subject for future inquiry, this study becomes the first research effort that exculsively documents student harassment of African American females. Our study brings to public view the barriers black women work against in teaching in institutions of higher education. Such "isms" as race, sex, age, and class, together with work safety, are issues in the forefront of this study.

The Environment of Harassment

The circumstances of harassment by students present serious problems for women faculty of African ancestry, who are more likely than any other group in the academy to experience it and least likely to report it. Also, these women faculty are vulnerable to harassment because frequently their appointment is precarious. Finally, the unholy triangle of racism, sexism, and the affirmative action label is always looming on the horizon.

What are the causes of harassment by students? Three models—the organizational, sociocultural, and sex-role spillover models—are helpful in explaining sexual harassment of female faculty.

Organizational Model

The organizational model suggests that institutions, by the nature of their structure and operation, provide opportunities for harassment. That is, harassment relates to colleges' hierarchical arrangement, which is based on power and authority.[3] The role of women faculty in higher education must be understood in the context of the organization and tradition of campus life. For years campuses have been rife with sexism and racism. Though some headway has been made in the past against these barriers to women, they appear to be on the rise again, in part because of the nation's economic doldrums and a regressive approach to equity and justice. Employment, or lack thereof, is a case in point. Despite a thirty-year struggle, in the academic year 1991–92, faculty members of African descent constituted only 4.7 percent of full-time faculty; whites constituted 87.6 percent of all college and university faculties in the United States. In addition, only 27.5 percent of all full-time faculty members were white females.[4] A recent study on the employment of faculty of color in colleges and universities revealed that in 1991, women of color accounted for 14 percent of full-time faculty women and 4 percent of all faculty.[5] It is quite evident that people of African ancestry, who comprise 12 percent of the population, and majority females are underrepresented in colleges and universities.

Apart from the gross underrepresentation of women of African ancestry in the academy, many of them are concentrated in "gypsy" positions: typically, appointments for a year, a quarter, or a semester. Those faculty in tenure-track positions are routinely denied tenure.[6] Furthermore, that venerable tradition, the "old boys' network," based on years of friendship and social contacts, exists primarily to assist white males, leaving black women without mentors and on the periphery of college life. Vulnerability to harassment by students is nearly guaranteed by these experiences.

Sociocultural Model

The sociocultural model posits that harassment in academia is a reflection of what happens in the larger society, premised on patriarchy.[7] The authors contend that women are likely to be victims of harassment because men want to assert their power. Since the campus is a microcosm of society, one can assume that the treatment of African American women in academia will reflect their similar experiences outside.

Another important factor that shapes the private and academic life of black females is race. Often people of European descent receive unearned advantages and dominance over racial minorities because of white skin privilege. Consequently, racism is still pronounced in the United States but is subtle and sometimes difficult to address. Further, stereotypes about Africans in the Diaspora still exist. The symbolism, and all of its implications, of domineering, unintelligent, and promiscuous women of African ancestry has not been eliminated. Such negative attitudes, stereotypes, and myths are commonly transported to college, especially by students who have had no previous contact with female teachers of African ancestry. These preconceived notions can, and do, result in harassment. Society's mirror renders female professors nearly impotent, thus inhibiting their professional growth.

Sex-Role Spillover Model

Gutek and Morasch proposed this last model, which consists of two versions.[8] Sex-role spillover refers to women who are in nontraditional occupations or nontraditional college majors, where they are seen as "tokens" and treated as deviants. The second type of spillover occurs among women in female-populated careers, where the harassment is field-driven rather than individual (sex-typing occupations). Sex-role spillover can definitely apply to black women. A black female professor may be seen by other faculty members and students as an intruder, or she may be perceived as a "token," an "affirmative action hire," and therefore deemed incompetent. These misconceptions add to the probability that she will have to struggle against many issues at some time in her career.

Harassment of women professors by students is a fact of campus life, but many faculty members and administrators learn to ignore the problem, and by ignoring it, they make it worse. Much of the research on sexual harassment, moreover, has failed in the efforts of inclusion of black women. Thus their victimization is unrecorded.

The Authors' Study

Methodology

In mid-1993 a nationwide mail survey was sent to the female members of the National Congress of Black Faculty and to some selected others. Two hundred instruments were distributed, and 95 women from universities and four-year colleges, including traditionally African American institutions, responded. The survey did not control for tenure, rank, length of time at the institution, or the holding of an earned doctorate. The women's responses were heartening and heart-rending. One could argue that, as relative newcomers in academia, many female faculty deserve combat pay, given the problems foisted on them by students and colleagues. Fifty-seven percent of the respondents preferred to carry out their contractual responsibilities without reporting the victimization.

Description of the Sample

Fifty-five percent of the respondents were 45 years and over, with 34 percent between 35 and 44 years of age and 11 percent 34 and under. Seventy percent held Ph.D. degrees, 21 percent had M.A. or M.S. degrees, 1 percent had the B.A. or B.S., and 2 percent had other specialized degrees such as juris doctor or doctor of medicine. Forty-seven percent were concentrated in the social sciences, 15 percent in humanities, 16 percent in professional studies, 12 percent in African-American studies, 8 percent in fine arts, and 2 percent in the natural sciences. Ninety-three percent of the respondents were African Americans, 4 percent were African Caribbeans, and 3 percent were Africans.

Findings

Nature of Harassment

Fifty-four percent of the respondents reported being subjected to harassment within twelve months of the study. Of these incidents, 90 percent consisted of verbal harassment, 8 percent involved physical threat, and 2 percent were sexual harassment. Of the verbal harassment, 59 percent of the incidents consisted of name calling, 24 percent involved questioning faculty members' authority, and 17 percent involved cursing and other disrespectful behavior. Some of the verbal comments included "Bitch, go back to Africa," "Black bitch," and other racially disrespectful statements such as "I don't want a colored teacher" and "You are here because of affirmative action." Other faculty members reported that students left offensive notes in their offices and displayed extremely arrogant body language, hostility, and disrespect toward them. One respondent had a mouse placed in her handbag; someone shot into her office; and she was subjected to derogatory remarks regarding her race and gender. Other forms of harassment included being stalked, threatened with physical harm, and propositioned by the student.

Eighty-eight percent of those victimized were subjected to the abuse between one and five times, while 22 percent experienced it more than five times. Nineteen percent of the victimized respondents reported that the incidents related only to race; 12 percent indicated they related to gender; and 69 percent stated that they were related to both gender and race.

We determined that the numbers relating to gender and race were critical to understanding the harassment. Forty-three percent involved only one student, 45 percent between two and five students, and 12 percent more than five students. Males were the main perpetrators: 50 percent of the incidents involved males only, 10 percent involved only females, and 30 percent involved both males and females. Seventy-one percent of the incidents involved white students only; 14 percent, students of African ancestry; and 14 percent, others such as Asian or Latino students.

There was a significant difference between the race of the students and the faculty members' departments (r-.33; p.< .01). Many faculty members of the African-American studies departments were harassed by white students. Fifty-five percent of the incidents occurred in offices, 38 percent in classrooms, and 7 percent in the hallways. The typical student harasser, as noted, was a white male. This was not surprising since 69 percent of those harassed reported that the incidents were related to race and gender. Finally, older women, rather than younger ones, were more prone to harassment.

It is not surprising that older female professors are targets. In the larger community, seniors' vulnerability is being documented; witness increasing or reported elderly abuse by relatives. Academia reflects society, and its influence is substantial. As illustrated in this research, societal norms, ills, and views accompany the students. It is logical that older professors would be singled out for abuse; this is another symptom of our nation's social pathology.

Response to the Harassment

Only forty-three percent of those harassed reported the incident, a statistic consistent with similar studies that focus on female victimization.[9]

The victims may have been reluctant to report the harassment because of their marginal position in the institution. Their position is so precarious that they may believe reporting these problems would endanger their chances for reappointment, tenure, promotion, or professional support from their colleagues. College is perceived as a white man's world, and one way to disturb that status quo is to raise issues regarding race and gender, as female victims of African descent are well aware. They may risk their own credibility and status in the institution if they report an incident of harassment. One respondent declared, "I was afraid to report the incident because I was untenured. I thought that if I did 'rock the boat,' I would not get tenure. I really needed the job."

Another reason for not reporting the harassment was that some victims did not believe that anything would be done to the perpetrators. For example, one respondent stated, "I didn't think that the college would have done anything, because they care very little about racism and sexism. The typical response to racial and sexual harassment on campus is inaction." Others feared possible escalation of the harassment or retaliation from students. One respondent states, "I was afraid that the student would organize a public campaign and encourage other students to harass me. Students have a lot of power here on this campus."

Sixty percent of those who failed to report incidents stated that they did not think anything would be done, 29 percent feared retaliation, 5 percent said they did not think that it was serious enough, and 5 percent stated that they handled it privately. Ninety-four percent of those women harassed did report incidents to the dean or chair, and 16 percent reported them to another faculty member. As a result of reports, 38 percent of the harassers were reprimanded and 28 percent were suspended; 34 percent of the complaints were ignored. Overall, 72 percent of those reporting the incidents were satisfied with the outcome.

Effects of Harassment

Long-term consequences, including physical, emotional, psychological, and cognitive problems, are suffered as a result of harassment. Like the victims of sexual harassment, those in our study exhibited symptoms of what Tong referred to as "sexual harassment syndrome."[10] The victims in our study exhibited the following symptoms: 46 percent said that they experienced emotional trauma, which included a sense of helplessness, powerlessness, and vulnerability; 51 percent suffered from psychological problems including depression, fear, anxiety, paranoia, and anger; 3 percent experienced physical disturbances including headaches, nervous stomach, and inability to sleep.

College Policy on Harassment

Until recently, colleges had no obligations to publicize statistics on harassment on their campuses. Further, individual institutions handle cases differently. Some institutions do not tolerate it, while others are reluctant to pursue the matter for fear that it will reflect poorly on the institution and have a negative impact on future admissions. Institutions can be subject to civil lawsuits, however, if they are negligent in protecting victims or fail to take action on harassment complaints.

Our research suggests that many institutions do have written policies and procedures, but these are inadequate to deal with unethical and unacceptable behavior. For instance, 91 percent of the sample reported that their institutions had harassment policies, which included regulations on sexual harassment (53 percent), general harassment (40 percent), and physical harassment (7 percent). But a significant number (30 percent) stated that these policies are not enforced. It is quite clear that the mere existence of a policy is not sufficient evidence of its overall effectiveness.

Recommendations

In order to prevent or deal effectively with campus harassment by students, administrators should (1) provide a clear written policy on all forms of harassment, defining them and providing specific examples of the behaviors involved, and circulate the policy college-wide through handbooks, bulletins, lectures, and workshops; (2) provide written procedures regarding filing grievances; (3) provide lectures and seminars with mandatory attendance for students, faculty, administrators, and law enforcement staff regarding the definition, nature, prevention, and institutional response to student harassment of faculty; (4) establish mechanisms to determine the nature of these forms of harassment against female professors of African descent; (5) respond swiftly and consistently to harassment of these faculty members (prompt action will encourage victims to report harassment); (6) become sensitive to all the vital needs and concerns of women faculty of African descent; and (7) be aware of the response of professors of African descent to harassment since their experiences with racism and sexism will determine whether or not these professors will report an incident; (8) have trained administrators to understand the dual nature of the harassment; and (9) conduct a comparative survey (polling females not of African ancestry as well as others in the institution) in one's own institutions to ascertain the existence or level of harassment by students.

Faculty need to respond to any kind of harassment and develop survival strategies to deal with it by doing the following: (1) They should learn to recognize harassment and become acquainted with the institutional policies on harassment and the mechanisms designed to address the issues. This may involve attending workshops and lectures or acquiring written information on the policy. (2) They must talk with other faculty members about similar incidents and the methods used to pursue such complaints. This will alert them to the successful courses of action as well as inappropriate ones. (3) They must avoid the assumption that the harassment will disappear if ignored. Harassment often increases when it is regarded as insignificant or not serious enough. The slightest form of harassment must be addressed immediately by indicating disapproval. (4) They should request orally that the behavior cease, and if oral requests are unsuccessful or deemed inappropriate, a written report should be submitted to the administration. If the harassment continues or escalates, a formal grievance to the appropriate office may be necessary. Women should maintain a personal file of dated documentation of any incident and possible witnesses vital to the case. (5) They should identify other avenues of recourse. Complaints could be made to an appropriate federal enforcement agency. Civil litigation against the offending student or the institution could be initiated. Women should obtain professional advice before proceeding with litigation. (6) They should take special precautions when dealing with students in enclosed private areas. The data showed that 55 percent of the harassment incidents occurred in faculty members' offices.

Summary

Our survey results suggest widespread student harassment of women faculty of African ancestry. This could arguably be termed an epidemic. Male students of European ancestry are the main culprits, but cultural and institutional factors are integral components of the problem. Administrators, colleagues, and other students must share responsibility for the increasing workplace terrorism perpetrated against women faculty of African descent. Official silence on this issue is akin to encouragement of and participation in victimization. Although society as a whole harbors the genesis of harassment and all social maladies, we must avoid apathy and impotence by responding forcefully and immediately to any call for assistance. Women faculty have the right to work in an emotionally and physically safe environment. Appropriate steps must be taken to make this a reality that takes us into the twenty-first century. Implementing these recommendations will enhance the quality of life on campus for everyone. Terrorism against one segment of the community jeopardizes the entire community.

This study has examined several factors regarding harassment of female faculty of African descent, but more needs to be done. Future research should detail the effects of harassment on women and the likelihood that specific females will be targeted—for example, those who are untenured. The institutional, structural, and departmental factors that predispose female faculty of African ancestry to harassment by students need to be investigated as well.

A thorough examination of the sexual harassment endured by female faculty of African ancestry is long overdue. It is our hope that this research will be useful in capturing and expanding the debate concerning the needs of these invisible, silent female professors of African descent. Furthermore, we trust that adoption of the measures we have suggested will accelerate the movement away from victimhood to an affirmation of our strengths and resilience.

Notes

1. Billie Wright Dziech and Linda Weiner, *The Lecherous Professor: Sexual Harassment on Campus* (Chicago: University of Chicago Press, 1984); Jean W. Adams et al., "Sexual Harassment of University Students," *Journal of College Personnel* 24 (1983): 484–90; Phyllis L. Crocker and Anne E. Simon, "Sexual Harassment in Education," *Capital University Law Review* 10 (1981): 541–84; Francis Hoffman, "Sexual Harassment in Academia: Feminist Theory and Institutional Practice," *Harvard Educational Review* 56 (1986): 105–21.

2. Darlene C. DeFour and Michelle A. Paludi, "Research on Sexual Harassment in the Academy: Definitions, Findings, Constraints, Responses," *Initiatives* 51 (Fall 1989): 43–49.

3. Sandra S. Tangri, Martha R. Burt, and Leonora B. Johnson, "Sexual Harassment at Work: Three Explanatory Models, *Journal of Social Issues* 38 (1982): 54.

4. Carrell Peterson Horton and Jessie Carney Smith, eds., *Statistical Record of Black America*, 3rd edition (Detroit: Gale Research, 1990).

5. Deborah J. Carter and Eileen M. O'Brien, "Employment and Hiring Patterns for Faculty of Color," *ACE Research Brief Series* 4, no. 6 (1993): 1.

6. Darlene C. DeFour, "The Interface of Racism and Sexism on College Campuses," in *Ivory Power: Sexual Harassment on Campus*, edited by Michele A. Paludi (Albany: State University of New York Press, 1995), 227.

7. Tangri, Burt, and Johnson, "Sexual Harassment at Work," 54.

8. Barbara Gutek and Bruce Morasch, "Sex Ratios, Sex-Role Spillover and Sexual Harassment of Women At Work," *Journal of Social Issues* 38 (1982): 55–74.

9. Dziech and Weiner, *The Lecherous Professor*; Elizabeth Grauerhol, "Sexual Harassment of Women Professors by Situ: Exploring the Dynamics of Power, Authority, and Gender in a University Setting," *Sex Roles* 21 (December 1989): 789–801.

10. Rosemarie Tong, *Women, Sex, and the Law* (Totowa, N.J.: Rowman and Allanheld, 1984), 65–89.

Part Six

Black Women in Diverse Academic Settings

While racial and gender silhouettes outline their corporeality, black women in diverse academic settings have disparate needs and concerns. The American Council on Education reported that about 47.7 percent of black faculty in 1989 were employed at HBCUs. Within HBCUs, the United Negro College Fund reported that black faculty members represented approximately 59 percent (33 percent males, 26 percent females) of the total faculty pool in 1992, compared to only 2.2 percent of the total full-time black faculty pool. In 1992 only 2.2 percent were in traditionally white institutions.

In HBCUs, black faculty often are isolated from mainstream academia, lack funds to travel to professional meetings, lack research opportunities, and have disproportionately heavy teaching loads.

Black faculty in white schools, depending on the type of institution, might also face lack of resources in addition to social isolation. Data from the American Council on Education indicate that the largest percentage of African American faculty was employed at four-year public colleges (46 percent in 1989). Twenty-two percent of African American faculty were employed at two-year public colleges, 17.6 percent at four-year independent colleges, only 8.5 percent at four-year public universities, and 4.6 percent at independent universities.

Research opportunities, salary, tenure, and teaching loads are affected by the type of institution in which one is employed. According to a 1989–90 faculty survey of the Higher Education Research Institute, faculty members in public and private universities published far more than professors in other institutions. In addition, more professors are tenured in public institutions than in private ones. Four-year private colleges place more emphasis on student developmental goals than do public colleges or public and private universities.

Saliwe M. Kawewe's "Black Women in Diverse Academic Settings: Gender and Racial Crimes of Commission and Omission in Academia" frames some issues facing black women despite diverse settings, such as the subverting of affirmative action in the recruitment, hiring, retention, and promotion process. Two voices are heard from public white universities—one a small university and the other a major research university. Delo E. Washington's "Another Voice from the Wilderness" and Josie R. Johnson's "An African American Female Senior-Level Administrator: Facing the Challenges of a Major Research University" emotionally connect the reader to issues faced by black women in educationally diverse milieus.

Brenda Hoke's "Women's Colleges: The Intersection of Race, Class, and Gender" and Mona T. Phillips's "'I Bring the History of My Experience': Black Women Professors at Spelman College Teaching out of Their Lives" allow the reader to share what it is like being at a white women's private institution and a black women's private institution, both in the South, and how these milieus— one of the same gender as the writer but a different race, one of the same race and gender—shape the contours of their everyday consciousness.

Finally, J. Nefta Baraka's insightful analysis entitled "The African American Female Administrator: A Change Agent" provides the reader with a critical perspective of the conditions of African American women in one small private white coeducational college. Using Molefi Kete Asante's framework of situation, resistance, and liberation, she explores racial attitudes of white faculty and administrators and acts of resistance by black women administrators.

Chapter 23

Black Women in Diverse Academic Settings
Gender and Racial Crimes of Commission and Omission in Academia

Saliwe M. Kawewe

Black women in general are seriously underrepresented in higher education as administrators and faculty. As faculty they "are usually in the lowest ranks, where promotion and tenure are rarely achieved. Yet, even among the small number of Blacks, Black women are the fewest of the few."[1]

Social relations and the interactional characteristic of power both influence bureaucratic decision making and judgments in academic settings. Because hiring, promotion, and retention are based on the perceptions of those hiring, there has been a tendency for those decisions and judgments to be made on the basis of homogeneous reproduction, which excludes women, African Americans, Native Americans, and other special populations. This homosocial reproduction, built on the basis of Western supremacy, devalues women in general, promotes the idea of racial superiority of Caucasians, and justifies such a stance. Thus within the academy, as in the larger society, black women face a double negative of being black and female, attributes within the affirmative action framework that scholars such as Robert J. Menges and William H. Exum had expected would yield positive results.[2] Instead, race and sex are the multiple negatives. In predominantly white colleges and universities, black women encounter both racism and sexism, while they face sexism in black institutions of higher education. In both settings, misconceptions and stereotypes about race and sex lead to the treatment of and interaction with the black woman as a label, thus mystifying the real person behind the stigma and encouraging self-fulfilling prophesies by the sex and race that hold power.

In his study, Steward found the following misconceptions of black female faculty by their white counterparts: while white faculty members perceived the black females as expressing the need for inclusion and intimacy, as not seeking leadership roles, and as not seeking structure and supervision, the black female faculty did not perceive themselves that way.[3]

It could be deduced, based on this study, that such incongruence in perception could lead to misunderstanding and miscommunication, resulting in great stress for both parties. Because the black woman relies on the evaluation of these colleagues in her pursuit of academic excellence and tenure, her stress is extraordinary. Hence this perceptual polarization can systematically isolate her at the departmental, professional, and institutional levels.

While some of the misconceptions and stereotypes are culturally based, others are based on misunderstanding that arises from affirmative action compliance. For example, one false assumption is that any award, recognition, honor, or promotion of black females is due to their special status of being black and female. What this implies is that being black and female is a passport for receiving preferential treatment. It further suggests that when universities recruit the black woman, they neither review nor value her credentials, past experiences, or potential for meeting high academic standards.

In both public and private, both black and white institutions, various efforts to combat racial and/or sexual discrimination in higher education have yielded limited results, in part because of these misconceptions and stereotypes. Affirmative action was one effort instituted to bring greater equity to higher education by promising equal opportunities regardless of race and sex. Though affirmative action programs have increased the representation of men and women of color and white women on campus, this chapter notes how colleges and universities have devised sophisticated internal mechanisms to subvert affirmative action in recruitment, hiring, retention, and promotion to the advantage of the privileged gender and race that dominate the academy. Thus the very law that was designed to ensure egalitarian principles in academia has been racist and sexist in its implementation.

Affirmative action in many universities mandates increasing the number of women and minority faculty through the recruitment of qualified minorities, including women. In some cases, universities specify "black women" and other minorities as one of the initiatives to meet the Equal Employment Opportunities Program (EEOP) requirements. While some institutions have enforced this program, others have subverted it. Enforcement was particularly weakened during the Reagan and Bush administrations, and the law is currently under attack by conservative political forces in this country.

The recruitment and hiring criteria are examples of how affirmative action is subverted. Although affirmative action has been endorsed by colleges, universities, some foundations, and boards of accreditation, the recruitment and hiring success rate varies and is limited by the deliberate use of subversive tactics at the university, college, department, and program levels.

Recruitment and Hiring

How is the recruitment of blacks done to meet EEOP guidelines? Before affirmative action programs, advertising for academic positions was done through the "old boys' network," which both intentionally and unwittingly barred women and minorities from access to academic employment. As a result of affirmative action, academic positions are advertised not only in mainstream sources but also in journals and newsletters particularly aimed at women and minorities.

The actual practice of hiring, recruiting, and retaining faculty through tenure can be manipulated and disguised by visible and invisible internal forces, thus making it difficult for others to understand exactly what these activities entail. Words and phrases such as "quota," "equal opportunity," "equity," "quality standards," "racism," and "sexism" can be used to describe opposite meanings, depending on whether the user assumes a position that favors or opposes affirmative action.[4] Often when universities and colleges advertise for minorities, they do not include African Americans. If the recruited faculty members are black, they are often temporary and permanent residents or citizens who initially came here as international students. This misrepresents the actual number of African Americans in the stratum classified as "black faculty hired." These black internationals from the Third World appear to have become the "privileged" among blacks, but they do not necessarily escape discrimination. To what extent these privileged blacks in academe are retained is unknown.

An evaluative analysis reflects that, since the inception of affirmative action, many programs, departments, and academic institutions have complied by hiring women, blacks, and other minorities, but they did not necessarily tenure them. Similarly, Eric W. George's longitudinal study on Kentucky universities, done at two-year intervals from 1975 to 1990, found that Kentucky universities reached record-high numbers in hiring women and blacks, but they also lost more tenure-track women during that period. The number of *black women* hired or lost during the period was negligible.[5] A literature review shows that universities are lagging in hiring women, let alone black women, for faculty jobs that lead to tenure.

Menges and Exum's study states that the percentage of minorities among women hired was greater than that of minorities among males. They also note that the actual number of females was smaller than the number of males. When statistics on minority women in the academy were broken down by ethnicity, the data showed that 2 percent were black, 4 percent were Asians, 4 percent were Hispanics, and less than 0.20 percent were Native Americans.[6] The pool from which universities recruit minority women is very limited.

Problems of Implementing in Hiring and Recruiting

The affirmative action program addresses the following: (1) the process and criteria that are utilized to estimate the number of marketable women and minorities with academic potential; (2) the criteria and process by which institutional goals for hiring are determined for different levels and whether these are minimum or maximum goals; (3) the general practice of setting hiring goals at an institutional level rather than at the department level and how these lower institutional levels determine their responsibilities to meet these goals; (4) the determinants of the type of information dissemination and recruitment practices utilized to fill vacant positions; (5) the criteria used for assessing women, blacks, and other minority candidates; (6) the considerations about whether blacks, other minorities, and women applicants are pitted against each other as they aggressively compete for these positions; (7) the degree of conscientiousness in monitoring pursuance of affirmative action; (8) the existence of a leadership that is positive in persuading and influencing programs and departments to recruit minorities and women; (9) the presence of enough qualified staff, power, and sufficient funding for an effective university affirmative action or equal opportunity office; (10) the degree of inefficiency of government, and the lack of enforcement stamina to monitor compliance.[7]

Retention and Promotion

Like hiring and recruiting, implementation of affirmative action in retaining and promoting black women is at the discretion of those in power. Perhaps academic institutions' most severe crimes of omission and commission stem from the vagueness of their standards for academic performance for retention and promotion. Teaching, research, and service are the areas evaluated, but too often the guidelines in these areas are subjective when applied to black women, other men and women of color, and white women.

Excellence in Teaching

Minority women report experiencing more difficulty in teaching than minority men experience. There is evidence that black females and other minorities are underrated when compared with white males.

When black and white women academics challenge the traditional philosophy of pedagogy and opt instead for collectively initiated learning that promotes egalitarian roles of student and teacher in contributing to and generating knowledge, they are criticized by those who espouse the patriarchal pursuance of meritocracy,[8] and thus their teaching may be adversely affected. Many black women, white women, and other minority professors view education as a means of student empowerment and a way of helping students learn to transform social life rather than a vehicle for acquiring limited vocational skills. Even when the status quo is followed and student evaluation of teaching reflects effectiveness, the privileged interpret this as meaning that students like the faculty member or she gives easy assignments and exams. There is rarely a recognition of the minority faculty's abilities.

Excellence in Scholarship and Research

White males in traditionally white colleges and universities and black males in traditionally black colleges and universities maintain control over faculty research processes, interviewing, criteria, and internal information networks. Thus black women academicians are placed in a double bind that prevents equal access to research funding sources, particularly at white universities. Further, the requirement by many sources of research grants that the applicant has a record of prior research sets the new entrant into academia at a disadvantage, especially if she or he does not possess the "right" racial and gender characteristics. Scholarly publications by black authors are often discounted because of white elitism. Moreover, such polarization by race and gender leaves blacks publishing in mainly black or feminist journals. Publication in such journals is considered unscholarly; thus the avenues for fulfilling the tenure and promotion requirement are further limited, and black faculty are denied tenure and promotion.

While black women and other females prefer research that integrates process and outcome, the dominant group values research with more emphasis on outcome than on process, thus forcing detachment from human endeavors in research. Further, it is vague as to what type of publication and research carries the most weight, and in many cases the teacher is not told how many publications are required for tenure.

Excellence in Service

Society has traditionally placed disproportionate responsibility for service on women. This is mirrored in academia. Also mirrored in academic settings is the mindset that service carries the least value. Faculty often find themselves juggling teaching, advising, committee work, and community service with time for the scholarly endeavors that reap the rewards. Blacks are seemingly used as ceremonial showcases in university functions, where they serve on innumerable task forces and committees to insure the black presence. Thus they are robbed of time they need to perform other responsibilities that weigh more toward tenure and promotion. In return, they are met with innuendoes that they receive preferential treatment in workloads.

Although this dichotomy is experienced by all faculty, it is more intense for women and minorities. Because of their scarcity and visibility, they are enticed and pressured to accept extra committee responsibilities, which are referred to as "opportunities." The black faculty woman finds herself torn between meeting the political correctness standards that satisfy department and college committees or declining such so-called opportunities that threaten her survival. Declining could be considered uncooperative and thus can lead to negative evaluations, low salary raises, and nonconsideration for tenure or promotion. The black woman in academe is overutilized, not only by formal academic systems but by the black students who seek her out for professional guidance and other concerns as she serves as a positive role model for female and minority students regardless of their race. Black women in academe stretch themselves to the limit with service, but it is not highly valued in the retention process.

Despite the claim by some proponents of academic elitism that the evaluation and review process affects all faculty equitably and produces equal discontent among all faculty, there are various findings to the contrary. Even though women are now engaged in publication more than ever before, they are still paid less than what their male faculty colleagues of the same cohort earn. The preferential treatment of white males throughout the evaluation process mirrors the choices and preferences of the white male model of academic excellence.

Conclusion

In sum, the affirmative action program opened opportunities for black women, other men and women of color, and white women in higher education. While it has increased the pool of candidates and applicants for recruitment and hiring, however, it has done little in monitoring retention, and black women faculty have benefited least. Thus higher education continues to reflect severely restricting elitism at the top. Furthermore, affirmative action has led to the creation of a permanent underclass of proletariats, a hidden stratum of teachers resembling untouchables. These are found at the bottom, while the quasielites, mostly white males, are found at the top. The academic proletariat consists of gypsy scholars who move from one institution to another because they have been denied tenure or have never been on the tenure track. They are mostly women and minorities who are overrepresented in the lower academic positions without seniority. When there is retrenchment in staffing, they are disproportionately vulnerable to layoffs, as they were the last hired. Thus the implementation of affirmative action has been hindered in higher education through covert internal mechanisms used to maintain the dominant, privileged gender and/or race in the college and university hierarchy.

Black women and other oppressed populations should wedge a more unified egalitarian effort that is more inclusive than exclusive as the outcome of affirmative action reflects more segmentation of people who are intended beneficiaries.

University leaders and administrators should also serve as society's role models by wholeheartedly enforcing affirmative action programs that include more black women. Moreover, university faculty members should serve as role models to their students by standing for the truth. Their students will fill various positions in different segments of society and pass on this influence to build a more just and equitable community. Ideally, the university community should reflect diversity rather than discrimination.

Notes

1. Jeanne Noble, "The Higher Education of Black Women in the Twentieth Century," in *Women and Higher Education in American History*, edited by John Mack Faragher and Florence Howe (New York: Norton, 1988), 101.

2. Robert J. Menges and William H. Exum, "Barriers to the Progress of Women and Minority Faculty," *Journal of Higher Education* 54, no. 2 (1983).

3. Robbie J. Steward, "Work Satisfaction and the Black Female Professional: A Pilot Study," unpublished manuscript, 7–9.

4. Harold Orlans, "Affirmative Action in Higher Education," *Annals of the American Academy of Political and Social Sciences* 523 (1992): 150.

5. Eric W. George, *Employment of Women Holding Tenure-System Teaching Positions at Kentucky's Universities and Community Colleges Hits Record High 1975–1990.* Staff Report 92-2 (Frankfort: Kentucky Commission on Human Rights, 1992).

6. Menges and Exum, "Barriers to the Progress of Women."

7. Alayne L. Parson, Roberta G. Sands, and Josann Duane, "Sources of Career Support for University Faculty," *Research in Higher Education* 33, no. 2 (1988): 129.

8. Robert Boice, "New Faculty Involvement for Women and Minorities," *Research in Higher Education* 34, no. 3 (1993): 328.

Chapter 24

Another Voice from the Wilderness

Delo E. Washington

Tell me, how did you feel when you come out the wilderness, come
out the wilderness, come out the wilderness?

Negro Spiritual

It is because I believe the American people to be conscientiously
committed to a fair trial and ungarbled evidence, and because I feel
essential to a perfect understanding and an equitable verdict that
truth from each standpoint be represented at the bar—that this little
voice has been added to the already full chorus.

Anna Julia Cooper, *A Voice from the South*

Finding a voice in the largest state system of public education in the world is
no small challenge. The search for that voice in California's postsecondary educational enterprise is, nevertheless, a beginning gesture. It signals movement
that is expected to "make new life and new growth possible." For a black woman,
it is a way—as Bell Hooks and Sidonie Smith have described it—of "talking
back."[1] The search for just the right tone is intended as a liberating exercise.
The need to maneuver my way through the California State University—a subsystem in a supersystem with 9 research-oriented universities, 20 state universities, and 120 community colleges—has required a certain commitment. My
allegiance has been expressed over twenty-three years of tenure. The 20 campuses of the state university subsystem, from Arcata in the northern part of the
state to San Diego in the southern part, have degrees, staff, student relations,
and collegial networks that are sensitive to an academic marketplace. During a
time when budgets are limited, competition for position and status is keen. In
that climate, in that marketplace, in that situation, where is the black woman
professor's voice?

The 117,000 faculty members and nearly 375,000 students make up a full chorus whose voices do not always harmonize for a variety of reasons. For one thing, the diversity of the population reflects the collection of sounds—the range of voices that are trained and untrained. A campus's geography, the characteristics of its resident population, and its identified mission are only a few of the features that must blend toward that end. The search for my own voice in this context is a search for just the right pitch and tone for the delivery I intend. I have been trained for this performance in an environment where, in the beginning, I was among unfamiliar groups of people. They became unwitting mentors. My training ground has been a place where I could observe and listen "up close" and at a distance. I could put myself in the picture—in the framework of the experiences of the traditional academy. I recognize that I, like any personal narrator, am a product of history and culture. It is necessary for me, like Hamabata, to consider my personal odyssey as I record the stages of my own identity.[2]

I was hired to teach African American studies full-time at a small state college (the student population was under 5,000 at the time) in the Central Valley during the spring of 1972. At the same time, I had been accepted at the University of California at Berkeley to pursue doctoral studies in higher education. The latter's interdivisional program allowed me to take courses outside of the Department of Education. That policy encouraged my association with Professor John Ogbu in anthropology and Herbert Blumer, professor in sociology. Ogbu had conducted fieldwork in Stockton. His dissertation, which was later published as *The Next Generation: Ethnography of an Urban Neighborhood*, reflected the work of a cultural anthropologist.[3] His participant-observer techniques were instructive. It was Blumer who had advised, "If it were not for the naive student of human behavior, a good deal of the research enterprise would not be undertaken. People who are familiar with pitfalls tend to avoid them." I became a naive participant-observer at the university where I pursued my own course of study and at the college where I began my college teaching career.

Armed with the confidence fostered by early childhood conditioning, I became a participant and an observer in unfamiliar surroundings. During the earliest years of my socialization, I had been encouraged and expected to "do it"—to overcome obstacles or odds. "We Shall Overcome" was the signature song of the civil rights movement; it had been inspired by workers in Charleston, South Carolina. In the old slave songs, voices were used to respond to a call. That memory about the South Carolina Sea Islanders prompts me to recall my own upbringing in that region, where I was born and spent the first seventeen years of my life. I had learned that the question that began "How did you feel . . . ?" had been directed to the illiterate many times. That unlettered seeker, who had searched for salvation in the thickets of the Deep South, responded with conviction. That same question could also have prompted Anna Julia Cooper, nearly thirty years after the Civil War freed the enslaved, to comment: "Tis woman's strongest vindication for speaking that the world needs to hear her voice. It would be subversive of every human interest that the cry of one-half the human family be stifled. . . . Hers is every interest that has lacked an interpreter and a defender. Her cause is linked with that of every agony that has been . . . every wrong that needs a voice."[4]

In more recent times, nearly a century after Cooper penned her words and two centuries after the slaves started singing their song, the need for the general message has not changed. Yolanda Moses, among others, laments the plight of black women professors, for example, in the traditionally white academy.[5] Women of color, these writers say, continue to face tremendous barriers when they seek full-participant roles as tenured teachers in institutions of higher education. This means, among other things, that it is time to speak up about the standards by which they are judged there. Role-taking behavior, under such conditions, lacks appropriate models for one who is expected to be a model herself for a variety of students and for a community she is thought to represent. Her prescribed roles, then, are different according to two sets of cultural standards—the one from her family of origin and the other from her new associates. She has inherited little if anything in the context of the academic social group's way of life.

Since the academy is a workplace that has historically favored white males, stories behind the statistical reality today are particularly telling. Phillip has pointed to Equal Employment Opportunity figures showing that white women staffers comprise 27.5 percent of full-time faculty, while black women comprise 2.7 percent.[6] Furthermore, black women's median earnings on eleven-month contracts were $1,500 less than that of white women of similar status. And so the story goes, with questionable implications for the worth and value of African American women under such conditions. The writer does point out that many more white women than black women are vocal about their predicament; in fact, their sounds have been shattering the glass ceilings around them. On the other side, black women in academia remain laden with the "burden of race, gender, and class discrimination."[7]

The 1990s are witnessing a turning point. Black women like Yolanda Moses and Marian Mobley are examples. Moses, president of the City University of New York, outlined issues and strategies regarding black women in academe in her 1989 study, sponsored by the Ford Foundation. Mobley, professor of African American and women's literature at George Mason University, says that being a black professor at a white institution obligates one to articulate her reality. For example, at times a black woman professor must explain her limitations to students by saying things that will deconstruct the strong Black woman myth.

When I started my college teaching career in the 1970s, the "new" students as well as "new" professors were arriving on college campuses. These new people were those whose ethnic, age, gender, and socioeconomic identities were different from those of the traditional student. The emergence on my campus of African American studies and Chicano studies paralleled this development. There was concern about nontraditional learning styles and about associating community service with classroom work — now considered appropriate features of teaching. This was especially true if the "new" students were to be successful. (Arthur Chickering and his associates have devoted a large volume, *The Modern American College*, to variations on a theme that relies on the developmental stages conceptual model in addressing such issues.)[8]

Another way that I would learn of framing my experiences as a new college teacher was described by Joseph Axelrod.[9] Imitating Axelrod, I tried to make sense of a teaching and learning environment where, among a population of approximately 4,500 students, only about 3 percent were African Americans. These students had essentially been recruited from the Los Angeles and East Bay areas of the state. Postsecondary education, with its three-tiered supersystem, was designed to address the needs of students who required a range of opportunities. The students who came to the campus where I worked were primarily interested in getting a bachelor's degree. Axelrod's theoretical degree system model was a reference point to which I could relate. It allowed me to construct a path in a cultural context that represented a wilderness of ideas and expectations. The model's six moving and interlocking elements represented guideposts. I felt that I could identify with any local campus's schema about the structure and functions associated with the elements of this model: (1) the course and its acknowledged content; (2) the schedule or the times when students and teachers met in "class" or outside of it; (3) the number of credits or units assigned (which give the course and the professor some assigned value); (4) the group-personal interaction, wherein the roles of "student" and "professor" were well defined, were distinctly different, and would remain relatively stable from the beginning of the course to its end; (5) the experiences students could expect; and (6) the authority-responsibility arrangement, a system in which freedom and controls are exercised by the learner and over the learners as they pursued their identifiable goal—the degree—and the goal cited in the college catalog and higher education in general, which is preparation for lifelong learning.

While I was influenced by the overall frame of reference inspired by the degree system model, I invariably became selectively attentive to three of its elements. I sought a more manageable way to succeed as a professor on campus, so I concentrated on developing (1) the content of African American studies courses; (2) ways to provide students with experiences that would address their learning needs and the needs outlined in the institution's mission; and (3) ways to accept an authority-responsibility arrangement inside and outside the ethnic studies program. The unevenness of that authority-responsibility arrangement could not escape the attention of the most naive participant-observer. The power dynamics in this arrangement were murky, but it soon became apparent that my feelings regarding my authority and power over all decisions affecting course offerings were burdened by more weighty responsibilities I had assumed. For starters, my limited salary influenced my decision to commute between the East Bay area and two Central Valley cities. The latter included the city where the largest population of African Americans and I resided and the city where my university's main campus was located. Besides, I was committed to a community outreach component to teaching. I come from a tradition whose theme can be explained by combined pieces of two African proverbs: "She who learns is expected to teach the whole village."

Rist made some observations that were fairly commonplace after the black studies programs got under way in the 1970s. Using Homan's model for framing the issue, he referred to a woman's "difficulty in simultaneously having allegiance to the norms and activities of two contradictory reference groups. [S]he will identify with one and dismiss the other."[10] The contradiction in roles, according to Rist, paralyzes activity. Reflecting on the early conditioning of my childhood as well as the reinforcement I received in a black women's college, I expected to find a way around the obstacles. This is not to say that my reality was the reality of others. According to Rist's frame of reference, membership in the black ethnic group suggests a subordinate relationship in the context of traditional white universities. Rist described the historical rift between the black community and the white university as one that is a basic and crucial aspect of race relations. To expect black studies programs to establish a department, to engage in scholarship and research of the kind done in traditional departments, and to develop special remedial programs for low-income, poorly prepared students, is in error. Today black women professors are expected to be, and usually are, particularly sensitive to these needs. Rist's treatment of the subject reflects an analysis based on popular sociological theory regarding social structures and their functions. His conclusions, however, continue to have constricted meaning for a black woman who thinks that she has, indeed, been prepared to "do it"—to succeed in her chosen profession, even when that profession is generally identified with a high-status college role or position.

Fleming identified the problems of black women convincingly,[11] referring to the social science literature that portrayed black women as "strong, competent, self-reliant, even dominant" matriarchs though, being black and female, they had to plow their way through a society that was racist as well as sexist. While the favored view of black women pointed to them as having "strength, self-reliance, and a strong achievement orientation," the making of this matriarchal image is associated with stereotypical thinking. There is another way to look at their situation: the fact that black women show "stronger work orientation, longer history of participation in the workforce, and stronger commitment to professional goals" is not sufficient reason to see them as successes in their chosen professional fields. These women have an extended history of taking care of both expressive and instrumental family functions. Researchers such as Epstein have reported that the double bind in which black women find themselves is associated with the negative statuses linked to blackness and femaleness, which makes them the most disadvantaged of the four sex-race groups. They are probably concentrated at the lower portion of the occupational ladder because they lack assertiveness and are content to endure racial and sexual injustices.[12]

More contemporary views of this situation aside, the dilemma that black women face in academic institutions can be likened to what W. E. B. Du Bois reportedly described as the Negro's "double consciousness" in the beginning of the twentieth century.[13] His chapter entitled "Of Our Spiritual Strivings" set the tone in The Souls of Black Folk, originally published in 1903. It provided an intimate, classic context for describing the plight of one group trying to identify with another group while retaining some of its own characteristics and traditions. He could easily have described the black woman as having a third dimension. She was not only "born with a veil . . . in this American world," which yields her no "true self-consciousness" but allows her to see herself only "through the revelation of the other world." She, Du Bois could easily have said, possessed a triple consciousness, encompassing her identities as an American, a black, and a woman. Certainly this applies today to the African American woman who is teaching in colleges and universities.

By the end of the 1970s, still a naive participant-observer, I was getting deeper into the "wilderness" of a set of relationships that were considered everyday

acts by "Old Guard" standards. Barely two years into my sojourn, the president
of the institution resigned. This was a man who had used his authority to support my enrollment in the research university while I taught classes at the college. The change of leadership at the top clouded an already murky vision
of things. It marked a change in the college's governance system, the system
through which all other systems are modified as a result of decision making on
or off campus.[14] The course of my study and my plans for continued employment had to be reevaluated in light of the president's move. Acknowledging
and participating in college governance directly and preparing for classes at the
college and the university were undertakings that a superwoman might have
easily taken into stride. For the more ordinary, aspiring woman who is also
black and single, the moral and social imperative to succeed was becoming
unbearable. I wanted to merge conflicting allegiances to a whole and healthy
self, to family, to community, to society, and to the academy. Would the differences always be irreconcilable?

By the 1980s California's state legislature, its governing boards of universities and colleges, and the committee for the Master Plan for Postsecondary
Education had turned their attention to preparing the state's population to live
in an increasingly diverse society. By the year 2000, it was anticipated, California would no longer have a majority ethnic group. Furthermore, the African
American population would comprise a very small percentage of groups who
were considered most underrepresented in areas of achievement and status.
Attention to a more multicultural university curriculum was consistent with
the focus of my work at the university. Having completed my doctoral degree
work in 1977, I could pay full attention to the challenge of developing the
African American component of the ethnic studies program. But the budgetary
crisis that was gripping the state put more pressure on all participants and
observers in California's postsecondary educational supersystem. The African
American studies component of ethnic studies (Chicano studies was the other
component) was becoming increasingly isolated from departmental informal
decisions, with questionable information provided for budgetary expenses, for
prioritizing a sequential offering of classes, and for coordinating efforts with
other faculty members whose courses could complement the limited African
American offerings. Administrative memos, academic senate resolutions, and
communications from book publishers, professional journals, and the like were
directing attention to the goal of educating multiethnic populations, whose diversity could be considered a positive trait instead of a negative one. A black
woman could choose her sides, so to speak. I had made the commitment to "do
it"—to achieve. Had I not received my undergraduate degree from the black

women's college that boasted "over a century of service to women who achieve?" But I had done so in a way that I paid an incredible price. Over the years— seventeen to be exact—I'd had to become familiar with the allocation of resources among competing interests when promotions were awarded. It took ten years for me to be awarded the rank of associate professor. During a period of spiraling inflation in the country, constricted merit step increases, and limited access to outside reward opportunities unless one made a personal investment, the black woman professor could easily become the invisible woman.

There continues to be an uncertain place for us out there. I can call it a wilderness. For black women professors in traditionally white institutions, that wilderness can be described as the overwhelming overgrowth of obstacles that continue to prevent her from achieving the status and rewards that others achieve and for getting them in the timely manner that others get them. For black women professors who do achieve in spite of overwhelming odds, Du Bois framed his philosophical view convincingly: "It is the doggedness of conviction about the promises of her [special space] which keeps [the black woman] from being torn asunder."[15] But the time has come to call on a stronger voice. There is a need to recall the voices of Anna Julia Cooper, Mary McLeod Bethune, and others like them from the past. Sometimes their voices seem too far away, too distant, too inaudible to make a difference in contemporary life. When a collective voice is heard, there is some hope. Another generation must hear the sounds. Our generation must make those sounds more audible.

Notes

1. Bell Hooks, *Ain't I a Woman* (Boston: South End Press, 1981); Sidonie Smith, "Who's Talking/Who's Talking Back: The Subject of Personal Narratives," *Signs* 18, no. 2 (Winter 1993).

2. Matthews Masayuki Hamabata, *Crested Kimono: Power and Love in the Japanese Business Family* (Ithaca, N.Y.: Cornell University Press, 1990).

3. John W. Ogbu, *The Next Generation: An Ethnography of Education in an Urban Neighborhood* (New York: Academic Press, 1974).

4. Anna Julia Cooper, *A Voice from the South by a Black Woman of the South* (1892; reprint, New York: Oxford University Press, 1988).

5. Yolanda T. Moses, "Black Women in Academe: Issues and Strategies," in *Project on the Status and Education of Women* (Washington, D.C.: Association of American Colleges, 1989).

6. Mary-Christine Phillip, "Feminism in Black and White, Part I," *Black Issues in Higher Education* 10, no. 1 (March 11, 1993): 12–17.

7. Ibid.

8. Arthur W. Chickering, *The Modern American College: Responding to the New Realities of Diverse Students and a Changing Society* (San Francisco: Jossey-Bass, 1981).

9. Joseph Axelrod, *The University Teacher as Artist* (San Francisco: Jossey-Bass, 1973).

10. Ray C. Rist, "Black Staff, Black Studies, and White Universities: A Study in Contradictions," *Journal of Higher Education* 41, no. 8 (November 1970): 618–29.

11. Jacqueline Fleming, "Black Women in Black and White College Environments: The Making of a Matriarch," *Journal of Social Science* 39, no. 3 (1983).

12. Cynthia Fuchs Epstein, "Positive Effects of the Multiple Negative: Explaining the Success of Black Professional Women," *American Journal of Sociology* 78 (1973): 913–18.

13. W. E. B. Du Bois, *The Souls of Black Folk* (1903; reprint New York: New York University Press, 1970), 16–17.

14. Axelrod, *The University Teacher as Artist.*

15. Du Bois, *The Souls of Black Folk*, 17.

Chapter 25

An African American Female
Senior-Level Administrator

Facing the Challenges of a Major Research University

Josie R. Johnson

In this age of declining resources and rising expectations that we improve the quality of higher education, it is very difficult for senior-level administrators in major research universities to balance competing interests in their efforts to accomplish their institutional mission without compromising academic excellence and diversity. The complexity of such an administrative position is further compounded if the administrator happens to be an African American woman in a major, predominantly white research university.

An African American female has a triple set of obstacles and barriers that get in the way of her working as a senior administrator. One is the negative attitude that exists in the larger society regarding the role of women in our society. Then there is the resistance to females that exists among today's academic community. Third, these challenges are compounded by being an African American. Not only does an African American woman have to understand how a major university system operates—its organization, structure, personality, and culture— she also has to know how to communicate with all of the segments and elements within the university community. She has to be aware of the problems, the challenges, and the barriers that exist for the institution in addition to understanding what that means relative to the success of minority faculty, students, and staff. She has to be multicultural; she has to know not only her own community but also the other communities so that she knows how to represent and communicate the needs of the diverse communities.

Before I discuss the problems of an African American woman serving in a high-level administrative position at a major research university, I need to provide a brief description of my institution and my duties as associate vice president for academic affairs and associate provost with special responsibility for minority affairs.

Founded in 1869 as a land grant institution, the University of Minnesota is a huge, comprehensive, international research university. It consists of four campuses: Twin Cities (Minneapolis–St. Paul), Duluth, Morris, and Crookston. Composed of twenty colleges, the Twin Cities campus is the largest and confers a full range of bachelor's, master's, and doctoral degrees including doctorates in medicine, dentistry, law, and veterinary medicine. One of the Big Ten institutions, the University of Minnesota ranks among the top twenty universities in the United States.

In fall 1993, the University of Minnesota system had 48,524 students and 3,111 tenured and tenure-track faculty members. Persons of color accounted for 9.8 percent of the student population and 8.9 percent of the regular faculty. The distribution of students was as follows:

Campus	Students of color		All other students		Total	
Twin Cities	4,173	(11.1%)	33,375	(88.9%)	37,548	(100.0%)
Duluth	321	(4.2%)	7,265	(95.8%)	7,586	(100.0%)
Morris	231	(12.0%)	1,702	(88.0%)	1,933	(100.0%)
Crookston	40	(2.7%)	1,417	(97.3%)	1,457	(100.0%)
Waseca	0	(0.0%)	51	(100.0%)	51	(100.0%)
Total	4,765	(9.8%)	43,759	(90.2%)	48,524	(100.0%)

Note: Although the Waseca Campus was officially closed on June 30, 1991, fifty-one students were allowed to enroll for the 1993–94 academic year to complete their degree programs.
Source: University of Minnesota Office of the Registrar, Minority Enrollment Report, Fall Quarter 1993 (October 1993).

The ethnic breakdown of students and faculty of color was as follows:

Ethnicity	Students		Faculty	
Asian/Pacific	2,493	(52.3%)	184	(66.4%)
African American	1,172	(24.6%)	42	(15.2%)
Chicano/Latino/Hispanic	679	(14.3%)	38	(13.7%)
American Indian	421	(8.8%)	13	(4.7%)
Total	4,765	(100.0%)	277	(100.0%)

Source: University of Minnesota Office of the Registrar, Minority Enrollment Report, Fall Quarter 1993 (October 1993); University of Minnesota Human Resources Information System, Counts of Regular Faculty by Sex and Race (October 1993).

Asian Pacific Americans were the largest ethnic group, constituting 52.3 percent of minority students and 66.4 percent of minority faculty.

In August 1988, the University of Minnesota created the office of the associate vice president for academic affairs and associate provost with special responsibility for minority affairs to lead and coordinate university-wide diversity efforts. In 1992 the university appointed me to this position for a three-year term through the target of opportunity hire. As associate vice president for academic affairs, I have systemwide jurisdiction over all academic matters pertaining to students and faculty of color as well as over all diversity issues. In the capacity of associate provost, I am responsible for academic affairs on the Twin Cities campus. I not only serve on the President's Cabinet and the Provost's Council but also participate in the Twin Cities deans' meetings to create a vehicle by which there is ongoing communication with all of the vice presidents. I work through the vice presidents to reach their deans, with the result that this office has taken on a different direction and organizational structure to produce institutional change.

When I accepted the current position, I tried to formulate a paradigm that would help us to evaluate what had happened under the direction of the first associate vice president. I established a vehicle by which all those efforts could be evaluated so that we could understand what works successfully for students and faculty of color and what does not. I have created a process by which funding and support for the successful programs could be maintained or increased and unsuccessful programs could be discontinued.

Challenges and Dilemmas of an African American Female Administrator

One of the major difficulties I face is helping people who are my peers and colleagues understand the historical nature of the experience that students of color have at a very large institution like this. Located in a predominantly white environment of the Upper Midwest, the University of Minnesota had very few students and faculty of color before 1968. Our institution experienced much of the same turmoil that other major institutions experienced in the late 1960s and the early 1970s in connection with student protests over the lack of student representation. The Afro-American Studies Department did not really materialize until 1968. The new department was met with a lot of resistance, resentment, and hostility from many of the academics within the University of Minnesota's collegiate units. As a result of the creation of the Afro-American Studies Department, the departments of Chicano studies, American Indian studies, and women's studies were also established.

I find myself in an environment where people have developed some attitudes about people of color based on their personal experience in the 1960s and 1970s and on what the system has taught them about people of color. One of the significant barriers for me, therefore, is the fact that most people want and expect a quick resolution to age-old historical problems. I try to encourage them to change the environment so that students of color feel welcomed and successful and have an opportunity to develop their own sense of self. Furthermore, the faculty of color must feel welcomed, respected, and supported by being given the tools and the vehicles they need to gain tenure. In addition to making efforts to be a person who understands the system, I can speak the language of the system and try to get the system to understand the language, culture, and needs of the communities of color. These are real, serious barriers that are hard to overcome.

I meet both with individuals and with groups of people. I examine requests that come to our office—requests for financial assistance and requests for evaluation of programs. In addition to meeting with my own staff, I meet with representatives of other university units to discuss projects that they may be undertaking. I also hold meetings with my other colleagues in the university to address the issues pertaining to the mission of this office, such as ways to remove the barriers that exist for students and faculty of color. I am here until eight or nine o'clock at night depending on the day; I either have evening meetings or stay in the office trying to catch up with things that need to be done each day. I also have other kinds of responsibilities that are more often than not related to issues of communication—communicating with my African American community and other communities that I am responsible for and feel very connected to, and meeting with community people who are majority group members. I speak to the state legislators not only during the legislative session but also when the legislature is not in session. As I must also meet with faculty and students, my day is full.

Even though I try very hard not to commit myself to weekends so that I can use them for reflection and recuperation, there are times when it is inevitable that I schedule meetings over a weekend. Because many of the people with whom I need to communicate are available only evenings and weekends, I find myself having to accommodate their schedules. Often I must also fulfill nonuniversity functions or responsibilities on the weekends because of my position here or because of my interest in specific cultural organizations. There are several diverse boards on which I serve. For example, I am working with the Harriet Tubman Women's Shelter, which is the only shelter in Minneapolis for battered women. I serve as chair of its capital campaign to raise six million dollars. I also sit on the board of directors of the Minneapolis Institute of Arts.

This work allows me to express the other part of who I am and gives me a sense of renewal. I serve as chair of the nominating committee for this organization.

I am very active with the Minneapolis Urban League. I closely work with a Jewish and black organization that was formed after my daughter, Patrice, and Representative Mickey Leyland were killed in August 1989 in a plane crash while inspecting the famine in Ethiopia. We raise money to send two African American high school seniors to Israel every summer to spend six weeks in a kibbutz to experience that environment. I belong to the National Council of Black Women and a national panel that reviews schools and the entire system of choice as a method of educating young people.

My busy schedule is often interrupted by crises that arise with or without warning. I sometimes spend an inordinate amount of time doing damage control. Granted that it is the nature of my job, such crises take a lot of time and energy away from my regular duties. Three examples may suffice. The first example concerns an initiative called "University 2000: A Road Map to the 21st Century," a comprehensive and ambitious plan to prepare the University of Minnesota for the twenty-first century by meeting the changing expectations of higher education; responding to changing demographics and to an increasingly diverse society; and enhancing the social, cultural, economic, and intellectual health of Minnesota. This plan has generated serious concerns in the communities of color, which feared that it would limit access by students of color to the University of Minnesota, one of whose colleges has maintained an open admission policy for over half a century.

Since the past changes have seldom included the communities of color, it is difficult to convince them that change does not necessarily mean exclusion but could very well mean inclusion. Minority groups' opposition to University 2000, however, could undermine or at least delay its planning and implementation. I have therefore been meeting with the representatives of minority communities to share what has actually happened and to explain what kinds of changes my office has been instrumental in promoting to enhance diversity on campus. I am trying to respond to the communities of color in ways that they need to hear.

The second example deals with the unrest of students of color. They are going through a time right now in which they are very uncertain about their own success. They are reacting to the inevitable environmental conditions that exist in a place like this, which make them feel insecure and unfulfilled. So I spend a great deal of time meeting with these students to address their anxieties and concerns.

The third example involves staff and faculty who feel that they have been discriminated against. We have a case of a faculty member who feels that she and several others have been targeted by their chair or their colleagues and are not being given the support they need to do the kind of scholarly work they are doing. We also have issues affecting staff. We are trying to communicate and hear the issues they have; to determine what rules, policies, and issues they must deal with; and to explicate to the staff how those impact the work they have to do. Crises abound on our campus.

In addition to numerous crises, many victims of actual and perceived discrimination come to my office, although the university has an official vehicle for handling discrimination cases. Because most members of the university community see us as the office of minority affairs rather than the office of academic affairs with special responsibility for minority affairs, many cases of racial discrimination and harassment are brought to my attention first. For this reason, I have to stop and take the time to either redirect them to the appropriate offices or directly handle them, so that the victims feel that they are not ignored and their complaints are promptly heard.

The racial problems are very complex because they are often not clear. They are not issues about which you can track what happened how and when and then offer a resolution. They are mixed with the faculty's and students' sense of being, of their history, of whether they have felt accepted or excluded from the mainstream in the university community. In one case, students were being called names in the dormitories. Such an issue does not directly come under the purview of my office, but it affects us because it impacts the students' performances. If we are talking about retention and graduation of students of color, we must insure that they are not shackled with additional barriers to overcome.

I face many dilemmas because of my background and the duties that I have to perform. The dilemmas fall into several categories. The mission, role, and responsibility of my office require that we address the issues of academic success for students of color and the recruitment and scholarly satisfaction of faculty of color, and these are the issues of concern in the academic area. In addressing areas of minority concerns, our society seldom exercises the discipline of understanding what are general issues of minority affairs and what are issues that deal explicitly with the responsibilities for faculty and students of color. This type of dilemma is caused by the lack of definition on the part of the larger society—that is, the university administration, the very people with whom I work.

Students and faculty of color may be partly responsible for creating another type of dilemma, partly because minority people are also looking for prompt answers to age-old problems. Even my colleagues, for example, find it very hard to understand the boundaries of my office, or how I distinguish between the boundaries of the office and what I know simply as a person who has had a lot of experience in this field. It goes beyond academic interest and information; my knowledge base is broader than that. The dilemma is whether I should limit my responses, observations, and concerns to just those areas that deal with students and faculty of color on the academic side of the house or should speak to all of the issues that may affect students and faculty of color.

Another category of dilemma deals with the blurry jurisdiction of my office. People are not clear as to whether we are in academic affairs or student affairs or financial aid. If a person of color is involved in any of these issues, others automatically assume that it is our job, no matter what. So the dilemma for us is how to assist our colleagues in focusing their attention on the relevant questions in order to permit my office to take care of what we were assigned to do rather than having larger expectations of us than the job description warrants.

The ironic part of this jurisdiction dilemma is that the other diversity representatives feel that their interests and concerns are not adequately heard because, in their opinion, my office deals with just the ethnic minority issues in spite of having funds, staff, and other resources. People come from a variety of perspectives, so I find myself trying to make sure that I am addressing the human element of each person who is not very well informed about diversity and who may have some questions about its value. I should, however, stimulate in these people a sense of responsibility and understanding of diversity. The dilemmas are very complex, and they are deeply woven into the fabric of our American life.

I believe that many things I did earlier in my life have converged to qualify me uniquely for this difficult yet rewarding task at a predominantly white major research university. I will describe some relevant parts of my background that I think helped prepare me for my current senior-level position at the University of Minnesota.

My Background

I was born in San Antonio, Texas, to parents who were both college graduates. The oldest of three children, I had two younger brothers. My maternal grandmother and step-grandfather, who was a pharmacist, lived in San Antonio, where they had a drugstore. After college, my father worked as a waiter on the railroad because that was about the level of employment opportunities available to African Americans with a college degree. A nursery school teacher, my mother worked in the early years as a private teacher to wealthy white women.

When I was about two years old, my parents moved from San Antonio to

Houston, where my father, a political activist, became a labor organizer. He worked for A. Philip Randolph in organizing the unionized dining car waiters. My father's labor organization office was located in the African American business community, and, as a young woman, I used to go with him to his office and watch and listen to him. He was also very involved in politics, and I trailed along with him in his political work as well. As a precinct judge, my father worked hard toward the elimination of the poll tax imposed on African American voters. He left the railroad in 1949 and opened a real estate company; I became his first secretary.

Education was stressed as an important value in my family. I attended a poor private Catholic school from kindergarten through the twelfth grade. When I finished high school, there was no doubt that I was going to college.

I attended Fisk University, a historically black college in Nashville, Tennessee, where I majored in sociology and minored in chemistry. It was a small, highly respected liberal arts college that was founded in 1866, shortly after the emancipation of the African American people. Fisk University gave its students a sense of belonging; we had a sense of pride. Many of the faculty were well-known figures in the black renaissance. On campus, we were exposed to distinguished visiting scholars and civil rights leaders who were on the cutting edge of the protest movements. My positive undergraduate experience at this historically black institution helped me become a well-rounded, self-confident, and open-minded person.

Immediately after graduation, I married and moved to Massachusetts because my husband received a scholarship to attend Massachusetts Institute of Technology to work for his Ph.D. in mathematics. While he was studying at MIT, I worked in one of the botany labs at Harvard University. In 1954 our eldest daughter was born and my husband was drafted. He was in the military for two years, during which time I moved to Texas and went back to school to work on my master's degree in sociology at Texas Southern University in Houston.

After his discharge, my husband took a job at Honeywell in Minnesota, where he was probably the third African American to hold a professional position. By then we had two daughters. I had not completed my master's program when we came to Minnesota; I still needed to write my thesis. I had received a teaching certificate, however, while I was enrolled at Texas Southern University. In Minnesota I became so involved in civic and community activities that I did not go back until much later to earn my master's degree and doctorate in education at the University of Massachusetts at Amherst. I had started the doctoral program in education at the University of Minnesota around 1970 but subsequently withdrew from the program because of a conflict of interest that arose when I was elected to the Board of Regents of the University of Minnesota.

Prior to becoming a regent, I was a lobbyist for the League of Women Voters and the Minnesota State Department of Civil Rights. As the chief lobbyist for the latter, we were able to get fair housing legislation through the Minnesota legislature in 1961. During the 1960s, when there was so much turmoil here, I was working for the Urban League as a community organizer. In the mid-1960s I took a leave of absence from the Urban League to work as an assistant to the mayor of Minneapolis. I was a liaison between the mayor's office and the African American community in those turbulent years.

I was a community organizer for a federally funded program called Project ENABLE, which was the first federally and privately funded agency in the nation. The project established a partnership among the Urban League, the Jewish Family Children's Service, the Minneapolis Family Children's Service, and the federal government to explore ways of assisting families with parenting skills and strengthening family life. I also served as acting director of the Minneapolis Urban League. I directed a mentoring program that was probably one of the first, if not the first, of its kind for young African American females.

In 1968, when the African American student movement spread throughout the country, we also had a student movement here, and a group of African American students occupied Morrill Hall, the central administration building of the University of Minnesota. Because of my work in the community as a lobbyist and a volunteer in the Minneapolis public schools, I became involved with the students, providing food and moral support for them. When the siege was over, the African American Studies Department was created, and I became a member of the first faculty. I taught courses on black families in white America and the welfare system and its impact on African American families.

In late 1970 or early 1971, I was encouraged to offer my name as a candidate for the Board of Regents of the University of Minnesota. I served as a regent for three years. I was the chair of the Student Affairs Committee and the cochair of the Health Sciences Committee. At that time there was a strong relationship between the Board of Regents and the University Hospital. We were a very close board, and I learned a lot about the university and its structure.

As a regent, I also had a chance to understand the university's budget process and organizational labyrinth. I had opportunities to visit all of the coordinate campuses of the University of Minnesota. I was very interested in the university's total scope of responsibilities. I became familiar with all of the campuses, where I visited with faculty and students and got to know them quite well. In 1973 I resigned from the Board of Regents because my husband was transferred to Denver. I was named regent emeritus before leaving Minnesota.

My experience as a former regent makes it easier for me to work with the regents in my current capacity as an associate vice president for academic affairs. Because I was a regent, the present regents appear to expect some rapport with me. They seem to think that being a former regent, I understand what they are doing and have some appreciation for the issues and the schedules that they face. The current board appears to exercise much more direct responsibility. In the early 1970s, however, the regents diligently attempted to be policy makers. We were extremely supportive of the university. We looked for ways to assist it and to be more engaged in policy issues rather than management. It is a strange feeling to be a former regent and current senior-level university administrator.

We moved to Denver in the winter of 1973, and I eventually met an African American state senator. I became involved in his successful campaign to become state lieutenant governor and accepted employment in his office after he was seated. We worked closely with labor unions and created opportunities for Chicano and African American contractors, helping to break the barriers confronting them, and making it possible for them to bid on government contracts. Our work enabled minority contractors to become members of the union, a possibility that had been denied to them in the past.

Subsequently, after the lieutenant governor's term had ended and after I returned to Nashville, where I became a deputy director in the Carter-Mondale campaign in Tennessee, I began to work simultaneously on my master's degree and doctorate in education at the University of Massachusetts at Amherst. While enrolled in the doctoral program, I had an opportunity to work with an expert in school desegregation who was the editor of *Integrated Education*, a magazine that we published to report on progress in the area of school desegregation. This magazine became a resource for my dissertation because I was looking at the education of African American children and the role of African American parents in the community. In 1985 I received my doctorate in educational policy and administration.

In 1989 the president of the University of Minnesota asked me to get involved in resolving a problem that had developed between the African American and Jewish communities. I decided that rather than doing what had been customary—that is, having a conference to deal with those issues—I wanted to create an opportunity for the Jewish people and African Americans to understand why these conflicts existed. I suggested that the African American faculty and the Jewish faculty look at these issues as research projects.

The first area to be examined was the oppression and discrimination that each group had experienced. The second area was the coping mechanisms each community had developed to survive oppression. And the third area to explore was whether those experiences would give the Jewish and African American communities different ways of looking at the world. The two groups could then share that information with each other and have an intellectual dialogue about their experiences.

As a natural progression from the Jewish–African American dialogue, I developed the All-University Diversity Forums to look at the history of the University of Minnesota and evaluate the diversity programs that had been undertaken over the years with a view to determining what was working and what was not.

The All-University Diversity Forums helped prepare me for the position of associate vice president for academic affairs and associate provost with special responsibility for minority affairs. I derived a great deal of information from diverse segments of the university community as well as from the larger community. My experience with the diversity forums reinforced what we already knew and helped us understand that we needed to continue to develop a set of strategies, which I called a paradigm for effectiveness.

My Plan, Approach, and Contributions

I feel strongly that we must seize the moment to effect systemic changes to enhance diversity in every facet of the university community and to make diversity a mainstream issue. The biggest challenge I face is to accomplish these aims during my tenure as associate vice president and associate provost. In order to achieve this diversity goal, we must translate our vast institutional knowledge and information about diversity issues into policies, programs, and initiatives that will have lasting impact. A systemic change needs to be worked into a regular university process. For instance, the issue of minority faculty must become the issue of the total university system; everyone must take ownership of and responsibility for the issue.

Slow and subtle systemic changes may not necessarily show dramatic results immediately. Although such fundamental changes require time, processes, and efforts, the communities of color may need to see some visible signs that changes are taking place in a positive and constructive way. We therefore need to establish both long-range goals to represent systemic changes, as indicated by an increased number of faculty of color, higher retention and graduate rates, improved environment, and enhanced cultural awareness and sensitivity; and short-range goals to illustrate what is happening now. The communities of color and students of color need to feel that something positive is happening, the legislature must be aware of the need for change, and the people with whom I work must feel that the long hours and hard work are paying off.

In order for me to be an effective and successful catalyst for systemic changes, several things must be in place. First, it is very important for us to understand the obstacles that we face. What are the issues of students, faculty, and staff? Second, we have to understand the system, the organizational matrix of the university, so that we know how it is structured, how it operates, and what the mechanism is for effecting change to promote the objectives and goals of my office. Third, I must have financial resources that will allow me to execute our goals and objectives, to hire adequate staff, and to acquire necessary space and facilities to provide a comfortable and attractive workplace, inasmuch as my position is a political job as well as an administrative job. My office is also a social place where people who visit need to feel comfortable and welcome. Fourth, I have to have a title that says I am at least a peer with other people who have authority. I have to be able to command the respect of my colleagues as well as loyalty and commitment from the people with whom I work on a day-to-day basis. Fifth and last, I have to be fair, honest, and direct. I need to be in a position to objectively evaluate the end result of our efforts. Since I should be able to show success, I must have goals that are achievable and reportable. Evaluation is a key, because if I do not know what I am doing, I cannot evaluate what I am doing.

As an African American senior-level administrator, I must be vigilant to insure that systemic changes contemplated under University 2000 are not made without taking diversity into consideration. I have contributed to incorporating into the planning and development of University 2000 a mechanism to enhance academic excellence through diversity in preparation for the twenty-first century. Under University 2000, budget allocations to university units are closely tied to the units' contributions to and success in promoting diversity at the University of Minnesota. I will continue to play a pivotal role in guiding the University of Minnesota's University 2000 planning and implementation procedures so that systemic changes to be effected will reflect diversity as one of the central and integral themes. Fundamental changes without diversity are not systemic changes.

Chapter 26

Women's Colleges

The Intersection of Race, Class, and Gender

Brenda Hoke

Until recently, African American women were excluded from professorial positions in predominantly white institutions of higher learning. Sociologist Lois
Benjamin says that "prior to World War II, Black faculty and administrators
were deliberately excluded by law or tradition from predominantly White universities."[1] Since the doors opened, many blacks have found life inside the academy to be fraught with numerous contradictions and dilemmas.[2]

Social science research on African American women in the academy focuses on the experiences of black faculty and administrators in predominantly
white coed settings.[3] Little is known, however, about African American women
professors on predominantly white women's college campuses. The objective
of this chapter is to describe the experiences of this particular group of academicians. A quote from Ruth Farmer's "The Race for Inclusion in Academe"
accurately describes their plight:

> It is difficult to talk about being Black in a White space, even though in
> the United States such is usually the case. The difficulty is to speak, to
> name, without appearing to whine, a near impossibility, since African
> American women are not expected to speak at all. It is particularly diffi-
> cult to be heard, since despite reality, the myth still prevails that African
> American women are making great professional strides. Enmeshed within
> this myth is the belief that even when African American women are suf-
> fering, obstacles are faced stoically and handled with a prayer, and a smile.
> In other words, we always overcome. We African American women are
> reluctant to dispel this myth for it is one of the positive stereotypes af-
> forded us.[4]

The data presented here are organized into several sections. In the first section, historical information will be provided to describe the women's college on which this chapter is based. Next, the experiences of a group of African American women professors at the women's college will be examined. The chapter concludes with a discussion of the ways college and university campuses will be transformed if more black women faculty members are recruited and retained.

Background

Women's Christian College (WCC; a pseudonym), the setting on which this chapter is based, was organized over a century ago for daughters of the planter aristocracy in the South. The group of religious leaders who organized WCC decided that an educational facility was needed to help young women develop "Christian character." The first enrollees were privileged young women whose families were members of the planter aristocracy. WCC's founding fathers developed a liberal arts program that resembled curricula found at women's colleges in the North. They structured other aspects of college life to help young women develop the "genteel image" of the southern woman.[5]

WCC, not unlike many other white coed institutions of higher learning throughout the South, admitted its first African American student during the mid-1960s. The first black student graduated during the early 1970s, and the college employed its first African American faculty member close to twenty years later.

Other changes involving the hiring of women to fill top positions at WCC also did not occur until recently. For example, WCC selected its first woman president during the early 1980s. A woman chair of the board was chosen around 1990. She has since been replaced by a man. These structural changes represent a pattern that appears to be uncharacteristic of women's colleges throughout the United States, especially those located in the North. Some northern women's colleges began selecting women presidents and board members over a hundred years ago (Wellesley and Bryn Mawr selected women presidents during the late 1800s). White male hegemony continues to exist in spite of the structural changes that have occurred since the 1980s.

Where and When We Enter

Unlike the case in many large predominantly white colleges and universities, where blacks are hired to work in special programs, WCC black women professors, all of whom are untenured, are members of traditional departments—two teach social science courses and Africana studies courses; one teaches sociology courses, some of which have been cross-listed with women's studies. Since racial and gender biases are prevalent in women's colleges, we are marginalized, as are other blacks who work at predominantly white coed colleges and universities. We are the "outsiders within." Sociologist Patricia Hill Collins proposes that "this unique status confers a certain advantage — it stimulates a special Black women's perspective."[6]

Social scientist Linda Carty expresses a similar point: "Black women have been more than victims; they have been actors, conscious builders of relations from which they benefit, and though confined certainly to a very limited sphere of the White patriarchal world, their very position affords them clear understanding of their oppression."[7] It is this special understanding of the intersection of race and gender that enables blacks to maintain their identity.

In our daily interactions with both colleagues and students, we are reminded that we are the "other." Whether we are ignored by our colleagues or our knowledge is challenged by students in the classroom, we are not surprised by the pervasiveness of racism and sexism. Many blacks learn during the socialization process to be always cognizant of the daily manifestations of racism that characterize our society. In fact, one of the respondents in Lois Benjamin's study accurately captured the sentiment of some of my former and current colleagues when he said, "I am never surprised by racism. I never assume there is a minimum of racism among White colleagues and friends, so I don't get angry when it comes up. My question is how is it going to be manifested? Is it going to be with a billy club or with knights in hoods, or will it be the subtle discrimination of talk at the faculty club?"[8] The faculty member's comment describes the feelings of many blacks in both predominantly white coeducational and noncoeducational college and university settings. In spite of the daily assaults of racism, blacks are able to keep their identity intact.

Black women faculty face not only racism but sexism as well. Sexism is widespread on the WCC campus; employment at a women's college does not shield black women faculty from it. As we experience the daily assaults of oppression in the academy, we ask whether our colleagues and students are responding to our color or our gender. We experience the role strain and role conflict that characterize the lives of our African American counterparts on predominantly white coed college and university campuses. All of the WCC black women faculty have worked at predominantly white coed institutions of higher learning. These experiences provide a framework from which we are able to make comparisons between the different settings.

Is it race or is it sex? Lois Benjamin provides the answer when she concludes that the women in her study "recognize the confluence of both race and sex as salient variables in their professional and social interactions."[9]

Sisterhood: An Illusion or Reality?

Bonnie Thornton Dill proposes that

> the concept of sisterhood has been an important unifying force in the contemporary women's movement. By stressing the similarities in women's secondary social and economic positions in all societies and in the family, it has been a binding force in the struggles against chauvinism and patriarchy. However, as we review the past decade, it becomes apparent that the cry "sisterhood is power" has engaged only a few segments of the female population in the United States. Black, Hispanic, Native American, and Asian-American women of all classes and many working-class women have not readily identified themselves as sisters of the white middle-class women who have been in the forefront of the movement.[10]

Dill's quote notes that few African American women on college and university campuses, or in the larger society, have identified with white middle-class women. Yet there are gender equity issues that black and white women share. Race, however, creates a schism that allows black and white women on college and university campuses to enjoy only a "fragile bond,"[11] threatened by persistent hostility, resentment, and suspicion. While working at universities in the Midwest and the Northeast, I have observed black and white women supporting each other on occasion. For example, at one Midwestern university, black women united with white women to sponsor several campuswide events that addressed gender equity issues throughout the university system. After the event, black and white women went their separate ways. Throughout such interactions, black women often ask themselves if they have been asked to participate because their input is valued or because their white colleagues need some tokens. Until these barriers are resolved satisfactorily, race remains a hurdle that white and black women will be unable to overcome.

Instead of a cross-racial sisterhood here at WCC, we have seen more intense bonds develop between women of the same racial groups. For example, white women establish close relationships with other white women. Likewise, black women develop "nurturant supportive feelings of attachment and loyalty to other black women" if they are available.[12] If a woman is the only black faculty member on her campus, such a relationship is not possible. My predecessor at WCC was the only black woman faculty member for several years. Having

been in a similar position, I can understand her feelings of isolation, invisibility, and fragmentation, of being an "outsider who is within." When confronted with this scenario, black women form fragile relationships with white female faculty members. These relationships usually are not a "bonding sisterhood," although many black women have been socialized to value them. As Dill notes, "We have institutionalized sisterhood in our churches, organized it through the club movements that began in the late 1880s, recited it in our numerous informational gatherings, and lived it in our extended family gatherings that frequently place great importance on female kinship ties."[13]

After several racial incidents on campus, WCC has learned that having one black woman faculty member does not successfully solve a moral dilemma or settle a justice issue. WCC has hired four full-time black faculty members, three women and one man. Additionally, four part-time and/or adjunct black faculty were hired, all of them women. This increase in faculty has allowed black women to create a bond of sisterhood.

Quite often the sisterly bond, regardless of the number of women included, is the only supportive network African American females find on both predominantly white coed and noncoed campuses. Relationships with other black women help us to reaffirm our positive black identity.

On some campuses I have noticed that whites appear to be suspicious of relationships that black faculty develop among themselves. For example, there have been times that I invited other blacks to my office and my white colleagues paced in front of my door several times, lingering briefly to stare. On several occasions we have been questioned regarding our conversations. These are indignities that our white counterparts do not experience.

The Influence of Cultural Images

White perceptions of African American women faculty are shaped by the controlling negative cultural images that have been created to symbolize black womanhood. Sociologist Cheryl Townsend Gilkes suggests that "black women's assertiveness and their use of every expression of racism to launch multiple assaults against the entire fabric of inequality have been a consistent, multifaceted threat to the status quo. As punishment, black women have been assaulted with a variety of negative images."[14] For example, "mammy" is one of the most pervasive images used to characterize black womanhood. This particular controlling image emerged during slavery. At its inception, mammy was depicted as a large, dark, submissive woman who was devoted to the white family that owned her. After emancipation, the image was modified to show mammy's submissiveness to her employer.

Over the years, the mammy image has evolved to a more contemporary form that continues to impact the lives of many African American females, including those black women who occupy professional positions on predominantly white college and university campuses. On a daily basis, the lives of African American women faculty members on the WCC campus are affected by the controlling mammy image. For instance, black women faculty who are supportive of students (both black and white) are described by their white colleagues as mothering, whereas these white colleagues describe their own supporting behavior as mentoring. The contrast between the two descriptions suggests that black women, regardless of educational attainment, are still perceived as nurturant domestic servants. As Benjamin notes, the mammy image has been transferred to the academy.[15] There are other controlling negative cultural images that shape whites' perception of African American women faculty members. Sociologist K. Sue Jewell provides the example of the "bad-black-girl." She proposes that this particular stereotype is an extension of the mammy image. The modern version of the bad-black-girl image is not necessarily someone with a fair complexion or European features, as described in the literature. Unlike the mammy image, the newly created bad-black-girl is characterized as being aggressive, independent, and decisive. The stereotype emphasizes "the hypersexuality of the African American woman who yearns for her sexuality."[16]

Daily interactions with white male colleagues on the WCC campus (and other institutions where I have worked) suggest that some men perceive African American women faculty members and students in terms of the bad-black-girl's cultural image. These men consistently make remarks with sexual overtones to black women faculty members and students. On several occasions, both at WCC and at a Midwestern university, white male colleagues have made such remarks to me.

There have been other situations in which white male professors have tried to touch me as well as other black women faculty and students. Several times on the elevator here at WCC a white colleague tried to rest his arm on my shoulder. Many men believe that their "whiteness" is a privilege that gives them a right to dominate black women faculty. While these men may not view their behavior as offensive, I suggest that it is inappropriate.

That African American women faculty members continue to be perceived in terms of these negative cultural images suggests that we have devalued status because of our gender and race. As Farmer notes, "An African American woman is viewed through lenses colored by gender and race biases; therefore, ideas, instructions, and feedback from her may be received with hostility in a patronizing manner, or sometimes blatantly ignored, with impunity."[17] She calls these strategies "the silencing mechanism whites use to denigrate the African American woman, to let her know that she does not belong, that she has no ideas worth hearing."[18]

Though most of the faculty members at WCC are women, a similar scenario occurs on our campus. African American women faculty members are treated as the "other," particularly by white men faculty, who are the most influential on the campus. Our opinions are not solicited unless our colleagues need information about racial issues. We are reminded frequently that we were brought to the campus because of our expertise in the area of race relations. Inquiries about gender concerns are usually directed to white women professors. The white males also use other strategies to remind us that we are the "other." Recent conversations with two black women administrators revealed the following information. One woman, who works at a large Southern university, reports that her dean, who is a white male, does not expect her to question any of his policy decisions. "If I raise questions regarding his handling of campus racial issues, in particular those involving black students, I am accused of being too sensitive." The second woman administrator from a Midwestern university expresses a similar problem in her daily interactions with her dean, a white woman. "I am not expected to challenge her on any issues. She always wants to be right." These accounts suggest that black women in the academy are expected to be submissive and obedient. The mammy role has been professionalized.

Some white male colleagues also regularly question the credentials of black women professors. The actions and comments of some white men at WCC indicate that they think the hiring of black women takes positions from other white men. I was hired over a white man, and I have heard through the campus grapevine that many students and faculty were, and continue to be, upset over the decision. Many white faculty view all appointments of black faculty as "affirmative action hires."

Teaching, Research, and Service

After WCC's first black woman professor left, the administrators hired more African American faculty in an attempt to address some of the racial problems students were experiencing on the campus. At the same time more faculty members were being hired, the college began recruiting more African American women students. This hiring practice was initiated in anticipation that African American faculty would serve as role models for currently enrolling African American students and others who are expected to come in the future. This personnel move should lend itself to the retention of both African American students and faculty.

At the present time, the climate at WCC is conducive to professional development. For example, the teaching load is fairly consistent with that of other universities where I have worked. Most women students in my classes have not resisted lectures and discussions that address the intersection of race, class, and gender. This is not to suggest the they do not challenge me as the "other" at times. But these challenges are not like those I have experienced in other places where the students were white males, mostly from middle-class families. One white male engineering major complained to me that my voice aggravated him. I am certain the student would not have made the same complaint to his white male engineering professors.

Upper-echelon administrators, all of whom are women, seem to be supportive of teaching that examines interlocking systems of oppression in the lives of people of color. Many other white male and female faculty members, however, tend to suppport more traditional paradigms and research methodologies. It remains to be seen how those who support using the more traditional approaches will evaluate me or any of the other African American women professors when it is time for our tenure and promotion reviews. To date, no African American faculty member has remained at WCC long enough to be considered for tenure and promotion.

Likewise, the administration provides financial support for research interests of all faculty. Priority is usually given to new faculty, most of whom are African American or Latin American. Most of the research interests of the new faculty focus on the intersection of the multiple systems of domination, race, class, and gender in the lives of people of color and/or underrepresented groups in the social scientific literature.

Since all new black faculty have been here at WCC less than two years, it remains to be determined whether our service to Afrocentric concerns will be given the same consideration in the tenure and promotion process as similar concerns of our white counterparts.

Recently the college has begun to offer more professional development support that emphasizes issues of multiculturalism. For example, the administration selected me to represent the college at a diversity and collaborative learning conference, selected another African American faculty member to attend a conference on infusion of diversity in the college curriculum, and chose still another to participate in an in-depth Latin American cultural studies program.

These administrative decisions seem to suggest a commitment by the college to expose both black and white faculty to activities of diversity.

Though some members of the WCC community have been supportive, it is difficult being among the first African American women to be hired. We are overscrutinized by faculty and students. It is as though many of the whites were waiting for us to make a mistake. I experienced these same responses at the Midwestern university where I worked. There I was the first African American woman faculty to be employed in the hundred years of the university's existence. Many times I have suspected that a majority of my students had not had any contact with African Americans before enrolling in my classes.

What Now? The Potential for Social Change

Black women initiate both individual and collective acts of resistance on WCC's campus. Many of the individual acts involve a female faculty member's providing advice to black students about how to handle racist and sexist comments made by white professors in the classroom. Black faculty seek advice from each other on how to handle racist and sexist behavior of male faculty members. The black faculty members are striving to initiate joint research ventures as a means of instituting change at WCC. Plans are under way to develop a minor in Africana studies, which is indeed a challenge for WCC faculty, students, and administration. More students are beginning to enroll in courses, and the college community seems more responsive to social change. For example, the college is preparing a core faculty to assist in the recruitment of Latina students, including Afro-Latina students, and in promoting curricular changes and sensitivity initiatives to welcome and retain these students.

Conclusions

This chapter suggests that black female faculty members on white women's college campuses face many of the same obstacles to success as their African American counterparts in coed settings. It is important that WCC and other colleges and universities that are beginning to employ more African American faculty and administrators understand the barriers that black females experience. Institutions of higher learning need to create policies and programmatic changes that will make the academic environment less hostile to and more supportive of black women faculty. Effective recruitment and retention of more black faculty will help transform the academy.

WCC's current attempt to address its lack of racial diversity has the potential to transform the campus. If the administration continues to recruit and retain more black women faculty members and other people of color, we can expect to observe a number of changes on our campus. For example, as black women faculty members begin to assume positions of authority on campus, we can expect the general climate to change, particularly for the students. As the campus climate changes from hostile to more supportive, we can expect the college to be able to recruit and retain more black female students. The addition of more African American women faculty members will provide role models for the female students. The black students will be able to look to the African American women faculty members for advice and counseling. The faculty can also assist students in setting goals for the future.

Not only will the black students benefit from the addition of more African American women faculty members; the entire WCC campus will gain. African American women faculty members will bring to academia different paradigms that are more inclusive of the experiences of women, people of color, and low-income groups. We can also expect the black women faculty members to utilize research methodologies that are more liberatory for people of color, women, and low-income groups than the traditional strategies used in the past to investigate the concerns of mostly white middle-class males.

The efforts of the black women faculty members will produce a new kind of knowledge that will enable students (and other members of the WCC community) to appreciate racial diversity. This knowledge can also be used to show the campus community new patterns of relating across racial lines. We are optimistic that our interactions with each other will set an example for the black women students. It is important for them to learn that unity in the academy is necessary because unity facilitates coordinated resistance.

Notes

1. Lois Benjamin, *The Black Elite: Facing the Color Line in the Twilight of the Twentieth Century* (Chicago: Nelson-Hall, 1991), 123.

2. Ibid., 123–41.

3. Ibid. See also Linda Carthy, "Black Women in Academia: A Statement from the Periphery," in *Unsettling Relations: The University as a Site of Feminist Struggles*, edited by Himani Bannerji et al. (Boston: South End Press, 1992), 13–44; Michelle Howard-Vital, "African-American Women in Higher Education Struggling to Gain Identity," *Journal of Black Studies* 20, no. 2 (1986): 180–91; and Yolanda Moses, *Black Women in Academe*, Project on the Status and Education of Women (Washington, D.C.: Association of American Colleges, 1989).

4. Ruth Farmer, "The Race for Inclusion in Academe," in *Spirit, Space, and Survival*, edited by Joy James and Ruth Farmer (New York: Routledge, 1993), 205.

5. John Lynxwiler and Michele Wilson, "The Code of the New Southern Belle: Generating Typifications to Structure Social Interaction," in *Southern Women*, edited by Caroline Matheny Dilman (New York: Hemisphere, 1988), 113–25.

6. Patricia Hill Collins, *Black Feminist Thought* (Cambridge, Mass.: Unwin Hyman, 1990), 11.

7. Linda Carthy, *Black Women in Academia*, 13–44. See also Robert Merton, "Insiders and Outsiders: A Chapter in the Sociology of Knowledge," *American Journal of Sociology* 78, (1972): 9–47; and Georg Simmel, "The Sociological Significance of the Stranger," in *Introduction to the Science of Sociology*, edited by Robert Park and Ernest Burgess (Chicago: University of Chicago Press, 1921).

8. Benjamin, *The Black Elite*, 126.

9. Ibid., 177.

10. Bonnie Thornton Dill, "On the Hem of Life: Race, Class and the Prospects for Sisterhood," in *Class, Race and Sex: The Dynamics of Control*, edited by Amy Swerdlow and Hanna Lessinger (Boston: G. K. Hall, 1983), 174.

11. Benjamin, *The Black Elite*, 183.

12. Dill, "On the Hem of Life," 175.

13. Ibid.

14. Cheryl Townsend Gilkes, "From Slavery to Social Welfare: Racism and the Control of Black Women," in *Class, Race and Sex*, 294.

15. Benjamin, *The Black Elite*, 189.

16. K. Sue Jewell, *From Mammy to Miss America and Beyond: Cultural Images and the Shaping of U. S. Social Policy* (New York: Routledge, 1993), 37–38.

17. Farmer, "The Race for Inclusion in Academe," 206.

18. Ibid.

Chapter 27

"I Bring the History of My Experience"

Black Women Professors at Spelman College Teaching out of Their Lives

Mona T. Phillips

Gloria Wade-Gayles recalls, in *Pushed Back to Strength: A Black Woman's Journey Home*, how she missed the professors at the historically black college in Memphis that she attended as an undergraduate, who "taught with passion" and inspired by example, when she first encountered "the cold whiteness" of the city of Boston, where she went as a graduate student. Wade-Gayles writes, "I missed them. I missed the small campus in Memphis which was resonant with the history of my people. I missed the lectures and convocations and conversations about mission which meant giving back to the place from whence you come. I missed the humanistic approach to education."[1]

Wade-Gayles recalls her experiences as a student with black professors committed to imparting those analytical skills and perspectives necessary for black students to function as subjects in the "cold whiteness" of the larger society and perhaps as agents for its transformation. Bell Hooks writes of a similar recollection, calling from childhood memory a Miss Annie Mae Moore, "who taught my mama and her sisters." Hooks remembers the woman as someone (along with other "progressive teachers") who taught not just from the books but from an "oppositional world view—different from that of our exploiters and oppressors, a world view that would enable us to see ourselves not through the lens of racism or racist stereotypes."[2]

Although Hooks and Wade-Gayles invoke memories from different points of their educational experiences, the people they remember have something in common: they used their teaching as a weapon against racism and sexism, offering a "liberatory pedagogy."[3] The effectiveness of these women teachers and professors is clear in the often cited statistics on retention rates of historically black colleges and universities as well as in the recent reconsideration of the ability of the segregated classrooms of the preintegration South to yield bountiful results. What is missing, however, are the women professors themselves—their own stories. These women disappear into the generic familiar figure of the strong, sustaining black woman.

In addition, the women are rendered invisible because of the "invisibility" (as defined by the larger academy) of black colleges and universities. Similarly to the segregated schools described by Hooks (which were deemed the expendable schools during the era of court-ordered desegregation), black colleges and universities are seen as operating at the "margins" of the larger academic community.[4] Because black colleges and universities are characterized within the larger academy as "isolated" institutions (isolated from places where the "real" activities of higher education occur), their professors are also viewed within the larger academy as isolated toilers, "stuck" there doing the necessary but essentially mindless work of the private sphere.

After centuries of misinterpretation of African American women's lives, many scholars have moved, as Kesho Scott writes, "to ensure . . . that women's stories are told in their own words."[5] Therefore the writing, collection, and examination of life histories and personal narratives have become important ways to begin to uncover the complexities of life for African American women at their point along the "matrix of domination" as those complexities are articulated by the women themselves.[6] In this chapter, based on in-depth, semistructured interviews with ten African American women professors at Spelman College, a historically black college for women, three women share their understanding of their own work experiences within the tradition of teaching for survival and change. The time the women spent in the college ranged from nine years to more than thirty years. I chose these three women because, as I listened to them talk, it seemed that they were having a conversation with one another about pedagogy and that this conversation was taking place across time (history), across individually located perspectives, and across historically located social experiences.

The interviews began with my asking the women to reflect on their lives and to think about the relationship (if there was any) of their own life histories to their work at Spelman College. Because African American women occupy a social space at the intersection of multiple, devalued statuses, the thoughts of the women reflected that particular position. The women did not separate their personal stories from the story of African Americans, from the stories of *women*, from the story of their work at a black women's college. What was revealed from the interviews was thus much more than a simple linear telling of the impact of the past on the present, which is what the opening question elicited.

What emerged instead were intricately woven stories of women's lives as those lives are embedded in and reflective of the life of a people.

The women talked about their experiences within supportive segregated childhoods and within sometimes less supportive desegregated schools; their encounters with racism and sexism; and how these experiences fashioned the contours of their hopes and passions for the young African American women they teach. Their descriptions of these experiences varied with the individuals *and* with the historical moment in which the experiences occurred.

But just as their memories and perspectives were shaped by differences, they were also shaped by continuities that have consistently affected African American women, from those writing the earliest slave narratives of the eighteenth century to those coming to adulthood in the 1990s.

Lois B. Moreland: Continuing the Tradition of Claiming Denied Space

The efforts of women at the turn of the century to define themselves, redefine dominant constructs, and then have themselves accepted as "ladies" or "women" are documented through the writings of educator Anna Julia Cooper; the auto-biography of Mary Church Terrell; the historical records of members, activities, and goals of the Colored Women's Club Movement; and various other historical documents.[7] Lois Moreland is firmly grounded in that tradition of claiming those "spaces" denied to African American women and men. Whether those denied spaces were womanhood, certain occupations, or simply "human-ity," Dr. Moreland spoke throughout the interview of "proving" the worth of African Americans to others.

Lois Moreland is the director of the International Affairs Center at Spelman College and founding chair of the Political Science Department of the college, over which she presided from 1966 to 1990. She received her undergradu-ate degree from Sarah Lawrence, her master's in political science from Howard University, and her Ph.D. from American University. She began her teaching career at Spelman College in 1959, when she was twenty-four years old. She has strong recollections of the dramas on the campus and the city that played out against the backdrop of the civil rights and black power movements and her own tenure as the Southeast regional youth field secretary for the NAACP.

Arriving for my appointment, I entered the office of this impeccably groomed, seemingly always self-possessed woman and noticed the Bible on the edge of the desk. She smiled warmly, invited me to sit down, and asked if I would like some coffee or tea. She listened very attentively as I told her the general frame-work of the interview, nodded when I finished, adjusted her half-moon glasses, and then began to speak in careful and precise language and in strong tones. "I was born in 1933, and I am not ashamed to say that. I am happy that I have lived so long. I must also say, first, that I am a Christian, and that influences all that I do and believe. . . . I grew up in segregated Washington, D.C., and among the things I remember most are our family discussions around the dining room table. We would talk about anything, and we were encouraged to do so by our parents. We were taught to question *everything*. Our ideas were important, and we were encouraged to talk them through."

It is clear that her parents were (and still are) important influences in her life. She speaks of them a great deal throughout the interview, and their names appear first on her vita. Memories of her mother are intertwined with memories of books, movie theaters, and parks. She recalled her mother "reading to me from the comics. I learned to read by the age of five, and I remember telling my mother, 'I can do it by myself now. . . .' My mother would take us to the library every Saturday and sometimes to the park. . . . As I think about those times now, I know that the park was segregated, but I just know that I had lovely times there with my mother and sister. I also remember my father taking my sister and me to work with him and showing us his work evaluations. . . . Both my parents are very bright people."

Throughout Lois Moreland's description of her years growing up in Washington, D.C., she does not conjure up a traumatized segregated experience. In addition to an intellectually stimulating and loving home environment, she recalls supportive schoolteachers who had only the highest expectations for her. She received a scholarship to Radcliffe at the end of her high school years but actually attended Sarah Lawrence. She recalls "not being afraid or intimidated by Sarah Lawrence":

> You see, I was accustomed to expressing my ideas around the table with my parents. . . . But I did have low self-esteem there. I did not feel pretty or smart. Now, that is not what others thought of me, because I later discovered that they all thought I was quite bright and attractive. But that is what the isolation of integration did [to me]. I remember being placed in a Spanish class, as I thought that I might become a linguist. I always enjoyed the languages. There was one other person in the class, and on the first day, we were asked to translate Lord Byron into Spanish. I had not heard of Lord Byron, and the little bit of Spanish I had. . . . Well, I was in a class with someone who traveled to Spain every summer and had had many years of the language. But I was determined to prove that I could do it.

Lois Moreland also recalled the first time she was "accosted by racism." She remembers going into a drugstore, asking for a BC headache powder and a Coca-Cola for her mother, and being told in a "cold manner" that she was not to stand at that end of the counter but should go down to the "colored" end. This happened when she was, as she recalls, "around nine years old," but she tells the story with the vivid details and emotions of an incident that might have occurred more recently.

Moreland shares an experience with sexism that happened during her studies at Howard University and involved a political science professor who, she says, was responsible for her going into that discipline. She remembers him fondly but also recalls that he did not look kindly upon women who did well on comprehensives. He referred to her as that "g.d. [goddamned] woman who got the highest scores on the comprehensive examinations." She states that this was her first remembered experience with sexism, asserting that "the first thing people see about me is my race, you see. And then they get to the woman."

While Lois Moreland sees her life's work as breaking down barriers between races and ethnic groups and expresses a firm belief in the basic humanity of all people, she also voices a firm commitment to African American people. She is convinced of the specialness she and other African American women bring to a classroom of African American women students: "The decline in the family requires black women teachers to bring to students the kind of understanding we have that's grown out of pain. . . . I know what they have been through. You remember I told you about the low self-esteem at Sarah Lawrence? I know what they will have to confront. I bring [to them] the history of my experience."

Lois Moreland describes her role at the college as "preparing African American women to be a part of the power base, the foundation of the society." She acknowledges what she herself calls the "conservatism" of her ideas ("As you get older, you get more conservative") but is firm in her belief that power lies not in being a "member of an organization protesting a law" but in being a "member of the legislative body that makes the law." She speaks proudly of her students who have "done well" and says that while her thrust at one time was to produce lawyers, her "focus now is on getting them to be Ph.D.s—but, of course, to choose their own fields." She says, "I love what I do. I love it when the light comes on. You can see it. It's like they're saying, 'I can do it by myself now.'"

As we came to the end of our interview, I asked Lois Moreland for her vita. She had this ready for me because "she thought I might want it." I left her office with that carefully typed representation of her life's agenda to prove that African Americans are "as good as anyone else": the listing of her book on rac-

ism and law, journal articles she's written, and her active participation and leadership in professional organizations. I am once again reminded of those women
who had come before her who — by pushing forcefully — carefully placed themselves and their people into those arenas that had been determined to be off-
limits to African Americans.

Judy Gebre-Hiwet: Finding Voice Away from the Dismissive Eye

Judy Gebre-Hiwet has been an instructor and lecturer in English at Spelman
College for twenty years. She graduated from Spelman in 1965, at what she
describes as the "tail-end" of the civil rights activism on the campus. She has
received a master's degree from the Columbia School of Journalism and another master's from Harvard University in literature.

I was determined to get an interview with this woman, whom one former
student (now an outspoken member of the city's school board) fondly remembers as the professor who wrote on her first college essay in big red letters, "What
is this madness?"

The analytical thread woven throughout the interview (which was filled with
references to the ideas of such diverse people as Alice Walker, John Milton,
Frederick Douglass, Adrienne Rich, June Jordan, and Benjamin E. Mays) is
her identification with and analysis of the forces in her life that attempted (sometimes successfully) to silence her and those forces that encouraged her to give
voice to who she was. Judy Gebre-Hiwet spoke passionately, sometimes elevat-
ing her voice, sprinkling declarative responses with queries such as "What do
you think?" Her words tumbled out, one almost on top of the other.

She described her own college experience as one in which there was a silence in the curriculum regarding African American women. She found her
college experience "rigidifying"; its dominant message was "Do what I tell you
to do; see what I tell you to see." She continued, "Seldom (even though the
classes were small) was there a teaching method other than lecture. Very seldom was there class discussion. [The message was] We are here to train you, to
show the white people you can do it, and you can do it in most cases better
than they can do it. Very seldom did I have the opportunity to think about what
I was thinking, and why I was thinking it, although my home life provided me
with some alternative."

Judy Gebre-Hiwet then spoke of her mother and grandmother as "saving"
influences in her life and described them as "careful thinkers . . . who were
always asking questions, even though we lived in a society . . . that didn't encourage black folk to ask *no* questions." She continued her description of her
mother and grandmother:

They always encouraged me to ask questions because they said that only in questioning can you clarify who you are and what you stand for. And it was very important in my family to formulate a position or a stand: What do you stand for? What are you about? What are your principles? So I went through the four-year experience as a professional automaton. . . . It was not difficult for me to give back what I was given — flawlessly. I think what saved me was the kind of background that I came from . . . my mother and grandmother always encouraging me to clarify what I stood for."

She also recalls going to school at the college laboratory nursery school. She especially remembers one teacher, a white woman, who was "very adept at bringing out your voice. She'd always tell us stories and these were white Anglo-Saxon, Protestant fairy tales, which always exalted the position of the little white girl or the little white boy. She would always say tell the story the way you see it, the way you feel it. Which I didn't recognize until much later on was a real serious call for my own voice."

She goes on to describe her time in Ethiopia, where she moved with her husband. They moved back to Atlanta after three years, and as Gebre-Hiwet talked, she illuminated the role of race and gender in shaping the contours of her and her husband's lives. She wryly stated that "Atlanta had no jobs for two aspiring black journalists." After living with her family for a while, she and her husband did end up with teaching jobs at Spelman. She describes her decision to attend Harvard as an escape from a failing marriage and also a move that came about as she "came to recognize" her desire to teach. "I had been running away from that call to teach. . . . My mother and grandmother were teachers, so I always had those models in front of me. And I really did have an investment in speaking to young women about that special burden . . . and in realizing that special burden that black women have in terms of liberating the race. And after the breakdown of a marriage, I began to understand the importance of the silence that had been imposed. . . . I guess that was my . . . self-awakening."

Judy Gebre-Hiwet returned from Harvard when her daughter was going into the sixth grade (the child had been living in Atlanta with her grandmother and great-grandmother). "I needed to get back to help with that transition, and when the money ran out, I came back home and began teaching literature."

She spoke of her time at Harvard as a period when she thought of herself as "an outsider, outside the circle of power. [I saw myself] as Sojourner Truth, or Harriet Tubman on an 'underground railroad mission.'" She describes her particular mission as bringing back the story of Harvard, demystifying it for the black women she taught, and beginning the conversation of how black people might live without valorizing all that is white. She remembers the Harvard library as "daunting," but she goes on to say that she, "as Alice [Walker] says, just kept whistling like a woman undaunted." Judy Gebre-Hiwet decries the importance that places like Harvard seem to have for her students, whom she sees as being "caught up in a culture of oppression and denial." As she describes what she calls "an irony within an irony," she locates in her students' parents the responsibility for her students' preoccupation with getting into the "right" graduate schools. These parents had become adults, as she had, during the 1960s, and, as she explained, "the thrust has been . . . we've got to show them. While we've taken the struggle off the streets and, shall we say, inside the boardrooms, there still is that apish mentality, that apish desire that we can show them, we can prove to them. . . . And they [whites] don't give a damn about us."

Du Bois wrote in 1903 of the double consciousness required of Negroes who were also Americans; that double-sightedness that is a function of having to attend to the dismissive eye of the larger society.[8] Judy Gebre-Hiwet is convinced that the double consciousness that fueled Lois Moreland distracts African American women from the necessary business of discovering "who we are and who we see ourselves as being." This conviction undergirds her critique of the institution in which she teaches and the students she teaches. She asserts that the dismissive eye has a particularly harsh view of black women: "There is a ceiling that is put over us . . . that is intended to diminish us in our minds. . . . I think we are taught we are nothing in a way that diminishes us to a level that . . . is a deadness. And so, when we go out . . . to meet these young women every day—and I think we need to be clear that this is what we are doing—we are going out to raise them from the dead. And the irony is that we are the walking dead—the near dead—attempting to raise the dead."

As Judy Gebre-Hiwet continued to talk, she made her "goals" for her students clear. It is important to her that they learn how to "negotiate [their] way through the world of thought" and to confront those realities around them (and inside of them) that are perhaps unpleasant and uncomfortable. She sees her very *being* as a personification of all that some of the students are "willing to turn away from." She laughed as she said, "I represent a whole different image to them. [They think] This big, black, curl-wearing woman. What can she possibly [teach me]? . . . I see it in their parents' eyes when they introduce me to them at graduation: Is *this* your teacher?"

Judy Gebre-Hiwet acknowledges that students may find her uncomfortable but insists that true learning does not occur in an environment of comfort. She is aware of her students' discomfort with her appearance, so, she says, "I bring it out. It's about an emptying in order to reach renewal." She also insists that the students turn a critical eye on the college itself and recognize what she describes as that "imitative, oppressive quality that permeates this whole environment."

Throughout the interview, Judy Gebre-Hiwet spoke with a direct intensity about the relationship between her life and the lives of the young women she faces in the classroom every day. She speaks about them (and to them) lovingly—even when she is harshly critical. Hers is not a romantic view of the dynamics and experience of teaching African American women at a historically black college. She says that "in this period of our development, of our overcoming, there are those [of us] who have to sacrifice ourselves without clear or sure-footed indication that we are going to overcome." Yet she expresses some belief in the possibility of change: "I guess . . . I really do believe that overcoming is possible. And I really have bought into the understanding of human history and progress . . . because it's not about whether I see it, or my daughter, but that it eventually happens."

Myra Burnett: Reclaiming the Tradition of "Functional Segregation"

The interviews with those women who came to adulthood during the last half of the 1970s revealed social and educational experiences that tended to be divided between segregated and desegregated environments. Caught in the crossroads of disappearing forced segregation and the broken promises of affirmative action, these women remembered being denied valedictorian spots in their graduation classes (because of their race) and the pressures of being "the only one" in desegregated elementary and high school classrooms. One woman spoke of the social isolation during her high school years because of the disappearance of black males when black schools disappeared. Some of the women worried about what impact teaching at a historically black college would have on their scholarly production. They spoke of the social and intellectual isolation of graduate school.

But these women also spoke of the encouragement and support they found in the corners of their lives that were, and remained, "segregated." They spoke of the significant black teachers who opened their eyes to the sciences or to the power of Langston Hughes. Some worried aloud about the future of their students, whom they did not see as having experienced the supportive communities (as opposed to isolated individuals or even isolated families) of women and men pushing them forward and helping them to make sense of their lives.

Myra Burnett graduated from Harvard in 1977, received her master's in psychology from Stanford, and then completed her Ph.D. in clinical psychology at Duke University in 1988. Her use of quiet, concise, yet passionate language communicates the sense that her ideas are carefully reasoned. But what is also evident throughout the interview is that she is constantly rethinking and reformulating her ideas.

Myra Burnett began teaching at Spelman in 1986. She said, "I had never thought much about teaching. Had I not gotten the job at Spelman, I would have worked at a hospital as an on-site clinical psychologist. What enticed me was the idea of teaching young black women." She describes herself as coming out of a background of what she calls "functional segregation." "I grew up in a working-to-middle-class segregated neighborhood in Fort Worth, Texas. . . . In my block, there were teachers and high school counselors (and my father, who was an electrician). We weren't in the ritzier neighborhood where the doctors or the principals lived . . . but it was very comfortable, orderly—as you can imagine back in the early '60s."

Throughout her interview, the consideration of "tradition" appeared over and over again. At one point, Myra Burnett laughed and said, "I guess I'm kind of into tradition." Her decision to teach at a historically black college was a decision to maintain the tradition of "functioning segregation—a tradition that has almost disappeared." "I see this place as something of a race haven—and a gender haven—where you can have people be themselves and think of ideas and, you would hope, be able to produce something in their work that would continue that development of the community as a whole."

She then went on to describe the discussion that her class had that very day as evidence that such a haven is necessary. "We were able to move away from learning what the lesson was for the day and talk about some issues that were very important to people—not the topic but issues about what we are all doing. How do we all fit into the big picture of what's happening in the community? What can we do, and what are we willing to do, to try to make a difference?"

Myra Burnett spoke most passionately about her hopes and her fears for her students in terms of what kinds of scholars they would become. In her own educational experience, as she describes it, she was taught one particular model of intellectual life, and she remembers "falling for it hook, line, and sinker." She says, "I felt that because psychology was so mechanistic, it was free of a lot of bias. And when I was hit with the fact that it is absolutely loaded with bias, in addition to just plain distortion, . . . I had to rethink all I had thought before in respect to psychology."

What she hopes for her students is that they think about the discipline on "the front end" and "gain a critical perspective." She insists that African American scholars should not function as autonomous individuals but should "represent our disciplines to our people. We have a responsibility to correct our disciplines."

Like other women I interviewed, Myra Burnett could recall one significant black woman teacher who "opened up the world" for her and her classmates by showing them pictures of Egypt and telling them that Egypt was in Africa. "Well, I thought, what was the debate? It's obvious it's in Africa. Who thinks otherwise? But she always emphasized that point, that Egypt is an African country. And I didn't appreciate until years later that she was setting us up to understand that some people would say that it was not."

In speaking of her own teaching, the examples Myra Burnett gave were often of students and teacher exploring possible answers to honest questions: that is, those questions for which she did not already have ready-made answers. Reflecting her feeling of great responsibility to the students not to be frivolous in their discussions about their relationship to the larger African American community, she expressed uncertainty about whether or not she was always "sure about what they should do." She was certain, however, about what she perceived as the detrimental effects of integration on African Americans. She was also clear that her presence at the historically black college for women was "meaningful" and that her impact was most evident to her when students would take the time to come back, call, or write after they had graduated. "I get the feeling that I'm doing something important. It's hard to know in life if you're doing something important—whatever you're doing, to know if it really matters or makes a difference. I think what I'm doing makes a difference."

Subjugated Knowledge: Passing It On

Patricia Hill Collins writes that African American women have developed a knowledge that "empowers people to resist domination";[9] this knowledge is formed out of what Deborah King calls multiple consciousness: an identity that is a composite of several simultaneously experienced statuses as woman and as member of the African American community.[10] The women in this chapter are clearly committed to the process of creating and disseminating a "knowledge" that will enable young African American women to "do well" in their lives—to the benefit of the larger African American community. While there were varied definitions of what "doing well" means in specific ideological and political terms, all of those I interviewed saw their teaching at Spelman College as a way to continue or reshape the tradition of "telling the tale" to other African American women.

Although all of the women spoke of a commitment to African American women, there are complexities embedded in their fulfilling their commitment to Spelman College. On the one hand, it is a place where it would seem to make sense to believe in an African American women's tradition. The dining hall walls are lined with portraits of well-known African American women. The campus bears the clear and central presence of women (like Dr. Moreland) who have "gone before" and are still actively engaged in their life's work of teaching African American women. Most of the women you encounter on any given day, in a variety of functions, are African American. Many of the guest speakers who come to the campus are well-known women scholars and activists of African descent. It is a place where, as Myra Burnett says, time can be "taken out" from the usual class proceedings to sort through the difficult issues of where "we" are going as a people and where "we" as African American women fit into various larger pictures. It is a place where forums are held about African American women's health, African American women's business opportunities, African American women's media images, and so on. Most of the women who were interviewed spoke of that special energy in the classroom that can exist because no one, student or professor, has to justify her presence on the campus. All of the women who were interviewed appreciated the unique context provided by a historically black women's college for their life's work of passing on subjugated knowledge.

On the other hand, most of the women who were interviewed also spoke in a forthright manner about those elements of the environment that make their work difficult, some of which are factors talked about by faculty members at other historically black colleges and universities.[11] For example, Beverly Guy-Sheftall, director of the Women's Resource Center at Spelman College, spoke of what she called the "tyranny of the norm": the reluctance of some members of the college community to move beyond what had been done in the past and to allow newer, younger faculty members to grow professionally and make an impact on the curriculum. That presence of those who have lived the tradition of African American women "teaching for liberation" may serve as both model and oppressive force for other black women on the faculty.

Others critiqued the degree to which double consciousness, or even an internalization of the judgments of the "dismissive eye," sometimes results in a "cruelty," a "suspicion," and lack of respect within the college community for the talents and abilities of its faculty members. They questioned the degree to which the "dismissive eye" dictated changes that had been made on the campus, and they wondered if the very uniqueness of an institution devoted to the education of African American women (a quality that newer members of the faculty found attractive) was being subverted by the "intrusion" of the concerns and trends of the larger academy. Younger faculty, attempting to balance their dedication to teaching African American women with the demands of their own professional development, also expressed concern with the tensions between their scholarship and their heavy teaching and mentoring responsibilities.

I chose to focus on three women for this chapter, but all of the women interviewed theorized about the layered complexity of their commitment to teaching African American women. The "subjugated knowledge" they are passing on is in the process of being shaped by the shifting tides of history, their individual experiencing of that history, and their African American women's "multiple consciousness." Their subjugated knowledge is not a static "body" of assertions but rather a living, breathing, and changing knowledge claim evolving out of the lives of their mothers, their grandmothers, and the women teachers they remember as having a "revolutionary feminist pedagogy."[12] It is a knowledge claim that is also evolving out of the life of their people—and their own lives.

Notes

1. Gloria Wade-Gayles, *Pushed Back to Strength: A Black Woman's Journey Home* (Boston: Beacon Press, 1993), 124.

2. Bell Hooks, *Talking Back: Thinking Feminist, Thinking Black* (Boston: South End Press, 1989), 49.

3. Ibid., 50.

4. Kenneth Jackson, "African American Faculty in Traditionally Black Institutions: Contemporary Problems Associated with Academic Growth," paper presented at the meeting of the Association of Black Sociologists, Pittsburgh, Penn., August 1992.

5. Kesho Scott, *The Habit of Surviving: Black Women's Strategies for Life* (New Brunswick, N.J.: Rutgers University Press, 1991), 10.

6. Patricia Hill Collins, *Black Feminist Thought: Knowledge, Consciousness, and the Politics of Empowerment* (New York: Routledge, 1991); see also Patricia Bell-Scott, *Life Notes: Personal Writings by Contemporary Black Women* (New York: Norton, 1994).

7. Mary Church Terrell, *A Colored Woman in a White World* (Washington, D.C.: Randsell, 1940); Anna Julia Cooper, *A Voice from the South by a Black Woman of the South* (1892; reprint New York: Oxford University Press, 1988); Fannie B. Williams, "The Club Movement among the Colored Women," *Voice of the Negro* 1 (March 1904): 99–102.

8. W. E. B. Du Bois, *The Souls of Black Folk* (1903; reprint, New York: Washington Square Press, 1970). See also Patricia Williams, *The Alchemy of Race and Rights* (Cambridge: Harvard University Press, 1991), 63.

9. Hill Collins, *Black Feminist Thought*, 234.

10. Deborah King, "Multiple Consciousness and Multiple Jeopardies: The Context of a Black Feminist Ideology," *Signs* 14 (1988): 42–72.

11. Kenneth Jackson, "Factors Associated with Alienation Among Black Faculty," *Research in Race and Ethnic Relations* 6: 123–44.

12. Ibid., 50.

Chapter 28

The African American Female Administrator

A Change Agent

J. Nefta Baraka

Analysis of the condition of African Americans within any setting or institution is made productive by the conceptual framework established by Molefi Kete Asante, who suggests a clear structure for effective resistance to attempts to subordinate them.[1] African Americans become agents of their own liberation by understanding the context in which they operate and their choices of responses. In predominantly white settings, intercultural interactions present opportunities for the black woman administrator either to actively assimilate into the existing culture or to look the other way and ignore sources of intergroup tensions. The African American woman then becomes subject to her own actions rather than the object of actions designed to oppress her. Asante's divisions of the African descendants' experiences into "situation, resistance, and liberation" are used here to discuss the black woman administrator in the academy.

The Situation

To paraphrase Anna Julia Cooper, when and where I enter, in the undisputed dignity of my African womanhood, with existential authority and authenticity, at that moment, the entire black race enters with me. This is the situation of the black woman in diverse academic settings as historically white colleges and universities across the nation prepare for survival into the next century by including populations previously excluded from their campuses. The African American woman administrator, in changing white academic settings, finds herself in multiple conflicting roles. She is both academic and activist, subject and object, central and marginal, advocate and accuser, conservator and change agent. Her very presence as a newcomer whose ancestors have no traditions in shaping Eurocentric American academies is an accusation of past institutional culpability. Whites respond defensively, as if the entire black race were putting them on trial, even though black women are often "the least institutionally empowered in academe . . . working as untenured assistant professors, lower-echelon administrators, and artist-in-residence instructors."[2] Thus the African American woman's personal power is derived from the truth, which describes the relationship between blacks and whites in the United States. No amount of change and adaptation on the part of African Americans will, therefore, bring about mutually respectful coexistence with white America since racism is a permanent feature of American society. This means that the American academy, as well as other institutions, is circumscribed by racist values and practices of people who are devoid of skills to effectively manage human differences—particularly differences of race, class, religion, and gender. The black woman administrator becomes, too often, the lightening rod and focal point of white America's dysfunctional attitudes toward differences.

The Changing Academy

Integration of the 1960s has been replaced by "cultural diversity" and "multicultural education" in the 1990s. Yet the process of cultural "inclusion" in the academy continues to exclude factors surrounding the major problem of America's color line, whether in the classroom, in hiring decisions, in policy formulation, in professional support organizations and conferences, or in canons of the academy.

The academy, which was designed to prepare white males for leadership, is flailing like a wounded animal as it tries procrustean measures to assimilate Africans, Asians, Latinos, and Native Americans without changing its basic premises. Administrations, faculties, curricula, and student bodies remain disproportionately white in areas with sizeable African American populations. While everyone is responsible, no one claims accountability for changing the fundamental character of institutions that are resistant to mutually respectful interaction with another racial and cultural worldview. Simultaneously, lip service is given to "cultural diversity."

For whites, solutions to intercultural communication are external to them and are a matter of the "right program, system, or technology." Interracial conflicts that occur are viewed by them as flaws in the character or perceptions of "the other"—never as the result of their own insensitivities developed by institutionalized white skin privilege. Blind spots are maintained by silence and avoidance or by exclusion of and hostile retaliation against black professionals who seek to shed light on fundamental sources of racial and cultural misunderstanding. Yet the African American professional who "looks the other way" when racial conflict occurs becomes part of the problem that maintains the status quo.

The Predominantly White Small Private Liberal Arts Campus

Institutionally buttressed white privilege exists in its most potent form in private institutions of higher learning. They are the training grounds for the white elite who move into the policy-making and power positions in society.

Small private liberal arts colleges are often inbred enclaves of overlapping professional and social relationships. Faculties and administrators usually are neighbors in the area immediately surrounding the campus and are intimately involved with each other's personal lives. Many employees of small private historically white colleges are graduates, or relatives of graduates, of the college, with little in their personal backgrounds or daily lives to prepare them for diversity beyond a superficial understanding of people of other races and cultures. They engage in cultural diversity activities with attitudes that range from smug self-confidence to high levels of anxiety.

Racial Attitudes in the Private College

The relationship of small college white students and faculty to the black race is generally distant and abstract. They come to campuses with backgrounds informed by notably fewer interactions with African Americans as compared to their central life experiences. Many white students and faculty members in private colleges report encounters with black people and their culture that, upon close observation, reveal their sometimes unconscious classification of those encounters as experiences with the exotic *only when they are ready* to be distracted from what, to them, is central and normative. White faculty and administrators amenable to multicultural education in both public and private institutions are generally aging "baby boomers" who participated in the civil rights and anti-war movements and now are caught between their desire to belong to their same-group associations and the belief that change is necessary to embrace and survive in a demographically different future.

Unlike African descendants in America, who adapt to a pervasive "white presence" in their lives, whites believe that they control when and where they interact with blacks and that they can, and do, according to Peggy McIntosh, choose not to experience such interactions whenever they please.[3] The privilege of that choice is the basis for whites' feeling annoyed or "forced" whenever they are held accountable to principles of racial equality and justice.

The response of historically white institutions to the "baby bust" and the movement of "minorities" into nonwhite majorities is to create positions and departments of "multicultural (or minority) affairs," responsible for administering the change process. These positions are most often occupied by African Americans, other people of color, or white women. Institutional racism is neither openly acknowledged nor understood in the narrow response of creating a position to handle diversity. Such a major social phenomenon, then, becomes conceptualized as another administrative role that functions according to standard operating procedure. But too often, manuals or documented procedures are nonexistent as methods of operating remain in the heads of long-time employees; and deliberate, comprehensive planning to manage diversity is scarce or nonexistent.

Black Identity in the Small Private College

African American faculty and administrators in these institutions are caught at the crossroads of the dual consciousness, described by Du Bois, with a choice of obliterating their racial and ethnic identity in exchange for a marginal place in the European hegemony or maintaining race and identity as a birthright.[4] Blacks who choose the latter path will be labeled troublemakers and described as "threatening," "militant," "difficult," and "not a team player." Mythology surrounds them, and they are stereotyped to the extent that they remain outsiders and can never reach the margins of European hegemony once they are typecast by the white majority. The presence of these outsiders is healthy for progress toward effective intercultural exchange.

The African American woman administrator in a predominantly white college cannot expect institutionally recognized position power and therefore must rely heavily on personal and spiritual power. To be African American in the private higher education setting is to be confronted directly with issues of personal integrity, self-determination, cultural, and economic survival and growth. Amid feverish activity to face challenges of changing higher education demographics arise issues of what it means to be African in America.

The newcomer in such a setting faces the test of "fitting in" to the existing professional and community order; and, in seeking information and support necessary to meet her professional duties, she is faced with the unspoken expectation that she confirm the sense of importance of established employees. When the African American woman suggests corrections, she is likely to be met with defensiveness, hostility, incredulity that she dares to think of herself as the source of innovative solutions, or with the pretense that steps are already being taken to remedy whatever problem is at hand. Seldom is her suggestion immediately taken at face value and implemented. It is submitted to general discussion and worked over until it reemerges as the idea of someone else (usually white and/or male), at which point everyone applauds herself and himself with self-congratulatory relish to whatever task results from the African American woman's suggestion. Whites find it difficult to permit blacks to exercise leadership except in racial issues—and even then they sometimes assume expertise on their own part. Lois Benjamin confirms the belief of many African Americans that they "are hired as interpreters for the needs of Black students, faculty, the Black community, and those of the White administrators, faculty, students, and the larger society."[5]

In this setting, for the African American woman to be unaware of her status as both woman and African is to invite persistent stress and conflict and professional failure. The institution compartmentalizes and fragments the African American woman to suit purposes that are often at odds with her own and those of her community of origin. Her location on the hierarchical chart away from the policy-making bodies places her in a position of having to implement programs and activities agreed upon without her participation in the decision-making process. Indeed, the very job description that predated her in the position represents white assumptions as to the best way to proceed toward inclusion of other cultures into campus life and curricula.

The Resistance

Resistance requires the honest naming of strategies and structures that suppress black people. The African American woman administrator must resist the temptation and the pressure of illusory acceptance that comes if she allows herself to be defined by a majority seeking to assimilate and neutralize her.

Effectiveness for the African American woman administrator in a predominantly white climate of the type described depends on her willingness to frame racial issues in their social and historical context and to verbalize, vocalize, and assert them in problem-solving and policy-making contexts. To do any less compounds the problem. It must be very clear to her that she will never fit in and become a part of the existing order. Benjamin reports that "most Black administrators in predominantly White universities are denied access to power and have limited authority, except for Black Studies and minority affairs."[6] Advocacy on behalf of African American students and faculty puts the black administrator at odds with the established practice of old-guard community members who validate each other and make themselves feel good no matter what their blunders and incompetencies might be.

The black woman must cultivate an Afrocentric worldview to resist negative definitions of herself and negative characterizations of her duties to her race as a burden. She is not a superwoman, but she is an extremely *able* woman who is up to the challenges before her. Through acceptance of the powers endowed to her by African heritage, and through her belief in her ability to access those powers within herself, the African American woman becomes a change agent toward humanizing her surroundings. She becomes an example for valuing interdependence and mutual aid over independence, cooperation over competition, spiritualism over materialism, elder reverence over youth worship, and inclusion over exclusion.[7] I turn now to some ways the African American female administrator can become that change agent.

Change Agent for White Faculty Abuse of Power

The black administrator on predominantly white campuses should be prepared not only to advocate respect for the voices and perspectives of African American students but also to interpret for the students their intercultural encounters and their experiences with racism. For example, a black administrator was host to an explosive eruption of pain when two African American students stormed into her office with nine papers—theirs and those they had collected from other classmates. Only one of the papers was from another African American student who had taken the class the previous quarter—the remainder of the papers belonged to angry white students.

They had been in the class of a white professor who liked to promote the notion that race is no longer an issue in U.S. society; that assimilation that destroys ethnic identity is necessary for one to be highly educated; and that ethnic identity is a threat to American unity. The professor inflamed the angry passions of both black and white students who accused him of trying to stifle and manipulate their thinking when he opposed their views. They wanted to know if their suspicion of racism was correct and what they should do. The administrator listened to the students vent for an hour, told them that she would do a content analysis of their papers and the professor's responses, and promised to get back to the students. She suggested that in the interim, they talk to the professor about how to improve their papers.

The African American woman administrator was appalled at what she found. The only A paper was that of a white male who agreed with the professor's bias. An A—/B+ was awarded to an African American male whose paper took a neutral position but had twenty grammatical errors noted. All of the white students who disagreed with the professor were given a B, with the exception of a white, feminist female who received a C—. The two African American students, who both took a stand against the loss of their ethnic identity through assimilation, both received a grade of C. The black administrator observed no qualitative differences between the writing styles of the black and white students. She encouraged the students to take her analysis to the top-ranking administrator and offered to accompany them if they so desired. The students took their complaints as high as the board of trustees. The professor was reprimanded and declined to teach the class again but managed to work similar ideas into other courses that he taught. Later a white male student reported that he too knew what was going on. He said he always got As and that he was the beneficiary of the grade discrimination that was happening in the professor's class.

The private school population of African American students has experienced middle-class privilege and aspirations. Many have attended predominantly white schools or lived in white neighborhoods and had white friends all of their lives. They have grown up with the illusion of racial equality. Most of their families of origin have instilled African values of hard work, respect for elders, and the rights and privacy of others. Many express pride in their heritage and a desire for solidarity with other African Americans. Yet they have also absorbed the Eurocentric views of rugged individualism and survival of the fittest as the preferred way to succeed in life. Many have earned high GPAs in high school and have learned to be afraid of naming racism for fear of being accused of "using it as an excuse." They generally blame themselves—totally—for their academic problems. Yet they maintain a vestige of the collective nature of African character when they refuse to reveal shortcomings or uncertainty in white settings for fear that "it will make all blacks look bad and prove they can't cut it in prestigious schools." These students face an inordinate amount of stress and trauma trying to manage their dual identities. Yet they are without the coping skills and mechanisms of the generations of African Americans before them. Hence no adult African American administrator "worth her salt" can afford to let these youngsters face such conditions alone.

Maintaining Eurocentric Hegemony Through Resource Allocation

In what is perhaps the most challenging and stressful part of her job, the African American woman administrator must confront and correct majority members of working groups on issues of race and culture. They expect her, as a representative of her race, to be the object of their discussions and, by her presence, to confine her role to legitimating and validating their goals of making no expenditures to achieve cultural diversity. The black woman and her race are expected to "take the hits," without notice or complaint, of daily racist salvos implied in the trivializing and discounting of the importance of black culture.

The Fiction of "Sisterhood" with White Women

White female administrators cannot be relied upon to behave any differently toward African American women than do white male administrators. The white feminist concept of sisterhood places white skin privilege before female solidarity.

For example, an African American woman with extensive experience, a track record of effectiveness, and an earned doctorate was hired as an administrator in a small private predominantly white college. She was given no budget and no orientation. There was no program, only her position description as a guide for what was expected of her. The diversity program developed and evolved under her leadership. The African American students were more organized and (according to old-timers) presented the best campus programming in anyone's memory. Forums were established for dialogue on racial issues; a lecture series featuring prominent African Americans from the surrounding local community was launched; faculty consulted the black woman administrator regularly on approaches to uncomfortable racial situations in the classroom and found her consultation to be valuable. When the time came for performance review, her supervisor, a white female, focused on her clashes with support staff and a sexist male administrator as indicators of "only satisfactory" performance and added "establish a good working relationship with [the sexist male]" as a goal for the next performance review. The director wrote a written rebuttal, pointing out her creation of an exemplary program, despite a lack of resources, and the improved performance of the Black Student Organization; she noted that she could not be held accountable for the attitudes and behavior of another professional unless there was some kind of reporting relationship between them. The offending remarks were removed or revised to more accurately reflect the performance and contributions of the director. Her relationship with her supervisor grew steadily more open and mutually respectful.

The Liberation

When the African American woman enters the halls of predominantly white institutions, she must bring with her a sense of self located firmly in the traditions of her ancestors, who prepared the way for her. Her objective must always be clearly focused on the strengthening of her community. She is needed, as Harriet Tubman was needed, to have courage in alien territory and to be tough in the presence of threats to African American dignity and expression. She, along with all similarly positioned African Americans and well-intentioned people of other races, has to confront repressive systems and behavior when she sees them. She must develop an immunity to the discomfort of whites and the hostility directed toward her by thinking of herself as a change agent for a more humane world.

Whites will be most comfortable with the African American woman as academic if she adheres to Eurocentric epistemologies and remains object and marginal in reference to themselves, ready to maintain their traditions and accept superficial assimilation. Those who have been tempted to take that path have found themselves marginal, distressed, and isolated in a no-woman's-land of artificial allegiances dedicated to the agendas and causes of others. A form of cultural and gender suicide is encouraged by the inability to see blackness and femaleness as one with the power to lead, elevate, and give insight for the betterment of humanity through its most ancient institutions.

To liberate herself from debilitating effects of encounters with racism, the African American woman administrator must first understand herself as a spiritual being connected to God through her ancestors. Second, she must actively seek knowledge of her own Afrocentric traditions. Third, she must define and name attempts to control and subordinate on the basis of race from a position of professional excellence. Fourth, she must point out alternatives to resist practices in documented form wherein she describes the offense and offers a course of action. Fifth, she should actively seek and build community through maintaining mutually supportive black friendships and networks. Finally, she should take responsibility to nurture and develop the young of her race with love and African traditions. Always the organizing question in the life of the liberated African American woman must be: Is this good for black people?

Notes

1. Molefi Kete Asante, *The Afrocentric Idea* (Philadelphia: Temple University Press, 1987).

2. Joy James and Ruth Farmer, *Spirit, Space and Survival: African American Women in (White) Academe* (New York: Routledge, 1993), 1.

3. Peggy McIntosh, *White Privilege and Male Privilege: A Personal Account of Coming to See Correspondences Through Work in Women's Studies.* Working Paper No. 189. (Wellesley, Mass.: Wellesley College Center for Research on Women, 1988), 2.

4. W. E. B. Du Bois, *The Souls of Black Folk* (1903; reprint New York: Penguin, 1989), 164–65.

5. Lois Benjamin, *The Black Elite: Facing the Color Line in the Twilight of the Twentieth Century* (Chicago: Nelson-Hall, 1991), 130.

6. Ibid., 131.

7. Nsenga Warfield-Coppock, "The Rites of Passage Movement: A Resurgence of African-Centered Practices for Socializing African American Youth," *Journal of Negro Education* 61, no. 4 (1992): 471.

Part Seven

The Future of Black Women in the Academy

Black women's voices and visions, offering alternative pedagogies, perspectives, and paradigms in administrative practices, leadership styles, and knowledge systems, are promising prospects toward authenticating the academy in the twenty-first century. Despite struggling with the Siamese twins of racism and sexism, Darlene Clark Hine, John A. Hannah Professor of American History at Michigan State University, gives us hope in her personal treatise, "The Future of Black Women in the Academy: Reflections on Struggle," that our strides can be longer and our voices stronger in the ivy halls of academe. She gives us faith too that Western cornerstones of the academy are relenting and that dim rays of sunshine are beginning to permeate the hallowed halls.

Mamie E. Locke, in "Striking the Delicate Balances: The Future of African American Women in the Academy," begins with a promising note of optimism that the academy is indeed relenting and removing the Siamese twins, but she ends on a cautionary note that racism and sexism remain joined in the academy.

If the academy is to move beyond racism, sexism, and other "isms" on the eve of the twenty-first century, it must begin seeing strength through diverse lenses rather than viewing it from divisive prisms. A mosaic community of scholars provides an opportunity for the academy to fulfill its promises to seek knowledge and truth, fairness and reason, and excellence. The academy can serve as a lighted torch for the larger community, showing us how to live with our deepest differences.

Chapter 29

The Future of Black Women in the Academy
Reflections on Struggle

Darlene Clark Hine

The surest way to a productive and fulfilling future for black women in any profession is paved with understanding of the experiences of those who went before. It is within this spirit of illuminating the road for those to come that I offer this meditation on my work as a black women's historian during my first few years as John A. Hannah Professor of American History at Michigan State University. Although several black women historians now hold endowed professorships, including Nell Irvin Painter at Princeton University and Mary Frances Berry at the University of Pennsylvania, this is a recent phenomenon. The professorship that I hold was created to honor Hannah's unique contributions to the institution's development while simultaneously facilitating the research agenda and interests of the faculty member selected to hold the position. I anticipate that the future, given the large number of black women now engaged in history graduate study, will witness increased numbers of endowed professorships held by black women academicians. Still, there remains considerable mystery surrounding these illustrious appointments.

As I lecture and travel around the country, I am frequently asked three questions: What is an endowed chair? Who was John A. Hannah? and How did I become a Hannah Professor? My answers vary depending upon the circumstances and the time I am given to respond. Usually I explain that John A. Hannah was president of Michigan State from 1941 to 1969 and that upon his retirement, six professorships were established in his name to recruit outstanding research scientists to the university. Hannah served a twelve-year stint as the first chairman of the United States Commission on Civil Rights during the Dwight D. Eisenhower and John F. Kennedy presidencies. He served one term as assistant secretary of the Department of Defense for Manpower in the Penta-gon.[1]

In spring 1987, key members of the history department—Fred Williams, Harold Marcus, Leslie Rout, and Gordon Stewart, to name only a few—nomi-nated me for the Hannah Professorship. Within months after my initial conver-sation with Harold Marcus, whom I met while I was a fellow at the National Humanities Center in Research Triangle, North Carolina, I was invited to cam-pus. I sat in the office of provost David Scott (himself a physicist and former Hannah Distinguished Professor and now chancellor of the University of Mas-sachusetts at Amherst) and questioned him about the John A. Hannah Profes-sorships. Although they had been in existence for almost two decades, no woman, black, or humanist had ever been appointed to a Hannah Professorship. Spe-cifically, I wanted to know what would be expected of me were I to accept this honor. As I listened to Scott's response, I imagined that I had died and gone to academic heaven. "Your acceptance of the John A. Hannah endowed chair in American History means," he said, "that it is up to you to decide how best you will serve Michigan State University." I remember thinking, "Wow! So this is what it's all about!" Words fail to adequately express my delight to have an opportunity to work on big research projects, but most important, to exist in the academy on my own terms.

An endowed professorship facilitated work in black women's history and on the multivolume project concerning the history of blacks in law, medicine, nursing, science, theology, and education that I had launched while at Purdue University. I was cognizant of how rare it was for a black woman scholar, espe-cially one who worked at the intersections of black and women's history, to be accorded such a prestigious position within the academy. After leaving Scott's office, I had had a brief conversation with John Eadie, dean of the College of Arts and Letters, about the powerful symbol of the receipt of the Hannah Chair as an acknowledgement that research and writing on black women have be-come a legitimate and valued part of the academy.

Even as I savored my good fortune, I was never so sanguine as to believe that, if I had written only about black women in the early stages of my career, I would have been accorded a chaired professorship at the relatively young age of forty. I had proven that I could produce more traditional male-biased/race relations/social problems–oriented history. By 1987 black women's history was still in its infancy and had not acquired widespread acceptance and legitimacy. Many in the profession considered it to be just a fad. My early work crossed fields and boundaries in political, constitutional, and legal history. Undoubt-edly race and gender worked to my advantage. Moreover, for six of my thirteen years at Purdue University, I had served in a variety of administrative capacities, including interim director of the Africana Studies and Research Center and vice provost. By the time I was offered the Hannah Professorship, I had written over thirty refereed articles and two monographs, edited three volumes, and served as a distinguished visiting professor at Arizona State University.

The other items on my curriculum vita that may have favorably impressed the Hannah Professorship selection committee included grants and fellowships from the Rockefeller and Ford Foundations, the American Council of Learned Societies, and the National Humanities Center. I had served on committees in all of the major professional organizations and on the advisory board of the *Journal of Negro History*, published by the Association for the Study of Afro-American Life and History. Fortuitously, while the negotiations were under way for the Hannah Chair, the *New York Times* published a long story about the Black Women in the Middle West archives-creation project. Nor did it hurt that I had worked as a senior academic advisor to Henry Hampton's *Eyes on the Prize*, part of the America's Civil Rights Years television documentary series, and had coedited, with Vincent Harding, Clayborne Carson, and David Garrow, a documentary history under the same title. Moreover, I had consulted with the producers and appeared in the Florentine Films production of *Sentimental Women Need Not Apply: A History of American Nursing*. These activities, along with a few good words from my friend the historian John Hope Franklin, among others, surely influenced the university's decision to grant me the Hannah Chair.

This record notwithstanding, I anticipated adjustment difficulties as I settled into the department. In other words, I refused to let my joy over the appointment blind me to the problematics of being a black woman in the academy. Jealousy and envy are human characteristics. In this day and age, it is still a challenge for some male colleagues to transcend their own bitterness about the lack of similar recognition of their work. This bitterness is often veiled behind attacks on affirmative action or windows of opportunity hires and laments about the so-called lowering of standards. I expected that a couple of my new colleagues would find my presence disconcerting.

I did not have long to wait. As I lunched with one colleague in the fall of my first term, he cautioned me not to let the Hannah Chair go to my head. He declared that although I had joined the department as the Hannah Distinguished Professor, there were at least five others who were equally, if not more, deserving. I smiled at this unsolicited advice and thinly veiled admonition that I should stay in my place. Humor is an effective technique to defuse unpleasant encounters. I responded, "Goodness! I thought I had met everyone in the department." It caught him off guard. We laughed to ease the tension and turned to more important concerns, such as the name of a good dentist and automobile mechanic. On the whole, I have been well received in the department.

Given that one of the many purposes of this volume, to which I was invited to contribute, is to help black women faculty and graduate students survive and flourish in the academy, it may be helpful to comment more fully on the first-year transition from Purdue University to Michigan State. I arrived at MSU ready to hit the ground running. There were the requisite receptions to attend and an inaugural address to be delivered, but beyond this, my most pressing task was to learn who the other black faculty and staff people were. Black faculty and administrators and women's studies faculty offered warm words of welcome, and many treated me to lunches. For an inaugural address, I decided to lecture on black women's relationship to and perspectives on the United States Constitution. It seemed a fitting topic, given the fact that everyone was celebrating the bicentennial of the Constitution, a document that had paved the way for the institutionalization of race and gender inequities while simultaneously providing an intellectual and political rationale for relentless resistance against injustice.

After the protocol obligations were fulfilled, I immediately went to work to establish a Ph.D. program in comparative black history. The idea for this field, which has now been approved by the department, took shape when I noticed the large number of colleagues in the department who were concerned with black subjects in their research and teaching: the department numbered four African Americanists, three Africanists, a U.S. Southern historian, a Latin Americanist, and a Mexican historian, all willing and able to become the core faculty of the new field. Throughout the seven years of endless meetings and mediation of personality conflicts and long-standing grievances, I derived enormous benefit from the insightful suggestions, advice, and comments of David Barry Gaspar of Duke University. Gaspar's expertise in Atlantic world history and his friendship and collaboration proved critical to the success of the new comparative black history program. Receipt of a Ford Foundation grant in 1991 made it possible for Professor Gaspar to serve as a visiting professor and to teach a seminar in Caribbean history.

Throughout the 1980s, and even more so since I arrived at Michigan State University, the bulk of my scholarly attention has focused on black women's history. It is ironic to note that when I first entered graduate school at Kent State University in 1968, the history of black women was the furthest topic from my mind. Accordingly, my entry into this field was somewhat serendipitous. In the preface to *Black Women in America: An Historical Encyclopedia*, which I edited with Elsa Barkley Brown and Rosalyn Terborg-Penn, I recount how in 1980 the primary school teacher Shirley Herd, who was also president of the local chapter of the National Council of Negro Women, successfully provoked me to abandon a research project on blacks in the medical profession to write a history of black women in Indiana. I am still embarrassed at my initial response to Herd. It is ironic that I had attended graduate school with the intent to become a historian so that I could contribute to the black struggle for social justice, yet I met with condescension Herd's request that I write a history of black women in Indiana. I had given little thought to black women as historical subjects with their own relations to the state's history. I thought Herd's request an extraordinary intrusion and informed her that she "could not simply call up a historian and order a book the way you drive up to Wendy's and order a hamburger." I assured her that no one could write such a book. I was both arrogant and wrong-headed.

History is more than an accumulation of facts, names, dates, and events, yet no one could write a worthwhile book without access to adequate primary sources. The historian's task is to make sense, to give order and coherence to disparate bits of data, to fashion a resonant narrative full of explanatory power. Only later did I concede how straightforward and reasonable had been Herd's request and invitation to redress a historical omission. Indeed, black women were conspicuous by their absence from the history of Indiana. None of the social studies texts or state histories that Herd had used to teach her students made mention of the contributions of black women. Since historians had left them out, she reasoned, only a "real" historian could put them in, and since I was the only tenured black woman historian in the state of Indiana at that time, the task was mine. Herd rejected my reservations, completely ignored my admonitions, and dismissed my assertions of personal ignorance about the history of black women in Indiana. My confession to having never studied the subject in any history course or examined any sources pertaining to their lives did not daunt her. Black women as historical subjects and agents were as invisible to me as they had been to school textbook writers.

A less determined black woman would have relented, but not Shirley Herd. She demanded that I connect my biology and autobiography, my race and gender, my being a black woman, to my skill as a historian and write, for her and the local chapter members of the National Council, a history of black women in Indiana. In the face of such determination, I gave in and wrote, as requested, the modest volume that was published as *When the Truth Is Told: Black Women's Culture and Community in Indiana, 1875–1950*. The process of writing the book humbled and astounded me. The array of rich primary source materials Herd, her best friend and fellow teacher Virtea Downey, and the other members of the Indianapolis club had spent two years collecting included diaries, club notes, church souvenir booklets, photographs, club minutes, letters, hand-written county and local histories, and birth, death, and marriage certificates. Collectively, this material revealed a universe I had never known existed, in spite of having lived with black women all of my life and being one myself. Or more accurately, black women had not penetrated my historical consciousness. Now, looking back over the past decade, I see clearly that I traveled along two paths, those of black history and women's history. I researched, wrote, and taught courses at the intersections of these fields, on the history of black women.

I am struck by how consuming were questions of race and race relations throughout my college education and the early years of my career as a profes-sional historian. Questions of race dominated virtually every academic conver-sation. The historian Evelyn Brooks Higginbotham persuasively argues that the metalanguage of race silences all other discourses.[2] This certainly reflects my own intellectual migrations. Rarely, if ever, were questions of the relationship between sex and class raised. I distinctly remember engaging in misguided and ill-informed discussions with fellow undergraduate students at Roosevelt Uni-versity in Chicago about the absence of a class structure within black America. To me and my undergraduate friends, black women stood "outside" of history and were not subjects of study.

The primary source materials Herd and her council members had so pains-takingly collected launched my transformation into a historian of black women, a true historian of the margin. In 1982, following the completion of *When the Truth Is Told*, Herd, Downey, and I, with the help of historian Patrick Bidelman, launched the Black Women in the Middle West (BWMW) project for the sole purpose of making a black women's history archive. With funds from a Na-tional Endowment for the Humanities grant and the help of some twelve hun-dred black women from all walks of life, we collected primary source materials from black women and their families throughout Indiana and Illinois and de-posited the bulk of them at the Chicago Historical Society and the Indiana Historical Society.

An unforeseen but invaluable benefit of the BWMW project was the rare opportunity it afforded me to talk with hundreds of ordinary community black women about their experiences, deeds, beliefs, and values. As I studied the dusty records, frayed diaries, yellowed club minutes, faded photographs, brittle newspaper clippings, and scores of obituaries; as I listened to oral interviews; and as I engaged in countless discussions with long-time residents of commu-nities in the Midwest, the sheer force of these everyday narratives and the urgency with which their authors spoke shocked me and left me questioning the very nature of history.

Imperceptively at first, I began to reconsider a great many of the cherished values and beliefs that I had internalized in graduate school concerning the nature of the historical enterprise and to reevaluate the profession's notions of historical merit and worthiness. As a black historian, I knew that the construction of history reflected the existing system of power relations. As long as privileged white males held the authority and power to define the nature and content of history, blacks would never secure more than a token hearing of representation before the academic canon. But I had never extended that analysis specifically to include black women. I had not asked questions, or even considered asking questions, about the processes that rendered them invisible to historians. Two things converged to force my awakening: Herd's call and the call from the American Historical Association.

By the 1980s the field of African American history had acquired legitimacy and respect. In 1983 the American Historical Association sponsored a major conference at Purdue University on the research and teaching of black history. I chaired the committee that organized the conference and edited the resultant volume, *The State of Afro-American History: Past, Present, and Future.* After the conference, the committee recommended that I write an essay to cover the one major theme that had been omitted or that remained inadequately addressed in other essays. More to the point, as we assessed the state of black history, it became patently clear that the history of black women was its least developed area and had the least amount of scholarship. If black history was to be fully representative and accurate, then it was essential that black women be included. These are the thoughts and commitments that I brought to fruition during my tenure at Michigan State University.

While in hindsight it is easy to explain why black women were omitted from both black and women's history, the issues and difficulties that challenge contemporary black women in the academy still beg excavation and analysis. As members of two subordinate groups in American society, black women fell between the cracks of black history and women's history. Historians assumed that whatever was said about black men applied with equal validity to black women and that the history of white women covered black women as well. Thus it was left to the small number of black women scholars to insist that black women's experiences, precisely because of their race, gender, and class, were different and distinct in fundamental ways from those of black men and white women and deserved to be studied in their own right. Black women historians argued that simply to add black women and stir was an unacceptable and inadequate response and that all of American history must be rewritten and reinterpreted from multiple perspectives. In 1989, two years after arriving at MSU, I joined forces with Ralph Carlson, who had founded his own publishing company. This collaboration generated two major reference works in black women's history. The first was a sixteen-volume series consisting of 248 previously published articles, 5 unpublished dissertations, and a proceedings volume of papers delivered at a conference on the role of black women in the civil rights movement. The second project that I helped to edit, with Elsa Barkley Brown and Rosalyn Terborg-Penn, was the two-volume *Black Women in America: An Historical Encyclopedia.* Shortly before the publication of these reference works, I published the monograph *Black Women in White: Racial Conflict and Cooperation in the Nursing Profession, 1890–1950,* which deals with the history of black women in the nursing profession.

Today black women professors comprise a small but emerging force in the academy. In many ways they are the most recent immigrants in an increasingly diverse professoriate. Two thousand black women attended the January 1994 Massachusetts Institute of Technology Conference on Black Women in the Academy, convened by historians Robin Kilson and Evelynn Hammonds. Only about a hundred black women possess Ph.D. degrees in history, however. A significant number of these individuals hold faculty positions at historically black colleges or in black studies programs and departments. Too few traditional departments in predominantly white colleges and universities, regardless of discipline, boast more than one black woman professor at any given time. Clearly there exists a need for many more black women academics, especially if black women's history is to have a secure place and space within American history and black studies curricula.

Becoming a member of the academy does not automatically translate into a successful and stress-free life full of honors and lots of free time. The problems and frustrations of black women academicians can be grouped into three clusters. First, there are the problems related to geographical isolation. Most of the predominantly white colleges and universities that provide career opportunities for a significant percentage of black women historians are located in small, predominantly white towns and cities. Places such as Bloomington and West Lafayette, Indiana; East Lansing and Ann Arbor, Michigan; and Urbana and Evanston, Illinois, are not known for large racially and culturally diverse populations. The options for the black woman academician to develop a viable social life outside of the academy remain limited in such places, especially if she is single. Black women faculty often must travel to secure intellectual stimulation, rest, and spiritual renewal or simply to find communities of other black scholars and like-minded people. There is very little that can be done about geography.

Limited social options promote a related set of problems for the black woman professor. While a number of white female colleagues rightly bemoan the need to balance demands of their families with the obligations of their careers, a significant percentage of black women will never have to confront that particular dilemma. Demographics and geographical isolation conspire to produce a sex-ratio imbalance among black academicians because of which few single black women professors of my generation have had the opportunity to encounter suitable partners, to marry, and to bear children. In short, too many first-generation black women academicians never had even the luxury of making a choice of whether to live alone.

While many unmarried black women academicians do not have to juggle the demands of family with those of career, that does not mean they have complete control over unlimited time. Rather, the demands of community, church, and social organizations are added to committee assignments and expectations within the academy. It is the isolation, the aloneness, the oneness of the black woman's position in the departments of institutions located in small white towns that cause her third set of problems and frustrations. All too frequently she is called upon to serve on every committee that needs the representation of a minority, a woman, or a black. She is stretched to the limits of physical and emotional endurance with endless professional service demands.

In addition to the service demands, the black woman professor is expected to be a role model and mentor for the black undergraduate and graduate students who seek her out for knowledge, advice, sympathy, and friendship. Of course, these students are often themselves feeling the adverse affects and consequences of living in isolated small white towns. Moreover, for the black woman academician, the role model obligations extend far beyond the physical boundaries of the campus. Local churches, women's groups, civic and rights organizations, cultural and social service agencies, and the media frequently appeal to her to speak and lecture on a variety of topics. While most black women professors willingly accommodate many of the service demands made upon their time within the academy, they are often frustrated by the knowledge that service counts for very little when it comes to achieving tenure and promotion or negotiating for higher wages. Nor is there the supportive understanding evidenced by administrators and colleagues that community and student service obligations are often performed at the expense of research and writing time. The future survival and success of black women in the academy depend on the extent to which institutions will provide them with course release time and greater financial support for their research.

It often requires an iron will and a strong constitution to do all the service, mentoring, and friendship work while continuing to produce scholarship. After I completed the Black Women in the Middle West project, and before producing the Carlson reference series, I turned to blacks in the medical profession. By then my focus had shifted from medicine to nursing. In 1989 I published *Black Women in White: Racial Conflict and Cooperation in the Nursing Profession, 1890–1950.* The history of black women health care professionals proved to be the ideal vehicle for studying gender relations and the problems growing out of the intersections of race and sex. Moreover, the study of this group of black women professionals has helped me to understand better the experiences of black women in the academy. There are, in other words, significant parallels, even though a century separates us.

My study focused on the earliest generation of activist black women who were also providers of nursing services—Harriet Tubman, Sojourner Truth, and Susie King Taylor nursed wounded black soldiers during the Civil War. By the 1890s, in countless farm and small city communities, black women helped to found training schools for nurses and operated local well-baby clinics.[3] The activism and institution-building work of the first generation of black nursing professionals were necessary to overcome the racial exclusion and discrimination rampant in the larger society and within the profession itself. In 1908 the black nurses organized the National Association of Colored Graduate Nurses. In 1980 black women historians founded the Association of Black Women Historians. Both groups used their organizations to forge professional identities and to help their members combat racial and sexual discrimination and exclusion.

The work on black health care concentrates on the institutional apparatus for training practitioners and highlights the accomplishments of several representative members of the twentieth-century health care profession. Black nurses' battles against racism and sexism prefigure the similarity of struggles that faced my own generation of black women professors.

It is true that almost a century of racial exclusion, class oppression, and sexual discrimination thwarted even the most ambitious black women as they searched for mainstream educational opportunities in nursing and medicine. For some black women professors, the struggle to win recognition for their scholarship, especially work that focuses on the historical experiences of black women, continues, in spite of noteworthy advances.

Black women professors must tackle head-on the problems of having their research and scholarship taken seriously. This is precisely the area in which they most share the frustrations and problems much discussed among white female colleagues, especially those who, during the early 1970s and 1980s, engaged the study of women. Although women's history has made great strides—and indeed, some of the most sophisticated historical scholarship being produced today is in this field—there persists the slightly raised brow about the legitimacy of black women's history, literature, and studies.

Black women scholars, however, remain sensitive and vigilant to the ways in which their scholarship is received. Many will privately comment on their almost total exclusion from the key thematic or general interest journals in the field. I am concerned about the lack of institutional and professional organizational interest in black women's development. Others eschew close working relations with white women scholars, expressing suspicion as to the depth of their commitment actually to transform the academy. But all is not doom and gloom. There are exceptional performers, to be sure. There are black women professors who have effectively demonstrated the possibilities of achieving respect, recognition, and reward for their work and will enjoy solid careers within the profession. Still, there are always costs. Some of these star performers would loathe to reveal inner anguish, doubt, anxiety, or the extent of their private battle scars resulting from racist and sexist encounters with privileged or "status threatened" white and black male colleagues.

In many ways the experiences of black women professors serve as a window onto the issues, problems, and frustrations most marginalized groups and women in general daily encounter in the academy. There is never enough time to devote to self. Too much of the service performed goes unrewarded and unrecognized. Too often, white male professors and administrators lack appreciation for scholarship produced. Black women professors in the academy still have to work twice as hard and be three times better just to be perceived as average and to win tenure and promotion.

Given the difficulties and challenges, the key question is: How can black women survive and flourish in institutions that were never created with them in mind? Important weapons that can never be overemphasized are friendship, networks, and mutual support. While a supportive and informed professional community of like-minded colleagues is critical to success within the academy, it is equally important to have friends, both within and outside of the ivory gates. Throughout my academic career, I have invested as much time and energy developing community among black historians and women's studies professors as I have employed in creating a body of black feminist scholarship. Phone calls, notes, letters, occasional visits, meeting at conferences, and attending conference sessions where black historians are presenting are the essential tools for building and sustaining personal and professional friendships. It is worth underscoring that black women should make a point of attending and participating in conferences of the relevant professional associations. This will give them and their work greater visibility. Attending annual meetings of the Association for the Study of Afro-American Life and History and participating as a life member in the Association of Black Women Historians were essential activities in both my professional development and intellectual evolution. These organizations provided a site for the sharing of war stories in the ongoing struggle against racism and sexism in the academy. Moreover, these groups and others are important advocacy agents for the teaching of African and American history and black women's history. They nurture the soul and spirit as well. Difficulties and personality conflicts occasionally surface, but for the most part, these organizations and others like them are the garrisons to which weary intellectual warriors retreat for healing, affirmation, renewal, and guidance.

To be even more personal in my illustration of the necessity of friendship, it is impossible to exaggerate the importance of my convention conversations with University of Illinois professor James D. Anderson. He informed me of all the records pertaining to black hospitals and medical and nursing training schools located at the Rockefeller Archive Center in Tarrytown, New York. Without this information, it would have been impossible for me to write my book on black nursing. Conversations with Alton Hornsby of Morehouse College led to my being invited to serve on the editorial board of the *Journal of Negro History*. Similarly, it was while attending meetings of the Association of Black Women Historians that my friendship took root and bloomed with black women historians Linda Reed, Sharon Harley, Evelyn Brooks Higginbotham, Nell Irvin Painter, Rosalyn Terborg-Penn, Elsie Barkley Brown, and Mary Frances Berry, among others. Their spoken words and writings have made the academy a much more hospitable site for black women's intellectual work.

I participated in other conferences and organizations to develop community with white feminist sisters whose works have influenced my own. The Berkshire Conference of Women Historians and the Southern Association of Women Historians afforded me an opportunity to become acquainted and form lasting, mutually supportive friendships with historians Susan Reverby, Gerda Lerner, Ann Firor Scott, and Betty Brandon, among others. Over the years we have read and commented on each other's manuscripts, grant proposals, and editing projects and offered invaluable moral support.

I know that in some circles it is fashionable to bash white males and to blame them for whatever ills and misfortunes befall those on the margins or all who remain excluded from the historical mainstream. While some of the laments are inarguably justified and must be aired before healthy relations can be constructed, it is important to acknowledge the value of friendships and essential support that cut across gender and race boundaries. Were it not for the friendship, advice, encouragement, and strategic support of William C. Hine of South Carolina State University; Harold Woodman and Donald Berthrong of Purdue University; Harold Hyman of Rice University; and Gordon Stewart, Harold Marcus, and William B. Hixson of Michigan State University, I certainly would not be in the position I enjoy today.

Finally, I am especially grateful to my colleague and friend Wilma King, who saved me from being the only black woman in the history department at MSU in much the same way that Gwendolyn Keita Robinson, my friend since our undergraduate days at Roosevelt University in Chicago, saved me from a similar fate at Purdue University. The future of black women in the academy is full of promise and exciting possibilities. Today I have under my direction six young black women working toward Ph.D. degrees. Perhaps these reflections will help ease their journey in the academy.

Notes

1. John A. Hannah, *A Memoir* (East Lansing: Michigan State University Press, 1980), 77.

2. Evelyn Brooks Higginbotham, "African American Women's History and the Meta-language of Race," *Signs* 17, no. 2 (Spring 1992): 251–74.

3. Darlene Clark Hine, *Black Women in White: Racial Conflict and Cooperation in the Nursing Profession, 1890–1950* (Bloomington: Indiana University Press, 1989); and Hine, Elsa Barkley Brown, and Rosalyn Terborg-Penn, eds., *Black Women in America: An Historical Encyclopedia* (Brooklyn: Carlson, 1993).

Chapter 30

Striking the Delicate Balances

The Future of African American Women in the Academy

Mamie E. Locke

> I was raised to be acutely conscious of the likelihood that, no matter
> what degree of professional or professor I became, people would
> greet and dismiss my black femaleness as unreliable, untrustworthy,
> hostile, angry, powerless, irrational and probably destitute.
> Patricia R. Williams, Columbia Law School

Over the past two decades, women have steadily entered careers in areas once considered to be exclusive male domains. Successes have been achieved in corporate America, the public sector, and academe. Yet despite the successes, the careers of women still lag behind those of men, especially in higher education.

Although the number of women in academe is increasing, racism and sexism remain a serious problem. Women faculty and administrators often find themselves stagnating at the lower ranks and salaries. They also find themselves constantly faced with an "old boys' network" that is impenetrable. This network exploits gender and race issues to create a glass ceiling. To succeed in the academy, African American female faculty and administrators must not only learn the tricks of the trade but also grasp the subtle and not so subtle nuances of the situations in which they find themselves. They must also learn all those characteristics that women are taught not to display, such as aggressiveness, assertiveness, and dynamism. This personality transformation must come in the face of inevitable criticisms from male and female colleagues.

African American women have long sought advancement through the acquisition of an education. Historically, they have been denied equal access to secondary schools, colleges, and universities. This has become a continuous challenge, especially for minority women.

Since racism and sexism have been constant obstacles to their advancement in higher education, what is the future of African American women in higher education? What are the problems and pitfalls? What is it that African American women want? The first two questions will be addressed throughout the remainder of this paper. The latter question can be summed up as follows: "What women are seeking is fairly easily stated and fairly easy to support. . . . Women on campus . . . seek open access to the opportunities to which their abilities, their interest, and their willingness to work entitle them."[1]

Problems and Pitfalls

Institutions of higher education have long been strongholds of segregation and employment discrimination. Although the number of women of color, including African Americans, has substantially increased, the numbers are not yet in proportion to the eligible population. Data show that the majority of women are primarily in community colleges and institutions considered to be low in prestige. Half of African Americans with careers in higher education are at historically black colleges and universities (HBCUs). Their presence at HBCUs does not preclude their disfranchisement; it is just as pronounced at HBCUs as on white college campuses. Reginald Wilson claims that "the counter question of what opportunities there are for leadership by women of color is left without an answer. Sexism in the minority communities is as great a barrier to the academic advancement of women of color as is racism in the broader society; both must be eradicated to achieve a truly just society."[2]

Limited progress has been made in faculty appointments and tenure for minority women. Minorities are heavily concentrated in the lower ranks and hold a small percentage of administrative positions. In fact, part-time and nontenure-track positions are the fastest growing area for women in higher education. Holding 45 percent of such positions, women have little opportunity to advance. If they have administrative positions, they are most likely to be in student affairs or affirmative action positions. African American women are least likely to be college or university presidents. As late as the early 1980s, only one black woman headed a black women's four-year college. Upon her retirement, she was replaced by a man.[3] Currently there are African American women heading the two female historically black colleges—Gloria Scott at Bennett in Greensboro, North Carolina, and Johnnetta Cole at Spelman in Atlanta, Georgia. A few African American women also serve as presidents and chief academic officers at several colleges and universities. Recent appointments include Barbara Hatton as president at South Carolina State University, Condoleeza Rice as provost at Stanford, and Yolanda Moses as president of the City University of New York.

In 1992 there were 454 women chief executive officers in U.S. colleges and universities. Of that number, 7.5 percent were African American and 85.6 percent were white. The accomplishments noted above notwithstanding, race and gender segregation remains evident in higher education, from the faculty to the administrative level.[4]

Given that only a small percentage of doctoral degrees are awarded to African Americans, the pool of higher education personnel is not a very large one. The applicant pool for African American women is small because of the small number of African American students graduating from high school and moving on to pursue college and graduate degrees. Of the students graduating from high school in 1991, 320,000 were black and 1,867,000 were white. Those graduating and going on to college show a significant difference between blacks and whites—146,000 blacks (45.6 percent) went on to college, and 1,207,000 whites (64.6 percent) did so. In terms of sex and race, the data show that the pool of African American faculty and administrators is shrinking. In 1990 there were 683,900 white women in graduate school but only 54,500 African American women. In 1989–90, African Americans earned 1,145 doctoral degrees of the 26,938 awarded that year to whites and African Americans, 612 (2.3 percent) of which went to black women and 533 (2.1 percent) to black men. There was a total of 25,793 doctoral degrees awarded to whites during the academic year. White men received 10,691 (39.6 percent) and white women 15,102 (56.0 percent). It is interesting to note that nonresident internationals had a higher number and percentage receiving doctoral degrees in the United States than African Americans: 8,875 (23.4 percent).[5]

African Americans also face difficulty in tenure and promotion considerations. In addition to the overriding theme of racism, there is also the problem of the role the African American scholar is expected to play in institutions. At the majority of institutions there are many demands placed on these faculty members' time. Beyond classes, they are expected to serve on committees, work with student groups, provide service to the community, and conduct research. There is the added obstacle of producing "acceptable" research and publishing in the "right" journals. Oftentimes white institutions and scholars feel that they have cornered the epistemological market. They tend to view research on race, gender, and ethnicity as not being "real" scholarship, particularly when it is presented from an Afrocentric perspective, and they have the same perception of journals that publish this research. Since research is an important component of tenure and promotion considerations, one need not guess the implications of such a perception of African American scholarly productivity.

White institutions also tend to search for the African American "superstar" in their recruitment efforts. Thus many applicants have no real chance of being hired. When blacks *are* hired, they are often placed in black studies programs or, if they are more fortunate, given a joint appointment. Many find themselves overburdened with being the minority representative on committees, the black spokesperson. They also suffer from social isolation.[6] There are some African American women who fit easily into the isolating world of the Eurocentric academy and are comfortable being the "only one." Many more, however, find the experience less than rewarding.

On the administrative level, women across the board are concentrated in areas that are viewed as traditional women's fields—they may be deans of nursing or social work, for example. They are also placed in positions deemed to be caretaking—made affirmative action officers or given other academic support roles such as financial aid director. Further up the administrative ladder, they are often locked into "assistant to" or "associate" positions that provide little opportunity for advancement. For minority women the picture is even more dismal.

Minority women are the least well represented among tenured faculty. According to data in *Black Issues in Higher Education* (March 25, 1993), the number of African American women who were full-time faculty members in 1991 was 11,460. This number is minuscule when compared to the 143,049 white full-time female faculty members. Tenured African American women faculty are negligible (6.6 percent) in comparison to white women tenured faculty (88.2 percent).[7] The numbers are not much better at the administrative level. Women hold few chief executive positions in U.S. colleges and universities. In 1992 there were 454 women serving as presidents. Of these, 184 were in private four-year institutions, 164 in public four-year institutions, and 106 in two-year colleges. Of the 454, 85.6 percent were white and 7.5 percent were African American.[8]

As indicated, women are more likely to hold high-level administrative positions in private institutions than in public ones. Also, they are least likely to be found in academic and administrative affairs. In 1987 only 27 percent of all deans in academic areas were women. Of those, 97 percent were in nursing. The lowest percentage (8 percent) was in law. Of all minority administrators, 44 percent were women, and only 2 percent were deans.[9]

African American women administrators have difficulty in gaining respect. They are often called by their first name and find it hard to exercise authority. When men are assertive, they are regarded as exercising authority, whereas women who assert themselves are likely to be considered pushy. Thus there is a tendency on the part of men to emphasize gender in interactions with women.

It is clear that the participation of African American women in higher education is characterized by gender and racial disparities. Mary Ann Williams has stated that "in academia, the glass ceiling is a silent invisible barrier to one's upward mobility in the professional and administrative ranks."[10] African American women often find themselves in what is referred to as a "victim bind," which occurs when the institutional structures and political culture of the academy create and shape their career patterns and images. What is being created and reinforced are stereotypical perceptions, which are part and parcel of the institutional systems of race, gender, and power relations.[11] Coupled with the historical ramifications of slavery and patriarchy, these stereotypes have helped to reinforce the marginality of African American women.

Future Outlook

With so many systemic obstacles, the future of African American women in higher education may appear to be dismal. This is not the case, however; we have reasons to be optimistic. Many barriers remain, but they can be broken by collective efforts and by commitments to diversify the academy.

In 1984 Joyce Young pointed out the need for career leadership development for women in academia.[12] The strategies she suggested then are still useful today. They included both career options and occupational concerns, with African American women exploring leadership roles at the professional and administrative levels. On the occupational level one needs to recognize the many problems confronting African American women in colleges and universities. These include difficulty with promotion and tenure, discrimination on the basis of race and sex, social isolation, and the lack of rewards for professional activities. These problems remain factors in the 1990s.

As has been stated previously, the paucity of African American women in faculty and administrative positions can be attributed to the few numbers in the doctoral pipeline. Until more African American women enter graduate programs and earn Ph.D.s, black representation in faculty and administrative posts will continue to be negligible. Beyond increasing and developing the talent pool, there are many other activities that will further enhance African American women's leadership, such as mentoring and networking.

Tenure, promotions, and appointments to more substantive administrative posts must inevitably become the rule rather than the exception. Institutions must move beyond the "we have one" tokenism that is so pervasive.

Part of the responsibility of institutions is to validate African American women's scholarship. Patricia Hill Collins has eloquently argued the necessity of establishing a black feminist epistemology.[13] She argues that since African

American women have been placed in marginal positions for so long, they must learn to become creative with their marginality—that is, they must use their "outsider within" status to create black feminist thought, an epistemology that reflects not only a special view of society but also a view of self and family. Armed with self-knowledge, African American women are strengthened to break the glass ceiling.

Mentoring is key to breaking the glass ceiling among African American women. A survey conducted by Felicenne Ramey found that many African American women cite having a mentor as key to their career development.[14] It is therefore critically important for administrative leaders to mentor young scholars who demonstrate the potential for assuming leadership positions. If the problem of too few African American women faculty and administrators is to be rectified, then a system of growing and developing future administrators and managers must become the responsibility of women who already have administrative skills and positions. Tenured faculty must begin to help establish younger scholars and equip them for the long, arduous task of preparing for tenure. African American women need to move beyond the "crabs in a barrel" syndrome and work collectively toward increasing their visibility in higher education as faculty and administrators.

More intensive career counseling is also needed for young African American women to pursue careers in academia. Washington and Newman point out that many African Americans do not enter institutions of higher education because they are pushed out of the educational system before they reach that level.[15] Nellie McKay, professor at the University of Wisconsin at Madison, reinforced this notion when she stated that "to be Black and female in the academy has its own peculiar frustration because it was never intended for us to be here. . . . We are in spaces that have been appropriated for us."[16] Thus career counseling and nurturing need to occur at all levels of education, from kindergarten through graduate school.

The future of African American women administrators and faculty in the academy lies in their learning to empower each other and to foster cooperation, thereby diminishing competition among their own ranks. Through mentoring and the formation of women's networks, the number of African American women in higher education will continue to increase. African American women faculty and administrators must learn to negotiate the maze, striking the delicate balances necessary to wipe away the glass ceiling and become effective, successful, contributing members of the academy.

Notes

1. Martha E. Peterson, "Women, Autonomy and Accountability in Higher Education," in *Women in Higher Education*, edited by W. Todd Furniss and Patricia Graham (Washington, D.C.: American Council on Education, 1974), 6.

2. Esmeralda Barnes, "The Black Female College Student: Striving to Make Her Mark," *Black Issues in Higher Education* 10 (March 25, 1993): 30.

3. Mariam K. Chamberlain, ed., *Women in Academe: Progress and Prospects* (New York: Russell Sage Foundation, 1988), 54.

4. Jane C. Ollenburger and Helen A. Moore, *A Sociology of Women: The Intersection of Patriarchy, Capitalism and Colonization* (Englewood Cliffs, N.J.: Prentice-Hall, 1992), 22.

5. "Statistical Indicators for Academic Women," *Black Issues in Higher Education* 10 (March 25, 1993): 28.

6. Lois Benjamin, *The Black Elite: Facing the Color Line in the Twilight of the Twentieth Century* (Chicago: Nelson-Hall, 1991).

7. "Statistical Indicators for Academic Women," 28.

8. *Black Issues in Higher Education* 10 (October 21, 1993): 24.

9. Judith G. Touchton and Lynne Davis, eds., *Fact Book on Women in Higher Education* (New York: Macmillan, 1991), 18.

10. Mary Ann Williams, "The Ultimate Negotiation: Communication Challenges for African American Women in Higher Education," in *Perspectives on Minority Women in Higher Education*, edited by Lynne Brodie Welch (New York: Praeger, 1992), 93.

11. Gloria Jones Johnson, "The Victim-Bind Dilemma of Black Female Sociologists in Academe," *American Sociologist* 19 (Winter 1988): 312–22.

12. Joyce Young, "Black Women Faculty in Academia: Strategies for Career Leadership Development," *Educational and Psychological Research* 4 (Summer 1984): 133–45.

13. Patricia Hill Collins, "Learning From the Outsider Within: The Sociological Significance of Black Feminist Thought," *Social Problems* 33 (October-December 1986): 14–32.

14. Felicenne Ramey, "Mentoring: Its Role in the Advancement of Women Administrators in Higher Education," *Black Issues in Higher Education* 10 (October 21, 1993): 116.

15. Valora Washington and Joanna Newman, "Setting Our Own Agenda: Exploring the Meaning of Gender Disparities Among Blacks in Higher Education," *Journal of Negro Education* 60 (1991): 19–35.

16. Quoted in Barnes, "The Black Female College Student," 24.

Contributors

Lois Benjamin, editor of this volume, is professor of sociology at Hampton University. She is the author of *The Black Elite: Facing the Color Line in the Twilight of the Twentieth Century.*

J. Nefta Baraka is director of multicultural affairs at Kalamazoo College and adjunct professor of sociology at Western Michigan University.

Rose M. Brewer is associate professor and chairperson of the African American and African Studies Department at the University of Minnesota, Minneapolis.

Norma J. Burgess is associate professor of child and family studies at Syracuse University.

Donna M. Cox is associate professor of music at the University of Dayton.

Elnora D. Daniel is professor of nursing and executive vice president and provost at Hampton University.

Martha E. Dawson, professor emerita of education and former vice president for academic affairs at Hampton University, is currently serving as vice provost and vice president of academic affairs at Virginia State University.

Francine Essien is professor of biological sciences at Rutgers University.

Gwendolyn Etter-Lewis is associate professor of English at Western Michigan University.

Phyllis Strong Green is the recently retired associate dean of the Graduate School of Public Policy at the University of California, Berkeley.

Beverly Guy-Sheftall is founding director of the Women's Research and Resource Center and Anna Julia Cooper Professor of English and Women's Studies at Spelman College.

Darlene Clark Hine is John A. Hannah Professor of American History at Michigan State University.

Brenda Hoke is assistant professor of sociology at Agnes Scott College.

Beverly M. John is associate professor and chair of sociology at Hampton University.

Josie R. Johnson is senior fellow in the College of Education and a recently retired from the position of associate vice president for academic affairs and associate provost at the University of Minnesota, Minneapolis.

M. Colleen Jones is assistant professor of management at the University of Nebraska at Lincoln.

Janice Joseph is associate professor of criminal justice at Richard Stockton College of New Jersey.

Saliwe M. Kawewe is associate professor of social work and graduate program director at Southern Illinois University, Carbondale.

Shelby F. Lewis is vice president for academic affairs at Morris Brown College.

Mamie E. Locke is dean of the School of Liberal Arts and Education and associate professor of political science at Hampton University.

Nellie Y. McKay is professor of American and Afro-American literature at the University of Wisconsin at Madison.

Julia R. Miller is professor of family and child ecology and dean of the College of Human Ecology at Michigan State University.

Yolanda T. Moses is president of the City College of New York and president of the American Anthropological Association.

Linda Williamson Nelson is associate professor of writing at Richard Stockton College of New Jersey.

Mona T. Phillips is associate professor of sociology at Spelman College.

Jacqueline Pope is associate professor of public administration and political science at Richard Stockton College of New Jersey.

Vernellia R. Randall is assistant professor of law at the University of Dayton.

Gladys Gary Vaughn is director of development for the American Home Economics Association Foundation in Alexandria, Virginia.

Vincene Verdun is associate professor of law at the Ohio State University College of Law.

Amina Wadud-Muhsin is assistant professor of philosophy and religious studies at Virginia Commonwealth University.

Delo E. Washington is professor of ethnic studies at California State University at Stanislaus.

Brunetta Reid Wolfman is a recently retired professor of education from George Washington University.

Index

Academe, 54; analogy of, and the plantation, 59; bureaucratic structure, 54; gender, race, power and identity in, 60; theoretical structure, 54; transformation of, 61

Academy: a microcosm of society, 15; and quality of life, 134; barriers to growth of black women in, 24; black women as change agents in, 76; challenging ways of the white, 116; cultural inclusion of, 316; dissemination of contaminated knowledge in, 50; establishment of hegemony in, 43; Eurocentric, 4, 50, 242; favoritism of white males in, 272; marginal status of black women in, 76; problems in the, 116; prospects toward authenticating, 325; race, class, and sex within, 17, 21; the changing, 316; the white, 11; transforming the, 115

Affirmative action: advertising academic positions through, 265; and age discrimination, 154; and conservative political forces, 264; black women and, 254; conflict in values over, 25; hired but not tenured through, 265; hiring as a duty through, 18, 154; implementing hiring and recruiting, 266; male bitterness over, 329; mechanisms to subvert, 264, 265; quality without quotas, 17; racism and sexism in implementation of, 264; retention and promotion through, 266; stereotypes caused by compliance with, 264

African American female, 279; obstacles and barriers of, 279; African American female executives, 179–88; analysis of leadership roles for, 180; effects of racism and sexism on, 179–81; impact of multilevels of organization on, 181; networking for survival and success, 182–83; study of, 180

African American female founders of institutions, 159

African American female music professors, 108–13; and student relationships, 110; as anomaly, 108; as role models for recruitment, 109; dual role expectations for, 108; in a limited domain, 109, 110; in research, scholarship, and service, 111–13; transformation of, 108

African American music, 103–13; college curriculum in, 103, 104; criteria for non-Western music, 106; gospel choirs, 107; gospel music in college curriculum, 106; in "major" and "minor" ensembles, 105; jazz, 105; lack of, in textbooks, 106

African American Studies, 273; conflict in goals of, 274; content of courses in, 274

African American women: as a unit of